THE UNITED NATIONS SYSTEM

A Reference Handbook

Other Titles in ABC-CLIO's
CONTEMPORARY
WORLD ISSUES
Series

Books in the Contemporary World Issues series address vital issues in today's society such as genetic engineering, pollution, and biodiversity. Written by professional writers, scholars, and nonacademic experts, these books are authoritative, clearly written, up to date, and objective. They provide a good starting point for research by high school and college students, scholars, and general readers as well as by legislators, businesspeople, activists, and others.

Each book, carefully organized and easy to use, contains an overview of the subject, a detailed chronology, biographical sketches, facts and data and/or documents and other primary-source material, a directory of organizations and agencies, annotated lists of print and nonprint resources, and an index.

Readers of books in the Contemporary World Issues series will find the information they need in order to have a better understanding of the social, political, environmental, and economic issues facing the world today.

THE
UNITED NATIONS
SYSTEM

A Reference Handbook

Chadwick F. Alger

**CONTEMPORARY
WORLD ISSUES**

A B C C L I O

Santa Barbara, California
Denver, Colorado
Oxford, England

Library of Congress Cataloging-in-Publication Data

Alger, Chadwick F., 1924–
    The United Nations system : a reference handbook / Chadwick F. Alger.
        p.   cm. — (Contemporary world issues)
    Includes bibliographical references and index.
    ISBN 1-85109-805-4 (hardcover : alk. paper) — ISBN 1-85109-806-2 (ebook)   1. United Nations--History.   I. Title.   II. Series.
JZ4986.A44 2005
341.23—dc22

                                                                    2005025406

09   08   07   06   /   10 9 8 7 6 5 4 3 2 1

This book is also available on the World Wide Web as an eBook. Visit abc-clio.com for details.

Production Team
    Acquisitions Editor: Mim Vasan
    Submissions Editor: Peter Westwick
    Production Editor: Anna R. Kaltenbach
    Editorial Assistant: Alisha Martinez
    Production Manager: Don Schmidt
    Manufacturing Coordinator: George Smyser

ABC-CLIO, Inc.
130 Cremona Drive, P.O. Box 1911
Santa Barbara, California 93116-1911

This book is printed on acid-free paper ∞.
Manufactured in the United States of America.

*For my wife, Elinor,
with deep respect for her devoted efforts
to develop social justice in local communities,
where seeds essential for global social justice
must be planted.*

Contents

Preface

This overview of the United Nations System includes not only the United Nations, with its 191 members and headquarters in New York City, but also many subsidiary organizations of the UN, Specialized Agencies and Related Organizations with headquarters in many cities around the world. This is a system of some fifty organizations. The UN System has emerged in response to the ever more rapid, and ever more distant, linkages among people across all political borders, through trade, migration, communication, and pursuit of natural resources. In addition, military weapons have been developed that have ever greater destructiveness and have ever more distant range. As a result, most significant public policy problems flow across all political borders. Therefore, most of the departments of the U.S. government in Washington, and those of all other countries, have counterparts in the UN System. Of course, coping with a growing array of problems that circle the globe is much more challenging than those confronting the governments of single countries. Indeed, the UN System can be viewed as a "laboratory" in which procedures are being developed for coping with this new type of agenda—a global agenda.

Many readers who confront the organization chart of the UN System for the first time will find it to be very confusing. It is the purpose of Chapter 1, "Background and History," to provide you with a basic understanding of the system. Media coverage of the UN System tends to be focused on occasions where violence requires the attention of the Security Council and the need for a peacekeeping force. But it is the remainder of the system that is engaged in long-term peace building that frequently prevents violence. At the same time, other parts of the system are facilitating orderly worldwide travel, communications, and trade that make significant contributions to the daily lives of all people. Of course, many of the organizations and activities of organizations in the UN System have limited influence because of their limited financial resources and limited support from member countries. But because of our ever more connected world the need for enhancing their contributions is growing significantly. Therefore, it is essential that we be aware of this potential.

Because of continual development of new technologies for worldwide trade, travel, communications, and armaments, the UN System is continually facing new challenges. Chapter 2, "Problems, Controversies, and Solutions," offers a brief overview of some of the current ones. Of course, all governments of member countries are also having difficulties in coping with the challenges of a changing world. In the case of the United States, the government of the richest country with the most powerful military often finds it preferable to avoid working through the UN System. Chapter 3 discusses "The Ambivalent Participation of the United states in the UN System" and the consequences of this ambivalence for both the United States and the UN System. After presenting this background, Chapter 4 takes on the difficult challenge of presenting a "Chronology of the Emergence and Development of the UN System." Our very brief descriptions of the historic roots of each organization in the UN System reveals that each has its distinctive history. Some have evolved out of conferences held as early as the eighteenth century, and a few have evolved out of organizations founded in the nineteenth century. Many more have been responsive to new challenges in the twentieth century, with a majority of them created after the founding of the United Nations in 1945. Thus the history of the UN System can be traced back to a number of occasions in human history when efforts were made to cope with a diversity of international problems. Although the UN Conference in San Francisco in 1945 was one of the most significant, the UN System has many other significant historic roots. Knowledge about the historic background of efforts to cope with global problems such as violence, poverty, poor health, environmental pollution, and human rights violations enables us to appreciate how much has been achieved. It also illuminates potential for making future progress and offers insights, based on past experience, on how this potential might be most effectively utilized.

Chapter 5 provides "Facts and Data" that will answer many questions that arise in the reading of other chapters. These include the names of the 191 members of the United Nations, the League of Nations Covenant, the UN Charter, the UN Declaration on Human Rights, human rights monitoring bodies, UN peacekeeping operations, international criminal tribunals, UN System counterterror efforts, financing the UN System, public links to the UN System, and many other items.

Chapter 6 offers an array of proposals for "Alternative Futures for the UN System." This chapter is essential because the UN System has constantly undergone changes ever since its founding in response to the dynamic world in which it operates. This will continue into the future. Thus it is necessary for those involved in UN affairs to have visions of preferred future changes. This chapter includes proposals for changing the Economic and Social Council (ECOSOC), the Security Council, relations with private organizations and social movements, peacekeeping operations, and other aspects of the UN System.

Chapter 7 provides a "Directory of Organizations, Associations, and Agencies" that are involved in activities related to the UN System. This includes organizations such as the UN Association of the United States of America, the Business Council for the UN, the American NGO Coalition for the International Criminal Court (ICC), and the Academic Council on the UN system (ACUNS).

Chapter 8 offers "Biographical Sketches" of twenty-three people who now serve as heads of UN System organizations. Recruited from twenty member states around the world, they no longer serve these states, but now preside over secretariats obligated to serve a worldwide membership. Many have already served as members of secretariats before becoming the head of an agency.

Chapter 9, the final chapter, offers "Selected Print and Nonprint Resources." The print resources include books, encyclopedias, yearbooks, and journals. The nonprint resources include many websites. The UN website, www.un.org, offers access to the websites of all organizations in the UN System. Among the other websites are a number of UN issue sites and a number organized by Non-Governmental Organizations (NGOs).

It is our hope that this volume will offer useful information with respect to the questions that motivated you to open its

pages. At the same time, we hope that it enhances your awareness of the relevance of organizations in the UN System to activities in which you are involved throughout your daily life. As a result we believe that questions will begin to emerge with respect
to whether, and how, you might become involved in shaping the
future directions of the UN System.

1

Background and History

R eaders of this volume are probably most acquainted with UN activities located at UN Headquarters in New York City, particularly the General Assembly (composed of all 191 UN member states); the Security Council (15 members); the Economic and Social Council (54 members); and the Secretariat, composed of international civil servants from around the world that support the work of these three bodies. These three representative bodies, the Secretariat, and the International Court of Justice, located in The Hague, are known as the Principal Organs of the United Nations. But the goals and activities of these bodies, created by the UN Charter, are deeply intertwined with a number of other organizations that together form the UN System. This system of some forty organizations is portrayed in the diagram in Figure 1.1.

The organizations that are linked with the main organizations by a solid line are all part of the United Nations. When we use the term *United Nations* in this volume we are referring to this array of organizations. In addition, there are Specialized Agencies and Related Organizations that are linked to main organs by dashes. These organizations were created by separate treaties. When we use the term *UN System* in this volume it is inclusive of all of the organizations in Figure 1.1.

Organizations in the UN System are located at headquarters around the world, as portrayed in Figure 1.2. All of the organizations located in New York City, the headquarters of the UN System, are part of the United Nations. Geneva, formerly the headquarters of League of Nations, is also a city with extensive UN System activity, as headquarters of five Specialized Agencies, one

Figure 1.1

The United

| Trusteeship Council | Security Council | General Assembly |

Subsidiary Bodies
Military Staff Committee
Standing Committee and ad hoc bodies
International Criminal Tribunal for the Former
  Yugoslavia
International Criminal Tribunal for Rwanda
UN Monitoring, Verification and Inspection
  Commission (Iraq)
United Nations Compensation Commission
Peacekeeping Operations and Missions

Subsidiary Bodies
Main committees
Other sessional committees
Standing committees and
  ad hoc bodies
Other subsidiary organs

Programmes and Funds

UNCTAD United Nations
Conference on Trade and
Development

   ITC International Trade Centre
   (UNCTAD/WTO)

UNDCP United Nations Drug
Control Programme[1]

UNEP United Nations
Environment Programme

UNICEF United Nations
Children's Fund

UNDP United Nations
Development Programme

   UNIFEM United Nations
   Development Fund for Women

   UNV United Nations
   Volunteers

   UN CDF United Nations
   Capital Development Fund

UNFPA United Nations
Population Fund

UNHCR Office of the United
Nations High Commissioner for
Refugees

WFP World Food Programme

UNRWA[2] United Nations Relief
and Works Agency for Palestine
Refugees in the Near East

UN-HABITAT United
Nations Human Settlements
Programme (UNHSP)

Research and Training Institutes

UNICRI United Nations
Interregional Crime and Justice
Research Institute

UNITAR United Nations
Institute for Training and
Research

UNRISD United Nations
Research Institute for Social
Development

UNIDIR[2] United Nations
Institute for Disarmament
Research

INSTRAW International
Research and Training Institute
for the Advancement of Women

Other UN Entities

OHCHR Office of the
United Nations High
Commissioner for
Human Rights

UNOPS United
Nations Office for
Project Services

UNU United Nations
University

UNSSC United
Nations System Staff
College

UNAIDS Joint United
Nations Programme on
HIV/AIDS

Notes: Solid lines from a Principal Organ indicate a direct reporting relationship; dashes indicate a non-subsidiary relationship.
[1]The UN Drug Control Programme is part of the UN Office on Drugs and Crime. [2]UNRWA and UNIDIR report only to the GA.
[3]The World Trade Organization and World Tourism Organization use the same acronym. [4]IAEA reports to the Security Council and
the General Assembly (GA). [5]The CTBTO Prep.Com and OPCW report to the GA. [6]Specialized agencies are autonomous
organizations working with the UN and each other through the coordinating machinery of the ECOSOC at the intergovernmental
level, and through the Chief Executives Board for coordination (CEB) at the inter-secretariat level.

Nations system

Economic and Social Council	International Court of Justice	Secretariat

Functional Commissions

Commissions on:
- Human Rights
- Narcotic Drugs
- Crime Prevention and Criminal Justice
- Science and Technology for Development
- Sustainable Development
- Status of Women
- Population and Development
- Commission for Social Development
- Statistical Commission

Regional Commissions

- Economic Commission for Africa (ECA)
- Economic Commission for Europe (ECE)
- Economic Commission for Latin America and the Caribbean (ECLAC)
- Economic and Social Commission for Asia and the Pacific (ESCAP)
- Economic and Social Commission for Western Asia (ESCWA)

Other Bodies

- Permanent Forum on Indigenous Issues (PFII)
- United Nations Forum on Forests
- Sessional and standing committees
- Expert, ad hoc and related bodies

Related Organizations

WTO[3]	World Trade Organization
IAEA[4]	International Atomic Energy Agency
CTBTO Prep.com[5]	PrepCom for the Nuclear-Test-Ban-Treaty Organization
OPCW[5]	Organization for the Prohibition of Chemical Weapons

Specialized Agencies[6]

ILO	International Labour Organization
FAO	Food and Agriculture Organization of the United Nations
UNESCO	United Nations Educational, Scientific and Cultural Organization
WHO	World Health Organization

World Bank Group

IBRD	International Bank for Reconstruction and Development
IDA	International Development Association
IFC	International Finance Corporation
MIGA	Multilateral Investment Guarantee Agency
ICSID	International Centre for Settlement of Investment Disputes
IMF	International Monetary Fund
ICAO	International Civil Aviation Organization
IMO	International Maritime Organization
ITU	International Telecommunication Union
UPU	Universal Postal Union
WMO	World Meterological Organization
WIPO	World Intellectual Property Organization
IFAD	International Fund for Agricultural Development
UNIDO	United Nations Industrial Development Organization
WTO[3]	World Tourism Organization

Departments and Offices

OSG	Office of the Secretary-General
OIOS	Office of Internal Oversight Services
OLA	Office of Legal Affairs
DPA	Department of Political Affairs
DDA	Department for Disarmament Affairs
DPKO	Department of Peace-keeping Operations
OCHA	Office for the Coordination of Humanitarian Affairs
DESA	Department of Economic and Social Affairs
DGACM	Department for General Assembly and Conference Management
DPI	Department of Public Information
DM	Department of Management
OHRLLS	Office of the High Representative for the Least Developed Countries, Landlocked Developing Countries and Small Island Developing States
UNSECOORD	Office of the United Nations Security Coordinator
UNODC	United Nations Office on Drugs and Crime
UNOG	UN Office at Geneva
UNOV	UN Office at Vienna
UNON	UN Office at Nairobi

Published by the UN Department of Public Information
DPI/2342—March 2004

Figure 1.2

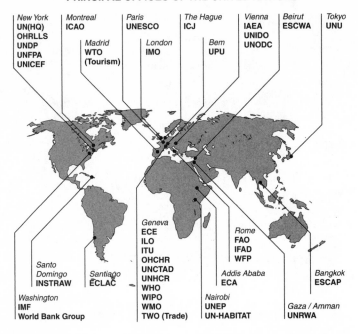

PRINCIPAL OFFICES OF THE UNITED NATIONS

New York	Montreal	Paris	The Hague	Vienna	Beirut	Tokyo
UN(HQ)	ICAO	UNESCO	ICJ	IAEA	ESCWA	UNU
OHRLLS				UNIDO		
UNDP	Madrid	London	Bem	UNODC		
UNFPA	WTO	IMO	UPU			
UNICEF	(Tourism)					

Geneva
ECE
ILO
ITU
OHCHR
UNCTAD
UNHCR
WHO
WIPO
WMO
TWO (Trade)

Rome
FAO
IFAD
WFP

Santo
Domingo
INSTRAW

Santiago
ECLAC

Addis Ababa
ECA

Bangkok
ESCAP

Washington
IMF
World Bank Group

Nairobi
UNEP
UN-HABITAT

Gaza / Amman
UNRWA

Related Organization, and four UN agencies. Other agency headquarters are located on all continents.

The UN System has arisen in response to two primary factors. First, new technologies for travel, communication, manufacturing, shipping, and investment are linking people around the world ever more rapidly across ever greater distances. As a result, a growing array of public policy problems are emerging that flow across all political borders. In response, organizations for coping with these problems are being created that reach to the borders of these problems. Second is growing understanding of the causes of seriously disruptive conflict and realization of the need to cope with these causes through long-term peace building. The roots of these conflicts are often found in an array of social problems that are on the agendas of organizations throughout the UN System.

Those viewing these two figures for the first time will find them exceedingly difficult to understand. It is the purpose of this volume to enable you to comprehend the usefulness of these diagrams for understanding the functioning of the UN System. Of course, upon reflection, we should not be too surprised at the growing scope of the UN System agenda. We are all linked throughout the world in our daily lives, as a result of the origins of clothes that we wear, the automobiles and electronic equipment that we use, the resources that we consume, foods that we eat, our e-mail and Internet linkages, and in many other ways. As a result, as you read this volume, we urge you to ponder which UN agencies have relevance to you in your daily life and to ponder what your response to this awareness should be. Table 1.1 offers you an alphabetical list of issues and functions that appear in the titles of organizations that appear in Figure 1.1. The purpose of this list is to provide a brief overview of the breadth and diversity of the titles of UN System agencies. It does not list all of the issues on the agendas of organizations in the UN System. As you read the list, ponder which subjects are most important to you in your daily life. Then, as you read this volume you will learn that the UN System is relevant to you in unexpected ways.

The UN System in Historical Perspective[1]

The foundation on which the drafters constructed the UN Charter in San Francisco in 1945 was built during a long historical process through which human inquisitiveness, restlessness, and acquisitiveness produced ever-increasing contacts among human settlements, across ever longer distances. If we look back in time from San Francisco, we readily see that the United Nations is a child of the League of Nations, founded in 1920. It incorporates important institutional developments of the League, such as the General Assembly, Security Council, a Secretariat, and the growth in importance of economic and social activities during the relatively brief history of the League.

The League, too, was not wholly a product of its founding conference, the Paris Peace conference of 1919. Inis L. Claude considers the century bounded by the Congress of Vienna (1815) and the outbreak of World War I (1914) as the "era of preparation for international organization."[2] He discerns three prime sources of the Leagues of Nations. First, the League Council evolved out of the Concert of Europe created by the Congress of Vienna

TABLE 1.1
Functions Appearing in Names of UN System Agencies in Figure 1

1. Agriculture (sa)	28. Labor (sa)
2. Atomic energy (ro)	29. Maritime (sa)
3. Banking (sa)	30. Monetary fund (sa)
4. Civil aviation (sa)	31. Meteorology (sa)
5. Children (ga)	32. Monetary (sa)
6. Chemical weapons (ro)	33. Narcotic drugs (fc)
7. Climate change	34. Nuclear test-ban (ro)
8. Crime prevention (fc)	35. Peacekeeping (sc)
9. Criminal tribunal (sc)	36. Population (fc) (ga)
10. Culture (sa)	37. Postal (sa)
11. Development (ga) (fc)	38. Reconstruction (sa)
12. Disarmament (ga)	39. Refugees (ga)
13. Drug control (ga)	40. Science (sa) (fc)
14. Education (sa)	41. Settle invest. disputes (sa)
15. Environment (ga)	42. Social development (ga)
16. Finance (sa)	43. Staff college (ga)
17. Food (sa) (ga)	45. Statistics (fc)
18. Forests (ecosoc)	45. Sustainable dev. (fc)
19. Health (sa)	46. Telecommunications (sa)
20. High technology	47. Tourism (sa)
21. HIV/AIDS (ga)	48. Trade (ga)
22. Human rights (fc)	49. Trade & dev. (ga)
23. Human settlements (ga)	50. Training & research (ga)
24. Industrial dev. (sa)	51. University (ga)
25. Investment guarantee (sa)	52. Volunteers (ga)
26. Indigenous issues(ecosoc)	53. Women (fc) (ga)
27. Intellectual property (sa)	54. World trade (ro)

sa Specialized Agency; **ga** Under General Assembly; **fc** Functional Commission under ECOSOC; **ecosoc** Other Bodies under ECOCOC; **sc** Under Security Council; **ro** Related Organization

(1815), convoked to create a new Europe out of the ruins of the Napoleonic Wars. Through the Concert of Europe, the great powers made themselves the self-appointed guardians of the European system of states. The Concert of Europe met sporadically, some thirty times before World War I, to deal with pressing political issues. While smaller states were sometimes present at Concert meetings, the Concert was dominated by the powerful. The League Covenant provided for a council with explicit authority, with the continuity of regular meetings, and with membership of both large and small states.

Second, the League also evolved out of the Hague System, instituted by conferences in 1899 and 1907. The League borrowed extensively from procedures for the peaceful settlement of conflicts codified by the Hague System. And the League reflected the Hague System's response to growing demands for universality, that is, that all states take part in international conferences. In the words of the president of the 1907 Hague Conference, "This is the first time that the representatives of all constituted States have been gathered together to discuss interests which they have in common and which contemplate the good of mankind."[3] The notion of universality meant not only the inclusion of smaller states but also participation by states outside Europe.

Third, the League also evolved out of international bodies founded in the nineteenth century, often referred to as public international unions, to deal with common problems that transcend the boundaries of states. These include the Rhine Commission, established by the Congress of Vienna in 1815, and the Danube Commission, established in 1848. Other examples are the International Telegraphic Union (1865); the Universal Postal Union (1874); and similar organizations dealing with health, agriculture, tariffs, railroads, standards of weight and measurement, patents and copyrights, narcotic drugs, and prison conditions. Through these organizations states acknowledged that problems were emerging that required periodic conferences where collaborative decisions would be made, to be implemented by secretariats on a day-to-day basis. The League borrowed extensively from this practice.

If we probe deeper into the past we find, of course, that the forces that fostered the antecedents of the League also had more distant beginnings. It is important to take note of these because we sometimes tend to forget them when we emphasize more recent forms of "globalization." The Industrial Revolution in the eighteenth century dramatically changed the technology of transportation, communication, and manufacturing. This in turn fostered the need for international organizations to deal with problems created by more rapid transportation and communication and by growth in international marketing, in importing of raw materials, and in the international interdependence of labor.

Some would say that humanity was placed on an irreversible path toward the League and the United Nations even earlier, in the late fifteenth century, when Europeans began a pattern of worldwide exploration that eventually led to extensive empires in Africa, Asia, and Latin America, and to Western domination of the world. William McNeill, in his "History of the Human Community," dates the "closure of global ecumene" as from 1500 to 1650: The result was to link the Atlantic face of Europe with the shores of most of the earth.

> What had always before been the extreme fringe of Eurasia became, within little more than a generation, a focus of the world's sea lanes, influencing and being influenced by every human society within easy reach of the sea.[4]

European-based empires eventually led to the creation of a worldwide system of states. In its early years, the United Nations was deeply involved in the creation of independent states out of former colonial empires. Much early twenty-first-century activity in the United Nations is concerned with the efforts of these new states to transcend their economic dependence on the West. In a fundamental sense, the conditions that fomented demands for a New International Economic Order (NIEO) in the 1970s, and for a New International Information and Communications Order (NIICO) in the 1980s, have their roots in the "closure of global ecumene" between 1500 and 1650. At the same time, the problems in what we now call "failed states" have roots in the fact that many of these states were created by European empire builders, not by people living in these areas.

In developing a historical perspective, it is worth remembering Claude's depiction of the century between 1815 and 1914 as the "era of preparation for international organization." How should we characterize the period between the founding of the League of Nations (1920) and the present? Very apt would be the "era of preparation for global governance." By "global governance" we do not mean a "world government" that is modeled after individual states that now make up the state system. Instead, we see "global governance" as something that is emerging out of experience in a UN System that is grappling with a continually expanding agenda of global problems. In other words, a form of governance that is relevant for an exceedingly diverse polity that reaches around the globe will emerge out of the "UN System laboratory."

What have the pioneers in this first era of global organizations left as their heritage for those now working on global governance?

First, they have achieved universality.

Second, they have created a network of global organizations responsive to a growing agenda of global problems.

Third, they have established a continuous, worldwide presence of this system of organizations, in some 134 cities on all continents but Antarctica.

Fourth, they have made multilateral decision making commonplace and have developed new procedures for achieving consensus.

Fifth, they have greatly increased the number of tools available for peace building.

Sixth, they have identified, and have made substantial progress in multilateral definition of, a set of fundamental global values, such as peace, human rights, development, and ecological balance.

Seventh, they have made some progress in breaking down barriers between the people of the world and global governmental organizations.

Emergence of New Tools for Peace Building

During the fourscore and four years prior to 2005, the League of Nations and the United Nations have demonstrated remarkable creativity in expanding the array of available tools for diminishing violence and peace building, and in experimenting with application of these tools. Figure 1.3 is an extremely simplified summary of the emergence of these peace tools.

Before the League was founded *diplomacy* (1) and *balance of power* (2) were the primary available tools. Because of the tendency of balance of power to result in arms races that ended in wars, the League Covenant attempted to replace it with *collective security* (3), through which military aggression would be prevented by the threat of response with overwhelming military force by members of the League. The Covenant made an effort to strengthen diplomacy by adding procedures for *peaceful settlement* (4) of disputes (through mediation, conciliation, and the World Court). The League also created procedures for *disarmament and arms control* (5). These approaches emphasized the use of, and control of, violence in the pursuit of peace, sometime referred to as "negative peace."

Figure 1.3 Emergence of Peace Tools in the League of Nations and the UN System

	19th Century	1919	1945	1950–1989	1990–	NGO/People's Movements
		League Covenant	UN Charter	UN Practice	UN Practice	
NEGATIVE PEACE	Diplomacy (1) Balance of Power (2) I	Collective Security (3) Peaceful Settlement (4) Disarmament / Arms Control (5) II	Collective Security Peaceful Settlement Disarmament / Arms Control	Collective Security Peacekeeping (9) Peaceful Settlement Disarmament / Arms Control	Collective Security Peacekeeping Peaceful Settlement Disarmament / Arms Control Humanitarian Intervention (15) Preventive Diplomacy (16)	Track II Diplomacy (17) Conversion (18) Defensive Defense (19) NonViolence (20)
POSITIVE PEACE			Functionalism (6) Self-Determination (7) Human Rights (8) III	Functionalism Self-Determination Human Rights Economic Development (10) Economic Equity (NIEO) (11) Communication Equity (12) Ecological Balance (13) Governance for Global Commons (14) IV	Functionalism Self-Determination Human Rights Economic Development Economic Equity (NIEO) Communication Equity Ecological Balance Governance for Global Commons V	Citizen Defense (21) Self Reliance (22) Feminist Perspective (23) Peace Education (24) VI

Practice under the League and some of the lessons of World War I, contributed to the drafting of the UN Charter in 1945. Significantly, these three approaches were again incorporated into the UN Charter in 1945, although with some changes—particularly the strengthening of collective security. The UN Charter authorizes nine of fifteen members of the Security Council to "take such action by air, sea, or land forces as may be necessary to maintain or restore international peace and security," so long as none of the permanent members (China, France, Russia, the United States, and the United Kingdom) vote against the resolution. The League of Nations required unanimity. Perhaps the greatest difference between the Covenant and the Charter are three peace strategies added to the latter by those assembled at San Francisco: *"functional" cooperation* (6) on economic and social issues, *self-determination* (7), and *human rights* (8). These approaches, in contrast to the earlier three, emphasize the creation of peaceful economic, social, and political relationships—sometimes referred to as "positive peace." The new Economic and Social Council (ECOSOC) was based on growth in functional activities of the League during its brief history. The Trusteeship Council continued League supervision over the treatment of colonies seized by the victors in war, but it was the Declaration Regarding Non-Self-Governing Territories (Chapter XI) that opened the way for future self-determination advances under the Charter. And the mention of human rights seven times in the Charter, including the second sentence of the preamble, was a dramatic departure from the League Covenant.

At the start of the twenty-first century the United Nations has existed three times as long as the League. As our most significant peace laboratory, the present UN System of organizations reflects very significant learning since its founding. We have learned that collective security—actually a form of deterrence—is as dangerous as any other deterrence strategy if it fails. The application of collective security in the Korean War, in which we tottered on the edge of World War III, taught us this. On the other hand, *peacekeeping* (7) forces are a useful new invention. With the UN Emergency Forces positioned between Egypt and Israel as prototypes (UNEF I, 1956–1967; UNEF II, 1973–1979), peacekeeping forces initially patrolled a neutral zone along a ceasefire line, employing only small arms in self-defense. More recent peacekeeping forces have been plunged into much more complicated situations involving civil war and ethnic strife. Thus, as the

United Nations faces new challenges, it is groping toward the development of a new peace tool that lies somewhere between peacekeeping and collective security.

Functional collaboration has flowered as the UN System has developed agencies that cope with a broad array of global issues, such as health, refugees, labor, education, clean water, communications, balance of payments, and housing. Self-determination has been one of the United Nations' greatest success stories, as it has assisted a multitude of states in Africa, Asia, and the Caribbean to independence and immediate UN membership.

With respect to human rights, under UN auspices the states assembled have drafted standards for human life on the planet through the Universal Declaration of Human Rights, and covenants on civil and political rights and economic, social, and cultural rights, and an array of other treaties on genocide, women's rights, elimination of racial discrimination, rights of children, rights of labor, environment, hunger and malnutrition, religious discrimination, and many others. Fortunately, the existence of these standards has now raised our expectations for fulfillment; unfortunately, progress in implementation of these standards has been very slow. But this should not prevent us from celebrating the tremendous achievements of the drafters of these new norms for human aspiration.

With the attainment of self-determination by states created by colonialism, the number of member states in the United Nations with widespread poverty grew rapidly. Difficulties in achieving successful functional cooperation in a United Nations in which wealth and resources are so unequally distributed among members soon became apparent. Thus began the effort to narrow the gap through *development* (10) programs in the poorer countries. Despite significant successes in some locations, the gap between the rich and the poor of the world has continued to grow, at the same time that the world economy has become increasingly interdependent.

As worldwide systems for exploitation of resources, production, marketing, and communications reached ever more intrusively into the most distant human settlements and rural areas, the peacelessness of population explosion in urban shantytowns in cities in the poorer countries provoked a searching dialogue on the meaning of development. This debate shifted the focus from development projects in the poorer countries to the inequities in the international economic system. A debate that began in the General Assembly grew into a UN Conference on Trade and Development (UNCTAD), to an UNCTAD organization, to a demand for a new international economic order (NIEO). In 1974 this campaign for *international economic equity* (11) produced a declaration for a NIEO, a plan of action for a NIEO, and a Charter of the Economic Rights and Duties of States.

Frustration over the unwillingness of the industrialized countries to conduct global negotiations over a NIEO contributed to demands for *international communications equity* (12) and emergence in the 1980s of the demand, centered in UNESCO, for a new international information and communications order (NIICO). The domination and control of worldwide communications by media corporations based in cities in the industrialized countries mirrors that of transnational corporations for resource exploitation, production, and marketing. As a consequence, leaders in the poorer countries complain that control of worldwide communications by corporations in Europe and North America prevent the people in the industrialized countries from learning about the actual condition of people in the poorer countries and the reasonableness of demands for a NIEO.

One could say that demands for a NIEO and a NIICO offered not only fuller understanding of the meaning of development, but that they in turn illuminated the full meaning of self-determination. Without changes in an international economic and communication system whose roots reach back into the days of colonial empires, the self-determination process will not be completed.

At the same time, the global dialogue on the meaning of development has challenged assumptions about the conditions under which functional cooperation could contribute to peace. It had been assumed that functional organizations such as UNESCO could provide arenas for collaboration among technical experts who would be isolated from political controversy. Bringing issues such as the NIICO into UNESCO has been viewed by some industrialized countries as "politicization" of agencies that should remain apolitical. But to many in the poorer countries, continued collaboration among technicians was intolerable so long as worldwide economic and communications structures were inequitable. From their perspective, this structure, and its impact on the outcome of functional cooperation, is an appropriate concern for agencies such as UNESCO. This dialogue has caused us to think in a more penetrating way about the relevance of equitable economic and communications relationships to fruitful functional collaboration in dealing with global problems.

Questions of *ecological balance* (13), too, can be seen as evolving out of global debate on the meaning of development. Ecological problems became a prominent issue on the agenda of the UN System beginning with the UN Environment Conference in Stockholm in 1972. The initiative came from the industrialized countries, and at first the environment was perceived to be their issue. Initially, many in the poorer countries even suspected that environmental initiatives from the industrialized countries were a covert strategy for preventing their development. But by the time of the UN Conference on Environment and Development (UNCED) in Rio de Janeiro in 1992, environmental issues were perceived to be a concern of people from all parts of the world. A new UN Commission on Sustainable Development (CSD) is leading the search in the early twenty-first century for meanings of development that can include ecological balance. At the same time, the squalor, disease, and death that result from destruction of the human habitat are increasingly judged to have the moral equivalence of similar peacelessness produced by weapons of war.

As new technology has enabled humankind to exploit more extensively the depth and the breadth of the commons (atmosphere, space, oceans, and the two polar regions), this activity becomes an ever greater threat to peace—threatening war, environmental disaster, inequitable sharing of resources of the commons, and inequitable access to the transportation and communications potential of the commons. Thus *governance for the global commons* (14) has emerged as a significant dimension of peace. Some consider the drafting of the United Nations Convention on Law of the Sea (1982) to be the most significant event in the struggle to develop peaceful governance for the commons. The convention sets territorial limits and provides regulations for ocean transit, for sharing of resources in and under the oceans, for control of pollution, and for scientific research. This was followed by the creation in 1994 of the International Seabed Authority, with its headquarters in Kingston, Jamaica, and the International Tribunal for Law of the Sea in Hamburg, Germany. Both have 145 member states.

The more recent emergence of *humanitarian intervention* (15) offers a striking example of how the emergence of new peace tools gradually reinterprets the UN Charter. Article 2.7 states:

"Nothing contained in the present Charter shall authorize the United Nations to intervene in matters which are essentially within the domestic jurisdiction of any state." Nevertheless, emerging human rights standards have been used to justify UN intervention in places such as Kosovo and Somalia. At the same time, interventions in the "failed states" of former colonies reveal how the achievements attained under one tool, in this case *self-determinism* (7) may lead to conditions that require the creation of another tool, such as humanitarian intervention.

At the same time, the recent emergence of *preventive diplomacy* (16) reveals a striking demand from many quarters for preventive measures that take a long-term perspective and thereby overcome the tendency to respond to threats of violence too late to prevent it. This has been accompanied by a remarkably rapid development of academic works that offer relevant insight.[5] The efforts of these researchers and others to make their work useful for policymakers are striking.

Our brief overview has revealed remarkable progress in fashioning tools that are now available for enhancing peace and well-being in the twenty-first century. Not only have functionalism, self-determination, and human rights been supplemented by economic development, economic and communications equity, ecological balance, and governance for the commons, but these new themes have deepened our insight on neglected dimensions of earlier approaches. We now understand better the full meaning of self-determination, as we have learned about its economic and communications dimensions. We now have insights on the ecological aspect of human rights. At the same time, new conflict resolution institutions, such as the International Seabed Authority and the International Tribunal for Law of the Sea, have been created.[6]

Organization of the UN System[7]

This brief overview of the historical roots of the UN System and the emergence of a growing array of peace tools has revealed the daily relevance of the entire system to the prevention of disruptive conflict and long-term peace building. We will now briefly describe significant aspects of the diagram of the UN System, Figure 1.1, beginning with the Principal Organs listed across the top.

General Assembly

The General Assembly consists of all member states, numbering 191 in 2005, listed in Chapter 5 on pages 153–155. It may consider any issue "within the scope of the present Charter or relating to the powers and functions of any organs," except for issues on the agenda of the Security Council. Voting procedures permit those present to vote "yes" or "no," or to abstain. Passage of substantive issues requires a two-thirds vote of those present and voting for or against the resolution. Votes on procedural issues require a simple majority of those voting for or against the resolution. The General Assembly begins its annual sessions on the second Tuesday in September of each year with a general debate in which heads of state and other high officials often participate. Those participating in the general debate may make comments on any issue.

Proposals of items for the General Assembly agenda are made to the General Committee, composed of the president of the General Assembly, twenty-one vice presidents, and the chairs of the six General Assembly main committees. The General Committee assigns accepted items to one of the six main committees. They are referred to both by a descriptive title and a number: (1) the Disarmament and International Security Committee, First; (2) the Economic and Financial Committee, Second; (3) the Social, Humanitarian, and Cultural Committee, Third; (4) the Special Political and Decolonization Committee, Fourth; (5) the Administrative and Budgetary Committee, Fifth; and (6) the Legal Committee, Sixth. Only rarely are issues sent directly to a plenary session of the Assembly.

In contrast to the practice of most legislative bodies, General Assembly committees are all committees of the whole, with representatives of all 191 member states. This challenges member states to have representation on six committees that often meet at the same time. Passage of resolutions in committees requires only a simple majority vote. As committees pass resolutions there are occasional meetings of the plenary to give final consideration to resolutions passed by committees. Those resolutions receiving only a simple majority in committee are the focus of much political activity before they reach the plenary, as efforts are made to attain a two-thirds majority.

Resolutions passed by the General Assembly are recommendations and do not have the force of law. On the other hand, they do have impact because of the legitimacy created by their passage. One example is the UN Declaration on Human Rights, which is treated as common law by courts in many countries. To give its provisions the explicit force of law, the Assembly drafted two conventions, one on civil and political rights and one on economic, social, and cultural rights. Individual states are not legally required to meet the standards defined in these conventions until they are ratified by their governments. Of course, General Assembly resolutions on the budgets and activities of UN agencies under General Assembly authority do have the force of law.

The General Assembly has more than a hundred issues on its agenda each year. Most require follow-up action by the Secretariat (the far right column in Figure 1.1) with offices that focus on a diversity of issues that include political matters, disarmament, peacekeeping, humanitarian concerns, economic and social problems, security, and drugs and crime. Particularly notable is the office created in 2001, Office of the High Representative for the Least Developed Countries, Landlocked Developing Countries, and Small Island Developing States (OHRLLS). Also included are offices of the Secetariat in Geneva, Vienna, and Nairobi.

The General Assembly has also found it necessary to establish the twenty-one units that are portrayed in the large box appearing in the bottom left-hand side of Figure 1.1. The names of these twenty-one units usefully reflect the growing breadth of the challenges confronted by the Assembly. We will make an effort to provide an overview by crudely classifying these offices, based on the three categories in the table, but it will be obvious to readers that the issues covered by them have a diversity of linkages.

The fourteen agencies classified as programs and funds could be divided into seven categories: (1) development (UNDP, UNIFEM, UNV, UNCDF, UNFPA, WFP); (2) refugees (UNHCR, UNRWA); (3) trade (UNCTAD, ITC); (4) environment (UNEP); (5) children (UNICEF); (6) drugs (UNDCP); and (7) human settlements (UN-HABITAT).

Of the five organizations classified as research and training institutes, one has a broad concern with training and research (UNITAR). The others are more specifically focused on (1) crime and justice (UNICRI), (2) social development (UNIDIR), (3) disarmament (UNUDIR), and (4) the advancement of women (INSTRAW).

The five other UN entities have a broad range of concerns: human rights (UNHCHR), HIV/AIDS (UNAIDS), UN Staff College (UNSSC), the UN University (UNU), and the UN Office for Project Services (UNOPS).

These fourteen agencies have seven locations in addition to those located where there are branches of the UN Secretariat (New York, Geneva, Vienna, and Nairobi). There are offices in Germany (Bonn), Italy (Rome, Turin), the Dominican Republic (Santo Domingo), Japan (Tokyo), Jordan (Amman), and Gaza.

Security Council

According to the Charter, the Security Council has "primary responsibility for the maintenance of international peace and security" (Article 24). It is organized to be able to function continuously, so a representative of each of its members must be present at all times at UN Headquarters. The Council has fifteen members: five permanent members (China, France, Russia, the United Kingdom, and the United States) and ten elected by the General Assembly for two-year terms. The presidency of the Council rotates monthly, according to the English alphabetical listing of its member states.

Each Council member has one vote. Decisions on procedural matters are made by an affirmative vote of at least nine of the fifteen members. Decisions on substantive matters also require nine votes, but no resolution passes if any permanent member votes against it. This power of permanent members is often referred to as the "veto" power.

Under the Charter, the functions and powers of the Security Council are: (1) to maintain international peace and security in accordance with the principles and purposes of the United Nations; (2) to investigate any dispute or situation that might lead to international friction; (3) to recommend methods of adjusting such disputes or the terms of settlement; (4) to formulate plans for the establishment of a system to regulate armaments; (5) to determine the existence of a threat to the peace or act of aggression and to recommend what action should be taken; (6) to call on members to apply economic sanctions and other measures not involving the use of force to prevent or stop aggression; (7) to take military action against an aggressor; (8) to recommend the admission of new members; (9) to exercise the trusteeship functions of the United Nations in "strategic areas"; (10) to recommend to the General Assembly the appointment of the secretary-general; and (11) together with the Assembly, to elect the judges of the International Court of Justice.

When a complaint concerning a threat to peace is brought before it, the Council's first action is usually to recommend that the parties try to reach agreement by peaceful means. In some cases, the Council itself undertakes investigation and mediation. It may appoint special representatives or request the secretary-general to do so or to use his or her good offices. It may set forth principles for a peaceful settlement.

A state that is a member of the United Nations, but not of the Security Council, may participate, without a vote, in the Council's discussions when the Council considers that that country's interests are affected. Both members of the United Nations and nonmembers if they are parties to a dispute being considered by the Council, are invited to take part, without a vote, in the Council's discussions; the Council sets the conditions for participation by a nonmember state.

On 18 May 2004 thirteen peacekeeping operations authorized by the Security Council were in the field, the highest number since 1995: three in Europe (Cyprus, Georgia, and Kosovo), six in Africa (the Ivory Coast, Liberia, the Democratic Republic of the Congo, Ethiopia/Eritrea, Sierra Leone, and Western Sahara), two in Asia (Eastern Timor and India/Pakistan), and two in the Middle East (the Golan Heights and Lebanon). These operations involved 53,000 peacekeepers (soldiers and police). Secretary General Kofi Annan observed on this day: "Many of these missions are large and complex. Most go beyond the limited military functions that have marked traditional peacekeeping missions."[8] There is also a UN truce supervision organization in the Middle East that performs observer functions in the area, serves as a go-between for hostile parties, and maintains offices in Beirut and Damascus.

Economic and Social Council

The Economic and Social Council (ECOSOC) consists of fifty-four representatives of member states that are elected by the General Assembly for three-year terms. Under the UN Charter, ECOSOC is responsible for: (1) promoting higher standards of living, full employment, and economic and social progress; (2) identifying solutions to international economic, social, and health problems; (3) facilitating international cultural and educational cooperation; and (4) encouraging universal respect for human rights and fundamental freedoms. ECOSOC's purview extends to over 70 percent of the human and financial resources of the entire UN System. Toward this end ECOSOC coordinates the work of the fourteen UN specialized agencies, nine functional commissions, and five regional commissions. It receives reports from eleven UN funds and programs and issues policy recommendations to the UN System and to member states. It is important to note that members of the coordinating bodies established by ECOSOC are representatives of member states. There is also a significant parallel effort at coordination carried out by representatives of the secretariats, the UN System Chief Executives Board (CEB).

As we provide a very brief inventory of the array of UN System agencies coordinated by ECOSOC, readers are urged to ponder which agencies are attempting to cope with activities in their personal daily lives that have global reach. A few obvious examples could be those with names that include these words: postal, telecommunications, civil aviation, intellectual property, tourism, environment, HIV/AIDS, trade, and the status of women. Each reader will no doubt identify others.

The fifteen Specialized Agencies (Figure 1.1) have a very special status. Each has been created by a separate treaty and has its own members, which tend to include most of the members of the organization created by the UN Charter. Each has its own assembly, council, and secretariat. The fact that they are largely autonomous makes efforts by ECOSOC to coordinate their activities of great importance. As we pointed out in our historical background, the roots of the Universal Postal Union (UPU), the International Telecommunications Union (ITU), and the World Health Organization (WHO) reach back into the nineteenth century. The International Labor Organization was founded in 1919. Headquarters of the specialized agencies are all located in Europe or North America: Geneva (ILO, WHO, ITU, WMO, WIPO), Vienna (UNIDO), Rome (FAO, IFAD), Paris (UNESCO), Washington (World Bank Group, IMF), Montreal (ICAO), London (IMO), and Bern (UPU).

The nine functional commissions (Figure 1.1) have a varying number of members, all representatives of member states. They focus on an array of issues that are on the agendas of the UN Secretariat and of separate units established by the General Assembly: human rights, narcotic drugs, crime prevention and criminal justice, science and technology for development, sustainable development, status of women, population and development, and social development. All of these issues are intertwined with issues on the agendas of a number of agencies in the UN System. Finally, the Statistical Commission responds to the need to achieve an integrated system in the collection, processing, and dissemination of statistics by a diversity of agencies within states and agencies throughout the UN System.

The five regional commissions (Figure 1.1), each with representatives from member states in a specific region of the world, were established to cope with issues that are regional in scope. Their headquarters are located in Addis Ababa, Bangkok, Beirut, Geneva, and Santiago (Chile).

Coordination of the work of the organizations in the UN System is also the responsibility of the UN System Chief Executives Board for Coordination (CEB), earlier called the Administrative Committee on Coordination (ACC). The CEB brings together the executive heads of twenty-four agencies to further coordination and cooperation on the whole range of substantive and management issues facing the UN System.

Chaired by the secretary-general of the United Nations, the CEB meets twice annually. It has two high-level committees of senior executives who are authorized to take decisions on behalf of their executive heads. The main function of the the High-Level Committee on Programs (HLCP) is to advise the CEB on policy and program and operational matters of systemwide importance and to foster interagency cooperation and coordination on these matters. The High-Level Committee on Management (HLCM) is the principal interagency body for coordination in the administration and management areas, particularly regarding financial and budgetary issues, human resources-related issues, information and communication technology (ICT) issues, and staff security within the UN System.

Trusteeship Council

In setting up an international trusteeship system, the Charter established the Trusteeship Council as one of the main organs of the United Nations and assigned to it the task of supervising the administration of trust territories placed under the trusteeship system. The major goals of the system were to promote the advancement of the inhabitants of trust territories and their progressive development toward self-government or independence. The aims of the trusteeship system have been fulfilled to such an extent that all trust territories have attained self-government or independence, either as separate states or by joining neighboring independent states. The Trusteeship Council suspended operation on 1 November 1994 with the independence of Palau, the last remaining UN trust territory, on 1 October 1994. By a resolution adopted on 25 May 1994, the council amended its rules of procedure to drop the obligation to meet annually and agreed to meet as occasion required—by its decision or the decision of its president, or at the request of a majority of its members or the General Assembly or the Security Council.

Secretariat

Our brief comments on the Secretariat will be limited to the Secretariat of the United Nations with headquarters in New York City. There are, of course, also secretariats at the headquarters of the fourteen autonomous Specialized Agencies with headquarters in other cities. The UN Secretariat, an international staff working in duty stations around the world, carries out the diverse day-to-day work of the organization. It services the other principal organs of the United Nations and administers the programs and policies laid down by them. At its head is the secretary-general, who is appointed by the General Assembly on the recommendation of the Security Council for a five-year renewable term.

The duties carried out by the Secretariat are as varied as the problems dealt with by the United Nations. These range from administering peacekeeping operations to mediating international disputes, from surveying economic and social trends and problems to preparing studies on human rights and sustainable development. Secretariat staff members also inform the world's communications media about the work of the United Nations, organize international conferences on issues of worldwide concern, and interpret speeches and translate documents into the organization's official languages.

The Secretariat has a staff of about 8,900 under the regular budget drawn from some 170 countries. As international civil servants, staff members and the secretary-general answer to the United Nations alone for their activities and take an oath not to seek or receive instructions from any government or outside authority. Under the Charter, each member state undertakes to respect the exclusively international character of the responsibilities of the secretary-general and the staff and to refrain from seeking to influence them improperly in the discharge of their duties.

Although headquartered in New York, the United Nations maintains a significant presence in Addis Ababa, Bangkok, Beirut, Geneva, Nairobi, Santiago, and Vienna, and has additional offices all over the world.

International Court of Justice

Chapter XIV of the UN Charter states that "[t]he International Court of Justice shall be the principal judicial organ of the United Nations." Its seat is at the Peace Palace in The Hague (Netherlands). It began work in 1946, when it replaced the Permanent Court of International Justice, which had functioned in the Peace Palace since 1922. The court has a dual role: to settle in accordance with international law the legal disputes submitted to it by states and to give advisory opinions on legal questions referred to it by duly authorized international organs and agencies.

The Court is composed of fifteen judges elected to nine-year terms of office by the UN General Assembly and Security Council sitting independently of each other. It may not include more than one judge of any nationality. Elections are held every three years for one-third of the seats, and retiring judges may be re-elected. The members of the court do not represent their governments but are independent magistrates.

Financing the UN System

The UN System is financed from two sources: the assessment of member states and voluntary contributions. Assessments are based on the wealth of each state. The United Nations has two forms of assessment, one for the regular budget and one for peacekeeping operations. Voluntary contributions are made to specific UN System agencies and activities. The Specialized Agencies have separate scales of assessment and also receive voluntary contributions. For the last year in which totals for the system were available, 2001, they were approximately US$ 12 billion. Of this total, 53 percent came from voluntary contributions.

With respect to UN assessments, it is notable that since 1992 the peacekeeping budget has surpassed the UN regular budget. In 2003 the peacekeeping budget equaled 67 percent of the assessments available to the United Nations. In 2004 the largest contributor, the United States, was assessed 24.5 percent, followed by Japan, Germany, the United Kingdom, France, Italy, Canada, and Spain. At the insistence of the U.S. Congress, the U.S. percentage was recently reduced to 21 percent. Were the United States to pay in accordance with its percentage of membership gross national product (GNP), it would be paying at a rate of 27 percent. The highest per capita contributors to the UN regular budget in rank order are: Luxembourg, Liechtenstein, Japan, Norway, Denmark, Monaco, Iceland, Germany, Austria, and Sweden. Their contributions range from $1.30 to $2.15 per capita. The U.S. per capita assessment is $0.98.

The very slow growth of the UN regular budget has not been responsive to its growing agenda. Particularly challenging for most agencies has been their significant dependence on voluntary contributions. For example, the Office of the High Commissioner for Human Rights (HCHR) depends on voluntary contributions for 67 percent of its budget. As a result, only 88 of its 155 personnel are financed by the regular budget. This dependence on voluntary contributions makes long-range planning difficult and prevents the OHCHR from making future commitments to valued personnel.

The challenges confronted by the UN System as a result of its limited financial resources is vividly demonstrated by comparing the UN System's US$ 12 billion-per-year budget with yearly world military expenditures of US$ 800 billion. This amount would finance the present UN System for sixty-five years. In 2005 the UN System's yearly budget is only 3 percent of that of the member state with the largest military budget. This imbalance challenges the UN System in two ways. First, it makes widespread tools of violence available to states for coping with conflict situations. Second, it withholds resources, from both states and the UN System, for the development of nonviolent procedures for coping with conflict and for long-term peace building.

The Political Process in the UN System

The emergence of organizations with universal membership has radically changed relations among states. In traditional diplomatic practice, it is only the large and wealthy states that have permanent representatives in most capitals of the world. The smaller and poorer states tend to accredit some of their ambassadors to a number of countries. But all member states tend to have permanent representatives at the main headquarters in the UN System. Another difference is that in capitals of states diplomats have no "common home," but at various UN System headquarters representatives of 191 states frequent the public and private meeting rooms, the lounges, hallways, dining facilities, bars, snack bars, libraries, and parking garages. In other words, when you wish to meet a representative of another state in a state capital, you plan it. In contrast, when you wish to avoid meeting a representative of a specific state at a UN System headquarters, you must plan it. These opportunities for apparently unplanned discussion can be particularly significant for representatives of states that are having unfriendly relationships or may not even have formal diplomatic relations.

Spending time at the headquarters of a UN agency offers representatives of states with a learning experience that is quite different from that acquired in the capital of a state. At a UN agency headquarters they are required to cope with an agenda of issues that has been developed by a political process in which states from around the world have been involved. At the same time, they must listen to public debate in which a vast array of different positions are taken on these issues. As they sit in alphabetical order in plenary and committee meetings, they find it difficult to avoid more private exchanges with nearby colleagues from other countries. In addition, small groups of delegates spend many hours in small meeting rooms attempting to develop a consensus on difficult issues that can be presented for consideration in public sessions. Thus, the atmosphere at the headquarters of many UN agencies is more akin to that of a parliament than that of traditional diplomacy. Indeed, Philip Jessup, who represented the United States in the UN in many capacities in the early days of the UN, gave the name "parliamentary diplomacy" to this process in the mid-1950s.[9] Members of UN secretariats are, of course, also important participants in the UN political process. They work with the elected officers of UN decision-making bodies in preparing the agenda. They often have a longer background of experience on issues being debated than do these officers. During public meetings they sit alongside the chairs of meetings and assist them as they attempt to cope with the dynamic political process by helping them to decide when to call a vote, when to adjourn, and when to make substantive or procedural recommendations to the participants.

In addition, in most of the places where representatives of states meet in parliamentary diplomacy, representatives of nongovernmental organizations (NGOs) may be present. Building on the Charter provision Article 71, providing for NGO consultation with ECOSOC, more than 2,400 NGOs have consultative status with ECOSOC in 2005. Access by some of these organizations has been extended to the General Assembly, the Security Council, and secretariats and decision-making bodies throughout the UN System. Finally, the media, too, have easy access to most of the places where representatives of states and secretariats are engaged in parliamentary diplomacy.

Conclusion

This opening chapter has emphasized that the UN System is an array of organizations that have emerged in response to two main factors. First, a growing number of global issues are emerging because of the impact of new technologies on travel, trade, communication, manufacturing, and investment. Second, there is growing understanding that overcoming violence and seriously disruptive conflict requires not only the capacity to respond when threats emerge, but also sustained efforts to cope with economic, social, cultural, and political issues at the roots of these conflicts—that is, long-term peace building. As a result, representatives of 191 states meet simultaneously every day in a number of headquarters, and members of secretariats work every day in some forty headquarters, in efforts to cope with these issues.

Because of these developments, we have termed this period of dynamic growth in the UN System to be the "era of preparation for global governance." We perceive the UN System to be a vast "laboratory" where representatives of states and members of secretariats are attempting to devise a form of governance relevant for people from a great diversity of cultures, religions, economies, and natural environments around the world.

Although a vast array of public policy issues now flow across all borders, as we ponder their global dimension it is important that we bear in mind that each has dimensions that must be attended to by local governments, regional governments within states, governments of states, and regional organizations of states, as well as organizations in the UN System. For example, coping with air pollution, human rights, health, and drug problems requires simultaneous efforts that reach from local to global governance. Of course, this also greatly complicates the challenges confronted by people who aspire to be responsible citizens. They must be informed of their responsibilities with respect to governments that represent them from the local to the global. It is our hope that the material that follows in this volume will challenge you to become more self-consciously aware of the world relations of your daily life and enhance your ability to become responsibly involved in emerging global governance.

Notes

1. This brief historical summary is based on Chadwick F. Alger, 1995, "The United Nations in Historical Perspective," in Chadwick F. Alger, Gene M. Lyons, and John E. Trent, eds., *The United Nations Systems: The Policies of Member States*. Tokyo: United Nations University, 3–40.

2. Inis Claude, Jr., 1971, *Swords into Ploughshares: The Problems and Progress of International Organizations*, 4th ed., New York: Random House, 41.

3. J. S. Scott., ed., 1971, *The Reports to the Hague Conference of 1899 and 1907*. Oxford: Humphren Milford, 201; cited by Claude, 29.

4. William McNeill, 1963, *The Rise of the West: A History of the Human Community*. Chicago: University of Chicago, 565.

5. Several titles of these works vividly illuminate this trend: *Preventive Measures: Building Risk Assessment and Crisis Early Warning*, 1998, by John L. Davies and Ted Robert Gurr; *Preventing Violent Conflicts: A Strategy for Preventive Diplomacy*, 1996, by Michael S. Lund; and *Preventing*

Deadly Conflict, 1998, by the Carnegie Commission on Preventing Deadly Conflict.

6. For a more comprehensive overview of the historical roots of the UN System see Chadwick F. Alger, "The Expanding Tool Chest for Peace-builders," 1999, in Ho-Won Jeong, ed., *The New Agenda for Peace Research. Aldershot, UK, and Brookfield, USA: Ashgate, 13–42.*

7. This brief overview of the UN System has drawn substantially on information available at the UN website at www.un.org.

8. www.UNWire.org, 18 May 2004.

9. Philip Jessup, 1956, *Parliamentary Diplomacy: An Examination of the Legal Quality of the Rules of Procedure of Organs of the United Nations. Leyden, Netherlands: A. W. Sijhoff.*

2

Problems, Controversies, and Solutions

fforts of the UN System to cope with a growing array of
global challenges are encountering problems that are resulting in many controversies and debates over what would be
the most effective solutions. This is to be expected because organizations in the UN System are attempting to cope with a dynamically changing social and natural global environment by developing procedures for what is increasingly called *global
governance*. This term is preferred in order to distinguish this process from *world government*, earlier associated with proposals for
a world government that tended to be modeled after existing
states. Instead, global governance is perceived to be emerging
out of learning acquired in efforts to cope with problems that
range across the borders of 191 states around the world.

Certainly, response to this challenge requires a form of governance that is quite different from that employed in single
states. Of course, this does not mean that what we have learned,
and are continually learning, from governing experience within
states will not be useful. But it does suggest that governance procedures in no single state will be a model for global governance.
Thus, for the most part, a useful model for global governance
must emerge primarily out of learning through practice. Certainly, practice in the UN System, or what could be called "the
UN System laboratory," will be exceedingly important.

A key challenge arises from the fact that people around the
world are increasingly linked in their daily lives as a result of factors such as the origins of the clothes they wear, the cars they

drive, the gas they consume, the fact that their employers may reside in distant states, the distant sources of pollutants in the air they breathe, and the distant sources of guns on their streets. But these linked people live in very different kinds of societies, cultures, and climates. Thus, attaining acceptable solutions to a diversity of global issues is certainly very challenging. For example, people everywhere aspire to acquire peace, human rights, development, and security. But people living in different circumstances tend to define these terms differently because their peace, human rights, development, and security are challenged by different factors.

Varied Definitions of Global Values

Peace is defined by many as the absence of violence, because it is the fear of war and other forms of violence that are perceived to be the greatest threat to a peaceful life. On the other hand, people in other circumstances may not see violence as the greatest threat to their peaceful existence. Because of their social and economic environment, the greatest threat may be lack of health care, lack of adequate housing, and lack of food. Indeed, many more people die around the world every year from the lack of these necessities than from violence. As a result of dialogue across cultures, some define the lack of violence as *negative peace*—that is, peace achieved by not doing something. *Positive peace* is defined as that which is achieved through availability of those things (such as health care, housing, and food) that remove the threats that prevent the fulfillment of a normal daily life. Availability of these human needs is inhibited by the ways societies are organized, or what is termed *structural violence*. On the other hand, the term *direct violence* is applied to wars and other forms of violence in which the perpetrator is more obvious.

Human rights are sought by all peoples. For some this term means what are often called civil and political rights, such as the rights to free speech, assembly, voting for governmental officials, equal legal protection for all, and the right to be presumed innocent until proven guilty. But people living in different circumstances assert that these rights cannot be enjoyed and protected without the underpinning of certain economic and social rights, such as the right to work, the right to education, the right to rest and leisure, and the right to a standard of living adequate for health and well-being. As a result, an increasing number of people believe that simultaneous attainment of civil/political and economic/social rights is necessary for either to be fulfilled.

Development is another human goal that has acquired different definitions as people living in different circumstances become involved in its definition. In the early days of UN development programs, many tended to define development as synonymous with industrialization. Thus, development programs emphasized the building of factories and the roads and airports needed to supply their production needs. But, sensing that this kind of development was not serving the needs of most of the people, some began to define development as meeting the basic needs of the people. Later, dissatisfied with the definition of basic needs imposed by external agencies, others began to assert that development must permit people to be self-reliant in defining their needs. Then, more recently, those concerned about the ecological consequences of development policies adopted the term *sustainable development,* meaning that long-term development can only be sustainable if it takes into account the ecological impact of development programs.

Until quite recently, in discourse on international issues, the term *security* tended to mean primarily security of the state from external aggression. But recently there has been an expansion of the definition of the beneficiaries of security. In 2005 the term *human security* was widely used, meaning that the goal of security is to protect the well-being of all people. It is obvious that the emergence of the human security concern has been affected by the broadened meanings of peace, human rights, and development. Each of these values, when defined in ways that are responsive to human needs around the world, tends to incorporate the factors contained in the other three values. In effect, this means that the goals of global governance—whether they be peace, human rights, development, or security—must be responsive to definitions espoused by people in different circumstances around the world. For example, an effort to achieve global peace cannot succeed if it is guided by a definition of peace adopted by one state or region of the world. Achievement of peace requires strategies that incorporate aspects of the definitions of peace that are emerging around the world.

In a similar way, organizations throughout the UN System are confronted by the need to contend with the links between global issues. For example, the lead UN agency for human rights is the High Commissioner for Human Rights. Nevertheless, programs of the UN Development Program (UNDP), the UN Development Fund for Women (UNIFEM), the UN High Commissioner for Refugees (UNHCR), and many other UN agencies affect the human rights of the people involved in their programs. This linkage between global issues makes challenging demands for widespread cooperation among UN agencies.

The Challenge of Global Complexity

The members of the United Nations, Specialized Agencies, and other Related Organizations are states, those institutions pictured so clearly in different colors on maps of the world. But the UN System must contend with the fact that the organization of humankind is much more complicated than suggested by the political map. This false simplicity has also been suggested by careless use of the terms *nation* and *nation-state*. Some groups with a strong national identity, such as the Kurds, flow across the borders of several states. Within some states—for example, the Democratic Republic of the Congo—there are nations that have never accepted their incorporation into a state whose borders were drawn by invaders from Europe. Thus, it would be more accurate to call some states *multination states*. A number of these states, now referred to as *failed states*, have recently been presenting the UN System with serious challenges.

The boundaries in the political map of the world also do not illuminate other boundaries, such as those of climate, resources, ecology, terrain, and concentrated locations of populations. These boundaries may reflect the existence of problems that can only be resolved by the collaboration of governments that reach to the borders of the problem. Some states involved in a specific problem area may give it high priority and others may consider it to be insignificant. For example, UN agencies may encounter great difficulty in attaining collaboration from representatives of a state when this problem area is distant from the capital of that state.

The Functions of Social Conflict

All political institutions, from those in small towns to global organizations, confront an array of problems in dealing with conflict among human beings. One challenge was revealed to me when sitting in the press gallery of the General Assembly one day when a strenuous debate between representatives of the Soviet Union and the United States took place. A member of the press said to me: "There they go again. This is supposed to be the United Nations, but they are fighting again." But vitally important was the fact that they were not fighting! They were waging conflict with words in a parliamentary body in which discussion followed agreed rules. Louis Coser, a sociologist who wrote in 1956 a classic in social theory, *The Functions of Social Conflict*, creatively argued that human beings live in an imperfect and dynamically changing world in which they are challenged by many problems. Conflict among those with different approaches to these problems is both inevitable and useful. The challenge is how to enable this conflict to take place in ways that attain widely accepted solutions. Too frequently people assume that it is the role of the UN System to end conflict. Instead, it is the role of the UN System to create institutions where conflict can be conducted without violence and serious disruption in ways that lead to widely accepted solutions.

The Need for Long-Term Peace Building

As we have emphasized in Chapter 1, experience in the League of Nations and the UN System has demonstrated that long-term peace building is required for preventing violence, instead of the tendency to employ short-term policies responsive to violence and threats of violence when it is too late to prevent them. Experience has also made it clear that the most effective approaches to avoidance of violence require efforts in local communities by governments of states and sometimes by regional organizations. On the other hand, it seems inevitable that, on some occasions, these efforts will fail and seriously disruptive conflicts will be placed on UN System agendas.

It is essential that we be aware of the challenges confronted by the UN System in its efforts to develop global governance procedures for long-term peace building. This requires monitoring potential areas of disruptive conflict, devising strategies that can overcome this potential, mobilizing people in the conflict area and UN member states to accept these strategies, and attaining the collaboration of UN agencies in implementing these strategies. Of course, there is no single formula for handling all cases of disruptive conflict because the roots of different conflicts may vary significantly, ranging across issues such as ethnic conflict, authoritarian rule, poverty, poor health, and environmental pollution, and often involve different combinations of these issues. Thus, different cases of disruptive conflict may require the involvement of different agencies in the UN System.

This approach to long-term peace building offers severe challenges when we ponder the need for collaboration among agencies of the UN System. In Chapter 1 we indicated that efforts are made to coordinate the system both by a body composed of heads of all agencies (the UN System Chief Executive Board for Coordination, CEB) and by representatives of states (ECOSOC) whose efforts are facilitated by nine functional commissions and five regional commissions. When we consider the entire UN System to be involved in long-term peace building, this offers an additional perspective on coordination among agencies. This means that all agencies in the UN System, as they develop their approach to specific global problems, must be aware of how their efforts could both contribute to and diminish long-term peace-building efforts. For example, efforts to cope with poverty by a certain form of economic assistance might come at severe ecological costs that will form the roots of another disruptive conflict.

One reason why we are emphasizing this approach to coordination in the UN System is in response to proposals that have been made for coping with coordination problems by developing a more centralized system. Some proposals would severely curtail the considerable autonomy of the specialized agencies and would even create a system primarily based in one place. On the other hand, we are inclined to see the decentralized system of global governance that is emerging out of experience to be more responsive to global needs. Certainly, the efforts of the CEB and ECOSOC are important and can be improved. But also vitally important is that peace builders throughout the system must be cognizant of the ways in which the success of their efforts requires a UN System perspective.

The Need for a
UN Standby Peacekeeping Force

In mid-2004 the UN's Department of Peacekeeping Operations was managing sixteen peacekeeping operations. Although the development of more effective long-term peace-building capacity in the UN System would decrease the need for peacekeeping operations, certainly there would still be need for peacekeeping forces. A serious challenge to the effectiveness of UN peacekeeping forces has been the lack of capacity for a rapid response. Over many years this has led to many proposals for the establishment of standby forces that would be prepared for quick deployment (Johansen 1998). Although no such force has been created, there are slowly moving efforts to meet this need.

One development has been the Standby Arrangements System (UNSAS) through which the UN Department of Peacekeeping Operations reports that nearly 70 countries have identified 88,000 potentially available troops. The UNSAS is based on conditional commitments by member states of specified resources within agreed response times for UN peacekeeping operations. These resources can be military formations, specialized personnel (civilian and military) services, as well as material and equipment. The resources agreed upon remain on "stand-by" in their home countries, where necessary preparation, including training, is conducted to prepare them to fulfill specified tasks or functions in accordance with UN guidelines. These stand-by forces and resources would be used exclusively for peacekeeping operations mandated by the Security Council. When specific needs arise, stand-by resources are requested by the Secretary-General and, if approved by participating member states, are rapidly deployed to set up new peacekeeping missions or to reinforce existing ones.

A multilateral effort in support of UNSAS has been created by fourteen European states (Austria, Denmark, Finland, Italy, Ireland, Lithuania, the Netherlands, Norway, Poland, Portugal, Romania, Slovenia, Spain, and Sweden) and Canada: the Steering

Committee of the Multinational Stand-by High Readiness Brigade for UN Operations (SHIRBRIG). With headquarters nineteen miles from Copenhagen, SHIRBRIG declared itself available to the United Nations in January 2000 (www.shirbrig.dk). It contributed to the UN Mission in Ethiopia and Eritrea (UNMEE) in November of that year and helped the United Nations to establish the mission there. In 2003 it helped to establish an interim headquarters in Liberia. The SHIRBRIG has been working with the African Union and the Economic Community of West African States (ECOWAS) toward developing a similar initiative on the African continent.

An effort to attain U.S. government support for the development of a UN rapid deployment force has been initiated by Congressman James P. McGovern from Massachusetts, the McGovern-Porter UN Rapid Deployment Police and Security Force Act of 2000. Cosponsored by 25 members of Congress, it calls for a military force under the command and control of the UN Security Council. This force of 6,000 would consist only of volunteers employed directly by the United Nations. It would be rapidly deployed as a "vanguard" unit sent to "contain conflict and stabilize the political situation, while giving regular peacekeeping units from member nations sufficient time to deploy" (www.unwatch.com). This resolution has been submitted to the House of Representatives International Relations Committee. At the time of the writing of this chapter, there was no indication that this bill would be accepted by the committee.

Are Changes in Security Council and General Assembly Voting and Security Council Membership Needed?

The Security Council has overwhelming power to take measures, including armed force, "with respect to threats to the peace, breaches of the peace, and acts of aggression" (Chapter VII, UN Charter). Some see the membership and voting procedures of the Security Council as a limitation on Council effectiveness. The Security Council is composed of five permanent members (China, France, Russia, the United Kingdom, and the United States) and ten rotating members serving two-year terms. But many claim that the legitimacy of the Council is limited by the fact that the permanent members, victorious powers in World War II, no longer have the legitimacy required for carrying out this task. Therefore, it is advocated that the permanent members should include member states from other regions, such as Brazil, Nigeria and India. It is also argued that the defeated states in World War II, Germany and Japan, now deserve to be permanent members.

To pass a substantive resolution, the Council requires nine votes and the absence of a negative vote from any of the permanent members, usually referred to as a "veto." Some proposing the addition of new permanent members would not give them the "veto" power. Others would limit the veto for existing permanent members to only those issues that have a direct bearing on the security of the state employing the veto.

Unlike the Security Council, resolutions of the General Assembly are only recommendations, although under certain circumstances these resolutions can have very significant influence. Each of the 191 members has one vote, with two-thirds of those casting "yes" or "no" votes required to pass a substantive resolution. As the membership of the United Nations has become universal, many states very small in area and population have become members. As a result, in 2005 there are more than thirty members with populations of less than 1,000.

Some believe that General Assembly resolutions would more accurately reflect the views of the people of the world if each state had a proportion of votes that reflected the size of its population. But this procedure would give the combined votes of only two states, China and India, one-third of all the votes. Others say that the votes of states should be weighted in conformity with the size of their assessed financial contributions. (In the World Bank and the International Monetary Fund member states have votes proportional to their financial assessments. In the case of the IMF, the five states with the largest votes have 40 percent of the votes: the United States, 17.4 percent; Japan, 6.15 percent; Germany, 6.01 percent; France, 4.96 percent; and the United Kingdom, 4.96 percent). If voting in the General Assembly were based on financial assessments, the United States would have 22 percent and Japan 19 percent of the votes, a total of 41 percent. Many would see either of these procedures giving too many votes to only two states.

Joseph E. Schwartzberg (Professor of Geography at the University of Minnesota), in *Revitalizing the United Nations: Reform through Weighted Voting,* has proposed combining the present General Assembly voting system with these two factors in order to develop a weighted voting (**WV**) proposal. The vote awarded to each state would be the average of its percentage of the UN membership (**M**), now 1/191, its percentage of total population (**P**) of UN members, and the percentage of its assessed financial contributions (**C**). Stated briefly this would be:

$$WV = \frac{P + C + M}{3}$$

Using this formula, sixteen states would receive at least 1 percent of the votes: the United States, 9.1 percent; China 7.7 percent, Japan, 7.3 percent; India, 6.0 percent; Germany, 3.8 percent; Italy, 2.2 percent; Canada, 1.2 percent; France, 2.6 percent; the United Kingdom, 2.3 percent; Brazil, 1.9 percent; Indonesia, 1.4 percent; Russia, 1.3 percent; Spain, 1.2 percent; Mexico, 1.1 percent; the Republic of Korea, 1.0 percent; and Pakistan, 1.0 percent.

Notable when this formula is applied is the fact that seven of the states receiving at least 1 percent of the votes would be from North America and Europe. There is no state from Africa, where Nigeria led the continent with 0.9 percent. Some would argue that this result indicates that population should have more weight than wealth. On the other hand, others would argue that the formula is more reflective of population than one vote for each state.

Schwartzberg has proposed applying this same formula in revising Security Council membership. His approach would first eliminate permanent members. Then he would make a fundamental change by permitting individual states to form like-minded blocs that are not necessarily contiguous. Then these blocs could be eligible for Security Council membership, which would be increased from fifteen to eighteen. Seats would first be awarded to all states with a **WV** exceeding 4 percent. Then blocs exceeding 4 percent **WV**, as well as with a total population in excess of 1 percent of all UN members, would be awarded Security Council seats. This formula would be applied up to a permissible total of seventeen seats. The remaining seat(s) would be reserved for one or more states not otherwise represented, and these seats would be filled by the General Assembly through an at-large election list composed of states not otherwise represented.

Schwartzberg's plan has two creative innovations. His **WV** formula for the first assignment of Security Council membership replaces the outmoded "victors in World War II" method of choosing permanent members. Also, his encouragement of the creation of like-minded blocs as candidates for Council membership offers a new method for states with a small **WV** percent to band together and attain seats that represent their key interests. It would seem that this formula would ensure Council membership that is more representative of all the people of the world than is the present system.

Alternative Modes for Financing the UN System

As we have indicated in Chapter 1, the annual UN System financial support of US$12 billion is only 3 percent of the military expenditures of one member state, the United States, a sum that is far short of that required for effectively fulfilling the organization's escalating responsibilities. In response, there have been a number of proposals for alternative means for financing the UN System by taxing activities that link people and enterprises involved in worldwide linkages. Included are currency transaction taxes, e-mail taxes, energy taxes, and aviation fuel taxes (www.globalpolicy.org).

Currency and e-mail taxes would tax those involved in international transactions that are dependent on UN System activities that help to make them possible. Global currency trade amounts to approximately $1.3 trillion per day. At least 80 percent of this is exchange-rate speculation, either short- or long-term profit-seeking transactions. Cross-border purchases of goods and services requiring foreign exchange account for only 2 percent. About 17 percent of foreign exchange trading takes place as a result of hedging against future exchange-rate fluctuations. A tax of only 0.25 percent would generate about $300 billion, twenty-five times the 2001 UN System budget of $12 billion.

An e-mail or Internet tax would tax the amount of data sent through the Internet. A person sending 100 e-mails a day, each containing a 10-kilobyte document, would pay a tax of just one cent. The UNDP Development Report 1999 reported that such a tax would have yielded $70 billion in 1996, almost six times the

2001 UN System budget. No doubt in 2005 this infinitesimal tax would bring in much more than this 1999 figure.

Aviation fuel and energy taxes would tax those who are responsible for global carbon emissions that are imposing environmental challenges on the UN System. Although airplane travel accounts for only 3 percent of global carbon emissions in 2005, it is expected to account for 15 percent by 2050. The European Parliament's Economic and Monetary Affairs Committee has urged the European Commission to pursue negotiations with the International Civil Aviation Organization toward the end of amending a 1944 Chicago convention allowing an exemption from taxes on air fuel. Although the United States and Australia oppose a worldwide levy on aviation fuel, many other countries have expressed interest. At the same time, some NGOs are pushing for increases in sales taxes on airline tickets and landing fees that could be devoted to financial support of the UN System.

There are also proposals for taxing more broadly carbon dioxide emissions resulting from combustion of fossil fuels that impose costs and challenges on governance that range from local to global. These proposals would tax carbon emissions from the burning of coal, oil, and natural gas. There is active debate on this issue now in the European Union. Some are proposing that at least a portion of such a tax be applied to UN financial needs.

Expanding Participation in Global Governance

Although the members of all organizations in the UN System are states, the broad array of global issues in which these organizations are involved are inevitably of concern to a diversity of other kinds of organizations. We will briefly examine the escalating involvement of nongovernmental organizations (NGOs), businesses, and local authorities in the UN System.

Non-governmental Organizations/ Civil Society

In addressing the Conference of NGOs at UN headquarters in 1994, Secretary-General Boutros Boutros Ghali began in this way:

> Madame President, ladies and gentlemen, dear friends,
> on behalf of the United Nations and for myself, I wel-
> come you. I want you to consider this your home.

The secretary-general's cordial greeting reflected the fact that the
number, roles, and importance of NGOs involved in the United
Nations had grown significantly since its founding almost fifty
years earlier. We have already indicated in Chapter 1 that Article
71 of the UN Charter provides the opportunity for NGOs to consult with ECOSOC and that this has led to NGO involvement
throughout the UN System. The NGOs involved in the UN System are nonprofit organizations that have as their mission the
achievement of specific goals on social issues. Although these organizations are referred to as NGOs in the UN System, others
tend to refer to them as "civil society." Building on consultation
with ECOSOC, NGOs have extended their involvement at UN
headquarters to relations with the General Assembly and the Security Council. In addition, NGOs also have wide-ranging involvement with members of the Secretariat. Furthermore, secretariats of organizations throughout the UN System have
established offices for facilitating collaboration with NGOs.
Thus, NGOs are making efforts to influence decision making in
organizations throughout the UN System (Alger 2003).

The practice of holding UN conferences focused on specific
global issues—such as environment, food, human rights, and
women's issues—at various sites around the world has had a significant impact on the development of NGO involvement in the
UN System in at least three respects. First, NGOs have held conferences that run parallel to the governmental conferences. These
parallel conferences have spurred the development of NGO collaboration in the development of policies on specific issues and
in presenting them to meetings composed of government representatives. Second, NGOs have become increasingly involved in
the preparatory phases of these UN conferences. This has offered
NGOs experience in wider involvement in the prepublic phases
of parliamentary diplomacy. Third, the fact that the sites of these
conferences have been scattered around the world has made
them accessible to a growing number of NGOs, particularly
those in the "less developed world" who have not had access to
meetings at various UN headquarters.

It is obvious that NGO involvement in UN conferences
away from headquarters and new relationships provided by the

Internet are having a feedback impact on the numbers and quality of NGO participation at various UN headquarters. They have tended to greatly increase not only the number of NGOs involved, but also to broaden geographic representation and the array of policy issues on the agendas of headquarters NGOs. At the same time, rules for NGO participation have often been more flexible away from headquarters, leading to demands for the same opportunities at headquarters. Finally, NGOs have also become important "laboratories" in which some NGO leaders have begun to envisage greatly enhanced roles for NGOs in global governance.

For example, one proposal advanced by NGOs would create a subsidiary organ of the General Assembly, a UN Commission on Peace and Crisis Prevention (UNCOPAC). It would be composed of "highly respected individuals from public life" from five regions of the world that would advise the General Assembly on strategies for preventing violent conflict. The proposal is motivated by the belief that many NGOs have had wide experience in coping with conditions that lead to violence and thereby have the experience needed to offer useful advice on violence prevention. Potential members of this commission would be nominated by UN-accredited NGOs, and the General Assembly would choose the members. The UNCOPAC would make recommendations to the General Assembly. "When there are signs that political developments could lead to violent conflict, genocide or crimes against humanity," UNCOPAC would "draw up detailed proposals for non-military measures appropriate to reverse the trend in this direction" (www.pro-uncopac.info).

For several decades there have been more ambitious proposals that call for a second general assembly composed either of representatives of nongovernmental organizations or of directly elected members. Some advocates of a second assembly see it as something that could evolve from an ad hoc annual event into a permanent organization that is eventually formally established by an amendment to the UN Charter (Childers and Urquhart 1994).

Those with this view saw an opportunity when plans were made to hold the Millennium Assembly of the UN General Assembly in 2000. Secretary-General Kofi Annan, in midsummer 1997, joined the call for a companion Peoples Millennium Assembly (PMA) in his reform report. This proposed assembly met on 22–26 May 2000 under the name Peoples Millennium Forum rather than "Assembly," no doubt a result of an effort by member states to clearly distinguish its role from that associated with the General Assembly. Participating in the Forum were 1,350 representatives of over 1,000 NGOs from more than 100 countries. The Forum issued a declaration with the title "We the Peoples Millennium Forum Declaration and Agenda for Action: Strengthening the United Nations for the Twenty-First Century." It declared the intent to build on UN world conferences and civil society conferences of the 1990s toward the goal of drawing "the attention of governments to the urgency of implementing the commitments they have made and to channel our collective energies by reclaiming globalization for and by the people." This was followed by a broad agenda for action in pursuit of a "vision of the world that is human-centered and genuinely democratic, where all human beings are full participants and determine their own destinies" (UN General Assembly A/54/959, 8 August 2000).

It is interesting that there seems to be no interest in applying the tripartite representation system of the International Labor Organization (ILO) to the General Assembly and Security Council of the United Nations, or the assemblies and councils of other Specialized Agencies. In the ILO assembly (Labor Conference) and council (Governing Body) each state is represented by two government delegates, one employers' delegate, and one labor delegate. Instead of proposing that member states add NGO representatives to their delegations there is a preference for adding a second assembly, either directly elected or composed of representatives of NGOs.

Businesses

The UN website (www.un.org) introduces UN relationships with businesses, that is, for-profit enterprises, in this way:

> The relationship with the business community has become more important as the role of business in generating employment and wealth through trade, investment and finance has grown and as UN member states have increasingly stressed the importance of private investment in development.
> The business community is increasingly appreciative of the role of the United Nations: Promoting peace and

security, providing norms and standards in such diverse areas as trade laws, shipping, aviation, telecommunication, postal services and statistics; addressing issues of vulnerability, poverty, environmental degradation and social conflict. All of this is seen as helping provide a stable and favorable framework for business and development.

In an address to the World Economic Forum on 31 January 1999, UN Secretary-General Kofi Annan challenged business leaders to join an international initiative—the Global Compact—that would bring companies together with UN agencies, labor, and civil society in support of ten principles in the areas of human rights, labor, and the environment. The ten principles are derived from: (1) the Universal Declaration of Human Rights, (2) the International Labor Organization's Declaration on Fundamental Principles and Rights at Work, (3) the Rio Declaration on Environment and Development, and (4) the UN Convention Against Corruption. The Global Compact's operational phase was launched at UN Headquarters in New York on 26 July 2000. Through the power of collective action, the Global Compact seeks to advance responsible corporate citizenship so that business can be part of the solution to the challenges of globalization. In this way, the private sector—in partnership with other social actors—can help realize the secretary-general's vision: a more sustainable and inclusive global economy. In 2005 hundreds of companies from all regions of the world, international labor, and civil society organizations are engaged in the Global Compact.

Local Authorities

For many years local authorities in towns, cities, and local regions have become increasingly aware of the involvement of people and organizations in their communities in activities that reach around the world. In response, many have seen a need to become more directly involved in developing policies that affect these relationships. As a result, there are a number of global organizations of local authorities that began with the creation of the International Union of Local Authorities (IULA) in 1913. It merged in 2004 with the World Federation of United Cities (FMCU-UTO) and Metropolis, an association of 81 cities with more than a million inhabitants, to form the United Cities and Local Government Organization (UCLG). There are also global organizations of local authorities focusing on environment, peace, poverty, children, and those sharing a common language. There are also regional organizations of local authorities composed of Asian, Latin American, African, and Arab participants. In 1996 these organizations collaborated in establishing a Federation of Global Organizations of Local Authorities (WACLAC). The WACLAC is asking for participation of cities and local authorities in the proceedings of the UNCHS (Habitat) and for membership on its Commission on Human Settlements (Alger 2003A, 96–103).

Cities are even on the agenda of Secretary-General Kofi Annan, who said that local governments should be given more authority to deal with problems that come with explosive growth as the world enters the "urban millennium." In January 2000 a UN Advisory Committee of Local Authorities was established in Venice at a meeting called by the head of the UNCHS (Habitat) and attended by mayors from all over the world and presidents of international associations of local authorities (UNCHS 2001).

The UNCHS (Habitat) has been a significant focus of local authority activity in the UN System. Before the Second UN Conference on Human Settlements (Habitat II), held in Istanbul in 1996, there was a World Assembly of Cities and Local Authorities (WACLA) that led to the formation of WACLAC (UNCHS 2000). Other examples of local concerns in the UN System include the Municipal Development Program (World Bank), World Alliance of Cities Against Poverty (UNDP), Mayors Defenders of Children Initiative (UNICEF), Environmental Management Systems for Local Authorities (UNEP), Alliance of Mayors Initiative for Community Action on AIDS at the Local Level (UNAIDS and UNESCO), Cities for Peace Network, and the Global Campaign on Urban Governance (UNCHS).

What Are Your Involvements and Responsibilities?

We have presented these brief accounts of the escalating involvement of NGOs, businesses, and local authorities in the UN System for two reasons. One is to underline three significant indicators of the dynamic expansion of actors involved in global governance in the UN System. The other is to illuminate for all readers the fact that they are personally involved in organizations and activities that are perceiving the need for wider involvement in global governance that is emerging in the UN System.

Our brief presentation of expanding participation in global governance by NGOs/civil society, businesses, and local authorities possibly challenged some readers to ponder their personal linkage to global governance. Probably most readers are members of NGO/civil society organizations that have representation at one or more UN organizations. Some may have investments in business organizations that are involved in the Global Compact. No doubt we all have dealings with business organizations that are either adhering to or violating UN human rights standards. Some readers are certainly living in cities that have membership in world organizations of local authorities. Some readers may wish to find out the degree to which they approve of the policies of those NGO/civil society organizations, business organizations, and local authorities that are representing them.

References

Alger, Chadwick F., 2003, "Escalating Roles of NGOs in Member State Decision-Making in the UN System," *Journal of Human Rights,* Vol. 2, No. 3, 407–424.

———, 2003A, "Searching for Democratic Potential in Emerging Global Governance," in Bruce Morrison, ed., *Transnational Democracy in Critical and Comparative Perspective: Democracy's Range Considered.* Aldershot, UK: Ashgate, 88–105.

Childers, Erskine, and Brian Urquhart, 1994, *Renewing the United Nations System.* Uppsala, Sweden: Dag Hammarskjold Foundation.

Coser, Louis, 1956, *The Functions of Social Conflict.* Glencoe, IL: Free Press.

Global Policy Forum, www.globalpolicy.org/finance.

Johansen, Robert, 1998, "Enhancing United Nations Peace-Keeping," in Chadwick F. Alger, ed., *The Future of the United Nations System: Potential for the Twenty-first Century.* Tokyo: UN University, 89–126.

Luck, Edward C., 2003, *Reforming the United Nations: Lessons from a History in Progress.* New Haven, CT: Academic Council on the UN Occasional Papers.

Schwartzberg, Joseph E., 2004, *Revitalizing the United Nations: Reform through Weighted Voting*. New York and The Hague: Institute for Global Policy, World Federalist Movement.

Multinational Stand-by High Readiness Brigade for United Nations Operations (SHIRBRIG), www.shirbrig.dk.

UN Commission on Peace and Conflict Prevention (UNCOPAC), www.pro-uncopac.info.

UN Watch, www.unwatch.com.

UNCHS (Habitat), 2000, "Mayors Support the World Charter for Local Self-Government and the Istanbul+5 Process," Press release CHS/00/14, Nairobi: 9 May 2000. www.unhabitat.org/committee/chs14.htm.

UNCHS (Habitat), 2001, "Third Meeting of the UN Advisory Committee of Local Authorities." Nairobi, 17 February 2001, www.unhabitat.org/committee/unacla3.pdf.

UN General Assembly, "UN reform measures and proposals: the Millennium Assembly of the United Nations, Fifty-Fourth Session, A/54/959, 8 August 2000, www.un.org/millennium/declaration.htm.

United Nations, www.un.org.

3

The Ambivalent Participation of the United States in the UN System

Historic Roots of U.S. Ambivalence

The participation of the United States in the UN System is fraught with contradictions that spring from deep historic roots. The settling of Europeans in North America was a prominent step in an irreversible globalization process. But at the same time, after an ocean separated them from Europe, many settlers aspired to be detached from involvement in Europe. Their sentiments were expressed by George Washington's desire to "steer clear of permanent alliances," and Thomas Jefferson's warning against "entangling alliances."

The spirit of these warnings endured as the United States long avoided entry into World Wars I and II. Nevertheless, extensive U.S. involvements in Europe and Asia eventually resulted in the United States sending many thousands of its young people into combat far across the Atlantic to the east and the Pacific to the west. In response to the World War I disaster, President Wilson pressed for the creation of a League of Nations that would unite the states of the world in the pursuit of peace. In response to the even more extensive World War II disaster, Presidents Roosevelt and Truman strongly supported U.S. leadership in founding the United Nations after the war's end. Despite the leadership of President Wilson in the creation of the League of Nations, the United States never joined the League. Because of the leadership of Presidents Roosevelt and Truman, and extensive mobilization of public support, the United States did join the United Nations (Schlesinger 2003). Nevertheless, U.S. enthusiasm that arose out of the ashes of World War II has been replaced by ambivalence often reminiscent of the days of the League.

The sentiments of George Washington and Thomas Jefferson are still cited today, despite the fact that the organization of the world has undergone fundamental changes in the last two hundred years. The emergence of the United States and the Soviet Union as contending world powers after World War II led to U.S. leadership in the creation of the North Atlantic Treaty Organization (NATO), a quite "permanent" and "entangling" alliance. After the end of the Cold War, the United States has become the world's only superpower. At the same time, as we have illuminated in Chapter 1, new technologies for transportation and communication quickly bridge the Atlantic and the Pacific in ways that immerse all who live in the United States in world relations throughout their daily lives.

When thinking about U.S. participation in the UN System, it is important that certain concepts be used carefully. The League of Nations and organizations in the UN System are not *alliances*. Washington's and Jefferson's use of this term referred to agreements among one or several states to cooperate with each other to resist possible aggression from other states. NATO is certainly an alliance. But the development of an organization open to all states that has the purpose of creating a peaceful world is a quite different kind of enterprise.

The term *sovereignty* also requires careful usage. The adherence of the United States to treaties is often challenged because it is asserted that they infringe on U.S. sovereignty. But if we mean by *sovereignty* the capacity to control one's own fate, international treaties can be required to attain sovereignty. For example, there are problems that range across all state borders, including polluted air, certain diseases, and some crimes. Even a state with the greatest economic and military power cannot alone attain sovereignty over these problems. Thus, sovereignty over these problems can only be attained by creating an organization that reaches to the borders of the problem.

Widespread criticism today from governments and people in many countries, including traditional allies, of the unilateralist spirit of the foreign policies of the U.S. government is primarily focused on the waging of "preventive war" in Iraq without Security Council approval. But these criticisms have roots in U.S. government unwillingness to ratify a host of widely supported treaties aimed at building a world ruled by law, including:

1. International Criminal Court (94 member states)
2. Convention on the prohibition of the use, stockpiling, production and transfer of antipersonnel mines and on their destruction (143 ratifications)
3. Convention on rights of the child (ratified by all states but the United States and Somalia)
4. Covenant on economic, social and cultural rights (146 ratifications)
5. Convention on the elimination of all forms of discrimination against women (177 ratifications)
6. The UN framework convention on climate change: Kyoto Protocol (124 ratifications)
7. International Seabed Authority (143 member states)
8. International Tribunal for Law of the Sea (143 member states)
9. Prohibition of nuclear testing (115 ratifications)

Puzzling to many is the fact that most of the states with whom the United States shares values on law and governance, in Europe and beyond, have ratified all of these treaties.

Factors Contributing to U.S. Government Unilateralism

Certainly, the fact that the United States in the early twenty-first century has overwhelming economic and military power is a contributing factor to the present unilateralist spirit. The mobilization of Security Council support for a military operation is a political process that usually takes much time and involves many frustrations. If you have the economic and military power that enables you to undertake an action alone, or with the support of a few like-minded states, this makes unilateral action very feasible.

Supportive of unilateral action is also the frequently cited belief by political leaders in United States of "exceptionalism." This spirit is rooted in understandable pride in the fact that this democracy is over 200 years old and has made progressive improvements in broadening political participation during this long history. Therefore, when it comes to making decisions on issues such as spurring the development of democracy in other parts of the world, some believe that the United States has an exceptional capacity to determine what would be the appropriate kind of interventions.

Senator J. William Fulbright, while chairman of the Senate Foreign Relations Committee, vividly evaluated the impact of overwhelming power combined with belief in U.S. exceptionalism on U.S. foreign policy in a 1966 volume, *The Arrogance of Power:*

> Power confuses itself with virtue and tends to take itself for omnipotence. Once imbued with the idea of a mission, a great nation easily assumes that it has the means as well as the duty to do God's work. The Lord, after all, surely would not chose you as His agent and then deny you the sword with which to work His will. . . . What I do fear is that [America] may be drifting into commitments which, though generous and benevolent in intent, are so far-reaching as to exceed even America's great capacities. (Fulbright 1966, 2–3)

When multilateral cooperation by the U.S. government requires Senate ratification of a treaty, U.S. constitutional treaty ratifying procedures are also a great restraint on U.S. multilateral capacity. The fact that approval by two-thirds of the 100 members of the U.S. Senate is required to ratify a treaty has prevented U.S. ratification of many treaties. In explaining recent U.S. policy in negotiations over climate treaties, Shardul Agrawala and Steinar Andresen believe this "explains why the United States has consistently set more modest negotiating goals than its European counterparts within the climate regime" (Agrawala and Andresen 1999, 466). Agrawala is at the Climate Applications Division of the International Research Institute for Climate Prediction at Columbia University. Andresen is a senior research fellow at the Fridtjof Nansen Institute in Lysaker, Norway. Furthermore, because of the demands of ratification procedures, many treaties supported by the president, State Department, and other executive departments are never submitted to the Senate because the time and effort that passage of a treaty would require must be carefully evaluated and ranked with other priorities.

Public Opinion on the United Nations

In our discussion of public opinion we shall usually use the term *United Nations*, rather than *UN System*, because this is the term normally used in this literature. It appears that some using this term are referring only to the United Nations based in New York, some are including UN activities based in Geneva and other places, and some are referring to the UN System. Perhaps pollsters justify this lack of precision because they realize that most of their respondents are not able to make these distinctions. But it is important that those attempting to interpret polling results be aware of it.

Often members of Congress who are not supportive of the United Nations claim that they are reflecting the wishes of their constituents, but a penetrating study by Steven Kull and I. M. Destler, *Misreading the Public: The Myth of a New Isolationism* (1999), challenges this view. Both Kull and Destler are at the University of Maryland, where Kull is Director of the Center for the Study of Policy Attitudes and Destler is Director of the Center for International and Security Studies. Kull and Destler interviewed and conducted workshops with eighty-three practitioners, consisting of executive branch officials, congressional staff, members of the press, and leaders of nongovernmental organizations. They also did a comprehensive analysis of all relevant polling data and held focus group discussions with representative samples of people in four cities. Based on this study they conclude:

> [O]n no topic do policy practitioners misread the U.S. public more than on the subject of the United Nations. The dominant view, especially among congressional interviewees was that most Americans have a negative attitude toward the UN, would oppose strengthening it, oppose paying UN dues, and resist using force as part of a UN military operation. Polls, however, paint a quite different picture of a majority that strongly supports the

UN and U.S. participation in it, would favor strengthening the UN, supports paying UN dues, and strongly prefers using military force through the UN over acting alone. (Kull and Destler 1999, 59)

Gene Lyons, a professor at Dartmouth College who has done extensive research on the UN, explains the fundamental difference between actual public opinion on the United Nations and contrary assertions by members of Congress in this way: "Members of Congress are thus more sensitive to the highly vocal and conservative lobbies that are anti-UN than to broad trends in public opinion that favor engagement, including active participation in the UN" (Lyons 1999, 505). Over many years public opinion polls have indicated that the public is quite supportive of the United Nations. Table 3.1 shows that from 1990 to 1998 only a small percentage of respondents, from 11 percent to 13 percent, thought that strengthening the UN was not important.

Very informative are responses to questions asking for comparison of UN performance with other political institutions. When asked in June 1995, "How much of the time do you think you can trust the UN to do what is right?" respondents averaged 47 percent for the United Nations and 24 percent for the U.S. government (ATIF June 1995, retrieved from www.americans-world.org). In June 1999, when asked whether several political institutions were "doing a good job or a poor job in trying to solve problems it has had to face" those responding very or mostly favorable gave a total of these percentages: United Nations, 70 percent; Congress, 56 percent; and the CIA, 49 percent (*Times Mirror*, June 1999, retrieved from www.americans-world.org). When asked how much of each year's budget is lost to waste, fraud, and abuse, for the United Nations the median response was 30 percent, and for the U.S. government the median was 40 percent (PIPA, June 1996, retrieved from www.americans-world.org).

Although the U.S. public has been consistently strong in its support of the United Nations over many years, support can diminish in response to the current domestic political context. A poll on 25–26 April 2004, in the midst of U.S. engagement in a war in Iraq, produced this result: favorable view of the United Nations, 28 percent; unfavorable, 44 percent; not sure, 19 percent. These results were closely tied to domestic political identities. Self-identified liberal voters had a 60 percent favorable view of

TABLE 3.1
Importance of Strengthening the UN

Year	Very important	Somewhat important	Not important
1990	46%	43%	11%
1994	53%	34%	13%
1998	47%	41%	12%

(Chicago Council on Foreign Relations, retrieved from www.americans-world.org)

the United Nations, and self-identified conservative voters were 20 percent favorable. Those who intended to vote for President Bush in November 2004 were 18 percent favorable and those who planned to vote for John Kerry were 59 percent favorable (Rasmussen Reports, 25–26 April 2004, retrieved from www.americans-world.org).

Polls measuring public opinion on specific kinds of UN activities have a tendency to attain results that diverge significantly from the unilateral tendencies of their government. With respect to use of military force, 89 percent of the respondents agreed with this statement in April 1995: "When there is a problem in the world that requires the use of military force, it is generally best for the U.S. to address the problem together with other nations working through the UN, rather than going it alone." When the same question was posed in this reverse fashion, 66 percent rejected it: "When there is a problem in the world that requires the use of military force, it is better for the U.S. to act on its own rather than working through the UN because the U.S. can move more quickly and probably more successfully" (PIPA, April 1995, retrieved from www.americans-world.org).

In a July 2000 poll, respondents favored U.S. participation in UN military forces to NATO and going it alone when asked: "As a general rule, when it becomes necessary for the U.S. to use military force, do you think it is best to act as part of a United Nations operation, part of a NATO operation, or act on its own?" The results were: UN, 53 percent; NATO, 28 percent; on its own, 18 percent (PIPA, July 2000, retrieved from Americans and the World, www.americans-world.org).

Despite the fact that the U.S. government has shown no interest in strengthening UN readiness to dispatch peacekeeping forces, public opinion polls take a different view on four means for moving in this direction:

1. Having UN members commit 1,000 troops to a rapid deployment force that the UN Security Council can call up on short notice, 79 percent favor.
2. Allowing the United Nations to possess permanent stocks of military equipment stored in different locations around the world, 68 percent favor.
3. Improving UN communication and command facilities, 69 percent favor.
4. "For the U.S. to move away from its role as world policeman and reduce the burden of its large defense budget, the U.S. should invest in efforts to strengthen the UN's ability to deal with potential conflicts in the world," 73 percent agreed. (PIPA, November 1995, retrieved from www.americans-world.org)

Likewise, although the U.S. government has taken a very negative position on the now established International Criminal Court, 66 percent of respondents agree with this statement: "The U.S. should support such a court because the world needs a better way to prosecute war criminals, many of whom go unpunished today" (PIPA, October 1999, retrieved from www. americans-world.org).

The U.S. government has for years used its influence to promote no-growth budgets for the United Nations. The consequences of this approach have led some to propose that the United Nations acquire the authority to tax specific international transactions in order to cope with its expanding responsibilities. The U.S. government opposes these efforts, but polls in 1995 and 1996 reveal that people in the United States would support this approach. Their response to questions about six different forms of taxation are as follows:

1. "on international arms sales with the money going to famine relief and humanitarian aid," 72 percent favor (ATIF, June 1995, retrieved from www.americans-world.org)
2. "on international oil sales dedicated to programs to . . . protect the world's environment," 72 percent favor

3. "on international sales of tobacco dedicated to programs to . . . improve health care," 71 percent favor
4. "on international arms sales dedicated to keeping peace in regional conflicts," 67 percent favor
5. "on international currency transactions dedicated to UN activities generally," 51 percent favor
6. "on international airline tickets," 33 percent favor (Wirthlin Group, 1996, retrieved from www.americans-world.org)

The divergence between public opinion on the United Nations and government policies in a democratic system leads to puzzling questions. Given the substantial public support for the United Nations revealed in public opinion polls, we are challenged to ponder why these views are rarely cited by government officials and why they are not significantly reflected in political campaigns and other aspects of the political process. Gene Lyons directs our attention to the fact that the overwhelming majority of those who have positive responses to questions about the United Nations in polls seem to be less active in advocating their views than opponents of the United Nations may be. He has concluded that "[t]he public favors the UN and the United States' active participation in an interdependent world. But, by and large, international issues are not high on their agenda" (Lyons 1999, 504).

Public Knowledge about the United Nations

Another reason for the discrepancy between public opinion polls on the United Nations and U.S. government policy could be because public opinions in the United States on the United Nations are based on very little knowledge about the United Nations. As a result, the public may not have the background knowledge required to place these questions on the public political agenda. For example, in response to questions about the UN budget in September 1996, 75 percent believed that the UN budget is four or more times larger than the actual budget of the UN System (PIPA poll, September 1996, retrieved from www.americans-world.org).

Table 3.2 offers modest insight on the knowledge of people in the United States about the United Nations compared to people in other countries. From 1989 to 1992 the United Nations sponsored public opinion polls on knowledge about the United Nations in thirty-six countries around the world. The survey shows that 92 percent of U.S. people have heard of the United Nations. Because the range of responses was from 32 percent to 99 percent, the United States ranks near the top. This is not surprising because of other poll results revealing widespread support of the United Nations by U.S. people. On the other hand, in responses to two other questions in the UN polls, U.S. people rank near the bottom of the thirty-six countries with respect to even minimal knowledge about the United Nations. From a list of five UN secretaries-general since 1945, respondents were asked to identify the current secretary-general. With only 15 percent of U.S. respondents able to select the right person, they ranked thirty-fifth. The mean correct response rate for all thirty-six countries was 45 percent. Respondents were also asked to name at least one UN agency. Only 16 percent of U.S. respondents were able to do so, giving them a rank of thirty-one.

It is indeed puzzling that U.S. people know so very little about the United Nations more than fifty years after its founding, and after its membership, component organizations, and agenda have expanded so greatly. It would seem that this public ignorance is deeply intertwined with attributes of the government, the media, and educational institutions in the United States. We say "deeply intertwined" because lack of attention to, and ignorance of, the United Nations by each of the four components—people, government, media, and educational institutions—affects the others. We have already discussed the fact that the United Nations is not high on the agenda of most relevant government officials in Washington. This contributes to, but is not entirely responsible for, the neglect of the United Nations by the media. Except for front-page attention given to occasional UN involvement in crises, particularly when peacekeeping forces are required, UN issues are rarely covered by U.S. media. Even press interest in long-term peacekeeping operations is very short-lived. We believe that educational institutions also contribute to lack of knowledge about the United Nations, and the larger UN System. Government officials, members of the media, and the public have learned very little about the United Nations in either precollegiate or collegiate education.

TABLE 3.2
US Response in Thirty-Six-Country Survey of Knowledge about UN

	Heard of UN	Know name of SG	Can name a UN agency
U.S.	92%	15%	16%
U.S. Rank	9	35	31
Range of Responses	32%–99%	7%–75%	7%–72%
Mean	82%	45%	34%

(UN Department of Public Information, Public Opinion Surveys, 1989–1992)

But even if the public does not bring their pro-UN and multilateral preference opinions into the political arena, why are they not a more significant part of the political agenda in Washington? Why are there not more officials in the executive branch and Congress who see the existence of substantial multilateral tendencies and pro-UN perspectives of the public as an opportunity to pursue similar views. Perhaps another factor is the inevitable competition between geographic domains of governance, as reflected in the competition between local authorities and governments of U.S. states, and between these state governments and the federal government in Washington. Is resistance to more creative participation in the UN System a result of the reluctance of Washington to support a more significant role in governance for UN agencies? Do they see this as a challenge to their control?

Seven Factors Contributing to U.S. Government Unilateralism

This analysis leaves us to conclude that the unilateralist tendencies of the U.S. government are a result of a number of intertwined factors, including: (1) the fear of foreign entanglements dating back to the Founders of the Republic, (2) belief in U.S. "exceptionalism," (3) fear by officials in Washington that enhanced UN authority will weaken their governing power, (4) overwhelming U.S. military and economic power, (5) the treaty ratification process required by the U.S. Constitution, (6) very limited coverage of the UN System by the media, and (7) limited public knowledge about the UN System that is a result of very limited education available in precollegiate and collegiate schools. This limited knowledge appears to prevent the public from bringing their pro-UN and multilateral opinions to bear in the political process.

Emerging Opportunities for Public Education and Participation

Nevertheless, significant opportunities have emerged through which the public can overcome the limited knowledge gained through educational institutions and the media. Very informative websites are easily accessible to many people. For example, UN-WIRE (un.wire@smartbrief.com) "is a free service sponsored by the United Nations Foundation which is dedicated to supporting the United Nations' efforts to address the most pressing humanitarian, socioeconomic and environmental challenges facing the world today." It provides the equivalent of a daily newspaper on the UN System. The foundation states its purpose as promoting "a more peaceful, prosperous, and just world through the support of the United Nations and its Charter. Through our grant-making and by building new and innovative public-private partnerships, the Foundation acts to meet the most pressing health, humanitarian, socioeconomic, and environmental challenges of the 21st century" (www.unfoundation.org).

The United Nations website (www.un.org) also provides daily news from the UN News Service at www.un.org/News. For those who have interest in specific agencies in the UN System, this website is a route to the latest news on agencies throughout the UN System. The websites of all organizations in the system can be accessed by pulling up the UN System organization chart and clicking on the name of a specific agency.

This site also offers quick access to those interested in UN System links with NGOs (civil society) and business organizations. It is necessary only to click on "Civil Society/Business" and then choose either "The United Nations & Civil Society" or "The United Nations & Business." The "United Nations & Civil Society" page "links to ways that the United Nations System works in partnership with civil society on issues of global concern." Available are the names of the 2,531 NGOs in consultative status with ECOSOC. "The United Nations & Business site provides information on partnerships and alliances between the UN and the private sector and foundations in furtherance of the UN Millennium Development Goals," as well as information on the Business Council for the United Nations (www.bcun.org).

A number of civil society websites are informative on activities of civil society organizations that are actively involved in issues on UN System agendas. We have space to mention only a few, but they offer links to many others.

Global Policy Forum (www.globalpolicy.org). "monitors policy making at the United Nations, promotes accountability of UN decisions, educates and mobilizes for global citizen participation, and advocates on vital issues of international peace and justice."

European Platform for Conflict Prevention and Transformation (www.conflict-prevention.net). "On this site you find information regarding: Conflicts, conflict prevention and peace building . . . efforts by people to prevent or resolve conflicts . . . details of international and local organisations working to prevent or resolve conflicts."

Global Partnership for the Prevention of Armed Conflict (www.gppac.net). "In 2003, in response to the UN Secretary-General's Recommendation 27 from his Report on the Prevention of Armed Conflict, the worldwide conflict prevention community joined to form a Global Partnership for the Prevention of Armed Conflict. . . . The Global Partnership is held together by a series of parallel regional processes and is in progress in fifteen regions worldwide."

Center for Defense Information (www.cdi.org). "The Center for Defense Information is dedicated to strengthening security through: international cooperation; reduced reliance on unilateral military power to resolve conflict; reduced reliance on nuclear weapons; a transformed and reformed military establishment; and, prudent oversight of, and spending on, defense programs."

Americans and the World (www.americans-world.org). This organization is "a source of comprehensive information on U.S. public opinion on international issues. The site includes *The Digest*, which provides comprehensive analyses of polling on various international topics."

Two organizations attempting to overcome lack of citizen knowledge about the UN System and their very limited participation in political efforts to implement their support for the UN deserve our attention. The United Nations Association of the

United States of America (UNA-USA) offers opportunities for those interested in becoming involved in efforts to strengthen U.S. participation in the UN system. It is a "not-for-profit, non-partisan organization that supports the work of the United Nations and encourages active civic participation in the most important social and economic issues facing the world today.... UNA-USA offers Americans the opportunity to connect with issues confronted by the U.N.—from global health and human rights to the spread of democracy, equitable development and international justice. Through its work, UNA-USA educates Americans about the work of the United Nations, and encourages public support for strong U.S. leadership in the United Nations" (www.unausa.org). The UNA-USA consists of a network of over 175 community-based chapters and divisions and a council of organizations with more than 100 members.

The UNA-USA is part of the World Federation of United Nations Associations (WFUNA), a network of UN associations around the world that comprises hundreds of thousands of people linked together in over 100 member states of the United Nations (www.wfuna.org).

The Academic Council on the United Nations System (ACUNS) is an organization of "scholars, teachers, practitioners, and others who are active in the work and study of the United Nations system and international organizations in general." Formed in 1987 at Dartmouth College, it has members from around the world. It is headquartered at Wilfrid Laurier University in Canada. The ACUNS is making important contributions in strengthening teaching and research on the UN System at universities and colleges in the United States through linking relevant scholars and graduate students. "The members share an interest in encouraging and supporting education, writing and research which contribute to the understanding of international issues and promote global cooperation. ACUNS has a number of ongoing projects, including research and policy workshops, an annual meeting which focuses on UN and international issues, a two-week summer workshop for younger scholars and practitioners organized in cooperation with the American Society for International Law (ASIL), and a dissertation awards program. The 900-member organization also co-sponsors an e-mail discussion listserver with Wilfrid Laurier University" (www.acuns.wlu.ca).

Conclusion

A dynamically changing world is presenting an escalating need for global governance. This is clearly illuminated in the growing demands placed on the UN System and in its efforts to cope with these demands. We have just presented an analysis of the challenges that this presents to the world's oldest democracy. It seems obvious that creative U.S. participation is the only option available to the U.S. government and the U.S. people. Toward this end, much is to be learned from the development of this democracy over two centuries. Essential is the fact that this democracy emerged out of a process that was founded on democratic local governments, then democratic state governments, and eventually a democratic central government that gradually reached to the boundary of the country on a growing agenda of issues. Virtually all national government issues in the United States must also be on the agendas of governments of U.S. states and local authorities.

Emerging regional governance and global governance are now adding larger territorial dimensions to this governing process as the boundaries of more and more policy problems reach around the world. It is essential that the United States creatively project its knowledge and democratic values into this process. The long-term security of the people in the United States, and people in the entire world, is dependent on this involvement. At the same time, long-term U.S. security depends on what will be learned from participation in this "laboratory for global governance" by people in the U.S. government, in U.S. civil society, and in U.S. businesses.

Our analysis suggests that foreign policy making may be the weakest aspect of this democracy because of the great gap between public opinion on the United Nations and the policies of their government. Creative involvement of the United States in the UN System will be dependent on greatly enhancing the knowledge of all the people in the United States about the UN System and about global governance issues. This is an essential step toward making it possible for significant growth in their participation in foreign policy making.

At the same time, we have learned about a great discrepancy between what government officials and other foreign policy elites believe about public opinion on UN issues and their actual beliefs. This must be overcome. This democracy may be able to gain insights on how this can be achieved by examining practices in other democracies where public involvement in foreign policy making is more dynamic. Obvious possibilities are the Scandinavian countries and the Benelux countries. They have been spared the unilateral temptations offered by overwhelming economic and military power. Use of this power unilaterally can lead to short-term advantages, but not to long-term security in an interdependent world in which each individual lives his or her daily life immersed in global connections.

References

Academic Council on the UN System (ACUNS), www.acuns.wlu.ca.

Agrawala, Shardul, and Steinar Andresen, 1999, "Indispensability and Indefensibility? The United States in the Climate Treaty Negotiations," *Global Governance*, Vol. 5, No. 4, 457–482.

Americans and the World, www.americans-world.org.

Business Council for the United Nations, www.un.org/partners/business.

Center for Defense Information (CDI), www.cdi.org.

Chicago Council on Foreign Relations, www.ccfr.org.

Debiel, Tobias, 2000, "Strengthening the UN as an Effective World Authority: Cooperative Security versus Hegemonic Crisis Management," *Global Governance*, Vol. 6, No. 1, 2000, 25–42.

European Platform for Conflict Prevention and Transformation, www.conflict-prevention.net.

Fulbright, J. William, 1966, *The Arrogance of Power*. New York: Vintage.

Global Partnership for the Prevention of Armed Conflict (GPPAC), www.gppac.net.

Global Policy Forum, www.globalpolicy.org.

Kull, Steven, and I. M. Destler, 1999, *Misreading the Public: The Myth of a New Isolationism*. Washington, DC: Brookings Institution.

Luck, Edward C., 1999, *Mixed Messages: American Politics and International Organization*. Washington, DC: Brookings Institution.

Lyons, Gene, 1999, "The UN and American Politics," *Global Governance*, Vol. 5, No. 4, 1999, 497–512.

Program on International Policy Attitudes (PIPA), University of Maryland, www.pipa.org.

Schlesinger, Stephen C., 2003, *Act of Creation: The Founding of the United Nations: A Story of Superpowers, Secret Agents, Wartime Allies and Enemies, and Their Quest for a Peaceful World*. Boulder, CO: Westview.

United Nations, www.un.org.

United Nations Association of the United States of America, www. unausa.org.

United Nations Department of Public Information, Public Opinion Surveys, 1989–1992.

United Nations System, www.unsystem.org.

UNWIRE, www.un.wire.com.

World Federation of UN Associations (WFUNA), www.wfuna.org.

4

Chronology of the Emergence and Development of the UN System

Historic Roots of the UN System

Deep Historic Roots

In the introduction to Chapter 1 we emphasized the importance of placing the UN System in a historical context in order to understand that it arose out of, and is continually evolving in response to, changing world conditions. Humankind has long had tendencies to travel, migrate, communicate, exchange, borrow, and dominate, and to invent ever new technologies that permit broadening the geographic scope of these activities. Brief examination of four dimensions of escalating human linkages, (1) travel, (2) industrialization, (3) communications, and (4) armaments, illustrates the challenges they present to governance of territorial units.

William McNeill, in *The Rise of the West: A History of the Human Community* (1963), has provided a very succinct summary of the impact of changing technology for travel on human connectedness. His chart of "The Shrinking World" (McNeill 1963, 766–767) is divided into four ecumenes. He uses the term "ecumene" to refer to an area in which there are contacts among human beings that reach across the entire area. First, there were land-centered ecumenes separated by oceans before 1500 A.D. Second, intercontinental ocean travel brought a closure of a

67

global ecumene between 1500 and 1650. Third, the development of steam ships and trains, and later automobiles, brought a mechanical, land, and sea transport ecumene from 1850 to 1950 in which travel was much faster. Fourth, the development of air transport, permitting travel over the poles, brought a polar centered ecumene after 1950. From the first to the fourth ecumene people traveled ever farther and ever faster.

Industrialization has long played a key role in the emergence of the global and polar ecumenes. William McNeill writes that the "technical aspect of the first phase of modern industrialization, in England in the mid-nineteenth century, can be summed up in two words: coal and iron" (McNeill 1953, 732). These resources were employed in the development of railroads, cotton mills, and hundreds of other machines. There was then a slow spread to the United States, northwest and central Europe, Russia, Japan, and the rest of the world. Industrial production spurred a need for raw materials from distant countries and the exporting of industrial products around the world. At the same time, the growing incomes of industrial workers spurred migration from other parts of the world to areas of industrialization.

In the nineteenth century new forms of communication emerged that added significant new dimensions to human linkages in the Global Ecumene. In 1844 Samuel Morse sent his first public message over a telegraph. The telephone was patented in 1876. Sound broadcasting began in 1920. In 1963 the first geostationary communications satellite permitted space radio communication. In the early twenty-first century, people in offices and homes throughout the world are in instantaneous contact by e-mail and have immediate access to websites around the world (Alleyne 1995).

In *From Crossbow to H-Bomb* (1973) Bernard and Fawn Brodie extensively illuminate the impact of scientific developments on the destructiveness and territorial reach of armaments. Bernard Brodie was an American military strategist and the author of books on naval power, nuclear strategy, and nuclear deterrence. His wife, Fawn Brodie, was a biographer of Richard Nixon, Joseph Smith, Thomas Jefferson and others. They emphasize how, as a result of the Industrial Revolution, "the civilian was now responsible for providing the industrial means of war, and the workshop became as vital a part of the struggle as the battlefield" (Brodie and Brodie 1973, 125). The global reach of sea power and air power, combined with weapons of ever more powerful and ever more distant reach, made world wars possible.

Ever more extensive human linkage driven by travel, industrialization, communication, and armaments has developed a need for enhanced forms for linkage among territorial governments. The dispatching of diplomatic envoys by the governments of one territorial political authority to another reaches deep into history. In the fifteenth century the first recorded permanent diplomatic mission was established by the duke of Milan at Genoa, beginning a practice that spread rapidly to the rest of Europe and beyond. It is important to note that a two-pronged system of representation developed and still exists. One is run by diplomats concerned with the public policy of their governments. The other is represented by the consular service, designed to expedite foreign trade and commerce. As global human linkage escalated, organizations were formed where representatives from a number of states could gather permanently to cope with specific topics. Then the need emerged for more general-purpose international organizations.

Nineteenth-Century Roots

Inis Claude, in a widely used textbook on international organizations, points to the Congress of Vienna in 1815 as an initiation of a "nineteenth-century conference system without precedent in the modern world" (Claude 1971, 25). At this conference the leaders of the major states of Europe constituted themselves as the Concert of Europe that held a series of conferences to deal with challenging political issues. These conferences were sporadic and confined to European states, but they began the development of new procedures for facilitating multilateral collaboration. Claude believes "the Concert of Europe produced the prototype of a major organ of modern international organization—the executive council of the great powers" (Claude 1971, 28). In other words, here we can see the roots of the UN Security Council.

In the nineteenth century more limited conferences also emerged that focused on specific issues concerned with the consequences of escalating linkages among people across political borders, such as telecommunications, trade, and health. Meetings held to cope with these problems became permanent conferences that were called permanent international unions. By World War I there were thirty public international unions with permanent administrative offices. In a book first published in 1911, Paul Reinsch, a University of Wisconsin–Madison political scientist, divides these unions into five categories: (1) communications, (2) economic interests, (3) sanitation and prison reform, (4) police powers, and (5) scientific purposes. A few of their titles offer a quick overview of the kinds of issues arising in the border-crossing activity of the evolving Global Ecumene: International Bureau of Weights and Measures, Wireless Telegraph Union, International Sugar Union, International Institute of Agriculture, Union for the Publication of Customs Tariffs, International Office of Public Health, Union for the Suppression of the African Slave Trade, International Opium Commission, and Central Bureau for the International Map of the World (Reinsch 1916). A number of these organizations created the roots for the Specialized Agencies of the UN System.

Gerard Mangone eloquently describes the nineteenth-century roots of international organizations:

> The [nineteenth-century] international agencies were only harbingers of a day in which hundreds of international organizations, employing thousands of people, should span the earth, touching in one guise or another the purse and prayer of every national citizen and prompting, pushing, or threatening every state toward some new task. . . . every one of the organizations had to wait through dreary arguments and often many years before its basic convention was signed and ratified. Only looking back from the twentieth century with its multitude of international offices, does the procession of organizations seem so steady in its gait, so certain of its future. (Mangone 1954, 90)

Initiated by Czar Nicholas II of Russia, "International Peace Conferences" held in the Hague in 1899 and 1907 began the movement toward universality in conferences focusing on political issues by including both small European states and many outside of Europe. The 1899 conference was attended by twenty-six states, mostly from Europe, but the 1907 conference involved forty-four states, including many from Latin America. Claude concludes: "Thus, the world achieved in 1907 its first General Assembly" (Claude 1971, 29). A significant item on the agenda of statesmen involved in the Hague Conferences was the creation of international judicial institutions. These efforts were precursors of the World Court of the League of Nations and the International Court of Justice of the United Nations. Participants in the Hague Conferences were moving toward the development of a permanent organization for the maintenance of world peace in a permanent home that had been promised by Andrew Carnegie, but World War I intruded before their next scheduled meeting in 1915.

League of Nations Roots

The overwhelming destructiveness of World War I spurred more rapid continuation of efforts by the Hague Conferences to create a permanent organization for the maintenance of world peace located in Geneva, Switzerland. The League of Nations was founded in 1920 and grew from thirty-two to forty-five members. Evolving out of nineteenth-century roots, the League had a Security Council that eventually included ten members and a General Assembly that grew from twenty-eight to forty-five members. The Secretariat, civil servants who would carry out the decisions of these two bodies, was largely built upon experience in the permanent offices of the nineteenth-century permanent international unions.

The League had very limited success when challenged by violent conflicts between Greece and Bulgaria and Bolivia and Paraguay, the Japanese invasion of Manchuria, and the Italian invasion of Ethiopia, and eventually was overwhelmed by World War II in 1939. On the other hand, Gerard Mangone concluded that "the League's international economic and social programs flowered in the fields of commerce, health, communications, and protection of helpless peoples. The Permanent Court sponsored by the League gained the respect of the world, and no reticulation of international law had ever spread so rapidly" (Mangone 1954, 153). Indeed, the League had begun to create the roots for an important second council of the United Nations, an economic and social council. In addition, the work of the Permanent Mandates Commission of the League of Nations was the forerunner of a third UN council, the Trusteeship Council. Both of these councils were established to provide oversight of those states who were entrusted with authority over colonies taken from defeated colonial powers in World Wars I and II.

(For a chronology of the League of Nations see www.unog.ch/
library/archives/lon/library/chrnlogy.htm).

Principal Organizations
of the United Nations

Because the UN Charter emerged out of experience with the first
general purpose world governmental organization, the League of
Nations, the UN Charter is three times longer than the League
Covenant. Charter provisions for the main organizations of the
United Nations are more detailed than those provided in the
League Covenant. Most of the League Covenant is devoted to
dispute settlement activities, while the UN Charter devotes much
attention to economic and social cooperation. In addition, the
Charter devotes much more attention to colonial issues and recognizes the significance of regional organizations in the settlement of disputes.

General Assembly (UN Charter, Chapter V)

As the body in which all member states are represented, each with
one vote, the General Assembly's membership has grown from
51 in 1945 to 191 sixty years later. Most issues on the General Assembly agenda are first discussed in one of the six main committees of the Assembly. The broad range of issues considered is
revealed by the names of the committees: First Committee—
Disarmament and International Security; Second Committee—
Economic and Financial; Third Committee—Social, Humanitarian
and Cultural; Fourth Committee—Special Political and Decolonization; Fifth Committee—Administrative and Budgetary; Sixth
Committee—Legal.

Voting in the UN General Assembly, when compared to the
League Assembly, reflects a significant trend toward majority
rule. In the League Assembly agreement of all states voting was
required for passage of a resolution, but procedural matters required only a majority. But in the UN General Assembly, only
two-thirds are required on "important questions." Procedural issues require only a simple majority. Furthermore, voting on all issues in committees of the UN General Assembly require only a
simple majority. But after passage by a committee, resolutions

must be submitted to a plenary session of the General Assembly. In plenary meetings, resolutions may be adopted by acclamation, that is, without objection or without a vote. A vote may be taken by roll call. In contrast with the Security Council, decisions of the General Assembly are only recommendations. On the other hand, they do carry the support of those voting for them and tend to have significant support of world opinion and have moral authority. Furthermore, General Assembly resolutions do determine the budgets, structure, and activities of the Secretariat and many subsidiary bodies established by the authority of the General Assembly.

Security Council
(UN Charter, Chapters V, VI, VII)

The Security Council has primary responsibility, under the Charter, for the maintenance of international peace and security, with its membership increased from eleven to fifteen members by Charter amendment. The functioning of the Security Council as provided for in the Charter is different from the League Covenant in three important respects. First, in order for the UN Security Council "to be able to function continuously" each member shall "be represented at all times at the seat of the Organization." The League Security Council was only required "to meet from time to time as occasion may require, and at least once a year." Second, reflecting a gradual movement away from required unanimous voting in international governmental organizations, nine votes are required in the UN Security Council for passing resolutions. Of course, a remaining limitation is the fact that a "no" vote from one of the five permanent members will defeat a resolution, except for procedural matters. Third, in contrast with the League Covenant, the UN Charter asserts that "while the Security Council is exercising in respect of any dispute or situation," the General Assembly may not make "any recommendations with respect to a dispute or situation unless the Security Council so requests" (Article 12).

In Chapter VI the Charter authorizes the Security Council to undertake "[p]acific settlement of disputes." When these measures are inadequate, Chapter VII authorizes the Council to take "[a]ction with respect to threats to the peace, breaches of the peace, and acts of aggression" that includes "such action by air, sea or land forces as may be necessary." While responding to challenges, the Council has developed a third approach not foreseen by the drafters of the Charter—peacekeeping. Initially, peacekeeping forces were deployed after parties to a conflict agreed to a cease-fire and approved the presence of UN troops that patrolled the cease-fire line. Often referred to as Chapter 6½, peacekeeping forces were intended to provide an environment facilitating diplomatic efforts to address the underlying causes of conflict. Between 1948 and August 2004 there were fifty-nine UN peacekeeping operations.

At the end of the Cold War, the Security Council established larger and more complex UN peacekeeping missions, often to help implement comprehensive peace agreements between protagonists in conflicts within states. As a result, peacekeeping has acquired more and more nonmilitary elements. United Nations Civilian Police now play a crucial role in UN peacekeeping operations and other UN field missions. In 2004 they participated in thirteen different missions around the globe. More than 7,000 police officers from eighty countries were on patrol, providing training, advising local police services, and helping to ensure compliance with human rights standards.

Economic and Social Council (UN Charter, Chapters IX, X)

Chapters IX (Economic and Social Cooperation) and X (The Economic and Social Council) represent a fundamental difference between the UN Charter and the League of Nations Covenant, which had only seven sentences (Article 23) on "Social and other activities." Nevertheless, this brief article did mention fair and humane conditions of labor for men, women, and children; traffic in women and children; drug traffic; freedom of communication; and equitable treatment of commerce. And League practice was leading toward the creation of an economic and social council before World War II.

Originally having eighteen members, in 2005 the Economic and Social Council (ECOSOC) has fifty-four members elected by the General Assembly for overlapping three-year terms. Seats are allotted based on geographical representation, with fourteen allocated to African states, eleven to Asian states, six to Eastern European states, ten to Latin American and Caribbean states, and thirteen to Western European and other states.

The Economic and Social Council attempts to coordinate the work of the nineteen UN specialized agencies, the nine functional commissions, and the five regional commissions (Table 4.1). It receives reports from eleven UN funds and programs and issues policy recommendations to the UN System and to member states. The UN Charter provides ECOSOC with a wide mandate of responsibilities that include promoting higher standards of living, full employment, and economic and social progress; identifying solutions to international economic, social, and health problems; facilitating international cultural and educational cooperation; and encouraging universal respect for human rights and fundamental freedoms. ECOSOC's purview extends to over 70 percent of the human and financial resources of the entire UN System.

Since the founding of the United Nations, the challenge provided by this broad agenda has been intensified by the growing linkages among the economies of states and almost fourfold expanded UN membership that has consisted primarily of economically poorer countries. In addition, growing concern about the impact of economic development on the environment has placed "sustainable development" on the ECOSOC agenda. Some insight on the range of economic and social issues confronted by ECOSOC can be attained by noting the names of its nine functional commissions: (1) crime prevention and criminal justice, (2) narcotic drugs, (3) population and development, (4) social development, (5) science and technology for development, (6) statistical support, (7) the status of women, (8) sustainable development, and (9) human rights. An ECOSOC panel of the chairpersons of functional commissions attempts to cope with issues that transcend each of these topics. One issue on their agenda has been "gender mainstreaming in the functional commissions of ECOSOC."

The great array of working groups created by the Human Rights Commission reflects the significant progress being made in placing human rights on the world political agenda since the days of the League of Nations, when the term *human rights* did not even appear in the League Covenant. The drafters of the UN Charter mentioned human rights seven times, including in the second sentence of the preamble and the instruction that ECOSOC establish a human rights commission (Article 68). This was quickly followed by the General Assembly's Universal Declaration of Human Rights (1948), a Covenant on Civil and Political Rights (entered into force in 1976), a Covenant on Economic, Social and Cultural Rights (entered into force in 1976), and nu-

TABLE 4.1
Subsidiary Bodies of the Economic and Social Council

Functional Commissions
1 Crime Prevention and Criminal Justice
2 Narcotic Drugs
   (1) Subcommission on Illicit Drug Traffic and Related Matters in the Near and Middle East
   (2) Meeting of Heads of National Drug Law Enforcement Agencies
3 Population and Development
4 Social Development
5 Science and Technology for Development
6 Statistical
7 Status of Women
8 Sustainable Development
9 Human Rights
   (1) The Group of Three established under the International Convention on the Suppression and Punishment of the Crime of **Apartheid**
   (2) Working Group on Enforced and Involuntary **Disappearances**
   (3) Working Group on Situations (which appear to reveal a consistent pattern of **gross violations** of human rights)
   (4) Working Group on **Arbitrary Detention**
   (5) Open-ended Working Group on the **Right to Development**
   (6) Open-ended Working Group on a Draft Optional Protocol to the Convention against **Torture** and Other Cruel, Inhuman or Degrading Treatment or **Punishment**
   (7) Open-ended Working Group on the Draft Declaration on the Rights of **Indigenous Peoples**
   (8) Open-ended Working Group established to elaborate policy guidelines on structural adjustments programs and **economic, social and cultural rights**
   (9) Subcommission on the Promotion and Protection of Human Rights
   (10) Working Group on the Rights of Persons Belonging to National or **Ethnic, Religious and Linguistic Minorities**
   (11) Working Group on Contemporary Forms of **Slavery**
   (12) Working Group on **Indigenous Populations**
   (13) Sessional Working Group on the methods of work of the Subcommission
   (14) Sessional Working Group on the **Administration of Justice**
   (15) Sessional Working Group on the working methods and activities of **transnational corporations**
   (16) Working Group on **Communications**

Regional Commissions
1 Economic Commission for **Africa** (ECA)
2 Economic and Social Commission for **Asia and the Pacific** (ESCAP)
3 Economic Commission for **Europe** (ECE)
4 Economic Commission for **Latin America and the Caribbean** (ECLAC)
5 Economic and Social Commission for **Western Asia** (ESCWA)

Standing Committees
1 Committee for Programme and **Coordination**
2 Commission on **Human Settlements**
3 Committee on **Non-Governmental Organizations**
4 Committee on Negotiations with **Intergovernmental Agencies**

merous other treaties focusing on genocide, torture, racial discrimination, the rights of women, the rights of children, and other issues. Then in 1997 the UN Center for Human Rights became the Office of the UN High Commissioner for Human Rights. The array of working groups created by the Human Rights Commission (Table 4.1) reflects the growing range of human rights concerns, including involuntary disappearances, arbitrary detention, the rights of indigenous peoples, the rights of ethnic and religious minorities, working methods of transnational corporations, and the right to development.

One of the most dynamic aspects of developments in the UN System has been growth in involvement of what the UN Charter refers to as nongovernmental organizations (NGOs) and many now refer to as civil society. Article 71 of the Charter states that ECOSOC:

> may make suitable arrangements for consultation with nongovernmental organizations which are concerned with matters within its competence. Such arrangements may be made with international organizations and, where appropriate, with national organizations after consultation with the Member of the United Nations concerned.

In response, ECOSOC created a Committee on Non-Governmental Organizations. In 2005 there are 2,531 NGOs in consultative status with ECOSOC and some 400 NGOs accredited to the Commission on Sustainable Development (CSD), a subsidiary body of ECOSOC. To qualify for consultative status, an NGO must have a democratic decision-making mechanism; be officially registered with the appropriate government authorities as nonprofit; and its basic resources must be derived primarily from contributions of the national affiliates, individual members, or other nongovernmental components.

Nongovernmental organizations that enjoy consultative status with ECOSOC with strong public information programs are also granted association with the UN Department of Public Information (DPI) upon written request to the DPI/NGO Section. NGOs can be associated with DPI without having consultative status with ECOSOC.

In order to strengthen their influence and competence at UN Headquarters in New York City, NGOs have created the Conference of NGOs in Consultative Relationship with the United Nations (CONGO). It "provides a forum for nongovernmental organizations with common interests to come together to study, plan, support, and act in relation to the principles and programs of the United Nations" (www.ngocongo.org).

Nongovernmental organization consultative status has spread to organizations throughout the UN System. In response, a small interagency program has been created, the United Nations Non-Governmental Liaison Service (NGLS) with offices in Geneva and New York. "The Non-Governmental Liaison Service (NGLS) promotes dynamic partnerships between the United Nations and non-governmental organizations. By providing information, advice, expertise and support services, NGLS is part of the UN's effort to strengthen dialogue and win public support for economic and social development" (www.un-ngls.org). In 2005 the NGLS is supported by seventeen UN System organizations.

Trusteeship Council (Chap. XII) Non-Self-governing Territories Declaration (Chap. XI)

The fact that the Trusteeship Council suspended operation in 1994 with the independence of Palau, the last remaining UN trust territory, reflects significant developments in the struggle for self-determination of peoples since the founding of the United Nations. The roots for these developments reach back to the founding of the League of Nations. The victorious states in World War I held on to their colonies. The fifteen colonies of the defeated states were placed in the hands of seven of the victorious states, but the mandatory system called for in the League Covenant placed some limitations on their authority. The seven states were required to report to the Permanent Mandates Commission each year "in reference to the territory committed to its charge."

Building on the experiences of the Permanent Mandates Commission, the UN Charter established a Trusteeship Council to oversee the mandated territories and the colonies of defeated states in World War II. The functions of the Trustee System were extended to include promotion of "the political, economic, social, and educational advancement of the inhabitants of the trust territories, and their progressive development towards self-government or independence as may be appropriate to the particular circumstances of each territory and its peoples" (Article 76).

A more significant indication of enhanced support for self-determination of peoples was Chapter XI of the Charter: "Declaration Regarding Non-Self-governing Territories." This declaration called on administrators of colonial territories "to develop self-government, to take due account of the political aspirations of the peoples, and to assist them in the progressive development of their free political institutions" (Article 73). This was only a "declaration" and did not define legal obligations of colonial administrations. But its spirit was again voiced by the General Assembly in December 1960 in an even stronger "Declaration on the Granting of Independence to Colonial Countries and Peoples." It declared that all peoples have the right to self-determination, that foreign rule is contrary to international law, and that the granting of independence to colonial peoples is to be initiated as soon as possible. This resolution received a positive vote of eighty-nine to zero in the General Assembly, with nine abstentions, including the United States. "There is no doubt that adoption of this declaration is a landmark in development of the United Nations' colonial policy. It is now clear that there is no moderating the pressure for UN action to see the last remnants of colonialism disappear" (Jacob et al. 1972, 543). In the same session, the General Assembly voted to admit seventeen new members, the largest number ever admitted in one year. All were former colonies, sixteen from Africa, along with Cyprus.

Significant UN success in advancing the self-determination of colonies has, unfortunately, placed new challenges on UN agendas with an escalating array of seriously disruptive conflicts and violence within former colonies, often referred to as "failed states." The borders of colonies now independent were established by colonial administrators, not by the people themselves. As a result, many newly independent states are actually multination states whose borders are not accepted by nations within their borders. Thus, the consequences of overseas colonialism remain as significant problems on the agendas of organizations throughout the UN System.

Secretariat (UN Charter, Chapter XV)

Differences between provisions in the League of Nations Covenant and the UN Charter with respect to secretariats reveal the significant progress that has been made in the development of an international civil service. The League Covenant had this very limited provision:

> The permanent Secretariat shall be established at the Seat of the League. The Secretariat shall comprise a Secretary-General and such secretaries and staff as may be required. (Article 6)

In contrast, the UN Charter includes these requirements for members of the Secretariat:

> In the performance of their duties the Secretary General and the staff shall not seek or receive instruction from any government or from any other authority external to the organization. They shall refrain from any action which might reflect on their position as international officials responsible only to the Organization.
> Each member of the United Nations undertakes to respect the exclusively international character of the responsibilities of the Secretary-General and the staff and not to seek to influence them in the discharge of their responsibilities. (Article 100)
> The paramount consideration in the employment of the staff and in the determination of the conditions of service shall be the necessity of securing the highest standards of efficiency, competence, and integrity. Due regard shall be paid to the importance of recruiting the staff on as wide a geographical basis as possible. (Article 101)

This is another example of how experience in the League "laboratory" provided insights useful to those writing the UN Charter. Although all members of the Secretariat come from member states, while working in the Secretariat they are expected to put aside any feelings of identity with that state and serve the United Nations. At the same time, the primary consideration when recruiting members of the Secretariat is to be their "efficiency, competence, and integrity." On the other hand, recruitment is to provide the Secretariat with "as wide a geographical basis as possible." Obviously, in some respects these two provisions are contradictory, but they can also be complementary. Experience has demonstrated that "competence" can include the capacity to understand how decisions affect widely different social, cultural, political, and geographic contexts. Thus, wide geographic representation in the secretariat can contribute to the ability of the Secretariat to take into consideration the worldwide impact of its actions. At the same time, wide geographic representation in the Secretariat also helps to strengthen the perceived legitimacy of its actions by member states and populations of member states. In fulfillment of this provision, the Secretariat includes people from some 170 countries.

The Secretariat administers the programs and policies laid down by the General Assembly, Security Council, and ECOSOC. Its responsibilities "range from administering peacekeeping operations to mediating international disputes, from surveying economic and social trends and problems to preparing studies on human rights and sustainable development. Secretariat staff also inform the world's communications media about the work of the United Nations; organize international conferences on issues of worldwide concern; and interpret speeches and translate documents into the Organization's official languages"(www.un.org). These programs and policies are carried out by some twenty-four organizations created by the General Assembly, with offices in New York and Geneva, a significant presence in Addis Ababa (Ethiopia), Bangkok, Beirut, Geneva, Nairobi (Kenya), Santiago (Chile), and Vienna, and other offices all over the world.

International Court of Justice (UN Charter, Chapter XIV)

The International Court of Justice (ICJ) was built on experience with the Permanent Court of International Justice (PCIJ) founded in 1920, the first international court with a worldwide reach. Unlike the ICJ, the PCIJ was not an organization of the League, although Article 14 of the League Covenant called on the League Council to formulate plans for the establishment of the PCIJ, and it was linked to the League through the election of its judges and its expenses. Similar to the PCIJ, the ICJ can settle, in accordance with international law, legal disputes submitted to it by states and give advisory opinions on legal questions referred to it by the General Assembly or Security Council. This has now been extended to include the twenty Specialized Agencies.

The ICJ is composed of fifteen judges elected to nine-year terms of office by both the General Assembly and Security Council. It may not include more than one judge of any nationality. Elections are held every three years for one-third of the seats, and retiring judges may be reelected. Of course, judges do not represent their governments but are independent magistrates. But when the court does not include a judge possessing the nationality of a state party to a case, that state may appoint a person to sit as an ad hoc judge for the purpose of the case. Only states may apply to and appear before the ICJ.

A serious limitation of the ICJ's jurisdiction is the fact that it is competent to entertain a dispute only if the states concerned have accepted its jurisdiction. Although all 191 members of the UN have ratified the statute of the court, only sixty-five accept the compulsory jurisdiction of the ICJ, not including the United States. But the number of cases before the ICJ has grown in recent decades. In the 1970s the ICJ had before it only one or two cases at any one time. Between 1990 and 1997 there were nine to thirteen. On 30 July 2004 there were twenty cases before the ICJ. Significantly, these cases had attained a global scope; four were from Africa, one from Asia, eleven from Europe, two from Latin America, and two were intercontinental (www.icj-cij.org).

Organizations Created by the General Assembly

We shall now help readers to acquire an understanding of the emergence of the complicated system of forty-seven organizations in the UN System. As we begin this task Table 4.2 provides a brief overview that reveals that twenty-three of these organizations were created by the General Assembly and twenty-four by separate treaties (twenty classified as Specialized Agencies and four as Related Organizations). To help the reader comprehend the activities of this array of organizations we have divided them into six categories. We recognize that these divisions are somewhat arbitrary and that other divisions are possible, but believe that these smaller categories enhance comprehension. As we present each group of organizations, we will indicate the year of their founding and often refer to their historic roots. This will underline the fact

TABLE 4.2
Overview of 47 Organizations in the UN System

Organizations Created by the General Assembly (23)
  Table 4.3   Programs and Funds (14)
  Table 4.4   Research and Training Institutes (8)
          Office for Project Services (UNOPS) (1)

Specialized Agencies (20)
  Table 4.5   Focus on Specific Economic and Social Issues (6)
  Table 4.6   Technical Organizations (8)
  Table 4.7   Financial and Monetary Organizations (6)

Related Organizations (4)
  Table 4.8   Related Organizations (4)

that emerging global governance is a dynamic process and that the UN System is constantly required to respond to new challenges.

We have divided the organizations created by the General Assembly into three categories. Fourteen are programs and funds, eight are research and training institutes, and the third consists only of the Office for Project Services (UNOPS). We have placed the five organizations categorized as "other UN entities" in the UN System organization chart in these categories.

Programs and Funds

The programs and funds (Table 4.3) began with four activities that can be broadly categorized as focused on human rights: the founding of UNICEF in 1946 and a human rights office in 1949 (now OHCHR) and the founding of two refugee organizations, one for Palestine refugees (UNRWA) in 1949 and the High Commissioner for Refugees (UNHCR) in 1950.

Between 1963 and 1964 four organizations emerged that were spurred by expansion of UN membership to include many states that placed development issues high on their agendas—the so-called underdeveloped states. These included the World Food Program (WFP) in 1963, the UN Conference on Trade and Development (UNCTAD) in 1964, the International Trade Center (ITC) in 1964, and the UN Development Program (UNDP) in 1965. Two more followed in 1970: the UN Population Fund (UNFPA) and the UN Volunteers (UNV).

TABLE 4.3
Programs and Funds (in order of founding date)

1946	UN Children's Fund (UNICEF), New York Founded as UN Children's Emergency Fund 1953 name changed to United Nations Children's Fund with same acronym
1949	Office of the UN High Commissioner for Human Rights (OHCHR), Geneva (HC for HR created in 1993, combined with the Center for HR in 1997) *(Under "Other UN Entities" in UN Organization Chart)*
1949	UN Relief and Works Agency for Palestine Refugees in the Near East (UNRWA), Gaza/Amman
1950	UN High Commissioner for Refugees (UNHCR), Geneva
1963	World Food Program (WFP), Rome
1964	UN Conference on Trade and Development (UNCTAD), Geneva
1964	International Trade Center (ITC) (Joint activity of UNCTAD & WTO), Geneva
1965	UN Development Program (UNDP), New York
1967	UN Population Fund (UNFPA), New York
1970	UN Volunteers (UNV), New York
1972	UN Environment Program (UNEP), Nairobi
1978	UN Human Settlements Program (UNHSP) (also called UN-Habitat), Nairobi
1985	UN Development Fund for Women (UNIFEM), New York Emerged from Voluntary Fund for the UN Decade for Women (VFDW) 1976
1995	Joint UN Program on HIV/AIDS (UNAIDS), Geneva (Founded by UNICEF, UNDP, UNFPA, UNESCO, WHO. Later UNODOC [1999], ILO [2001],WFP [2003]) *(Under "Other UN Entities" in UN Organization Chart)*

The founding of the UN Environment Program (UNEP) in 1972 reflects the emergence of a significant issue in the UN System that did not appear in the UN Charter. In that year the Declaration of the United Nations Conference on the Human Environment, held in Stockholm, recognized "the need for a common outlook and common principles to inspire and guide peoples of the world in the preservation and enhancement of the human environment." Gradually, the environment issue merged with the development issue and presented "sustainable development" as a significant UN System issue.

The creation of the UN Human Settlements Program (UNHSP) in 1978 was in response to recognition of the growing impact of urbanization on human life on the planet at a UN conference in Vancouver, Canada, in that year known as Habitat I. But support for UNHSP developed very slowly, and Habitat II was not held until 1996. Only after six more years, in 2002, was the agency's mandate strengthened and its status elevated to that of a fully fledged program of the UN System by a UN General Assembly resolution (A/56/206). In this way the Assembly recognized that when the UN was founded, two-thirds of humanity was still rural, but by 2002 half the world had become urban.

The emergence of the UN Development Fund for Women (UNIFEM) in 1976 indicates the rising significance of women's issues on UN System agendas. It was also in response to the UN World Conference on Women held in Mexico City in 1975, which was attended by many women's organizations around the world. In the same year, as will be indicated in our next category, an International Research and Training Institute for the Advancement of Women (INSTRAW) was created.

In 1995 another new global issue achieved prominence in the UN System: acquired immuno-deficiency syndrome, or AIDS. The epidemic spurred the creation of the Joint UN Program on HIV/AIDS (UNAIDS). The UNAIDS secretariat operates as a catalyst and coordinator of action on AIDS in the UN System, rather than as a direct funding or implementing agency. Toward this end, it is an example of remarkable cooperation among agencies in the UN System. It was founded by five agencies: UNICEF, UNDP, UNFPA, UNESCO, and WHO. This group has been joined by five more: UNHCR, the World Bank, UNODOC, ILO, and WFP.

Research and Training Institutes

The emergence of eight organizations involved in research and training (Table 4.4) reflects the need of the UN System to support its programs with expertise on approaching policy issues with a global perspective. Those focused on specific topics range across a broad range of UN System issues, including social development, crime and justice, advancement of women, disarmament, and drugs and crime. Three organizations that tend to emphasize research are focused on social development (UN Research Institute for Social Development, UNRISD), crime and justice

TABLE 4.4
Research and Training Institutes (in order of founding date)

1963	UN Research Institute for Social Development (UNRISD), Geneva
1965	UN Institute for Training and Research (UNITAR), Geneva
1968	UN Interregional Crime and Justice Research Institute (UNICRI), Turin (established as UN Social Defense Research Institute, in Rome; became UNICRI, 2000, in Turin)
1973	UN University (UNU), Tokyo *(Under "Other UN entities" in UN Organization Chart)*
1976	International Research and Training Institute for the Advancement of Women (INSTRAW), Santo Domingo
1980	UN Institute for Disarmament Research (UNIDIR), Geneva
1997	United Nations Office on Drugs and Crime (UNODC), Vienna
2002	UN System Staff College (UNSSC), Turin *(Under "Other UN Entities" in UN Organization Chart)*

(UN Interregional Crime and Justice Research Institute, UNICRI), and disarmament (UN Institute for Disarmament Research, UNIDIR). A fourth, the UN University (UNU), has a research agenda that reaches across the UN System. Two organizations range across training and research. One is focused on women, the International Research and Training Institute for the Advancement of Women (INSTRAW). The other is the UN Institute for Training and Research (UNITAR), with a broad issue agenda. One organization emphasizes only training, the UN System Staff College (UNSSC).

Two types of training that are offered deserve special attention. The UN Institute for Training and Research (UNITAR) conducts "training programs in multilateral diplomacy and international cooperation for diplomats accredited to the United Nations and national officials involved in work related to United Nations activities" (www.unitar.org). The UN System Staff College (UNSSC) focuses on these five tasks: (1) providing training and learning services to UN staff members, (2) delivering management solutions to UN organizations, (3) supporting interagency collaboration within the UN System, (4) encouraging cooperation with the private sector and civil society, and (5) promoting good management practices throughout the UN System (www.unssc.org).

UN Office for Project Services (UNOPS), New York

The evolving functions of the UN Office for Project Services (UN-OPS) offer useful insight on the progressive development of linkage among organizations in the UN System. In 1973 the UN Development Program (UNDP) established a Projects Execution Division (PED), responsible for managing programs and projects of UNDP. In 1988 it became UNOPS, to reflect the service-oriented nature of its activities. By this time it had evolved from a small division executing UNDP-funded projects to a provider of services on behalf of UNDP and a dozen other clients, including the World Bank and individual donor states. In 1995 the General Assembly made UNOPS an instrument of the UN System at large "for high-quality, cost-effective management of projects." By this time UNOPS had a diversified portfolio valued at more than $3 billion. In 1996 UNOPS began decentralizing by establishing offices in Geneva and Copenhagen. In 2004 it also had offices in Dakar (Senegal), Nairobi, Rome, Tokyo, San Salvador (El Salvador), Asela (Ethiopia), Guatemala City, Vienna, Dili (Indonesia), Kinshasa (Democratic Republic of the Congo), Lima, and Buenos Aires. The broad scope of UNOPS services range "from land mine awareness to public sector reform, from informatics solutions to eradicating poverty. These services include selecting and hiring project personnel, procuring goods, organizing training, managing financial resources and administering loans. In the field of development, UNOPS is the largest service provider in the United Nations System, working on behalf of more than thirty UN departments and organizations. But UNOPS also offers services to bilateral donors, international financial institutions, developing country governments and others, at their request" (www.unops.org).

UN Specialized Agencies

At the same time that the UN General Assembly has been establishing new organizations under its authority to cope with new problems on its ever broader agenda, the United Nations has been developing relationships with "various specialized agencies, established by intergovernmental agreement and having wide international responsibilities, as defined in their basic instruments, in economic, social, cultural, educational, health, and related fields" (UN Charter, Article 57). The Charter also states that ECOSOC "may co-ordinate the activities of the specialized agencies" and "may take appropriate steps to obtain regular reports from the specialized agencies" (UN Charter, Article 63). These Specialized Agencies total twenty in 2005, sometimes reported as fifteen when the six agencies of the World Bank group are counted as one organization. To develop a more easily comprehended overview of this complicated array of organizations, we have arbitrarily divided them into three groups: (1) six focus on specific economic and social fields; (2) eight are technical organizations; and (3) six are financial and monetary organizations.

Focus on Specific Economic and Social Fields

The six specialized agencies that focus on specific economic and social fields range across agriculture, culture, education, food, labor, health, industrial development, and science. The dates of their founding range from 1919 to 1977, all with headquarters in Europe (Table 4.5).

The **International Labor Organization (ILO)**, created in 1919 at the end of the First World War, became the first specialized agency of the UN System in 1946. The need for such an organization had been advocated in the nineteenth century by two industrialists, Robert Owen (1771–1853) of Wales and Daniel Legrand (1783–1859) of France. The International Association for Labor Legislation, founded in Basel in 1901, contributed ideas that were included in the constitution of the International Labor Organization.

It is indeed remarkable that almost a century ago the preamble of the ILO constitution expressed ideas that were a motivation for many of the creative innovations in the development of the UN System in 2005. The constitution expresses humanitarian concern that "conditions of labour exist involving . . . injustice, hardship and privation to large numbers of people" (www.ilo.org/public/english/about/iloconst.htm). Then the preamble recognizes that an industry or country may resist adopting social reform because it may result in disadvantage vis-à-vis its competitors by stating that: "the failure of any nation to adopt humane conditions of labour is an obstacle in the way of other nations which desire to improve the conditions in their own

TABLE 4.5
Specialized Agencies:
Focus on Specific Economic and Social Fields

1919	International Labor Organization (ILO), Geneva (UN Spec Ag 1946)
1945	Food and Agriculture Organization (FAO), Rome (UN Spec Ag 1946)
1946	UN Educational, Science and Cultural Organization (UNESCO), Paris (UN spec Ag 1946)
1948	World Health Organization (WHO), Geneva (UN Spec Ag 1948)
1966	UN Industrial Development Organization (UNIDO), Vienna (UN Spec Ag 1985)
1977	International Fund for Agricultural Development (IFAD), Rome (UN Spec Ag 1977)

countries." These concerns are then placed in a remarkably broad social context by noting that injustice produces "unrest so great that the peace and harmony of the world are imperiled" and that "universal and lasting peace can be established only if it is based upon social justice" (www.ilo.org).

The ILO has an unusual tripartite form of representation that extends beyond governmental representation. In the International Labor Conference, where all 177 members are represented, each state is represented by two government members and one each from labor and business organizations. The Governing Body (similar to UN councils) consists of fifty-six persons, twenty-eight representing governments, fourteen representing employers, and fourteen representing workers.

The ILO was an early innovator in the development of laws with respect to universal human rights. At the first International Labor Conference in 1919, six conventions were adopted that dealt with hours of work in industry, unemployment, maternity protection, night work for women, minimum age, and night work for young persons in industry. In 1926 the International Labor Conference set up a Committee of Experts on the Application of Conventions and Recommendations, independent of member states, to supervise adherence to these conventions. Each year they examine reports made by states that have ratified ILO conventions and make a report to the ILO Conference. There are 180 ILO labor conventions as of 2005. The United States has ratified seventeen. The ILO considers eight of them to be "fundamental" conventions: two dealing with freedom of association, two with abolition of forced labor, two with equality, and two with elimination of child labor. The United States has ratified one dealing with forced labor and one with the elimination of child labor.

The **Food and Agriculture Organization (FAO)** was founded in Rome in 1945 and became a UN Specialized Agency in 1946. It replaced the Institute of Agriculture, founded in Rome in 1905 by the International Congress of Agriculture, composed of forty-one states. An unofficial International Agricultural Congress had been held in Budapest in 1896. A key figure in the development of the Institute of Agriculture had been David Lubin, son of a Polish immigrant on the West Coast of the United States. Regarded as a "crank" by the U.S. Department of Agriculture, he "secured an audience with the King of Italy in 1904" that led to the 1905 conference (Mangone 1954, 88).

With 187 member states FAO declares: "We help developing countries and countries in transition modernize and improve agriculture, forestry and fisheries practices and ensure good nutrition for all. Since our founding in 1945, we have focused special attention on developing rural areas, home to 70 percent of the world's poor and hungry people" (www.fao.org/UNFAO/about/index_en.html). The FAO's activities comprise four main areas: (1) putting information within reach, (2) sharing policy expertise, (3) providing a meeting place for nations, and (4) bringing knowledge to the field. Restructuring of FAO since 1994 reflects some of the recent trends in the UN System: increased emphasis on food security, transferring more staff from headquarters to the field, increasing use of experts from developing countries, broadening links with the private sector and NGOs, and greater electronic access to FAO statistical databases and documents (www.fao.org).

The UN System agricultural activity was extended in 1977 as a result of the 1974 World Food Conference, organized in response to the food crises of the early 1970s that primarily affected the Sahelian countries of Africa. One of the most important insights emerging from the conference was that food insecurity and famine were not primarily a result of food production failures, but were caused by structural problems relating to poverty and to the concentration of the developing world's poor populations in rural areas. The conference decided that an International Fund for Agricultural Development (IFAD) should be established immediately for the purpose of financing the development of food production projects in the developing countries." The International Fund for Agricultural Development (IFAD) became a specialized agency of the United Nations in 1977. Its target groups "are the poorest of the world's people: small farmers, the rural landless, nomadic pastoralists, artisanal fisherfolk, indigenous people and rural poor women" (www.ifad.org).

The **UN Educational, Scientific and Cultural Organization (UNESCO),** with 190 member states in 2005, had three main predecessors: (1) the International Committee of Intellectual Co-operation (CICI), Geneva 1922–1946; (2) its executing agency, the International Institute of Intellectual Co-operation (IICI), Paris, 1925–1946; and (3) the International Bureau of Education (IBE), Geneva, 1925–1968. The IBE was founded in Geneva as a private, nongovernmental organization in 1925. In 1929, under new statutes, the IBE extended membership to governments and eventually became the first intergovernmental organization in the field of education. In 1969 the IBE became part of the UNESCO secretariat under its own statutes.

The preamble of the UNESCO constitution declares: "Since wars begin in the minds of men, it is in the minds of men that the defences of peace must be constructed." Since its founding UNESCO has followed an ever more broad range of topics that shape "the minds of men." It very briefly summarizes its interests into five thematic areas: (1) education, (2) natural sciences, (3) social and human sciences, (4) culture, and (5) communication and information. In addition, it lists a number of special focus issues that range as broadly as the culture of peace, HIV/AIDS, indigenous people, and world heritage.

UNESCO espouses "a single unifying theme—contributing to peace and human development in an era of globalization through education, the sciences, culture and communication." Toward this end it has three main strategic thrusts:

1. Developing and promoting universal principles and norms, based on shared values, in order to meet emerging challenges in education, science, culture and communication and to protect and strengthen the "common public good" ;
2. Promoting pluralism, through recognition and safeguarding of diversity together with the observance of human rights;

3. Promoting empowerment and participation in the emerging knowledge society through equitable access, capacity-building and sharing of knowledge. (www.unesco.org)

In working toward these ends, UNESCO has become increasingly decentralized. In 2005 it had twenty-four national offices (focused on one state), twenty-seven cluster offices (which cover various domains for a cluster of states), twelve regional bureaus, and twelve institutes and centers (for example, theoretical physics, water, and capacity building in Africa) (www.unesco.com).

One root of the **World Health Organization (WHO)** can be traced to the outbreak of cholera in Europe in 1830, which claimed the lives of thousands of people in different countries. This was followed by several health conferences: the First International Sanitary Conference in Paris (1851), the International Sanitary Conference for Repression of Epidemic Disease in Dresden (1883), and the Sanitary Conference against Plague in Venice (1898). Soon two international health organizations were formed: the International Sanitary Bureau in Washington (1902), and the Office International d'Hygiene Public (OIP) in Paris. Then in 1919 the Health Organization of the League of Nations was established in Paris.

The WHO constitution proclaims that "the enjoyment of the highest attainable standard of health" is "one of the fundamental human rights of every human being without distinction for race, religion, political belief, economic or social condition" and that "the health of all peoples is fundamental in the attainment of peace and security and is dependent upon the fullest cooperation of individuals and states." It defines health very broadly as a state of complete physical, mental, and social well-being and not merely the absence of disease or infirmity. With 192 member states, WHO has assistant director-generals for HIV/AIDS, tuberculosis and malaria, communicable diseases, noncommunicable diseases and mental health, sustainable development and health environment, health technology and pharmaceuticals, and family and community health (www.who.int).

Disappointed with its inability to fulfill the goals of its constitution, in 1978 WHO launched a Health for All program that recognized that large numbers of people, and even whole countries, were not enjoying an acceptable standard of health. WHO has also become significantly decentralized by establishing regional offices for Africa, the Americas, Southeast Asia, Europe, the Eastern Mediterranean, and the Western Pacific. Of course, concern for health is not confined to WHO. For example, the World Bank has taken note of health conditions in the poor countries and urged their health ministries to pool their resources and target the delivery of health services to their neediest populations.

The emergence of the **United Nations Industrial Development Organization (UNIDO)** as a Specialized Agency is a result of the large expansion of the number of UN member states with very limited industrialization. In response to their demands, the name of the UN Center for Industrial Development, then a part of the UN Secretariat, was changed to the UN Industrial Development Organization in 1966. It was made an autonomous organization, although the desire that it be a Specialized Agency was rejected. But in 1985 UNIDO became a Specialized Agency and in 2005 had 171 member states, although the United States was not a member.

UNIDO's mandate is to support the industrial competence and capacity of the poorer countries. It has been active in practically all fields of industry, frequently through programs of exchange and training. Carlos Magariños, the director-general of UNIDO who is from Argentina, believes that the "ultimate task of UNIDO is to contribute to a better future for those people presently excluded from globalization. This can be done most effectively by decentralizing, ensuring transparency and concentrating our efforts on a selected set of development goals in order to achieve concrete results" (www.unido.org/doc/3358).

UNIDO has an active presence in the poorer member states, including representatives in thirty states and a number of offices in these states focused on specific topics: seventeen investment and technology promotion offices (ITPOs) and ten international technology centers. Jointly with the UN Environment Program (UNEP), it has established thirty national cleaner production centers (NCPCs) (www.unido.org).

Technical Organizations

The eight specialized agencies that we have classified as technical organizations in Table 4.6 have founding years that range from 1878, sixty-seven years before the founding of the United Nations, to 2003. This list of their foci reflects the growing dimen-

TABLE 4.6
Specialized Agencies: Technical Organizations

1878	Universal Postal Union (UPU), Bern (UN Spec Ag 1948)
1934	International Telecommunication Union (ITU), Geneva (UN Spec Ag 1947)
1944	International Civil Aviation Organization (ICAO), Montreal (UN Spec Ag 1947)
1950	World Meteorological Organization (WMO), Geneva (UN Spec Ag 1951)
1946	United Nations Atomic Energy Commission, Vienna (Dissolved in 1952)
1958	International Maritime Organization (IMO), London (UN Spec Ag 1959)
1970	World Industrial Property Organization (WIPO), Geneva (UN Spec Ag 1974)
2003	World Tourism Organization (WTO), Madrid

sions of human linkage between 1865 and 2003: postal services, telecommunications, civil aviation, meteorology, atomic energy, maritime shipping, copyrights and patents, and tourism.

The **Universal Postal Union (UPU)**, established in 1874 in the Swiss capital of Bern, has 190 members. During the seventeenth and eighteenth centuries, the exchange of mail between countries was largely governed by bilateral postal agreements, but by the nineteenth century, these complex arrangements began to impede rapidly developing trade and commercial sectors. In 1863 U.S. Postmaster General Montgomery Blair called a conference in Paris, where delegates from fifteen European and American countries met, but they were not able to reach an international postal agreement. The Swiss government convened an international conference in Bern in 1874, attended by representatives from twenty-two states. On 9 October of the same year—a day now celebrated throughout the world as World Post Day—the Treaty of Bern established the General Postal Union. Membership in the union grew so quickly that its name was changed to the Universal Postal Union in 1878. The barriers and frontiers that had impeded the free flow and growth of international mail had finally been removed.

The postal service forms part of the daily life of people all over the world. Even in the digital age, the Post remains, for millions of people, the most accessible means of communication and message delivery available. The postal services of the Universal Postal Union's 190 member countries form the largest physical distribution network in the world. More than six million postal employees work in over 700,000 postal outlets to ensure that some 430 billion mail items are processed and delivered each year to all corners of the world. (www.upu.int/about_us)

Services provided by the UPU include annual statistical data that provide an overview of postal development in over 200 countries and territories and includes approximately 100 indicators of postal development. The UPU Technical Standards publication gives an overview of all technical standards that have been adopted through the UPU's standards approval process. In order to strengthen the quality of postal service to the poorer countries, the UPU has established the Quality of Service Fund (QSF) that is funded by increases in dues payments made by industrialized member states. The QSF is used to support specific quality-of-service improvement projects (www.upu.int).

The roots of the **International Telecommunication Union (ITU)** emerged on 24 May 1844, when Samuel Morse sent his first public message over a telegraph line between Washington, D.C., and Baltimore, Maryland, thereby initiating a telecommunication age that would be followed by the telephone, radio, television, and the Internet. In 1865 the International Telegraphic Union was established in Paris, followed by the creation of the International Radiotelegraph Conference in Berlin in 1906. These two organizations merged into the International Telecommunication Union in 1934, following a 1932 conference in Madrid. In 1947 the ITU became a specialized agency of the UN.

When the first geostationary communications satellite (Syncom–1) was put into orbit in 1963, a new age of challenges confronted the ITU. In 1992 allocations were made for the first time to serve the needs of a new kind of space service using nongeostationary satellites, known as global mobile personal communications by satellite (GMPCS). In this year the ITU also developed global standards for digital mobile telephony. It is expected that commercial implementation early in this new millennium will harmonize the incompatible mobile systems now in use around the world and provide high-speed wireless devices capable of handling voice, data, and connection to online services such as the Internet.

The Kyoto Plenipotentiary Conference in 1994 established the World Telecommunication Policy Forum (WTPF), an ad hoc meeting that encourages the free exchange of ideas and information on emerging policy issues arising from the changing telecommunication environment. The first WTPF was held in Geneva in 1996 on the theme of global mobile personal communications by satellite; the second in Geneva in 1998 on trade in telecommunication services; and the third in 2001, also in Geneva, on Internet protocol (IP). "As the world becomes ever more reliant on telecommunication technologies for commerce, communication and access to information, ITU's role in standardizing emerging new systems and fostering common global policies will be more vital than ever before" (www.itu.int).

The **International Civil Aviation Organization (ICAO)**, established at a Chicago conference in 1944, became a UN Specialized Agency in 1947 and has 187 members as of 2005. "Safe and efficient air transport is in the interest of all states, but it can only be achieved in cooperation, since most destinations of the national airlines are located in foreign countries and often third states have to be overflown to reach the destination. This might account for the astonishing fact that ICAO was able to function relatively undisturbed throughout the Cold War" (Volger 2002, 275). Because operational and technical problems vary greatly in different parts of the world, the ICAO has established eight regional offices.

The ICAO's services include aviation security (AVSEC), which "develops AVSEC principles, communicates and promotes such principles worldwide and assists ICAO in contracting States in implementing them" (www.icao.org/atb/avsec/index). A TRAINAIR program serves "to improve safety and efficiency of air transport through the establishment and maintenance of high standards of training and competency for aviation personnel on a worldwide basis and in a cost effective manner" (www.icao.org). There are also units on the environment, aviation medicine, navigation, air transport, legal affairs, and technical cooperation.

The **World Meteorological Organization (WMO),** with 187 members as of 2005, is "the UN system's authoritative voice on the state and behavior of the Earth's atmosphere, its interaction with the oceans, the climate it produces and the resulting distribution of water resources (www.wmo.int). In 1853 the first International Meteorological Conference was held in Brussels, followed by the founding of the semigovernmental International Meteorological Organization in 1873. It was succeeded in 1950 by the creation of the WMO that in 1951 became a UN Specialized Agency.

In addition to its headquarters in Geneva, the WMO secretariat has regional offices for Africa (Burundi), for Asia and the Southwest Pacific (Switzerland), and for the Americas (Paraguay); and subregional offices in West Africa (Nigeria), eastern and southern Africa (Kenya), the Southwest Pacific (Samoa), and for North and Central America and the Caribbean (Costa Rica).

Six regional associations (Africa, Asia, South America, North America, Central America and the Caribbean, the Southwest Pacific, and Europe), composed of member states, coordinate meteorological and related activities within their respective regions.

Eight technical commissions, composed of experts within their specific areas of competence, have been established for (1) basic systems, (2) instruments and methods of observation, (3) atmospheric sciences, (4) aeronautical meteorology, (5) agricultural meteorology, (6) hydrology, (7) climatology, (8) oceanography, and (9) marine meteorology. The last is a joint effort with the International Oceanographic Commission (IOC) of UNESCO.

The **International Maritime Organization (IMO)** was founded in 1948 by an international conference in Geneva. The original name was the Inter-Governmental Maritime Consultative Organization (IMCO), but the name was changed in 1982 to the International Maritime Organization. The convention entered into force in 1958 and the new organization met for the first time the following year. The purposes of the organization, as summarized by the convention, are "to provide machinery for cooperation among Governments in the field of governmental regulation and practices relating to technical matters of all kinds affecting shipping engaged in international trade; to encourage and facilitate the general adoption of the highest practicable standards in matters concerning maritime safety, efficiency of navigation and prevention and control of marine pollution from ships"(www.imo.org/home.asp).

Recent technological innovations have presented new opportunities to the IMO. These include a Global Maritime Distress and Safety System (GMDSS) and an International Mobile Satellite Organization (IMSO) that improves communication with ships. New challenges include growth in the amount of oil being transported by sea and in the size of oil tankers. "The most important convention regulating and preventing marine pollution by ships is the IMO International Convention for the Prevention of Pollution from Ships, 1973, as modified by the Protocol of 1978 relating thereto (MARPOL 73/78). It covers accidental and operational oil pollution as well as pollution by chemicals, goods in packaged form, sewage, garbage and air pollution" (www.imo.org).

"The IMO's International Convention on Standards of Training, Certification and Watchkeeping for Seafarers (STCW), 1978, was the first internationally agreed-upon convention to address the issue of minimum standards of competence for seafarers. The World Maritime University (WMU), established in Sweden in 1983, operates under the auspices of the International Maritime Organization. The IMO's Technical Co-operation Program helps "developing countries improve their ability to comply with international rules and standards relating to maritime safety and the prevention and control of maritime pollution, giving priority to technical assistance programs that focus on human resources development and institutional capacity-building" (www.imo.org).

The roots of the **World Intellectual Property Organization (WIPO)** are in the Paris Convention for the Protection of Industrial Property of 1883 and the Berne Convention for the Protection of Literary and Artistic Works of 1886. Each had an international bureau to carry out their administrative tasks. In 1893 these two small bureaus united to form an international organization called the United International Bureaux for the Protection of Intellectual Property (best known by its French acronym BIRPI), based in Berne, Switzerland. In 1970 BIRPI became the World Industrial Property Organization (WIPO). In 1974 WIPO became a Specialized Agency of the UN System, having 181 member states as of 2005. It administers twenty-three international treaties dealing with different aspects of intellectual property protection.

WIPO's activities and services include establishing international standards for intellectual property laws and practices and providing registration services that allow patents, trademarks, and designs to be protected in many countries. WIPO also offers assistance to developing countries in facilitating resolution of intellectual property disputes. As a result of rapid development of new communications technologies, WIPO is facing many new challenges in the twenty-first century. One of the most urgent is the need for both the organization and its member states to adapt to and benefit from rapid change in the field of information technology and the Internet (www.wipo.int).

The emergence of the **World Tourism Organization (WTO)** offers deep insight into the ways in which human activities that cross state borders eventually emerge as organizations in the UN System. It was founded as a nongovernmental organization, the International Congress of Official Tourist Traffic Associations, in 1925 in The Hague. It was renamed the International Union of Official Travel Organizations (IUOTO) after World War II and moved to Geneva. In 1967 IUOTO became an intergovernmental body and in 1975 it became the WTO. In 1976 it became an executing agency of the UN Development Program (UNDP). In 2003 the WTO became a UN Specialized Agency. Its membership is comprised of member states, seven territories, and more than 300 affiliate members representing the private sector, educational institutions, tourism associations, and local tourism authorities. The United States is not a member.

"At the start of the new millennium, tourism is firmly established as the number one industry in many countries and the fastest-growing economic sector in terms of foreign exchange earnings and job creation. International tourism is the world's largest export earner and an important factor in the balance of payments of most nations. Tourism has become one of the world's most important sources of employment." The WTO promotes "the development of responsible, sustainable and universally accessible tourism, with the aim of contributing to economic development, international understanding, peace, prosperity and universal respect for, and observance of, human rights and fundamental freedoms" (www.world-tourism.org). The WTO pays particular attention to the interests of developing countries, promotes technology transfers, and stimulates the development of public-private sector partnerships. It encourages the implementation of the Global Code of Ethics for Tourism, "with a view to ensuring that member countries, tourist destinations and businesses maximize the positive economic, social and cultural effects of tourism." Regional representatives, based at the Madrid headquarters, "hold regional conferences on problems that are shared by many countries so that members can exchange experiences and work towards common goals" (www.world-tourism.org). Conferences have included these topics: the challenge of globalization in the Middle East, human resource development in East Asia and the Pacific, the Euro and tourism in Europe, and quality standards in the Americas region.

Financial and Monetary Organizations

In July 1944 the UN Monetary and Financial Conference was convened at Bretton Woods, New Hampshire, in response to the need for international cooperation in dealing with monetary and financial problems that affect financial stability. The conference created articles of agreement that were ratified by forty-four states and went into force in December 1945. Two organizations emerged out of this conference, the International Monetary Fund (IMF) and the International Bank for Reconstruction and Development (IBRD) (Table 4.7).

The roots of the **International Monetary Fund (IMF)** go back as early as 1867 when the Monetary Conference was held in Paris, followed by the 1878 Monetary Diplomatic Conference that established a permanent bureau in Berne. Then the forty-five states represented at the Bretton Woods Conference in 1944 developed the IMF primarily to establish a means to avoid repetition of the economic policies that had contributed to the Great Depression of the 1930s. Toward this end the IMF was "established to promote international monetary cooperation, exchange stability, and orderly exchange arrangements; to foster economic growth and high levels of employment; and to provide temporary financial assistance to countries to help ease balance of payments adjustment" (www.imf.org). The IMF had 184 members by 2005.

"More generally, the IMF is responsible for ensuring the stability of the international monetary and financial system—the system of international payments and exchange rates among national currencies that enables trade to take place between countries. The Fund seeks to promote economic stability and prevent crises; to help resolve crises when they do occur; and to promote growth and alleviate poverty." It employs three main functions. The first is surveillance, defined by the IMF thus: "A core responsibility of the IMF is to promote a dialogue among its member countries on the national and international consequences of their economic and financial policies. This process of monitoring and consultation, normally referred to as 'surveillance,' has evolved rapidly as the world economy has changed. IMF surveillance has also become increasingly open and transparent in recent years." The second function is technical assistance, and the third is lending (www.imf.org).

Financial resources for pursuing these goals are acquired from member states, with each contributing according to a quota

TABLE 4.7
Specialized Agencies:
Financial and Monetary Organizations

1945	International Monetary Fund (IMF) Washington (UN Spec Ag 1947)

World Bank Group, Washington

1945	International Bank for Reconstruction and Development (IBRD), (UN Spec Ag 1947)
1956	International Finance Corporation (IFC)
1960	International Development Association (IDA), (UN Spec Ag 1961)
1966	International Center for Settlement of Investment Disputes (ICSID)
1988	Multilateral Investment Guarantee Agency (MIGA)

that reflects their wealth. A member's quota determines both its financial assessment and its voting power. The United States has the largest quota, 17.1 percent and Palau has the smallest, .013 percent.

The **International Bank for Reconstruction and Development (IBRD)** began operating in 1946 to help reconstruct the war-ravaged economies of Western Europe. After this had been achieved, the bank turned its attention to the developing countries, which led to its primary purpose of promoting poverty reduction and sustainable development by lending to the governments of developing countries. In 2004 the World Bank provided $20.1 billion for 245 projects in developing countries worldwide, with its finance and/or technical expertise aimed at helping these countries reduce poverty. The IBRD is financed through the sale of World Bank bonds. In fiscal 2004 it raised $13 billion in financial markets. The IBRD now has 184 member states in 2005 and more than 100 offices in these states (www.worldbank.org).

Members of the IBRD are represented on a Board of Governors. The number of shares each county has is based roughly on the size of its economy. The United States is the largest single shareholder, with 16.41 percent of votes, followed by Japan (7.87 percent), Germany (4.49 percent), the United Kingdom (4.31 percent), and France (4.31 percent). The rest of the shares are divided among the other member countries.

To cope with emerging financial challenges, four additional organizations were created alongside the IBRD that form the World Bank Group. These include the International Finance Corporation (IFC), the International Development Association (IDA), the International Center for Settlement of Investment Disputes (ICSID), and the Multilateral Investment Guarantee Agency (MIGA).

The **International Finance Corporation (IFC)** was established in 1956 to promote sustainable private-sector investment in developing countries as a way to reduce poverty and improve people's lives. To join IFC, a country must first be a member of the IBRD. The IFC is the largest multilateral source of loan and equity financing for private-sector projects in the developing world. It promotes sustainable private-sector development primarily by financing private-sector projects, helping private companies in the developing world mobilize financing in international financial markets, and providing advice and technical assistance to businesses and governments. The IFC has 178 member states (www.ifc.org).

By the 1950s it became clear that the poorest countries needed softer financial terms than those offered by the IBRD. To provide special attention to challenges confronted in lending to the poorest countries, the **International Development Association (IDA)** was formed in 1960. The IBRD and the IDA share the same staff and headquarters and report to the same president, but draw on different resources for their lending. The IDA is primarily funded by contributions from the wealthier countries in loans that mature in thirty-five to forty years and begin with a ten-year grace period during which there is a service charge of only 0.75 percent. In fiscal year 2004 the IDA provided $9 billion in financing for 158 projects in sixty-two low-income countries (www.worldbank.org/ida). Some forty rich countries provide the money for this funding by making contributions every four years. The IDA had 165 member states in 2005. All members of IDA are members of the IBRD.

In 1966 the **International Center for Settlement of Investment Disputes (ICSID)** was created to cope with investment disputes. It facilitates international financial settlements by providing conciliation and arbitration of investment disputes between nationals of different member countries. Recourse to ICSID conciliation and arbitration is entirely voluntary. However, once the parties have consented to arbitration under the ICSID convention, neither can unilaterally withdraw its consent.

"The creation of the International Center for Settlement of Investment Disputes (ICSID) in 1966 was in part intended to relieve the President and the staff [of the IBRD] of the burden of becoming involved in such disputes. But the Bank's overriding consideration in creating ICSID was the belief that an institution specially designed to facilitate the settlement of investment disputes between governments and foreign investors could help to promote increased flows of international investment" (www. worldbank.org/icsid). One hundred and fifty-five states had ratified the ICSID convention in May 2005.

In 1988 the **Multilateral Investment Guarantee Agency (MIGA)** was founded to help developing countries attract private and public foreign investments. MIGA membership is open to all IBRD members. The MIGA provides guarantees against commercial risk such as expropriation and war, and consultative and advisory services to improve the climate for foreign investment in member states. The MIGA has 164 member states that it divides into twenty-two industrialized and forty-two developing states (www.miga.org).

Related Organizations

Four organizations in the UN System that were established between 1957 and 1997 and created by separate treaties among member states are not classified as Specialized Agencies, but as Related Organizations. Three are concerned with military weapons, including atomic energy, nuclear test bans, and chemical weapons. The fourth focuses on world trade (Table 4.8).

The **International Atomic Energy Agency (IAEA)** was created in 1957 in response to the overwhelming challenges presented to the world by the development of nuclear weapons. "By 1958 it had become politically impracticable for the IAEA to begin work on some of the main tasks foreseen in its Statute. But in the aftermath of the 1962 Cuban missile crisis, the USA and the USSR began seeking common ground in nuclear arms control" (www.iaea.org).

The IAEA states that "three main pillars underpin IAEA's mission: 1. Safety and security: "The IAEA helps countries to upgrade nuclear safety and to prepare for and respond to emergencies. Work is keyed to international conventions, standards, and guidance. The main aim is to protect people and the environment from harmful radiation exposure." 2. Science and technology: "The IAEA is the world's focal point for scientific and technical cooperation in nuclear fields. The work contributes to fighting poverty, sickness, and pollution of the earth's environment, and to other global 'Millennium Goals' for a safer and better future." 3. Safeguards and verification: "The IAEA is the

TABLE 4.8
Related Organizations

1957	International Atomic Energy Agency (IAEA), Vienna
1995	World Trade Organization (WTO), Geneva
1996	The Preparatory Commission for the Comprehensive Nuclear Test-Ban Treaty Organization (CTBTO Preparatory Commission), Vienna
1997	Organisation for the Prohibition of Chemical Weapons (OPCW), The Hague

world's nuclear inspectorate, with more than four decades of verification experience. Inspectors work to verify that safeguarded nuclear material and activities are not used for military purposes. The Agency is additionally responsible for the nuclear file in Iraq" (www.iaea.org).

As of 2005 the IAEA had 137 member states with a staff from more than 90 countries. It reports to both the Security Council and the General Assembly. In addition to headquarters in Vienna, the IAEA has offices in Geneva, New York, Toronto, and Tokyo. The IAEA runs or supports research centers and scientific laboratories in Vienna and Seibersdorf (Austria), Monaco, and Trieste (Italy).

An example of the IAEA's involvement in peaceful uses of atomic energy occurred in 1988 when the IAEA and the UN Food and Agricultural Organization joined with other agencies to eradicate the New World screwworm—which spreads a deadly livestock disease. The radiation-based technology to eradicate the worm was developed at the agency's Seibersdorf laboratory. A more recent challenge confronting the IAEA is the need to develop countermeasures against the threat of nuclear terrorism.

The **World Trade Organization (WTO)**, like the IMF, has roots in efforts to prevent a repetition of the world economic chaos of the 1930s. ECOSOC wished to create an organization similar to the IMF for trade and convened a UN conference on trade and employment in Havana, Cuba, which drew up the Havana Charter in 1948 that called for the creation of an International Trade Organization (ITO). This charter "established a comprehensive institutional and substantial order for international economic relations, which is of unparalleled density and almost prophetic foresight. In addition to tariffs and trade, it addressed questions of economic development, trade in natural resources and even questions of anti-trust relations" (Stoll 2000, 691). In order to hasten the lowering of customs duties a special agreement was concluded: the General Agreement on Tariffs and Trade (GATT). The Havana Charter never came into force but the world trade order developed on the basis of GATT. Thus the future international trading system was developed through a series of trade negotiations, or rounds, held under GATT. The first rounds dealt mainly with tariff reductions, but later negotiations included other areas, such as antidumping and nontariff measures. The last round—the 1986–1994 Uruguay Round—led to the creation of the WTO, having 148 members in 2005.

The WTO's "overriding objective is to help trade flow smoothly, freely, fairly and predictably. It does this by: acting as a forum for trade negotiations, administering trade agreements, settling trade disputes, reviewing national trade policies, assisting developing countries in trade policy issues, through technical assistance and training programs, and cooperating with other international organizations" (www.wto.org).

The WTO's multilateral trading agreements are negotiated and signed by a large majority of the world's trading nations and ratified in their parliaments. These agreements cover a wide range of activities, including agriculture, textiles and clothing, banking, telecommunications, government purchases, industrial standards and product safety, food sanitation regulations, and intellectual property. They provide the legal ground rules for international commerce (www.wto.org).

The **Preparatory Commission for the Comprehensive Nuclear Test-Ban Treaty Organization (CTBTO)** is carrying out the necessary preparations for the implementation of the Nuclear Test-Ban Treaty that was adopted by the General Assembly in 1996. The treaty will enter into force after it has been ratified by forty-four states that possess nuclear power or research reactors, as listed in a treaty Annex. By 2005, 175 states have signed the treaty, of which 121 have also ratified it. The United States signed the treaty in 1996, but has not ratified it. The CTBTO reports to the General Assembly.

All states that have signed the treaty are members of the Preparatory Commission and fund its activities. The commission's main tasks are the establishment of a 337-facility international monitoring system and the International Data Center and the development of operational manuals, including those for on-site inspections (www.ctbto.org).

Roots of the **Organization for the Prohibition of Chemical Weapons (OPCW)** can be found in the 1899 international conference held in The Hague that led to an agreement prohibiting the use of projectiles filled with poison gas. But this was followed by an overwhelming setback in World War I, when toxic chemicals accounted for the deaths of 90,000 soldiers and more than a million casualties. The 1925 Geneva Protocol banned the use of chemical weapons in war, but did not prohibit the development, production, or possession of such weapons. Finally, in 1992 negotiators in Geneva agreed on the text of the Convention on the Prohibition of Development, Production, Stockpiling, and Use of Chemical Weapons and on Their Destruction.

The OPCW entered into force in 1997 and has 168 member states in 2005. It reports to the General Assembly. OPCW programs "have four broad aims: to ensure a credible, transparent regime to verify the destruction of chemical weapons and prevent their reemergence in any Member State, while also protecting legitimate national security and proprietary interests; to provide protection and assistance against chemical weapons; to encourage international cooperation in the peaceful uses of chemistry; and to bring about universal membership of the OPCW by facilitating international cooperation and national capacity building" (www.opcw.org). Inspections to verify that treaty obligations are being honored by member states are carried out at military sites and at industrial and research sites by 181 inspectors from 53 countries.

UN World Conferences

World conferences under UN auspices that are focused on specific global problems have emerged as a significant means for drawing widespread attention to issues such as the environment, women, human rights, human settlements, and peaceful use of outer space. A significant aspect of these gatherings is not only a formal conference of representatives of states, but also the presence of international and local NGOs and many other interested parties. Also significant is the fact that these conferences have been held in many cities around the world, thereby making them accessible to people worldwide.

Some 30,000 people were in Istanbul, Turkey, to seek solutions to urban problems at the Habitat II Conference (1996); nearly 50,000 were in Beijing for the Fourth World Conference on Women (1995); and some 47,000 were in Rio de Janeiro to find a better balance between environmental protection and economic development at the Earth Summit (1992). Some believe these large-scale United Nations conferences are wasteful, but a German scholar has concluded that they have these five "functions and impacts": (1) they provide fora for international communications exchange for a diversity of people concerned with a specific issue; (2) they make possible important learning opportunities, particularly across the poor and industrialized state divide; (3) they perform an important educational and information function as a result of media attention; (4) many of their nonbinding decisions eventually acquire normative force; and (5) many states do voluntarily comply with the decisions reached (Nuscheler 2002, 687–688).

Coordination of the UN System

Coordination of the UN System—an array of organizations with a global agenda and members from around the globe—has never been easy, and growth in the UN System in response to a dramatically changing world has made the task ever more challenging. A brief outline of the UN Millennium Declaration of the General Assembly (A/55/L.2) in September 2000 offers a useful snapshot of the agenda of the system in the early twenty-first century:

  I. We consider certain fundamental values to be essential in the twenty-first century. These include: freedom, equality, solidarity, tolerance, respect for nature, shared responsibility.
  In order to translate these shared values into actions, we have identified key objectives to which we assign special significance.
 II. Peace, security and disarmament,
III. Development and poverty eradication,

IV. Protecting our common environment,
V. Human rights, democracy and good governance,
VI. Protecting the vulnerable,
VII. Meeting the special needs of Africa,
VIII. Strengthening the United Nations.

Obviously, efforts to achieve any one of these values, such as poverty eradication, depends on the activities of several agencies in the UN System. At the same time, efforts that focus on one value, such as development, can significantly affect efforts to protect other values, such as the environment, health, and human rights.

In the UN System coordination requires efforts both by representatives of states in various decision-making bodies and by members of secretariats. Very important with respect to the first are the efforts of the Economic and Social Council to coordinate the work of the nineteen UN specialized agencies, nine functional commissions, and eleven UN funds and programs. At the same time, while the regional commissions (for Africa, Latin America and the Caribbean, Asia and the Pacific, Western Asia, and Europe) are coping with different regional conditions, ECOSOC must coordinate their efforts. Of course, the General Assembly has the main responsibility for coordinating the efforts of the eleven funds and programs that it has created.

In 1946, at the request of ECOSOC, the Administrative Committee on Coordination (ACC) was formed to bring together the executive heads of UN organizations for the purpose of coordinating their activities. The main purpose of the committee was to supervise the implementation of the agreements between the United Nations and the Specialized Agencies. Since then, its mandate has grown and it has been replaced by the UN System Chief Executives Board (CEB) for Coordination to further coordination and cooperation on the whole range of substantive and management issues facing the UN System. Expanded from ACC's original four members (UN, ILO, FAO, and UNESCO), the CEB in 2005 comprises twenty-eight member organizations, including UN funds and programs, as well as Specialized Agencies and the WTO. Chaired by the secretary-general of the United Nations, the board meets twice annually. It is composed of the executive heads of the member organizations and is assisted by two high-level committees, the High-Level Committee on Programs (HLCP) and the High-Level Committee on Management (HLCM).

In conclusion, this chapter has illuminated that the roots of the UN System are to be found not only in the UN Charter and treaties creating the Specialized Agencies and Related Organizations, but also in the diversity of historical roots of human linkage that transcend all political borders. In the world in which we now live, new technologies are making these linkages ever more rapid and ever more far-reaching. As a result, the demands placed on local governments, local regions, UN member states, and the UN System are constantly changing. This governmental fluidity is continually confronting officials in these political institutions with new challenges.

Of course, the same is true for all people, particularly those living in democracies who aspire to control their own fate. We hope that we have illuminated where in the UN System potential exists for coping with problems on UN System agendas that are most significant to you, and why these problems are on UN System agendas. What is your evaluation of how the UN System is trying to cope with these problems? What is your evaluation of how your federal and state governments and the governing bodies in your local region and community are contributing to the solution of these problems? When you find there are shortcomings, we hope that we have enabled you to begin to find ways in which you can become involved in efforts to overcome these deficiencies.

References

Alger, Chadwick F., 1995, "The United Nations in Historical Perspective," in Chadwick F. Alger, Gene M. Lyons, and John E. Trent, eds., *The UN System: The Policies of Member States*. Tokyo: UN University, 3–40.

Alger, Chadwick F., and Steven J. Brams, 1967, "Patterns of Representation in National Capitals and Intergovernmental Organizations," *World Politics*, Vol. 19, No. 4, 646–663.

Alleyne, Mark D., 1995, *International Power and International Communication*. New York: St. Martin's.

Brodie, Bernard, and Fawn Brodie, 1973, *From Crossbow to H-Bomb*, revised and enlarged ed. Bloomington: Indiana University.

Claude, Inis L., Jr., 1971, *Swords into Ploughshares: The Problems and Progress of International Organization*, 4th ed. New York: Random House.

Conference of NGOs in Consultative Relationship with the United Nations (CONGO), www.ngocongo.org.

Food and Agriculture Organization, www.fao.org.

International Atomic Energy Agency, www.iaea.org.

International Bank for Reconstruction and Development, www.worldbank.org.

International Center for Settlement of Investment Disputes, www.worldbank.org/icsid.

International Civil Aviation Organization, www.icao.org.

International Court of Justice, www.icj-cij.org.

International Development Association, www.worldbank.org/ida.

International Finance Corporation, www.ifc.org.

International Fund for Agricultural Development, www.ifad.org.

International Labor Organization, www.ilo.org.

International Maritime Organization, www.imo.org.

International Monetary Fund, www.imf.org.

International Telecommunications Organization, www.itu.int.

Jacob, Philip E., Alexine L. Atherton, and Arthur M. Wallenstein, 1972, *The Dynamics of International Organization*, revised ed. Homewood, IL: Dorsey.

Leonard, L. Larry, 1951, *International Organization*. New York: McGraw-Hill.

Mangone, Gerard J., 1954, *A Short History of International Organization*. New York: McGraw-Hill.

McNeill, William, 1963, *The Rise of the West: A History of the Human Community*. Chicago: University of Chicago.

Multilateral Investment Guarantee Agency, www.miga.org.

Nuscheler, Franz, 2002, "World Conferences," in Helmut Vogler, ed., *A Concise Encyclopedia of the United Nations*, 684–688.

Organization for the Prohibition of Chemical Weapons. www.opcw.org.

Preparatory Commission for the Comprehensive Nuclear Test-Ban Treaty Organization, www.ctbto.org.

Reinsch, Paul S., 1916, *Public International Unions*, 2d ed. Boston: World Peace Foundation.

Stoll, Peter Tobias, 2002, "WTO—World Trade Organization, GATT—General Agreement on Tariffs and Trade," in Helmut Vogler, ed., *A Concise Encyclopedia of the United Nations*, 691–697.

United Nations, www.un.org.

UN Educational, Scientific and Cultural Organization, www.unesco.org.

UN Industrial Development Organization, www.unido.org.

UN Institute for Training and Research, www.unitar.org.

United Nations Non-Governmental Liaison Service (NGLS), www. un-ngls.org.

United Nations Office for Project Services, www.unops.org.

Universal Postal Union, www.org.int.

Vogler, Helmut, ed., 2002, *A Concise Encyclopedia of the United Nations.* The Hague: Kluwer Law International.

World Health Organization, www.who.int.

World Industrial Property Organization, www.wipo.int.

World Meterological Organization, www.wmo.ch.

World Tourism Organization, www.world-tourism.org.

World Trade Organization, www.wto.org.

To quickly access other UN System Websites, go to www.unorg, *then "welcome," then "about the UN," then "organization chart of the UN system," then click on an organization's name to access its Website.*

5

Facts and Data

I t is a very challenging task to select the most useful facts and data about the network of organizations and their extensive overlapping functions that make up the UN System. The compilation that follows was chosen after consideration of many options. Presented first are the League of Nations Covenant, the UN Charter, and a list of the member states of the UN.

This is followed by broad coverage of human rights, an activity that is defining recognized global values that guide the activities of the entire UN System. Included are values relevant to civil, political, economic, social, cultural, labor, educational, nutritional, health, environmental, refugees, poverty, and other issues. Facts and data in this section reveal the growing understanding that agencies throughout the UN System have regarding human rights responsibilities.

Presented next are facts and data on UN peacekeeping, peacemaking, peace building, and international criminal tribunals. This section reveals organizational developments in response to learning about ways to cope with violence and severe violations of human rights.

A section on UN System efforts to counter terrorism follows. It is included because of widespread public and governmental concern about this issue. Here it is revealed that terrorism has long been a UN issue and that organizations throughout the system have important roles to play.

The following section on UN financing illuminates the challenges that the UN System confronts in attempting to cope with an ever widening array of responsibilities, while working with limited financial resources and uncertainty based on dependence on voluntary contributions and late payment of member state assessments. A response has been proposals for alternative sources of financing.

Next come an array of basic facts and data on secretaries-general, presidents of the General Assembly, UN System Nobel Peace Prizes, the extensive array of UN conferences, former trust territories and remaining non-self-governing territories.

Following this, information provided on public links to the UN System reveal the growing efforts by the UN System to reach out to civil society and efforts by civil society to become involved in the UN System. This includes not only nongovernmental organizations, but also businesses. In addition, local government authorities are growing in their awareness of the relevance of the UN System to local governance.

The last two sections are useful in placing the evolving UN System in the context of its historical roots and possible futures. Proposals for strengthening the UN System are followed by a concluding section on the nineteenth-century roots of organizations in the UN System.

Table of Contents

League of Nations Covenant

Following World War I, the Covenant of the League of Nations was adopted in the first phase of the Paris Peace Conference on 28 April 1919. On 10 January 1920 the League formally came into existence. The League was dissolved on 19 April 1946, one year after the founding of the United Nations.

Covenant of the League of Nations (Including Amendments adopted to December 1924)

THE HIGH CONTRACTING PARTIES,

In order to promote international co-operation and to achieve international peace and security by the acceptance of obligations not to resort to war, by the prescription of open, just and honourable relations between nations, by the firm establishment of the understandings of international law as the actual rule of conduct among Governments, and by the maintenance of justice and a scrupulous respect for all treaty obligations in the dealings of organised peoples with one another, Agree to this Covenant of the League of Nations.

ARTICLE 1   The original Members of the League of Nations shall be those of the Signatories which are named in the Annex to this Covenant and also such of those other States named in the Annex as shall accede without reservation to this Covenant. Such accession shall be effected by a Declaration deposited with the Secretariat within two months of the coming into force of the Covenant. Notice thereof shall be sent to all other Members of the League.

Any fully self-governing State, Dominion or Colony not named in the Annex may become a Member of the League if its admission is agreed to by two-thirds of the Assembly, provided that it shall give effective guarantees of its sincere intention to observe its international obligations, and shall accept such regulations as may be prescribed by the League in regard to its military, naval and air forces and armaments.

Any Member of the League may, after two years' notice of its intention so to do, withdraw from the League, provided that all its international obligations and all its obligations under this Covenant shall have been fulfilled at the time of its withdrawal.

ARTICLE 2   The action of the League under this Covenant shall be effected through the instrumentality of an Assembly and of a Council, with a permanent Secretariat.

ARTICLE 3   The Assembly shall consist of Representatives of the Members of the League.

The Assembly shall meet at stated intervals and from time to time as occasion may require at the Seat of the League or at such other place as may be decided upon.

The Assembly may deal at its meetings with any matter within the sphere of action of the League or affecting the peace of the world. At meetings of the Assembly each Member of the League shall have one vote, and may have not more than three Representatives.

ARTICLE 4   The Council shall consist of Representatives of the Principal Allied and Associated Powers, together with Representatives of four other Members of the League. These four Members of the League shall be selected by the Assembly from time to time in its discretion. Until the appointment of the Representatives of the four

Members of the League first selected by the Assembly, Representatives of Belgium, Brazil, Spain and Greece shall be members of the Council.

With the approval of the majority of the Assembly, the Council may name additional Members of the League whose Representatives shall always be members of the Council; the Council, with like approval may increase the number of Members of the League to be selected by the Assembly for representation on the Council.

The Council shall meet from time to time as occasion may require, and at least once a year, at the Seat of the League, or at such other place as may be decided upon.

The Council may deal at its meetings with any matter within the sphere of action of the League or affecting the peace of the world.

Any Member of the League not represented on the Council shall be invited to send a Representative to sit as a member at any meeting of the Council during the consideration of matters specially affecting the interests of that Member of the League.

At meetings of the Council, each Member of the League represented on the Council shall have one vote, and may have not more than one Representative.

ARTICLE 5   Except where otherwise expressly provided in this Covenant or by the terms of the present Treaty, decisions at any meeting of the Assembly or of the Council shall require the agreement of all the Members of the League represented at the meeting.

All matters of procedure at meetings of the Assembly or of the Council, including the appointment of Committees to investigate particular matters, shall be regulated by the Assembly or by the Council and may be decided by a majority of the Members of the League represented at the meeting.

The first meeting of the Assembly and the first meeting of the Council shall be summoned by the President of the United States of America.

ARTICLE 6   The permanent Secretariat shall be established at the Seat of the League. The Secretariat shall comprise a Secretary General and such secretaries and staff as may be required.

The first Secretary General shall be the person named in the Annex; thereafter the Secretary General shall be appointed by the Council with the approval of the majority of the Assembly.

The secretaries and staff of the Secretariat shall be appointed by the Secretary General with the approval of the Council.

The Secretary General shall act in that capacity at all meetings of the Assembly and of the Council.

The expenses of the League shall be borne by the Members of the League in the proportion decided by the Assembly.

ARTICLE 7   The Seat of the League is established at Geneva.

The Council may at any time decide that the Seat of the League shall be established elsewhere.

All positions under or in connection with the League, including the Secretariat, shall be open equally to men and women.

Representatives of the Members of the League and officials of the League when engaged on the business of the League shall enjoy diplomatic privileges and immunities.

The buildings and other property occupied by the League or its officials or by Representatives attending its meetings shall be inviolable.

ARTICLE 8   The Members of the League recognise that the maintenance of peace requires the reduction of national armaments to the lowest point consistent with national safety and the enforcement by common action of international obligations.

The Council, taking account of the geographical situation and circumstances of each State, shall formulate plans for such reduction for the consideration and action of the several Governments. Such plans shall be subject to reconsideration and revision at least every ten years.

After these plans shall have been adopted by the several Governments, the limits of armaments therein fixed shall not be exceeded without the concurrence of the Council.

The Members of the League agree that the manufacture by private enterprise of munitions and implements of war is open to grave objections. The Council shall advise how the evil effects attendant upon such manufacture can be prevented, due regard being had to the necessities of those Members of the League which are not able to manufacture the munitions and implements of war necessary for their safety.

The Members of the League undertake to interchange full and frank information as to the scale of their armaments, their military, naval and air programmes and the condition of such of their industries as are adaptable to war-like purposes.

ARTICLE 9   A permanent Commission shall be constituted to advise the Council on the execution of the provisions of Articles 1 and 8 and on military, naval and air questions generally.

ARTICLE 10   The Members of the League undertake to respect and preserve as against external aggression the territorial integrity and existing political independence of all Members of the League. In case of any such aggression or in case of any threat or danger of such aggression the Council shall advise upon the means by which this obligation shall be fulfilled.

ARTICLE 11   Any war or threat of war, whether immediately affecting any of the Members of the League or not, is hereby declared a matter of concern to the whole League, and the League shall take any action that may be deemed wise and effectual to safeguard the peace of nations. In case any such emergency should arise the Secretary General shall on the request of any Member of the League forthwith summon a meeting of the Council.

It is also declared to be the friendly right of each Member of the League to bring to the attention of the Assembly or of the Council any circumstance whatever affecting international relations which threatens to disturb international peace or the good understanding between nations upon which peace depends.

ARTICLE 12   The Members of the League agree that, if there should arise between them any dispute likely to lead to a rupture they will submit the matter either to arbitration or judicial settlement or to enquiry by the Council, and they agree in no case to resort to war until three months after the award by the arbitrators or the judicial decision, or the report by the Council. In any case under this Article the award of the arbitrators or the judicial decision shall be made within a reasonable time, and the report of the Council shall be made within six months after the submission of the dispute.

ARTICLE 13   The Members of the League agree that whenever any dispute shall arise between them which they recognise to be suitable for submission to arbitration or judicial settlement and which cannot be satisfactorily settled by diplomacy, they will submit the whole subject-matter to arbitration or judicial settlement.

Disputes as to the interpretation of a treaty, as to any question of international law, as to the existence of any fact which if established would constitute a breach of any international obligation, or as to the extent and nature of the reparation to be made for any such breach, are declared to be among those which are generally suitable for submission to arbitration or judicial settlement.

For the consideration of any such dispute, the court to which the case is referred shall be the Permanent Court of International Justice, established in accordance with Article 14, or any tribunal agreed on by the parties to the dispute or stipulated in any convention existing between them.

The Members of the League agree that they will carry out in full good faith any award or decision that may be rendered, and that they will not resort to war against a Member of the League which complies therewith. In the event of any failure to carry out such an award or decision, the Council shall propose what steps should be taken to give effect thereto.

ARTICLE 14   The Council shall formulate and submit to the Members of the League for adoption plans for the establishment of a Permanent Court of International Justice. The Court shall be competent to hear and determine any dispute of an international character which the parties thereto submit to it. The Court may also give an advisory opinion upon any dispute or question referred to it by the Council or by the Assembly.

ARTICLE 15   If there should arise between Members of the League any dispute likely to lead to a rupture, which is not submitted to arbitration or judicial settlement in accordance with Article 13, the Members of the League agree that they will submit the matter to the Council. Any party to the dispute may effect such submission by giving notice of the existence of the dispute to the Secretary General, who will make all necessary arrangements for a full investigation and consideration thereof.

For this purpose the parties to the dispute will communicate to the Secretary General, as promptly as possible, statements of their case with all the relevant facts and papers, and the Council may forthwith direct the publication thereof.

The Council shall endeavour to effect a settlement of the dispute, and if such efforts are successful, a statement shall be made public giving such facts and explanations regarding the dispute and the terms of settlement thereof as the Council may deem appropriate.

If the dispute is not thus settled, the Council either unanimously or by a majority vote shall make and publish a report containing a statement of the facts of the dispute and the recommendations which are deemed just and proper in regard thereto.

Any Member of the League represented on the Council may make public a statement of the facts of the dispute and of its conclusions regarding the same.

If a report by the Council is unanimously agreed to by the members thereof other than the Representatives of one or more of the parties to the dispute, the Members of the League agree that they will not go to war with any party to the dispute which complies with the recommendations of the report.

If the Council fails to reach a report which is unanimously agreed to by the members thereof, other than the Representatives of one or more of the parties to the dispute, the Members of the League reserve to themselves the right to take such action as they shall consider necessary for the maintenance of right and justice.

If the dispute between the parties is claimed by one of them, and is found by the Council, to arise out of a matter which by international law is solely within the domestic jurisdiction of that party, the Council shall so report, and shall make no recommendation as to its settlement.

The Council may in any case under this Article refer the dispute to the Assembly. The dispute shall be so referred at the request of either party to the dispute, provided that such request be made within fourteen days after the submission of the dispute to the Council.

In any case referred to the Assembly, all the provisions of this Article and of Article 12 relating to the action and powers of the Council shall apply to the action and powers of the Assembly, provided that a report made by the Assembly, if concurred in by the Representatives of those Members of the League represented on the Council and of a majority of the other Members of the League, exclusive in each case of the Representatives of the parties to the dispute, shall have the same force as a report by the Council concurred in by all the members thereof other than the Representatives of one or more of the parties to the dispute.

ARTICLE 16   Should any Member of the League resort to war in disregard of its covenants under Articles 12, 13 or 15, it shall ipso facto be deemed to have committed an act of war against all other Members of the League, which hereby undertake immediately to subject it to the severance of all trade or financial relations, the prohibition of all intercourse between their nationals and the nationals of the covenant-breaking State, and the prevention of all financial, commercial or personal intercourse between the nationals of the covenant-breaking State and the nationals of any other State, whether a Member of the League or not. It shall be the duty of the Council in such case to recommend to the several Governments concerned what effective military, naval or air force the Members of the League shall severally contribute to the armed forces to be used to protect the covenants of the League.

The Members of the League agree, further, that they will mutually support one another in the financial and economic measures which are taken under this Article, in order to minimise the loss and inconvenience resulting from the above measures, and that they will mutually support one another in resisting any special measures aimed at one of their number by the covenant-breaking State, and that they will take the necessary steps to afford passage through their territory to the forces of any of the Members of the League which are co-operating to protect the covenants of the League.

Any Member of the League which has violated any covenant of the League may be declared to be no longer a Member of the League by a vote of the Council concurred in by the Representatives of all the other Members of the League represented thereon.

ARTICLE 17   In the event of a dispute between a Member of the League and a State which is not a Member of the League, or between States not

Members of the League, the State or States not Members of the League shall be invited to accept the obligations of membership in the League for the purposes of such dispute, upon such conditions as the Council may deem just. If such invitation is accepted, the provisions of Articles 12 to 16 inclusive shall be applied with such modifications as may be deemed necessary by the Council.

Upon such invitation being given the Council shall immediately institute an inquiry into the circumstances of the dispute and recommend such action as may seem best and most effectual in the circumstances.

If a State so invited shall refuse to accept the obligations of membership in the League for the purposes of such dispute, and shall resort to war against a Member of the League, the provisions of Article 16 shall be applicable as against the State taking such action.

If both parties to the dispute when so invited refuse to accept the obligations of membership in the League for the purposes of such dispute, the Council may take such measures and make such recommendations as will prevent hostilities and will result in the settlement of the dispute.

ARTICLE 18   Every treaty or international engagement entered into hereafter by any Member of the League shall be forthwith registered with the Secretariat and shall as soon as possible be published by it. No such treaty or international engagement shall be binding until so registered.

ARTICLE 19   The Assembly may from time to time advise the reconsideration by Members of the League of treaties which have become inapplicable and the consideration of international conditions whose continuance might endanger the peace of the world.

ARTICLE 20   The Members of the League severally agree that this Covenant is accepted as abrogating all obligations or understandings inter se which are inconsistent with the terms thereof, and solemnly undertake that they will not hereafter enter into any engagements inconsistent with the terms thereof.

In case any Member of the League shall, before becoming a Member of the League, have undertaken any obligations inconsistent with the terms of this Covenant, it shall be the duty of such Member to take immediate steps to procure its release from such obligations.

ARTICLE 21   Nothing in this Covenant shall be deemed to affect the validity of international engagements, such as treaties of arbitration or regional understandings like the Monroe doctrine, for securing the maintenance of peace.

ARTICLE 22   To those colonies and territories which as a consequence of the late war have ceased to be under the sovereignty of the States which formerly governed them and which are inhabited by peoples not yet able to stand by themselves under the strenuous conditions of the modern world, there should be applied the principle that the well-being and development of such peoples form a sacred trust of civilisation and that securities for the performance of this trust should be embodied in this Covenant.

The best method of giving practical effect to this principle is that the tutelage of such peoples should be entrusted to advanced nations who by reason of their resources, their experience or their geographical position can best undertake this responsibility, and who are willing to accept it, and that this tutelage should be exercised by them as Mandatories on behalf of the League.

The character of the mandate must differ according to the stage of the development of the people, the geographical situation of the territory, its economic conditions and other similar circumstances.

Certain communities formerly belonging to the Turkish Empire have reached a stage of development where their existence as independent nations can be provisionally recognized subject to the rendering of administrative advice and assistance by a Mandatory until such time as they are able to stand alone. The wishes of these communities must be a principal consideration in the selection of the Mandatory.

Other peoples, especially those of Central Africa, are at such a stage that the Mandatory must be responsible for the administration of the territory under conditions which will guarantee freedom of conscience and religion, subject only to the maintenance of public order and morals, the prohibition of abuses such as the slave trade, the arms traffic and the liquor traffic, and the prevention of the establishment of fortifications or military and naval bases and of military training of the natives for other than police purposes and the defence of territory, and will also secure equal opportunities for the trade and commerce of other Members of the League.

There are territories, such as South-West Africa and certain of the South Pacific Islands, which, owing to the sparseness of their population, or their small size, or their remoteness from the centres of civilisation, or their geographical contiguity to the territory of the Mandatory, and other circumstances, can be best administered under the laws of the Mandatory as integral portions of its territory, subject to the safeguards above mentioned in the interests of the indigenous population.

In every case of mandate, the Mandatory shall render to the Council an annual report in reference to the territory committed to its charge.

The degree of authority, control, or administration to be exercised by the Mandatory shall, if not previously agreed upon by the Members of the League, be explicitly defined in each case by the Council.

A permanent Commission shall be constituted to receive and examine the annual reports of the Mandatories and to advise the Council on all matters relating to the observance of the mandates.

ARTICLE 23 Subject to and in accordance with the provisions of international conventions existing or hereafter to be agreed upon, the Members of the League:

(a) will endeavour to secure and maintain fair and humane conditions of labour for men, women, and children, both in their own countries and in all countries to which their commercial and industrial relations extend, and for that purpose will establish and maintain the necessary international organisations;

(b) undertake to secure just treatment of the native inhabitants of territories under their control;

(c) will entrust the League with the general supervision over the execution of agreements with regard to the traffic in women and children, and the traffic in opium and other dangerous drugs;

(d) will entrust the League with the general supervision of the trade in arms and ammunition with the countries in which the control of this traffic is necessary in the common interest;

(e) will make provision to secure and maintain freedom of communications and of transit and equitable treatment for the commerce of all Members of the League. In this connection, the special necessities of the regions devastated during the war of 1914–1918 shall be borne in mind;

(f) will endeavour to take steps in matters of international concern for the prevention and control of disease.

ARTICLE 24 There shall be placed under the direction of the League all international bureaux already established by general treaties if the parties to such treaties consent. All such international bureaux and all commissions for the regulation of matters of international interest hereafter constituted shall be placed under the direction of the League.

In all matters of international interest which are regulated by general convention but which are not placed under the control of international bureaux or commissions, the Secretariat of the League shall, subject to the consent of the Council and if desired by the parties, collect and distribute all relevant information and shall render any other assistance which may be necessary or desirable.

The Council may include as part of the expenses of the Secretariat the expenses of any bureau or commission which is placed under the direction of the League.

ARTICLE 25   The Members of the League agree to encourage and promote the establishment and co-operation of duly authorised voluntary national Red Cross organisations having as purposes the improvement of health, the prevention of disease and the mitigation of suffering throughout the world.

ARTICLE 26   Amendments to this Covenant will take effect when ratified by the Members of the League whose Representatives compose the Council and by a majority of the Members of the League whose Representatives compose the Assembly.

No such amendments shall bind any Member of the League which signifies its dissent therefrom, but in that case it shall cease to be a Member of the League.

(Available at www.ola.bc.ca/online/cf/documents/ 1924LeagueNations.html)

UN Charter

The Charter of the United Nations was drafted in a conference that began on 25 April 1945 in San Francisco. On 21 June representatives of all fifty participating states signed the Charter. The United Nations officially came into existence on 24 October 1945, when the Charter had been ratified by China, France, the Soviet Union, the United Kingdom, the United States, and a majority of other participating states. The General Assembly met for its first session on 10 January 1946.

Charter of the United Nations

We the peoples of the United Nations determined to save succeeding generations from the scourge of war, which twice in our lifetime has brought untold sorrow to mankind, and to reaffirm faith in fundamental human rights, in the dignity and worth of the human person, in the equal rights of men and women and of nations large and small, and to establish conditions under which justice and respect for the obligations arising from treaties and other sources of international law can be maintained, and to promote social progress and better standards of life in larger freedom,

And for these ends to practice tolerance and live together in peace with one another as good neighbours, and to unite our strength to maintain international peace and security, and to ensure, by the acceptance of principles and the institution of methods, that armed force shall not be used, save in the common interest, and to employ international machinery for the promotion of the economic and social advancement of all peoples,

Have resolved to combine our efforts to accomplish these aims

Accordingly, our respective Governments, through representatives assembled in the city of San Francisco, who have exhibited their full powers found to be in good and due form, have agreed to the present Charter of the United Nations and do hereby establish an international organization to be known as the United Nations.

Chapter I: Purposes and Principles

Article 1 The Purposes of the United Nations are:

1. To maintain international peace and security, and to that end: to take effective collective measures for the prevention and removal of threats to the peace, and for the suppression of acts of aggression or other breaches of the peace, and to bring about by peaceful means, and in conformity with the principles of justice and international law, adjustment or settlement of international disputes or situations which might lead to a breach of the peace;

2. To develop friendly relations among nations based on respect for the principle of equal rights and self-determination of peoples, and to take other appropriate measures to strengthen universal peace;

3. To achieve international cooperation in solving international problems of an economic, social, cultural, or humanitarian character, and in promoting and encouraging respect for human rights and for fundamental freedoms for all without distinction as to race, sex, language, or religion; and

4. To be a center for harmonizing the actions of nations in the attainment of these common ends.

Article 2 The Organization and its Members, in pursuit of the Purposes stated in Article 1, shall act in accordance with the following Principles.

1. The Organization is based on the principle of the sovereign equality of all its Members.

2. All Members, in order to ensure to all of them the rights and benefits resulting from membership, shall fulfill in good faith the obligations assumed by them in accordance with the present Charter.

3. All Members shall settle their international disputes by peaceful means in such a manner that international peace and security, and justice, are not endangered.

4. All Members shall refrain in their international relations from the threat or use of force against the territorial integrity or political independence of any state, or in any other manner inconsistent with the Purposes of the United Nations.

5. All Members shall give the United Nations every assistance in any action it takes in accordance with the present Charter, and shall refrain from giving assistance to any state against which the United Nations is taking preventive or enforcement action.

The Organization shall ensure that states which are not Members of the United Nations act in accordance with these Principles so far as may be necessary for the maintenance of international peace and security.

6. Nothing contained in the present Charter shall authorize the United Nations to intervene in matters which are essentially within the domestic jurisdiction of any state or shall require the Members to submit such matters to settlement under the present Charter; but this principle shall not prejudice the application of enforcement measures under Chapter VII.

Chapter II: Membership

Article 3   The original Members of the United Nations shall be the states which, having participated in the United Nations Conference on International Organization at San Francisco, or having previously signed the Declaration by United Nations of January 1, 1942, sign the present Charter and ratify it in accordance with Article 110.

Article 4

1. Membership in the United Nations is open to all other peace-loving states which accept the obligations contained in the present Charter and, in the judgment of the Organization, are able and willing to carry out these obligations.

2. The admission of any such state to membership in the United Nations will be effected by a decision of the General Assembly upon the recommendation of the Security Council.

Article 5   A member of the United Nations against which preventive or enforcement action has been taken by the Security Council may be suspended from the exercise of the rights and privileges of membership by the General Assembly upon the recommendation of the Security Council. The exercise of these rights and privileges may be restored by the Security Council.

Article 6   A Member of the United Nations which has persistently violated the Principles contained in the present Charter may be expelled from the Organization by the General Assembly upon the recommendation of the Security Council.

Chapter III: Organs
Article 7

1. There are established as the principal organs of the United Nations: a General Assembly, a Security Council, an Economic and Social Council, a Trusteeship Council, an International Court of Justice, and a Secretariat.

2. Such subsidiary organs as may be found necessary may be established in accordance with the present Charter.

Article 8   The United Nations shall place no restrictions on the eligibility of men and women to participate in any capacity and under conditions of equality in its principal and subsidiary organs.

Chapter IV: The General Assembly

Composition
Article 9

1. The General Assembly shall consist of all the Members of the United Nations.

2. Each member shall have not more than five representatives in the General Assembly.

Functions and Powers

Article 10   The General Assembly may discuss any questions or any matters within the scope of the present Charter or relating to the powers and functions of any organs provided for in the present Charter, and, except as provided in Article 12, may make recommendations to the Members of the United Nations or to the Security Council or to both on any such questions or matters.

Article 11

1. The General Assembly may consider the general principles of cooperation in the maintenance of international peace and security, including the principles governing disarmament and the regulation of armaments, and may make recommendations with regard to such principles to the Members or to the Security Council or to both.

2. The General Assembly may discuss any questions relating to the maintenance of international peace and security brought before it by any Member of the United Nations, or by the Security Council, or by a state which is not a Member of the United Nations in accordance with Article 35, paragraph 2, and, except as provided in Article 12, may make recommendations with regard to any such questions to the state or states concerned or to the Security Council or to both. Any such

question on which action is necessary shall be referred to the Security Council by the General Assembly either before or after discussion.

3. The General Assembly may call the attention of the Security Council to situations which are likely to endanger international peace and security.

4. The powers of the General Assembly set forth in this Article shall not limit the general scope of Article 10.

Article 12 While the Security Council is exercising in respect of any dispute or situation the functions assigned to it in the present Charter, the General Assembly shall not make any recommendation with regard to that dispute or situation unless the Security Council so requests.

The Secretary-General, with the consent of the Security Council, shall notify the General Assembly at each session of any matters relative to the maintenance of international peace and security which are being dealt with by the Security Council and shall similarly notify the General Assembly, or the Members of the United Nations if the General Assembly is not in session, immediately the Security Council ceases to deal with such matters.

Article 13

1. The General Assembly shall initiate studies and make recommendations for the purpose of:

a. promoting international cooperation in the political field and encouraging the progressive development of international law and its codification;

b. promoting international cooperation in the economic, social, cultural, educational, and health fields, and assisting in the realization of human rights and fundamental freedoms for all without distinction as to race, sex, language, or religion.

2. The further responsibilities, functions and powers of the General Assembly with respect to matters mentioned in paragraph 1(b) above are set forth in Chapters IX and X.

Article 14 Subject to the provisions of Article 12, the General Assembly may recommend measures for the peaceful adjustment of any situation, regardless of origin, which it deems likely to impair the general welfare or friendly relations among nations, including situations resulting from a violation of the provisions of the present Charter setting forth the Purposes and Principles of the United Nations.

Article 15

1. The General Assembly shall receive and consider annual and special reports from the Security Council; these reports shall include an

account of the measures that the Security Council has decided upon or taken to maintain international peace and security.

2. The General Assembly shall receive and consider reports from the other organs of the United Nations.

Article 16   The General Assembly shall perform such functions with respect to the international trusteeship system as are assigned to it under Chapters XII and XIII, including the approval of the trusteeship agreements for areas not designated as strategic.

Article 17

1. The General Assembly shall consider and approve the budget of the Organization.

2. The expenses of the Organization shall be borne by the Members as apportioned by the General Assembly.

3. The General Assembly shall consider and approve any financial and budgetary arrangements with specialized agencies referred to in Article 57 and shall examine the administrative budgets of such specialized agencies with a view to making recommendations to the agencies concerned.

Voting
Article 18

1. Each member of the General Assembly shall have one vote.

2. Decisions of the General Assembly on important questions shall be made by a two-thirds majority of the members present and voting. These questions shall include: recommendations with respect to the maintenance of international peace and security, the election of the non-permanent members of the Security Council, the election of the members of the Economic and Social Council, the election of members of the Trusteeship Council in accordance with paragraph 1(c) of Article 86, the admission of new Members to the United Nations, the suspension of the rights and privileges of membership, the expulsion of Members, questions relating to the operation of the trusteeship system, and budgetary questions.

3. Decisions on other questions, including the determination of additional categories of questions to be decided by a two-thirds majority, shall be made by a majority of the members present and voting.

Article 19   A Member of the United Nations which is in arrears in the payment of its financial contributions to the Organization shall have no vote in the General Assembly if the amount of its arrears equals or exceeds the amount of the contributions due from it for the preceding two full years. The General Assembly may, nevertheless, permit such a Member to vote if it is satisfied that the failure to pay is due to conditions beyond the control of the Member.

Procedure

Article 20   The General Assembly shall meet in regular annual sessions and in such special sessions as occasion may require. Special sessions shall be convoked by the Secretary-General at the request of the Security Council or of a majority of the Members of the United Nations.

Article 21   The General Assembly shall adopt its own rules of procedure. It shall elect its President for each session.

Article 22   The General Assembly may establish such subsidiary organs as it deems necessary for the performance of its functions.

Chapter V: The Security Council
Article 23

1. The Security Council shall consist of fifteen Members of the United Nations. The Republic of China, France, the Union of Soviet Socialist Republics, the United Kingdom of Great Britain and Northern Ireland, and the United States of America shall be permanent members of the Security Council. The General Assembly shall elect ten other Members of the United Nations to be non-permanent members of the Security Council, due regard being specially paid, in the first instance to the contribution of Members of the United Nations to the maintenance of international peace and security and to the other purposes of the Organization, and also to equitable geographical distribution.

2. The non-permanent members of the Security Council shall be elected for a term of two years. In the first election of the non-permanent members after the increase of the membership of the Security Council from eleven to fifteen, two of the four additional members shall be chosen for a term of one year. A retiring member shall not be eligible for immediate re-election.

3. Each member of the Security Council shall have one representative.

Functions and Powers
Article 24

1. In order to ensure prompt and effective action by the United Nations, its Members confer on the Security Council primary responsibility for the maintenance of international peace and security,

and agree that in carrying out its duties under this responsibility the Security Council acts on their behalf.

2. In discharging these duties the Security Council shall act in accordance with the Purposes and Principles of the United Nations. The specific powers granted to the Security Council for the discharge of these duties are laid down in Chapters VI, VII, VIII, and XII.

3. The Security Council shall submit annual and, when necessary, special reports to the General Assembly for its consideration.

Article 25   The Members of the United Nations agree to accept and carry out the decisions of the Security Council in accordance with the present Charter.

Article 26   In order to promote the establishment and maintenance of international peace and security with the least diversion for armaments of the world's human and economic resources, the Security Council shall be responsible for formulating, with the assistance of the Military Staff Committee referred to in Article 47, plans to be submitted to the Members of the United Nations for the establishment of a system for the regulation of armaments.

Voting
Article 27

1. Each member of the Security Council shall have one vote.

2. Decisions of the Security Council on procedural matters shall be made by an affirmative vote of nine members.

3. Decisions of the Security Council on all other matters shall be made by an affirmative vote of nine members including the concurring votes of the permanent members; provided that, in decisions under Chapter VI, and under paragraph 3 of Article 52, a party to a dispute shall abstain from voting.

Procedure
Article 28

1. The Security Council shall be so organized as to be able to function continuously. Each member of the Security Council shall for this purpose be represented at all times at the seat of the Organization.

2. The Security Council shall hold periodic meetings at which each of its members may, if it so desires, be represented by a member of the government or by some other specially designated representative.

3. The Security Council may hold meetings at such places other than the seat of the Organization as in its judgment will best facilitate its work.

Article 29   The Security Council may establish such subsidiary organs as it deems necessary for the performance of its functions.

Article 30   The Security Council shall adopt its own rules of procedure, including the method of selecting its President.

Article 31   Any Member of the United Nations which is not a member of the Security Council may participate, without vote, in the discussion of any question brought before the Security Council whenever the latter considers that the interests of that Member are specially affected.

Article 32   Any Member of the United Nations which is not a member of the Security Council or any state which is not a Member of the United Nations, if it is a party to a dispute under consideration by the Security Council, shall be invited to participate, without vote, in the discussion relating to the dispute. The Security Council shall lay down such conditions as it deems just for the participation of a state which is not a Member of the United Nations.

Chapter VI: Pacific Settlement of Disputes
Article 33
1. The parties to any dispute, the continuance of which is likely to endanger the maintenance of international peace and security, shall, first of all, seek a solution by negotiation, enquiry, mediation, conciliation, arbitration, judicial settlement, resort to regional agencies or arrangements, or other peaceful means of their own choice.

2. The Security Council shall, when it deems necessary, call upon the parties to settle their dispute by such means.

Article 34   The Security Council may investigate any dispute, or any situation which might lead to international friction or give rise to a dispute, in order to determine whether the continuance of the dispute or situation is likely to endanger the maintenance of international peace and security.

Article 35
1. Any Member of the United Nations may bring any dispute, or any situation of the nature referred to in Article 34, to the attention of the Security Council or of the General Assembly.

2. A state which is not a Member of the United Nations may bring to the attention of the Security Council or of the General Assembly any dispute to which it is a party if it accepts in advance, for the purposes of the dispute, the obligations of pacific settlement provided in the present Charter.

3. The proceedings of the General Assembly in respect of matters brought to its attention under this Article will be subject to the provisions of Articles 11 and 12.

Article 36

1. The Security Council may, at any stage of a dispute of the nature referred to in Article 33 or of a situation of like nature, recommend appropriate procedures or methods of adjustment.

2. The Security Council should take into consideration any procedures for the settlement of the dispute which have already been adopted by the parties.

3. In making recommendations under this Article the Security Council should also take into consideration that legal disputes should as a general rule be referred by the parties to the International Court of Justice in accordance with the provisions of the Statute of the Court.

Article 37

1. Should the parties to a dispute of the nature referred to in Article 33 fail to settle it by the means indicated in that Article, they shall refer it to the Security Council.

2. If the Security Council deems that the continuance of the dispute is in fact likely to endanger the maintenance of international peace and security, it shall decide whether to take action under Article 36 or to recommend such terms of settlement as it may consider appropriate.

Article 38 Without prejudice to the provisions of Articles 33 to 37, the Security Council may, if all the parties to any dispute so request, make recommendations to the parties with a view to a pacific settlement of the dispute.

Chapter VII: Action with Respect to Threats to the Peace, Breaches of the Peace, and Acts of Aggression

Article 39 The Security Council shall determine the existence of any threat to the peace, breach of the peace, or act of aggression and shall make recommendations, or decide what measures shall be taken in accordance with Articles 41 and 42, to maintain or restore international peace and security.

Article 40 In order to prevent an aggravation of the situation, the Security Council may, before making the recommendations or deciding upon the measures provided for in Article 39, call upon the parties concerned to comply with such provisional measures as it deems necessary or desirable. Such provisional measures shall be without prejudice to the rights, claims, or position of the parties concerned. The Security Council shall duly take account of failure to comply with such provisional measures.

Article 41   The Security Council may decide what measures not involving the use of armed force are to be employed to give effect to its decisions, and it may call upon the Members of the United Nations to apply such measures. These may include complete or partial interruption of economic relations and of rail, sea, air, postal, telegraphic, radio, and other means of communication, and the severance of diplomatic relations.

Article 42   Should the Security Council consider that measures provided for in Article 41 would be inadequate or have proved to be inadequate, it may take such action by air, sea, or land forces as may be necessary to maintain or restore international peace and security. Such action may include demonstrations, blockade, and other operations by air, sea, or land forces of Members of the United Nations.

Article 43

1. All Members of the United Nations, in order to contribute to the maintenance of international peace and security, undertake to make available to the Security Council, on its call and in accordance with a special agreement or agreements, armed forces, assistance, and facilities, including rights of passage, necessary for the purpose of maintaining international peace and security.

2. Such agreement or agreements shall govern the numbers and types of forces, their degree of readiness and general location, and the nature of the facilities and assistance to be provided.

3. The agreement or agreements shall be negotiated as soon as possible on the initiative of the Security Council. They shall be concluded between the Security Council and Members or between the Security Council and groups of Members and shall be subject to ratification by the signatory states in accordance with their respective constitutional processes.

Article 44   When the Security Council has decided to use force it shall, before calling upon a Member not represented on it to provide armed forces in fulfillment of the obligations assumed under Article 43, invite that Member, if the Member so desires, to participate in the decisions of the Security Council concerning the employment of contingents of that Member's armed forces.

Article 45   In order to enable the United Nations to take urgent military measures Members shall hold immediately available national air-force contingents for combined international enforcement action. The strength and degree of readiness of these contingents and plans for their combined action shall be determined, within the limits laid down in the special agreement or agreements referred to in Article 43, by the Security Council with the assistance of the Military Staff Committee.

Article 46   Plans for the application of armed force shall be made by the Security Council with the assistance of the Military Staff Committee.

Article 47

1. There shall be established a Military Staff Committee to advise and assist the Security Council on all questions relating to the Security Council's military requirements for the maintenance of international peace and security, the employment and command of forces placed at its disposal, the regulation of armaments, and possible disarmament.

2. The Military Staff Committee shall consist of the Chiefs of Staff of the permanent members of the Security Council or their representatives. Any Member of the United Nations not permanently represented on the Committee shall be invited by the Committee to be associated with it when the efficient discharge of the Committee's responsibilities requires the participation of that Member in its work.

3. The Military Staff Committee shall be responsible under the Security Council for the strategic direction of any armed forces placed at the disposal of the Security Council. Questions relating to the command of such forces shall be worked out subsequently.

4. The Military Staff Committee, with the authorization of the Security Council and after consultation with appropriate regional agencies, may establish regional subcommittees.

Article 48

1. The action required to carry out the decisions of the Security Council for the maintenance of international peace and security shall be taken by all the Members of the United Nations or by some of them, as the Security Council may determine.

2. Such decisions shall be carried out by the Members of the United Nations directly and through their action in the appropriate international agencies of which they are members.

Article 49   The Members of the United Nations shall join in affording mutual assistance in carrying out the measures decided upon by the Security Council.

Article 50   If preventive or enforcement measures against any state are taken by the Security Council, any other state, whether a Member of the United Nations or not, which finds itself confronted with special economic problems arising from the carrying out of those measures shall have the right to consult the Security Council with regard to a solution of those problems.

Article 51   Nothing in the present Charter shall impair the inherent right of individual or collective self-defense if an armed attack occurs against a Member of the United Nations, until the Security Council has taken measures necessary to maintain international peace and security. Measures taken by Members in the exercise of this right of self-defense shall be immediately reported to the Security Council and shall not in any way affect the authority and responsibility of the Security Council under the present Charter to take at any time such action as it deems necessary in order to maintain or restore international peace and security.

Chapter VIII: Regional Arrangements
Article 52
1. Nothing in the present Charter precludes the existence of regional arrangements or agencies for dealing with such matters relating to the maintenance of international peace and security as are appropriate for regional action, provided that such arrangements or agencies and their activities are consistent with the Purposes and Principles of the United Nations.

2. The Members of the United Nations entering into such arrangements or constituting such agencies shall make every effort to achieve pacific settlement of local disputes through such regional arrangements or by such regional agencies before referring them to the Security Council.

3. The Security Council shall encourage the development of pacific settlement of local disputes through such regional arrangements or by such regional agencies either on the initiative of the states concerned or by reference from the Security Council.

4. This Article in no way impairs the application of Articles 34 and 35.

Article 53
1. The Security Council shall, where appropriate, utilize such regional arrangements or agencies for enforcement action under its authority. But no enforcement action shall be taken under regional arrangements or by regional agencies without the authorization of the Security Council, with the exception of measures against any enemy state, as defined in paragraph 2 of this Article, provided for pursuant to Article 107 or in regional arrangements directed against renewal of aggressive policy on the part of any such state, until such time as the Organization may, on request of the Governments concerned, be

charged with the responsibility for preventing further aggression by such a state.

2. The term enemy state as used in paragraph 1 of this Article applies to any state which during the Second World War has been an enemy of any signatory of the present Charter.

Article 54 The Security Council shall at all times be kept fully informed of activities undertaken or in contemplation under regional arrangements or by regional agencies for the maintenance of international peace and security.

Chapter IX: International Economic and Social Co-operation

Article 55 With a view to the creation of conditions of stability and well-being which are necessary for peaceful and friendly relations among nations based on respect for the principle of equal rights and self-determination of peoples, the United Nations shall promote:

1. higher standards of living, full employment, and conditions of economic and social progress and development;

2. solutions of international economic, social, health, and related problems; and international cultural and educational co-operation; and

3. universal respect for, and observance of, human rights and fundamental freedoms for all without distinction as to race, sex, language, or religion.

Article 56 All Members pledge themselves to take joint and separate action in cooperation with the Organization for the achievement of the purposes set forth in Article 55.

Article 57

1. The various specialized agencies, established by intergovernmental agreement and having wide international responsibilities, as defined in their basic instruments, in economic, social, cultural, educational, health, and related fields, shall be brought into relationship with the United Nations in accordance with the provisions of Article 63.

2. Such agencies thus brought into relationship with the United Nations are hereinafter referred to as specialized agencies.

Article 58 The Organization shall make recommendations for the coordination of the policies and activities of the specialized agencies.

Article 59 The Organization shall, where appropriate, initiate negotiations among the states concerned for the creation of any new specialized agencies required for the accomplishment of the purposes set forth in Article 55.

Article 60   Responsibility for the discharge of the functions of the Organization set forth in this Chapter shall be vested in the General Assembly and, under the authority of the General Assembly, in the Economic and Social Council, which shall have for this purpose the powers set forth in Chapter X.

Chapter X: The Economic and Social Council

Composition

Article 61

1. The Economic and Social Council shall consist of fifty-four Members of the United Nations elected by the General Assembly.

2. Subject to the provisions of paragraph 3, eighteen members of the Economic and Social Council shall be elected each year for a term of three years. A retiring member shall be eligible for immediate re-election.

3. At the first election after the increase in the membership of the Economic and Social Council from twenty-seven to fifty-four members, in addition to the members elected in place of the nine members whose term of office expires at the end of that year, twenty-seven additional members shall be elected. Of these twenty-seven additional members, the term of office of nine members so elected shall expire at the end of one year, and of nine other members at the end of two years, in accordance with arrangements made by the General Assembly.

4. Each member of the Economic and Social Council shall have one representative.

Functions and Powers

Article 62

1. The Economic and Social Council may make or initiate studies and reports with respect to international economic, social, cultural, educational, health, and related matters and may make recommendations with respect to any such matters to the General Assembly, to the Members of the United Nations, and to the specialized agencies concerned.

2. It may make recommendations for the purpose of promoting respect for, and observance of, human rights and fundamental freedoms for all.

3. It may prepare draft conventions for submission to the General Assembly, with respect to matters falling within its competence.

4. It may call, in accordance with the rules prescribed by the United Nations, international conferences on matters falling within its competence.

Article 63

1. The Economic and Social Council may enter into agreements with any of the agencies referred to in Article 57, defining the terms on which the agency concerned shall be brought into relationship with the United Nations. Such agreements shall be subject to approval by the General Assembly.

2. It may coordinate the activities of the specialized agencies through consultation with and recommendations to such agencies and through recommendations to the General Assembly and to the Members of the United Nations.

Article 64

1. The Economic and Social Council may take appropriate steps to obtain regular reports from the specialized agencies. It may make arrangements with the Members of the United Nations and with the specialized agencies to obtain reports on the steps taken to give effect to its own recommendations and to recommendations on matters falling within its competence made by the General Assembly.

2. It may communicate its observations on these reports to the General Assembly.

Article 65   The Economic and Social Council may furnish information to the Security Council and shall assist the Security Council upon its request.

Article 66

1. The Economic and Social Council shall perform such functions as fall within its competence in connection with the carrying out of the recommendations of the General Assembly.

2. It may, with the approval of the General Assembly, perform services at the request of Members of the United Nations and at the request of specialized agencies.

3. It shall perform such other functions as are specified elsewhere in the present Charter or as may be assigned to it by the General Assembly.

Article 67

1. Each member of the Economic and Social Council shall have one vote.

2. Decisions of the Economic and Social Council shall be made by a majority of the members present and voting.

Procedure

Article 68   The Economic and Social Council shall set up commissions in economic and social fields and for the promotion of human rights, and such other commissions as may be required for the performance of its functions.

Article 69   The Economic and Social Council shall invite any Member of the United Nations to participate, without vote, in its deliberations on any matter of particular concern to that Member.

Article 70   The Economic and Social Council may make arrangements for representatives of the specialized agencies to participate, without vote, in its deliberations and in those of the commissions established by it, and for its representatives to participate in the deliberations of the specialized agencies.

Article 71   The Economic and Social Council may make suitable arrangements for consultation with non-governmental organizations which are concerned with matters within its competence. Such arrangements may be made with international organizations and, where appropriate, with national organizations after consultation with the Member of the United Nations concerned.

Article 72

1. The Economic and Social Council shall adopt its own rules of procedure, including the method of selecting its President.

2. The Economic and Social Council shall meet as required in accordance with its rules, which shall include provision for the convening of meetings on the request of a majority of its members.

Chapter XI: Declaration Regarding Non-Self-Governing Territories

Article 73   Members of the United Nations which have or assume responsibilities for the administration of territories whose peoples have not yet attained a full measure of self-government recognize the principle that the interests of the inhabitants of these territories are paramount, and accept as a sacred trust the obligation to promote to the utmost, within the system of international peace and security established by the present Charter, the well-being of the inhabitants of these territories, and, to this end:

1. to ensure, with due respect for the culture of the peoples concerned, their political, economic, social, and educational advancement, their just treatment, and their protection against abuses;

2. to develop self-government, to take due account of the political aspirations of the peoples, and to assist them in the progressive development of their free political institutions, according to the particular circumstances of each territory and its peoples and their varying stages of advancement;

3. to further international peace and security;

4. to promote constructive measures of development, to encourage research, and to cooperate with one another and, when and where appropriate, with specialized international bodies with a view to the practical achievement of the social, economic, and scientific purposes set forth in this Article; and

5. to transmit regularly to the Secretary-General for information purposes, subject to such limitation as security and constitutional considerations may require, statistical and other information of a technical nature relating to economic, social, and educational conditions in the territories for which they are respectively responsible other than those territories to which Chapters XII and XIII apply.

Article 74   Members of the United Nations also agree that their policy in respect of the territories to which this Chapter applies, no less than in respect of their metropolitan areas, must be based on the general principle of good-neighborliness, due account being taken of the interests and well-being of the rest of the world, in social, economic, and commercial matters.

Chapter XII: International Trusteeship System

Article 75   The United Nations shall establish under its authority an international trusteeship system for the administration and supervision of such territories as may be placed thereunder by subsequent individual agreements. These territories are hereinafter referred to as trust territories.

Article 76   The basic objectives of the trusteeship system, in accordance with the Purposes of the United Nations laid down in Article 1 of the present Charter, shall be:

1. to further international peace and security;

2. to promote the political, economic, social, and educational advancement of the inhabitants of the trust territories, and their progressive development towards self-government or independence as may be appropriate to the particular circumstances of each territory and its peoples and the freely expressed wishes of the peoples concerned, and as may be provided by the terms of each trusteeship agreement;

3. to encourage respect for human rights and for fundamental freedoms for all without distinction as to race, sex, language, or religion,

and to encourage recognition of the interdependence of the peoples of the world; and

4. to ensure equal treatment in social, economic, and commercial matters for all Members of the United Nations and their nationals and also equal treatment for the latter in the administration of justice without prejudice to the attainment of the foregoing objectives and subject to the provisions of Article 80.

Article 77

1. The trusteeship system shall apply to such territories in the following categories as may be placed thereunder by means of trusteeship agreements:

a. territories now held under mandate;

b. territories which may be detached from enemy states as a result of the Second World War; and

c. territories voluntarily placed under the system by states responsible for their administration.

2. It will be a matter for subsequent agreement as to which territories in the foregoing categories will be brought under the trusteeship system and upon what terms.

Article 78   The trusteeship system shall not apply to territories which have become Members of the United Nations, relationship among which shall be based on respect for the principle of sovereign equality.

Article 79   The terms of trusteeship for each territory to be placed under the trusteeship system, including any alteration or amendment, shall be agreed upon by the states directly concerned, including the mandatory power in the case of territories held under mandate by a Member of the United Nations, and shall be approved as provided for in Articles 83 and 85.

Article 80

1. Except as may be agreed upon in individual trusteeship agreements, made under Articles 77, 79, and 81, placing each territory under the trusteeship system, and until such agreements have been concluded, nothing in this Chapter shall be construed in or of itself to alter in any manner the rights whatsoever of any states or any peoples or the terms of existing international instruments to which Members of the United Nations may respectively be parties.

2. Paragraph 1 of this Article shall not be interpreted as giving grounds for delay or postponement of the negotiation and conclusion of agreements for placing mandated and other territories under the trusteeship system as provided for in Article 77.

Article 81   The trusteeship agreement shall in each case include the terms under which the trust territory will be administered and designate the authority which will exercise the administration of the trust territory. Such authority, hereinafter called the administering authority, may be one or more states or the Organization itself.

Article 82   There may be designated, in any trusteeship agreement, a strategic area or areas which may include part or all of the trust territory to which the agreement applies, without prejudice to any special agreement or agreements made under Article 43.

Article 83

1. All functions of the United Nations relating to strategic areas, including the approval of the terms of the trusteeship agreements and of their alteration or amendment, shall be exercised by the Security Council.

2. The basic objectives set forth in Article 76 shall be applicable to the people of each strategic area.

3. The Security Council shall, subject to the provisions of the trusteeship agreements and without prejudice to security considerations, avail itself of the assistance of the Trusteeship Council to perform those functions of the United Nations under the trusteeship system relating to political, economic, social, and educational matters in the strategic areas.

Article 84   It shall be the duty of the administering authority to ensure that the trust territory shall play its part in the maintenance of international peace and security. To this end the administering authority may make use of volunteer forces, facilities, and assistance from the trust territory in carrying out the obligations towards the Security Council undertaken in this regard by the administering authority, as well as for local defense and the maintenance of law and order within the trust territory.

Article 85

1. The functions of the United Nations with regard to trusteeship agreements for all areas not designated as strategic, including the approval of the terms of the trusteeship agreements and of their alteration or amendment, shall be exercised by the General Assembly.

2. The Trusteeship Council, operating under the authority of the General Assembly, shall assist the General Assembly in carrying out these functions.

Chapter XIII: The Trusteeship Council

Composition

Article 86

1. The Trusteeship Council shall consist of the following Members of the United Nations:

    a.   those Members administering trust territories;

    b.   such of those Members mentioned by name in Article 23 as are not administering trust territories; and

    c.   as many other Members elected for three-year terms by the General Assembly as may be necessary to ensure that the total number of members of the Trusteeship Council is equally divided between those Members of the United Nations which administer trust territories and those which do not.

2. Each member of the Trusteeship Council shall designate one specially qualified person to represent it therein.

Functions and Powers

Article 87   The General Assembly and, under its authority, the Trusteeship Council, in carrying out their functions, may:

1. consider reports submitted by the administering authority;

2. accept petitions and examine them in consultation with the administering authority;

3. provide for periodic visits to the respective trust territories at times agreed upon with the administering authority; and

4. take these and other actions in conformity with the terms of the trusteeship agreements.

Article 88   The Trusteeship Council shall formulate a questionnaire on the political, economic, social, and educational advancement of the inhabitants of each trust territory, and the administering authority for each trust territory within the competence of the General Assembly shall make an annual report to the General Assembly upon the basis of such questionnaire.

Voting

Article 89

1. Each member of the Trusteeship Council shall have one vote.

2. Decisions of the Trusteeship Council shall be made by a majority of the members present and voting.

Procedure
Article 90

1. The Trusteeship Council shall adopt its own rules of procedure, including the method of selecting its President.

2. The Trusteeship Council shall meet as required in accordance with its rules, which shall include provision for the convening of meetings on the request of a majority of its members.

Article 91
The Trusteeship Council shall, when appropriate, avail itself of the assistance of the Economic and Social Council and of the specialized agencies in regard to matters with which they are respectively concerned.

Chapter XIV: The International Court of Justice

Article 92
The International Court of Justice shall be the principal judicial organ of the United Nations. It shall function in accordance with the annexed Statute which is based upon the Statute of the Permanent Court of International Justice and forms an integral part of the present Charter.

Article 93

1. All Members of the United Nations are ipso facto parties to the Statute of the International Court of Justice.

2. A state which is not a Member of the United Nations may become a party to the Statute of the International Court of Justice on conditions to be determined in each case by the General Assembly upon the recommendation of the Security Council.

Article 94

1. Each Member of the United Nations undertakes to comply with the decision of the International Court of Justice in any case to which it is a party.

2. If any party to a case fails to perform the obligations incumbent upon it under a judgment rendered by the Court, the other party may have recourse to the Security Council, which may, if it deems necessary, make recommendations or decide upon measures to be taken to give effect to the judgment.

Article 95
Nothing in the present Charter shall prevent Members of the United Nations from entrusting the solution of their differences to other tribunals by virtue of agreements already in existence or which may be concluded in the future.

Article 96

1. The General Assembly or the Security Council may request the International Court of Justice to give an advisory opinion on any legal question.

2. Other organs of the United Nations and specialized agencies, which may at any time be so authorized by the General Assembly, may also request advisory opinions of the Court on legal questions arising within the scope of their activities.

Chapter XV: The Secretariat

Article 97   The Secretariat shall comprise a Secretary-General and such staff as the Organization may require. The Secretary-General shall be appointed by the General Assembly upon the recommendation of the Security Council. He shall be the chief administrative officer of the Organization.

Article 98   The Secretary-General shall act in that capacity in all meetings of the General Assembly, of the Security Council, of the Economic and Social Council, and of the Trusteeship Council, and shall perform such other functions as are entrusted to him by these organs. The Secretary-General shall make an annual report to the General Assembly on the work of the Organization.

Article 99   The Secretary-General may bring to the attention of the Security Council any matter which in his opinion may threaten the maintenance of international peace and security.

Article 100

1. In the performance of their duties the Secretary-General and the staff shall not seek or receive instructions from any government or from any other authority external to the Organization. They shall refrain from any action which might reflect on their position as international officials responsible only to the Organization.

2. Each Member of the United Nations undertakes to respect the exclusively international character of the responsibilities of the Secretary-General and the staff and not to seek to influence them in the discharge of their responsibilities.

Article 101

1. The staff shall be appointed by the Secretary-General under regulations established by the General Assembly.

2. Appropriate staffs shall be permanently assigned to the Economic and Social Council, the Trusteeship Council, and, as required,

to other organs of the United Nations. These staffs shall form a part of the Secretariat.

3. The paramount consideration in the employment of the staff and in the determination of the conditions of service shall be the necessity of securing the highest standards of efficiency, competence, and integrity. Due regard shall be paid to the importance of recruiting the staff on as wide a geographical basis as possible.

Chapter XVI: Miscellaneous Provisions

Article 102

1. Every treaty and every international agreement entered into by any Member of the United Nations after the present Charter comes into force shall as soon as possible be registered with the Secretariat and published by it.

2. No party to any such treaty or international agreement which has not been registered in accordance with the provisions of paragraph I of this Article may invoke that treaty or agreement before any organ of the United Nations.

Article 103
In the event of a conflict between the obligations of the Members of the United Nations under the present Charter and their obligations under any other international agreement, their obligations under the present Charter shall prevail.

Article 104
The Organization shall enjoy in the territory of each of its Members such legal capacity as may be necessary for the exercise of its functions and the fulfillment of its purposes.

Article 105

1. The Organization shall enjoy in the territory of each of its Members such privileges and immunities as are necessary for the fulfillment of its purposes.

2. Representatives of the Members of the United Nations and officials of the Organization shall similarly enjoy such privileges and immunities as are necessary for the independent exercise of their functions in connection with the Organization.

3. The General Assembly may make recommendations with a view to determining the details of the application of paragraphs 1 and 2 of this Article or may propose conventions to the Members of the United Nations for this purpose.

Chapter XVII: Transitional Security Arrangements

Article 106   Pending the coming into force of such special agreements referred to in Article 43 as in the opinion of the Security Council enable it to begin the exercise of its responsibilities under Article 42, the parties to the Four-Nation Declaration, signed at Moscow October 30, 1943, and France, shall, in accordance with the provisions of paragraph 5 of that Declaration, consult with one another and as occasion requires with other Members of the United Nations with a view to such joint action on behalf of the Organization as may be necessary for the purpose of maintaining international peace and security.

Article 107   Nothing in the present Charter shall invalidate or preclude action, in relation to any state which during the Second World War has been an enemy of any signatory to the present Charter, taken or authorized as a result of that war by the Governments having responsibility for such action.

Chapter XVIII: Amendments

Article 108   Amendments to the present Charter shall come into force for all Members of the United Nations when they have been adopted by a vote of two-thirds of the members of the General Assembly and ratified in accordance with their respective constitutional processes by two-thirds of the Members of the United Nations, including all the permanent members of the Security Council.

Article 109

1. A General Conference of the Members of the United Nations for the purpose of reviewing the present Charter may be held at a date and place to be fixed by a two-thirds vote of the members of the General Assembly and by a vote of any seven members of the Security Council. Each Member of the United Nations shall have one vote in the conference.

2. Any alteration of the present Charter recommended by a two-thirds vote of the conference shall take effect when ratified in accordance with their respective constitutional processes by two thirds of the Members of the United Nations including all the permanent members of the Security Council.

3. If such a conference has not been held before the tenth annual session of the General Assembly following the coming into force of the present Charter, the proposal to call such a conference shall be placed on the agenda of that session of the General Assembly, and the conference shall be held if so decided by a majority vote of the members of the General Assembly and by a vote of any seven members of the Security Council.

Chapter XIX: Ratification and Signature
Article 110
1. The present Charter shall be ratified by the signatory states in accordance with their respective constitutional processes.

2. The ratifications shall be deposited with the Government of the United States of America, which shall notify all the signatory states of each deposit as well as the Secretary-General of the Organization when he has been appointed.

3. The present Charter shall come into force upon the deposit of ratifications by the Republic of China, France, the Union of Soviet Socialist Republics, the United Kingdom of Great Britain and Northern Ireland, and the United States of America, and by a majority of the other signatory states. A protocol of the ratifications deposited shall thereupon be drawn up by the Government of the United States of America which shall communicate copies thereof to all the signatory states.

4. The states signatory to the present Charter which ratify it after it has come into force will become original Members of the United Nations on the date of the deposit of their respective ratifications.

Article 111   The present Charter, of which the Chinese, French, Russian, English, and Spanish texts are equally authentic, shall remain deposited in the archives of the Government of the United States of America. Duly certified copies thereof shall be transmitted by that Government to the Governments of the other signatory states.

IN FAITH WHEREOF the representatives of the Governments of the United Nations have signed the present Charter.

DONE at the city of San Francisco the twenty-sixth day of June, one thousand nine hundred and forty-five.

The UN Charter is available at www.un.org/aboutun/charter.

Additional Information

The Statute of the International Court of Justice is an integral part of the Charter. It is available at www.icj-cij.org/icjwww/ibasicdocuments/Basetext/istatute.htm.

Amendments to Articles 23, 27, and 61 of the Charter were adopted by the General Assembly on 17 December 1963 and came into force on 31 August 1965. A further amendment to Article 61 was adopted by the General Assembly on 20 December 1971, and came into force on 24 September 1973. An amendment to Article 109, adopted by the General Assembly on 20 December 1965, came into force on 12 June 1968.

The amendment to Article 23 enlarges the membership of the Security Council from eleven to fifteen. The amended Article 27 provides that decisions of the Security Council on procedural matters shall be made by an affirmative vote of nine members (formerly seven) and on all other matters by an affirmative vote of nine members (formerly seven), including the concurring votes of the five permanent members of the Security Council.

The amendment to Article 61, which entered into force on 31 August 1965, enlarged the membership of the Economic and Social Council from eighteen to twenty-seven. The subsequent amendment to that Article, which entered into force on 24 September 1973, further increased the membership of the Council from twenty-seven to fifty-four.

The amendment to Article 109, which relates to the first paragraph of that Article, provides that a General Conference of Member States for the purpose of reviewing the Charter may be held at a date and place to be fixed by a two-thirds vote of the members of the General Assembly and by a vote of any nine members (formerly seven) of the Security Council. Paragraph 3 of Article 109, which deals with the consideration of a possible review conference during the tenth regular session of the General Assembly, has been retained in its original form in its reference to a "vote, of any seven members of the Security Council," the paragraph having been acted upon in 1955 by the General Assembly, at its tenth regular session, and by the Security Council. (Available at www.hnmun.org/2005/websys.exe?file=refdesk/uncharter.html.)

Member States (191) of the United Nations with Dates on which They Joined

UN membership grew from fifty-one in 1946, to ninety-nine in 1960, 127 in 1970, 154 in 1980, and 159 in 1990. Having 191 members in 2005, the UN achieved universal membership.

Because the twenty Specialized Agencies and the four Related Organizations were created by separate treaties, their membership is slightly different from that of the United Nations.

Afghanistan (19 November 1946)
Albania (14 December 1955)
Algeria (8 October 1962)
Andorra (28 July 1993)
Angola (1 December 1976)
Antigua and Barbuda
(11 November 1981)
Argentina (24 October 1945)
Armenia (2 March 1992)
Australia (1 November 1945)
Austria (14 December 1955)
Azerbaijan (2 March 1992)

Bahamas (18 September 1973)
Bahrain (21 September 1971)
Bangladesh (17 September 1974)
Barbados (9 December 1966)
Belarus (24 October 1945)
Belgium (27 December 1945)
Belize (25 September 1981)
Benin (20 September 1960)
Bhutan (21 September 1971)
Bolivia (14 November 1945)
Bosnia and Herzegovina
(22 May 1992)
Botswana (17 October 1966)
Brazil (24 October 1945)
Brunei Darussalam (21 September 1984)
Bulgaria (14 December 1955)
Burkina Faso (20 September 1960)
Burundi (18 September 1962)

Cambodia (14 December 1955)
Cameroon (20 September 1960)
Canada (9 November 1945)
Cape Verde (16 September 1975)
Central African Republic (20 September 1960)
Chad (20 September 1960)
Chile (24 October 1945)
China (24 October 1945)

Colombia (5 November 1945)
Comoros (12 November 1975)
Congo (20 September 1960)
Costa Rica (2 November 1945)
Côte d'Ivoire (20 September 1960)
Croatia (22 May 1992)
Cuba (24 October 1945)
Cyprus (20 September 1960)
Czech Republic (19 January 1993)

Democratic People's Republic of
Korea (17 September 1991)
Democratic Republic of the Congo
(20 September 1960)
Denmark (24 October 1945)
Djibouti (20 September 1977)
Dominica (18 December 1978)
Dominican Republic (24 October 1945)

Ecuador (21 December 1945)
Egypt (24 October 1945)
El Salvador (24 October 1945)
Equatorial Guinea (12 November 1968)
Eritrea (28 May 1993)
Estonia (17 September 1991)
Ethiopia (13 November 1945)

Fiji (13 October 1970)
Finland (14 December 1955)
France (24 October 1945)

Gabon (20 September 1960)
Gambia (21 September 1965)
Georgia (31 July 1992)
Germany (18 September 1973, the
Federal Republic of Germany and
the German Democratic Republic
were admitted. On 3 October 1990
they formed one state.)
Ghana (8 March 1957)

Greece (25 October 1945)
Grenada (17 September 1974)
Guatemala (21 November 1945)
Guinea (12 December 1958)
Guinea-Bissau (17 September 1974)
Guyana (20 September 1966)

Haiti (24 October 1945)
Honduras (17 December 1945)
Hungary (14 December 1955)

Iceland (19 November 1946)
India (30 October 1945)
Indonesia (28 September 1950)
Iran (Islamic Republic of)
    (24 October 1945)
Iraq (21 December 1945)
Ireland (14 December 1955)
Israel (11 May 1949)
Italy (14 December 1955)

Jamaica (18 September 1962)
Japan (18 December 1956)
Jordan (14 December 1955)

Kazakhstan (2 March 1992)
Kenya (16 December 1963)
Kiribati (14 September 1999)
Kuwait (14 May 1963)
Kyrgyzstan (2 March 1992)

Lao People's Democratic Republic
    (14 December 1955)
Latvia (17 September 1991)
Lebanon (24 October 1945)
Lesotho (17 October 1966)
Liberia (2 November 1945)
Libyan Arab Jamahiriya
    (14 December 1955)
Liechtenstein (18 September 1990)
Lithuania (17 September 1991)
Luxembourg (24 October 1945)

The former Yugoslav Republic of
    Macedonia (8 April 1993)
Madagascar (20 September 1960)
Malawi (1 December 1964)
Malaysia (17 September 1957)
Maldives (21 September 1965)
Mali (28 September 1960)
Malta (1 December 1964)
Marshall Islands (17 September
    1991)
Mauritania (27 October 1961)
Mauritius (24 April 1968)
Mexico (7 November 1945)
Micronesia (Federated States of)
    (17 September 1991)
Monaco (28 May 1993)
Mongolia (27 October 1961)
Morocco (12 November 1956)
Mozambique (16 September
    1975)
Myanmar (19 April 1948)

Namibia (23 April 1990)
Nauru (14 September 1999)
Nepal (14 December 1955)
Netherlands (10 December 1945)
New Zealand (24 October 1945)
Nicaragua (24 October 1945)
Niger (20 September 1960)
Nigeria (7 October 1960)
Norway (27 November 1945)

Oman (7 October 1971)

Pakistan (30 September 1947)
Palau (15 December 1994)
Panama (13 November 1945)
Papua New Guinea (10 October
    1975)
Paraguay (24 October 1945)
Peru (31 October 1945)
Philippines (24 October 1945)

Poland (24 October 1945)
Portugal (14 December 1955)

Qatar (21 September 1971)

Republic of Korea (17 September
1991)
Republic of Moldova (2 March
1992)
Romania (14 December 1955)
Russian Federation (24 October
1945)
Rwanda (18 September 1962)

Saint Kitts and Nevis
(23 September 1983)
Saint Lucia (18 September 1979)
Saint Vincent and the Grenadines
(16 September 1980)
Samoa (15 December 1976)
San Marino (2 March 1992)
Sao Tome and Principe (16
September 1975)
Saudi Arabia (24 October 1945)
Senegal (28 September 1960)
Serbia and Montenegro (1
November 2000)
Seychelles (21 September 1976)
Sierra Leone (27 September 1961)
Singapore (21 September 1965)
Slovakia (19 January 1993)
Slovenia (22 May 1992)
Solomon Islands (19 September
1978)
Somalia (20 September 1960)
South Africa (7 November 1945)
Spain (14 December 1955)
Sri Lanka (14 December 1955)
Sudan (12 November 1956)
Suriname (4 December 1975)

Swaziland (24 September 1968)
Sweden (19 November 1946)
Switzerland (10 September 2002)
Syrian Arab Republic (24 October
1945)

Tajikistan (2 March 1992)
Thailand (16 December 1946)
Timor-Leste (27 September 2002)
Togo (20 September 1960)
Tonga (14 September 1999)
Trinidad and Tobago
(18 September 1962)
Tunisia (12 November 1956)
Turkey (24 October 1945)
Turkmenistan (2 March 1992)
Tuvalu (5 September 2000)

Uganda (25 October 1962)
Ukraine (24 October 1945)
United Arab Emirates (9 December
1971)
United Kingdom of Great Britain
and Northern Ireland
(24 October 1945)
United Republic of Tanzania
(14 December 1961)
United States of America (24
October 1945)
Uruguay (18 December 1945)
Uzbekistan (2 March 1992)

Vanuatu (15 September 1981)
Venezuela (15 November 1945)
Viet Nam (20 September 1977)

Yemen (30 September 1947)

Zambia (1 December 1964)
Zimbabwe (25 August 1980)

(Source: www.un.org/Overview/unmember.html)

International Bill of Human Rights

The International Bill of Human Rights consists of the Universal Declaration of Human Rights; the International Covenant on Economic, Social and Cultural Rights; and the International Covenant on Civil and Political Rights and its two optional protocols.

"Human rights" is mentioned seven times in the UN Charter, the first appearing in the third phrase of the preamble. Building on these references in the Charter, on 10 December 1948 the General Assembly passed the Universal Declaration of Human Rights. The rights expressed in the declaration were placed in treaty form by the General Assembly in two covenants. The Covenant on Economic, Social and Cultural Rights was adopted by the General Assembly on 16 December 1966 and entered into force on 3 January 1976. The International Covenant on Civil and Political Rights and its first optional protocol, which allows individuals to submit complaints to the Human Rights Committee, were adopted by the General Assembly on 16 December 1966 and entered into force on 23 March 1976. The second optional protocol to the International Covenant on Civil and Political Rights, which aims at the abolition of the death penalty, was adopted on 15 December 1989 and entered into force on 11 July 1991. (All components of the International Bill of Human Rights are available at www.ohchr.org/english/about/publications/docs/fs2.htm)

Universal Declaration of Human Rights

On December 10, 1948 the General Assembly of the United Nations adopted the Universal Declaration of Human Rights and called upon all member countries to publicize the text of the Declaration and "to cause it to be disseminated, displayed, read and expounded principally in schools and other educational institutions, without distinction based on the political status of countries or territories."

THE UNIVERSAL DECLARATION OF HUMAN RIGHTS

Preamble

Whereas recognition of the inherent dignity and of the equal and inalienable rights of all members of the human family is the foundation of freedom, justice and peace in the world,

Whereas disregard and contempt for human rights have resulted in barbarous acts which have outraged the conscience of mankind, and the advent of a world in which human beings shall enjoy freedom of speech and belief and freedom from fear and want has been proclaimed as the highest aspiration of the common people,

Whereas it is essential, if man is not to be compelled to have recourse, as a last resort, to rebellion against tyranny and oppression, that human rights should be protected by the rule of law,

Whereas it is essential to promote the development of friendly relations between nations,

Whereas the peoples of the United Nations have in the Charter reaffirmed their faith in fundamental human rights, in the dignity and worth of the human person and in the equal rights of men and women and have determined to promote social progress and better standards of life in larger freedom,

Whereas Member States have pledged themselves to achieve, in co-operation with the United Nations, the promotion of universal respect for and observance of human rights and fundamental freedoms,

Whereas a common understanding of these rights and freedoms is of the greatest importance for the full realization of this pledge,

Now, Therefore THE GENERAL ASSEMBY proclaims THIS UNIVERSAL DECLARATION OF HUMAN RIGHTS as a common standard of achievement for all peoples and all nations, to the end that every individual and every organ of society, keeping this Declaration constantly in mind, shall strive by teaching and education to promote respect for these rights and freedoms and by progressive measures, national and international, to secure their universal and effective recognition and observance, both among the peoples of Member States themselves and among the peoples of territories under their jurisdiction.

Article 1   All human beings are born free and equal in dignity and rights. They are endowed with reason and conscience and should act towards one another in a spirit of brotherhood.

Article 2   Everyone is entitled to all the rights and freedoms set forth in this Declaration, without distinction of any kind, such as race, colour, sex, language, religion, political or other opinion, national or social origin, property, birth or other status. Furthermore, no distinction shall be made on the basis of the political, jurisdictional or international status of the country or territory to which a person belongs, whether it be independent, trust, non-self-governing or under any other limitation of sovereignty.

Article 3   Everyone has the right to life, liberty and security of person.

Article 4 No one shall be held in slavery or servitude; slavery and the slave trade shall be prohibited in all their forms.

Article 5 No one shall be subjected to torture or to cruel, inhuman or degrading treatment or punishment.

Article 6 Everyone has the right to recognition everywhere as a person before the law.

Article 7 All are equal before the law and are entitled without any discrimination to equal protection of the law. All are entitled to equal protection against any discrimination in violation of this Declaration and against any incitement to such discrimination.

Article 8 Everyone has the right to an effective remedy by the competent national tribunals for acts violating the fundamental rights granted him by the constitution or by law.

Article 9 No one shall be subjected to arbitrary arrest, detention or exile.

Article 10 Everyone is entitled in full equality to a fair and public hearing by an independent and impartial tribunal, in the determination of his rights and obligations and of any criminal charge against him.

Article 11
(1) Everyone charged with a penal offence has the right to be presumed innocent until proved guilty according to law in a public trial at which he has had all the guarantees necessary for his defence.
(2) No one shall be held guilty of any penal offence on account of any act or omission which did not constitute a penal offence, under national or international law, at the time when it was committed. Nor shall a heavier penalty be imposed than the one that was applicable at the time the penal offence was committed.

Article 12 No one shall be subjected to arbitrary interference with his privacy, family, home or correspondence, nor to attacks upon his honour and reputation. Everyone has the right to the protection of the law against such interference or attacks.

Article 13
(1) Everyone has the right to freedom of movement and residence within the borders of each state.
(2) Everyone has the right to leave any country, including his own, and to return to his country.

Article 14

(1) Everyone has the right to seek and to enjoy in other countries asylum from persecution.

(2) This right may not be invoked in the case of prosecutions genuinely arising from non-political crimes or from acts contrary to the purposes and principles of the United Nations.

Article 15

(1) Everyone has the right to a nationality.

(2) No one shall be arbitrarily deprived of his nationality nor denied the right to change his nationality.

Article 16

(1) Men and women of full age, without any limitation due to race, nationality or religion, have the right to marry and to found a family. They are entitled to equal rights as to marriage, during marriage and at its dissolution.

(2) Marriage shall be entered into only with the free and full consent of the intending spouses.

(3) The family is the natural and fundamental group unit of society and is entitled to protection by society and the State.

Article 17

(1) Everyone has the right to own property alone as well as in association with others.

(2) No one shall be arbitrarily deprived of his property.

Article 18
Everyone has the right to freedom of thought, conscience and religion; this right includes freedom to change his religion or belief, and freedom, either alone or in community with others and in public or private, to manifest his religion or belief in teaching, practice, worship and observance.

Article 19
Everyone has the right to freedom of opinion and expression; this right includes freedom to hold opinions without interference and to seek, receive and impart information and ideas through any media and regardless of frontiers.

Article 20

(1) Everyone has the right to freedom of peaceful assembly and association.

(2) No one may be compelled to belong to an association.

Article 21

(1) Everyone has the right to take part in the government of his country, directly or through freely chosen representatives.

(2) Everyone has the right of equal access to public service in his country.

(3) The will of the people shall be the basis of the authority of government; this will shall be expressed in periodic and genuine elections which shall be by universal and equal suffrage and shall be held by secret vote or by equivalent free voting procedures.

Article 22   Everyone, as a member of society, has the right to social security and is entitled to realization, through national effort and international co-operation and in accordance with the organization and resources of each State, of the economic, social and cultural rights indispensable for his dignity and the free development of his personality.

Article 23

(1) Everyone has the right to work, to free choice of employment, to just and favourable conditions of work and to protection against unemployment.

(2) Everyone, without any discrimination, has the right to equal pay for equal work.

(3) Everyone who works has the right to just and favourable remuneration ensuring for himself and his family an existence worthy of human dignity, and supplemented, if necessary, by other means of social protection.

(4) Everyone has the right to form and to join trade unions for the protection of his interests.

Article 24   Everyone has the right to rest and leisure, including reasonable limitation of working hours and periodic holidays with pay.

Article 25

(1) Everyone has the right to a standard of living adequate for the health and well-being of himself and of his family, including food, clothing, housing and medical care and necessary social services, and the right to security in the event of unemployment, sickness, disability, widowhood, old age or other lack of livelihood in circumstances beyond his control.

(2) Motherhood and childhood are entitled to special care and assistance. All children, whether born in or out of wedlock, shall enjoy the same social protection.

Article 26

(1) Everyone has the right to education. Education shall be free, at least in the elementary and fundamental stages. Elementary education shall be compulsory. Technical and professional education shall be made generally available and higher education shall be equally accessible to all on the basis of merit.

(2) Education shall be directed to the full development of the human personality and to the strengthening of respect for human rights and fundamental freedoms. It shall promote understanding, tolerance and friendship among all nations, racial or religious groups, and shall further the activities of the United Nations for the maintenance of peace.

(3) Parents have a prior right to choose the kind of education that shall be given to their children.

Article 27

(1) Everyone has the right freely to participate in the cultural life of the community, to enjoy the arts and to share in scientific advancement and its benefits.

(2) Everyone has the right to the protection of the moral and material interests resulting from any scientific, literary or artistic production of which he is the author.

Article 28   Everyone is entitled to a social and international order in which the rights and freedoms set forth in this Declaration can be fully realized.

Article 29

(1) Everyone has duties to the community in which alone the free and full development of his personality is possible.

(2) In the exercise of his rights and freedoms, everyone shall be subject only to such limitations as are determined by law solely for the purpose of securing due recognition and respect for the rights and freedoms of others and of meeting the just requirements of morality, public order and the general welfare in a democratic society.

(3) These rights and freedoms may in no case be exercised contrary to the purposes and principles of the United Nations.

Article 30   Nothing in this Declaration may be interpreted as implying for any State, group or person any right to engage in any activity or to perform any act aimed at the destruction of any of the rights and freedoms set forth herein.

International Covenant on Economic Social and Cultural Rights

Adopted and opened for signature, ratification, and accession by General Assembly resolution 2200A (XXI) of 16 December 1966, this covenant entered into force 3 January 1976, in accordance with article 27.

Preamble

The States Parties to the present Covenant,

Considering that, in accordance with the principles proclaimed in the Charter of the United Nations, recognition of the inherent dignity and of the equal and inalienable rights of all members of the human family is the foundation of freedom, justice and peace in the world,

Recognizing that these rights derive from the inherent dignity of the human person,

Recognizing that, in accordance with the Universal Declaration of Human Rights, the ideal of free human beings enjoying freedom from fear and want can only be achieved if conditions are created whereby everyone may enjoy his economic, social and cultural rights, as well as his civil and political rights,

Considering the obligation of States under the Charter of the United Nations to promote universal respect for, and observance of, human rights and freedoms,

Realizing that the individual, having duties to other individuals and to the community to which he belongs, is under a responsibility to strive for the promotion and observance of the rights recognized in the present Covenant,

Agree upon the following articles:

PART I

Article 1

1. All peoples have the right of self-determination. By virtue of that right they freely determine their political status and freely pursue their economic, social and cultural development.

2. All peoples may, for their own ends, freely dispose of their natural wealth and resources without prejudice to any obligations arising out of international economic co-operation, based upon the principle of mutual benefit, and international law. In no case may a people be deprived of its own means of subsistence.

3. The States Parties to the present Covenant, including those having responsibility for the administration of Non-Self-Governing and Trust Territories, shall promote the realization of the right of self-

determination, and shall respect that right, in conformity with the provisions of the Charter of the United Nations.

PART II

Article 2

1. Each State Party to the present Covenant undertakes to take steps, individually and through international assistance and co-operation, especially economic and technical, to the maximum of its available resources, with a view to achieving progressively the full realization of the rights recognized in the present Covenant by all appropriate means, including particularly the adoption of legislative measures.

2. The States Parties to the present Covenant undertake to guarantee that the rights enunciated in the present Covenant will be exercised without discrimination of any kind as to race, colour, sex, language, religion, political or other opinion, national or social origin, property, birth or other status.

3. Developing countries, with due regard to human rights and their national economy, may determine to what extent they would guarantee the economic rights recognized in the present Covenant to non-nationals.

Article 3

The States Parties to the present Covenant undertake to ensure the equal right of men and women to the enjoyment of all economic, social and cultural rights set forth in the present Covenant.

Article 4

The States Parties to the present Covenant recognize that, in the enjoyment of those rights provided by the State in conformity with the present Covenant, the State may subject such rights only to such limitations as are determined by law only in so far as this may be compatible with the nature of these rights and solely for the purpose of promoting the general welfare in a democratic society.

Article 5

1. Nothing in the present Covenant may be interpreted as implying for any State, group or person any right to engage in any activity or to perform any act aimed at the destruction of any of the rights or freedoms recognized herein, or at their limitation to a greater extent than is provided for in the present Covenant.

2. No restriction upon or derogation from any of the fundamental human rights recognized or existing in any country in virtue of law, conventions, regulations or custom shall be admitted on the pretext that the present Covenant does not recognize such rights or that it recognizes them to a lesser extent.

PART III
Article 6
1. The States Parties to the present Covenant recognize the right to work, which includes the right of everyone to the opportunity to gain his living by work which he freely chooses or accepts, and will take appropriate steps to safeguard this right.

2. The steps to be taken by a State Party to the present Covenant to achieve the full realization of this right shall include technical and vocational guidance and training programmes, policies and techniques to achieve steady economic, social and cultural development and full and productive employment under conditions safeguarding fundamental political and economic freedoms to the individual.

Article 7 The States Parties to the present Covenant recognize the right of everyone to the enjoyment of just and favourable conditions of work which ensure, in particular:

(a) Remuneration which provides all workers, as a minimum, with:

(i) Fair wages and equal remuneration for work of equal value without distinction of any kind, in particular women being guaranteed conditions of work not inferior to those enjoyed by men, with equal pay for equal work;

(ii) A decent living for themselves and their families in accordance with the provisions of the present Covenant;

(b) Safe and healthy working conditions;

(c) Equal opportunity for everyone to be promoted in his employment to an appropriate higher level, subject to no considerations other than those of seniority and competence;

(d) Rest, leisure and reasonable limitation of working hours and periodic holidays with pay, as well as remuneration for public holidays.

Article 8
1. The States Parties to the present Covenant undertake to ensure:

(a) The right of everyone to form trade unions and join the trade union of his choice, subject only to the rules of the organization concerned, for the promotion and protection of his economic and social interests. No restrictions may be placed on the exercise of this right other than those prescribed by law and which are necessary in a democratic society in the interests of national security or public order or for the protection of the rights and freedoms of others;

(b) The right of trade unions to establish national federations or confederations and the right of the latter to form or join international trade-union organizations;

(c) The right of trade unions to function freely subject to no limitations other than those prescribed by law and which are necessary in a democratic society in the interests of national security or public order or for the protection of the rights and freedoms of others;

(d) The right to strike, provided that it is exercised in conformity with the laws of the particular country.

2. This article shall not prevent the imposition of lawful restrictions on the exercise of these rights by members of the armed forces or of the police or of the administration of the State.

3. Nothing in this article shall authorize States Parties to the International Labour Organisation Convention of 1948 concerning Freedom of Association and Protection of the Right to Organize to take legislative measures which would prejudice, or apply the law in such a manner as would prejudice, the guarantees provided for in that Convention.

Article 9   The States Parties to the present Covenant recognize the right of everyone to social security, including social insurance.

Article 10   The States Parties to the present Covenant recognize that:

1. The widest possible protection and assistance should be accorded to the family, which is the natural and fundamental group unit of society, particularly for its establishment and while it is responsible for the care and education of dependent children. Marriage must be entered into with the free consent of the intending spouses.

2. Special protection should be accorded to mothers during a reasonable period before and after childbirth. During such period working mothers should be accorded paid leave or leave with adequate social security benefits.

3. Special measures of protection and assistance should be taken on behalf of all children and young persons without any discrimination for reasons of parentage or other conditions. Children and young persons should be protected from economic and social exploitation. Their employment in work harmful to their morals or health or dangerous to life or likely to hamper their normal development should be punishable by law. States should also set age limits below which the paid employment of child labour should be prohibited and punishable by law.

Article 11

1. The States Parties to the present Covenant recognize the right of everyone to an adequate standard of living for himself and his family, including adequate food, clothing and housing, and to the continuous improvement of living conditions. The States Parties will take appropriate steps to ensure the realization of this right, recognizing to this effect the essential importance of international co-operation based on free consent.

2. The States Parties to the present Covenant, recognizing the fundamental right of everyone to be free from hunger, shall take, individually and through international co-operation, the measures, including specific programmes, which are needed:

(a) To improve methods of production, conservation and distribution of food by making full use of technical and scientific knowledge, by disseminating knowledge of the principles of nutrition and by developing or reforming agrarian systems in such a way as to achieve the most efficient development and utilization of natural resources;

(b) Taking into account the problems of both food-importing and food-exporting countries, to ensure an equitable distribution of world food supplies in relation to need.

Article 12

1. The States Parties to the present Covenant recognize the right of everyone to the enjoyment of the highest attainable standard of physical and mental health.

2. The steps to be taken by the States Parties to the present Covenant to achieve the full realization of this right shall include those necessary for:

(a) The provision for the reduction of the stillbirth-rate and of infant mortality and for the healthy development of the child;

(b) The improvement of all aspects of environmental and industrial hygiene;

(c) The prevention, treatment and control of epidemic, endemic, occupational and other diseases;

(d) The creation of conditions which would assure to all medical service and medical attention in the event of sickness.

Article 13

1. The States Parties to the present Covenant recognize the right of everyone to education. They agree that education shall be directed to the full development of the human personality and the sense of its dignity, and shall strengthen the respect for human rights and fundamental freedoms. They further agree that education shall enable all persons to participate effectively in a free society, promote understanding, tolerance and friendship among all nations and all racial, ethnic or religious groups, and further the activities of the United Nations for the maintenance of peace.

2. The States Parties to the present Covenant recognize that, with a view to achieving the full realization of this right:

(a) Primary education shall be compulsory and available free to all;

(b) Secondary education in its different forms, including technical and vocational secondary education, shall be made generally available and accessible to all by every appropriate means, and in particular by the progressive introduction of free education;

(c) Higher education shall be made equally accessible to all, on the basis of capacity, by every appropriate means, and in particular by the progressive introduction of free education;

(d) Fundamental education shall be encouraged or intensified as far as possible for those persons who have not received or completed the whole period of their primary education;

(e) The development of a system of schools at all levels shall be actively pursued, an adequate fellowship system shall be established, and the material conditions of teaching staff shall be continuously improved.

3. The States Parties to the present Covenant undertake to have respect for the liberty of parents and, when applicable, legal guardians to choose for their children schools, other than those established by the public authorities, which conform to such minimum educational standards as may be laid down or approved by the State and to ensure the religious and moral education of their children in conformity with their own convictions.

4. No part of this article shall be construed so as to interfere with the liberty of individuals and bodies to establish and direct educational institutions, subject always to the observance of the principles set forth in paragraph 1 of this article and to the requirement that the education given in such institutions shall conform to such minimum standards as may be laid down by the State.

Article 14   Each State Party to the present Covenant which, at the time of becoming a Party, has not been able to secure in its metropolitan territory or other territories under its jurisdiction compulsory primary education, free of charge, undertakes, within two years, to work out and adopt a detailed plan of action for the progressive implementation, within a reasonable number of years, to be fixed in the plan, of the principle of compulsory education free of charge for all.

Article 15

1. The States Parties to the present Covenant recognize the right of everyone:

(a) To take part in cultural life;

(b) To enjoy the benefits of scientific progress and its applications;

(c) To benefit from the protection of the moral and material interests resulting from any scientific, literary or artistic production of which he is the author.

2. The steps to be taken by the States Parties to the present Covenant to achieve the full realization of this right shall include those necessary for the conservation, the development and the diffusion of science and culture.

3. The States Parties to the present Covenant undertake to respect the freedom indispensable for scientific research and creative activity.

4. The States Parties to the present Covenant recognize the benefits to be derived from the encouragement and development of international contacts and co-operation in the scientific and cultural fields.

PART IV

Article 16

1. The States Parties to the present Covenant undertake to submit in conformity with this part of the Covenant reports on the measures which they have adopted and the progress made in achieving the observance of the rights recognized herein.

2. (a) All reports shall be submitted to the Secretary-General of the United Nations, who shall transmit copies to the Economic and Social Council for consideration in accordance with the provisions of the present Covenant;

(b) The Secretary-General of the United Nations shall also transmit to the specialized agencies copies of the reports, or any relevant parts therefrom, from States Parties to the present Covenant which are also members of these specialized agencies in so far as these reports, or parts therefrom, relate to any matters which fall within the responsibilities of the said agencies in accordance with their constitutional instruments.

Article 17

1. The States Parties to the present Covenant shall furnish their reports in stages, in accordance with a programme to be established by the Economic and Social Council within one year of the entry into force of the present Covenant after consultation with the States Parties and the specialized agencies concerned.

2. Reports may indicate factors and difficulties affecting the degree of fulfilment of obligations under the present Covenant.

3. Where relevant information has previously been furnished to the United Nations or to any specialized agency by any State Party to the present Covenant, it will not be necessary to reproduce that information, but a precise reference to the information so furnished will suffice.

Article 18   Pursuant to its responsibilities under the Charter of the United Nations in the field of human rights and fundamental freedoms, the Economic and Social Council may make arrangements with the specialized agencies in respect of their reporting to it on the progress made in achieving the observance of the provisions of the present Covenant falling within the scope of their activities. These reports may include particulars of decisions and recommendations on such implementation adopted by their competent organs.

Article 19   The Economic and Social Council may transmit to the Commission on Human Rights for study and general recommendation or, as appropriate, for information the reports concerning human rights submitted by States in accordance with articles 16 and 17, and those concerning human rights submitted by the specialized agencies in accordance with article 18.

Article 20   The States Parties to the present Covenant and the specialized agencies concerned may submit comments to the Economic and Social Council on any general recommendation under article 19 or reference to such general recommendation in any report of the Commission on Human Rights or any documentation referred to therein.

Article 21   The Economic and Social Council may submit from time to time to the General Assembly reports with recommendations of a general nature and a summary of the information received from the States Parties to the present Covenant and the specialized agencies on the measures taken and the progress made in achieving general observance of the rights recognized in the present Covenant.

Article 22   The Economic and Social Council may bring to the attention of other organs of the United Nations, their subsidiary organs and specialized agencies concerned with furnishing technical assistance any matters arising out of the reports referred to in this part of the present Covenant which may assist such bodies in deciding, each within its field of competence, on the advisability of international measures likely to contribute to the effective progressive implementation of the present Covenant.

Article 23   The States Parties to the present Covenant agree that international action for the achievement of the rights recognized in the present Covenant includes such methods as the conclusion of conventions, the adoption of recommendations, the furnishing of technical assistance and the holding of regional meetings and technical meetings for the purpose of consultation and study organized in conjunction with the Governments concerned.

Article 24   Nothing in the present Covenant shall be interpreted as impairing the provisions of the Charter of the United Nations and of the constitutions of the specialized agencies which define the respective responsibilities of the various organs of the United Nations and of the specialized agencies in regard to the matters dealt with in the present Covenant.

Article 25   Nothing in the present Covenant shall be interpreted as impairing the inherent right of all peoples to enjoy and utilize fully and freely their natural wealth and resources.

PART V

Article 26

1. The present Covenant is open for signature by any State Member of the United Nations or member of any of its specialized agencies, by any State Party to the Statute of the International Court of Justice, and by any other State which has been invited by the General Assembly of the United Nations to become a party to the present Covenant.

2. The present Covenant is subject to ratification. Instruments of ratification shall be deposited with the Secretary-General of the United Nations.

3. The present Covenant shall be open to accession by any State referred to in paragraph 1 of this article.

4. Accession shall be effected by the deposit of an instrument of accession with the Secretary-General of the United Nations.

5. The Secretary-General of the United Nations shall inform all States which have signed the present Covenant or acceded to it of the deposit of each instrument of ratification or accession.

Article 27

1. The present Covenant shall enter into force three months after the date of the deposit with the Secretary-General of the United Nations of the thirty-fifth instrument of ratification or instrument of accession.

2. For each State ratifying the present Covenant or acceding to it after the deposit of the thirty-fifth instrument of ratification or instrument of accession, the present Covenant shall enter into force three months after the date of the deposit of its own instrument of ratification or instrument of accession.

Article 28   The provisions of the present Covenant shall extend to all parts of federal States without any limitations or exceptions.

Article 29

1. Any State Party to the present Covenant may propose an amendment and file it with the Secretary-General of the United Nations. The Secretary-General shall thereupon communicate any proposed amendments to the States Parties to the present Covenant with a request that they notify him whether they favour a conference of States Parties for the purpose of considering and voting upon the proposals. In the event that at least one third of the States Parties favours such a conference, the Secretary-General shall convene the conference under the auspices of the United Nations. Any amendment adopted by a majority of the States Parties present and voting at the conference shall be submitted to the General Assembly of the United Nations for approval.

2. Amendments shall come into force when they have been approved by the General Assembly of the United Nations and accepted by a two-thirds majority of the States Parties to the present Covenant in accordance with their respective constitutional processes.

3. When amendments come into force they shall be binding on those States Parties which have accepted them, other States Parties still being bound by the provisions of the present Covenant and any earlier amendment which they have accepted.

Article 30   Irrespective of the notifications made under article 26, paragraph 5, the Secretary-General of the United Nations shall inform all States referred to in paragraph 1 of the same article of the following particulars:

(a) Signatures, ratifications and accessions under article 26;

(b) The date of the entry into force of the present Covenant under article 27 and the date of the entry into force of any amendments under article 29.

Article 31

1. The present Covenant, of which the Chinese, English, French, Russian and Spanish texts are equally authentic, shall be deposited in the archives of the United Nations.

2. The Secretary-General of the United Nations shall transmit certified copies of the present Covenant to all States referred to in article 26.

(Available at www.ohchr.org/english/law/cescr.htm)

International Covenant on Civil and Political Rights

Adopted and opened for signature, ratification, and accession by General Assembly resolution 2200A (XXI) of 16 December 1966, this covenant entered into force 23 March 1976, in accordance with Article 49.

Preamble

The States Parties to the present Covenant,

Considering that, in accordance with the principles proclaimed in the Charter of the United Nations, recognition of the inherent dignity and of the equal and inalienable rights of all members of the human family is the foundation of freedom, justice and peace in the world,

Recognizing that these rights derive from the inherent dignity of the human person,

Recognizing that, in accordance with the Universal Declaration of Human Rights, the ideal of free human beings enjoying civil and political freedom and freedom from fear and want can only be achieved if conditions are created whereby everyone may enjoy his civil and political rights, as well as his economic, social and cultural rights,

Considering the obligation of States under the Charter of the United Nations to promote universal respect for, and observance of, human rights and freedoms,

Realizing that the individual, having duties to other individuals and to the community to which he belongs, is under a responsibility to strive for the promotion and observance of the rights recognized in the present Covenant,

Agree upon the following articles:

PART I
Article 1

1. All peoples have the right of self-determination. By virtue of that right they freely determine their political status and freely pursue their economic, social and cultural development.

2. All peoples may, for their own ends, freely dispose of their natural wealth and resources without prejudice to any obligations arising out of international economic co-operation, based upon the principle of mutual benefit, and international law. In no case may a people be deprived of its own means of subsistence.

3. The States Parties to the present Covenant, including those having responsibility for the administration of Non-Self-Governing and Trust Territories, shall promote the realization of the right of self-

determination, and shall respect that right, in conformity with the provisions of the Charter of the United Nations.

PART II
Article 2

1. Each State Party to the present Covenant undertakes to respect and to ensure to all individuals within its territory and subject to its jurisdiction the rights recognized in the present Covenant, without distinction of any kind, such as race, colour, sex, language, religion, political or other opinion, national or social origin, property, birth or other status.

2. Where not already provided for by existing legislative or other measures, each State Party to the present Covenant undertakes to take the necessary steps, in accordance with its constitutional processes and with the provisions of the present Covenant, to adopt such laws or other measures as may be necessary to give effect to the rights recognized in the present Covenant.

3. Each State Party to the present Covenant undertakes:

(a) To ensure that any person whose rights or freedoms as herein recognized are violated shall have an effective remedy, notwithstanding that the violation has been committed by persons acting in an official capacity;

(b) To ensure that any person claiming such a remedy shall have his right thereto determined by competent judicial, administrative or legislative authorities, or by any other competent authority provided for by the legal system of the State, and to develop the possibilities of judicial remedy;

(c) To ensure that the competent authorities shall enforce such remedies when granted.

Article 3   The States Parties to the present Covenant undertake to ensure the equal right of men and women to the enjoyment of all civil and political rights set forth in the present Covenant.

Article 4

1. In time of public emergency which threatens the life of the nation and the existence of which is officially proclaimed, the States Parties to the present Covenant may take measures derogating from their obligations under the present Covenant to the extent strictly required by the exigencies of the situation, provided that such measures are not inconsistent with their other obligations under international law and do not involve discrimination solely on the ground of race, colour, sex, language, religion or social origin.

2. No derogation from articles 6, 7, 8 (paragraphs 1 and 2), 11, 15, 16 and 18 may be made under this provision.

3. Any State Party to the present Covenant availing itself of the right of derogation shall immediately inform the other States Parties to the present Covenant, through the intermediary of the Secretary-General of the United Nations, of the provisions from which it has derogated and of the reasons by which it was actuated. A further communication shall be made, through the same intermediary, on the date on which it terminates such derogation.

Article 5

1. Nothing in the present Covenant may be interpreted as implying for any State, group or person any right to engage in any activity or perform any act aimed at the destruction of any of the rights and freedoms recognized herein or at their limitation to a greater extent than is provided for in the present Covenant.

2. There shall be no restriction upon or derogation from any of the fundamental human rights recognized or existing in any State Party to the present Covenant pursuant to law, conventions, regulations or custom on the pretext that the present Covenant does not recognize such rights or that it recognizes them to a lesser extent.

PART III

Article 6

1. Every human being has the inherent right to life. This right shall be protected by law. No one shall be arbitrarily deprived of his life.

2. In countries which have not abolished the death penalty, sentence of death may be imposed only for the most serious crimes in accordance with the law in force at the time of the commission of the crime and not contrary to the provisions of the present Covenant and to the Convention on the Prevention and Punishment of the Crime of Genocide. This penalty can only be carried out pursuant to a final judgment rendered by a competent court.

3. When deprivation of life constitutes the crime of genocide, it is understood that nothing in this article shall authorize any State Party to the present Covenant to derogate in any way from any obligation assumed under the provisions of the Convention on the Prevention and Punishment of the Crime of Genocide.

4. Anyone sentenced to death shall have the right to seek pardon or commutation of the sentence. Amnesty, pardon or commutation of the sentence of death may be granted in all cases.

5. Sentence of death shall not be imposed for crimes committed by persons below eighteen years of age and shall not be carried out on pregnant women.

6. Nothing in this article shall be invoked to delay or to prevent the abolition of capital punishment by any State Party to the present Covenant.

Article 7   No one shall be subjected to torture or to cruel, inhuman or degrading treatment or punishment. In particular, no one shall be subjected without his free consent to medical or scientific experimentation.

Article 8

1. No one shall be held in slavery; slavery and the slave-trade in all their forms shall be prohibited.

2. No one shall be held in servitude.

3. (a) No one shall be required to perform forced or compulsory labour;

(b) Paragraph 3 (a) shall not be held to preclude, in countries where imprisonment with hard labour may be imposed as a punishment for a crime, the performance of hard labour in pursuance of a sentence to such punishment by a competent court;

(c) For the purpose of this paragraph the term "forced or compulsory labour" shall not include:

(i) Any work or service, not referred to in subparagraph (b), normally required of a person who is under detention in consequence of a lawful order of a court, or of a person during conditional release from such detention;

(ii) Any service of a military character and, in countries where conscientious objection is recognized, any national service required by law of conscientious objectors;

(iii) Any service exacted in cases of emergency or calamity threatening the life or well-being of the community;

(iv) Any work or service which forms part of normal civil obligations.

Article 9

1. Everyone has the right to liberty and security of person. No one shall be subjected to arbitrary arrest or detention. No one shall be deprived of his liberty except on such grounds and in accordance with such procedure as are established by law.

2. Anyone who is arrested shall be informed, at the time of arrest, of the reasons for his arrest and shall be promptly informed of any charges against him.

3. Anyone arrested or detained on a criminal charge shall be brought promptly before a judge or other officer authorized by law to exercise judicial power and shall be entitled to trial within a reasonable time or to release. It shall not be the general rule that persons awaiting

trial shall be detained in custody, but release may be subject to guarantees to appear for trial, at any other stage of the judicial proceedings, and, should occasion arise, for execution of the judgment.

4. Anyone who is deprived of his liberty by arrest or detention shall be entitled to take proceedings before a court, in order that that court may decide without delay on the lawfulness of his detention and order his release if the detention is not lawful.

5. Anyone who has been the victim of unlawful arrest or detention shall have an enforceable right to compensation.

Article 10

1. All persons deprived of their liberty shall be treated with humanity and with respect for the inherent dignity of the human person.

2. (a) Accused persons shall, save in exceptional circumstances, be segregated from convicted persons and shall be subject to separate treatment appropriate to their status as unconvicted persons;

(b) Accused juvenile persons shall be separated from adults and brought as speedily as possible for adjudication.

3. The penitentiary system shall comprise treatment of prisoners the essential aim of which shall be their reformation and social rehabilitation. Juvenile offenders shall be segregated from adults and be accorded treatment appropriate to their age and legal status.

Article 11   No one shall be imprisoned merely on the ground of inability to fulfil a contractual obligation.

Article 12

1. Everyone lawfully within the territory of a State shall, within that territory, have the right to liberty of movement and freedom to choose his residence.

2. Everyone shall be free to leave any country, including his own.

3. The above-mentioned rights shall not be subject to any restrictions except those which are provided by law, are necessary to protect national security, public order (ordre public), public health or morals or the rights and freedoms of others, and are consistent with the other rights recognized in the present Covenant.

4. No one shall be arbitrarily deprived of the right to enter his own country.

Article 13   An alien lawfully in the territory of a State Party to the present Covenant may be expelled therefrom only in pursuance of a decision reached in accordance with law and shall, except where compelling reasons of national security otherwise require, be allowed to submit the reasons against his expulsion and to have his case reviewed by, and be represented for the purpose before, the competent authority or a person or persons especially designated by the competent authority.

Article 14

1. All persons shall be equal before the courts and tribunals. In the determination of any criminal charge against him, or of his rights and obligations in a suit at law, everyone shall be entitled to a fair and public hearing by a competent, independent and impartial tribunal established by law. The press and the public may be excluded from all or part of a trial for reasons of morals, public order (ordre public) or national security in a democratic society, or when the interest of the private lives of the parties so requires, or to the extent strictly necessary in the opinion of the court in special circumstances where publicity would prejudice the interests of justice; but any judgement rendered in a criminal case or in a suit at law shall be made public except where the interest of juvenile persons otherwise requires or the proceedings concern matrimonial disputes or the guardianship of children.

2. Everyone charged with a criminal offence shall have the right to be presumed innocent until proved guilty according to law.

3. In the determination of any criminal charge against him, everyone shall be entitled to the following minimum guarantees, in full equality:

(a) To be informed promptly and in detail in a language which he understands of the nature and cause of the charge against him;

(b) To have adequate time and facilities for the preparation of his defence and to communicate with counsel of his own choosing;

(c) To be tried without undue delay;

(d) To be tried in his presence, and to defend himself in person or through legal assistance of his own choosing; to be informed, if he does not have legal assistance, of this right; and to have legal assistance assigned to him, in any case where the interests of justice so require, and without payment by him in any such case if he does not have sufficient means to pay for it;

(e) To examine, or have examined, the witnesses against him and to obtain the attendance and examination of witnesses on his behalf under the same conditions as witnesses against him;

(f) To have the free assistance of an interpreter if he cannot understand or speak the language used in court;

(g) Not to be compelled to testify against himself or to confess guilt.

4. In the case of juvenile persons, the procedure shall be such as will take account of their age and the desirability of promoting their rehabilitation.

5. Everyone convicted of a crime shall have the right to his conviction and sentence being reviewed by a higher tribunal according to law.

6. When a person has by a final decision been convicted of a criminal offence and when subsequently his conviction has been reversed or he has been pardoned on the ground that a new or newly discovered fact shows conclusively that there has been a miscarriage of justice, the person who has suffered punishment as a result of such conviction shall be compensated according to law, unless it is proved that the non-disclosure of the unknown fact in time is wholly or partly attributable to him.

7. No one shall be liable to be tried or punished again for an offence for which he has already been finally convicted or acquitted in accordance with the law and penal procedure of each country.

Article 15

1. No one shall be held guilty of any criminal offence on account of any act or omission which did not constitute a criminal offence, under national or international law, at the time when it was committed. Nor shall a heavier penalty be imposed than the one that was applicable at the time when the criminal offence was committed. If, subsequent to the commission of the offence, provision is made by law for the imposition of the lighter penalty, the offender shall benefit thereby.

2. Nothing in this article shall prejudice the trial and punishment of any person for any act or omission which, at the time when it was committed, was criminal according to the general principles of law recognized by the community of nations.

Article 16   Everyone shall have the right to recognition everywhere as a person before the law.

Article 17

1. No one shall be subjected to arbitrary or unlawful interference with his privacy, family, home or correspondence, nor to unlawful attacks on his honour and reputation.

2. Everyone has the right to the protection of the law against such interference or attacks.

Article 18

1. Everyone shall have the right to freedom of thought, conscience and religion. This right shall include freedom to have or to adopt a religion or belief of his choice, and freedom, either individually or in community with others and in public or private, to manifest his religion or belief in worship, observance, practice and teaching.

2. No one shall be subject to coercion which would impair his freedom to have or to adopt a religion or belief of his choice.

3. Freedom to manifest one's religion or beliefs may be subject only to such limitations as are prescribed by law and are necessary to protect public safety, order, health, or morals or the fundamental rights and freedoms of others.

4. The States Parties to the present Covenant undertake to have respect for the liberty of parents and, when applicable, legal guardians to ensure the religious and moral education of their children in conformity with their own convictions.

Article 19

1. Everyone shall have the right to hold opinions without interference.

2. Everyone shall have the right to freedom of expression; this right shall include freedom to seek, receive and impart information and ideas of all kinds, regardless of frontiers, either orally, in writing or in print, in the form of art, or through any other media of his choice.

3. The exercise of the rights provided for in paragraph 2 of this article carries with it special duties and responsibilities. It may therefore be subject to certain restrictions, but these shall only be such as are provided by law and are necessary:

(a) For respect of the rights or reputations of others;

(b) For the protection of national security or of public order (ordre public), or of public health or morals.

Article 20

1. Any propaganda for war shall be prohibited by law.

2. Any advocacy of national, racial or religious hatred that constitutes incitement to discrimination, hostility or violence shall be prohibited by law.

Article 21

The right of peaceful assembly shall be recognized. No restrictions may be placed on the exercise of this right other than those imposed in conformity with the law and which are necessary in a democratic society in the interests of national security or public safety, public order (ordre public), the protection of public health or morals or the protection of the rights and freedoms of others.

Article 22

1. Everyone shall have the right to freedom of association with others, including the right to form and join trade unions for the protection of his interests.

2. No restrictions may be placed on the exercise of this right other than those which are prescribed by law and which are necessary in a

democratic society in the interests of national security or public safety, public order (ordre public), the protection of public health or morals or the protection of the rights and freedoms of others. This article shall not prevent the imposition of lawful restrictions on members of the armed forces and of the police in their exercise of this right.

3. Nothing in this article shall authorize States Parties to the International Labour Organisation Convention of 1948 concerning Freedom of Association and Protection of the Right to Organize to take legislative measures which would prejudice, or to apply the law in such a manner as to prejudice, the guarantees provided for in that Convention.

Article 23

1. The family is the natural and fundamental group unit of society and is entitled to protection by society and the State.

2. The right of men and women of marriageable age to marry and to found a family shall be recognized.

3. No marriage shall be entered into without the free and full consent of the intending spouses.

4. States Parties to the present Covenant shall take appropriate steps to ensure equality of rights and responsibilities of spouses as to marriage, during marriage and at its dissolution. In the case of dissolution, provision shall be made for the necessary protection of any children.

Article 24

1. Every child shall have, without any discrimination as to race, colour, sex, language, religion, national or social origin, property or birth, the right to such measures of protection as are required by his status as a minor, on the part of his family, society and the State.

2. Every child shall be registered immediately after birth and shall have a name.

3. Every child has the right to acquire a nationality.

Article 25 Every citizen shall have the right and the opportunity, without any of the distinctions mentioned in article 2 and without unreasonable restrictions:

(a) To take part in the conduct of public affairs, directly or through freely chosen representatives;

(b) To vote and to be elected at genuine periodic elections which shall be by universal and equal suffrage and shall be held by secret ballot, guaranteeing the free expression of the will of the electors;

(c) To have access, on general terms of equality, to public service in his country.

Article 26   All persons are equal before the law and are entitled without any discrimination to the equal protection of the law. In this respect, the law shall prohibit any discrimination and guarantee to all persons equal and effective protection against discrimination on any ground such as race, colour, sex, language, religion, political or other opinion, national or social origin, property, birth or other status.

Article 27   In those States in which ethnic, religious or linguistic minorities exist, persons belonging to such minorities shall not be denied the right, in community with the other members of their group, to enjoy their own culture, to profess and practise their own religion, or to use their own language.

PART IV
Article 28
1. There shall be established a Human Rights Committee (hereafter referred to in the present Covenant as the Committee). It shall consist of eighteen members and shall carry out the functions hereinafter provided.

2. The Committee shall be composed of nationals of the States Parties to the present Covenant who shall be persons of high moral character and recognized competence in the field of human rights, consideration being given to the usefulness of the participation of some persons having legal experience.

3. The members of the Committee shall be elected and shall serve in their personal capacity.

Article 29
1. The members of the Committee shall be elected by secret ballot from a list of persons possessing the qualifications prescribed in article 28 and nominated for the purpose by the States Parties to the present Covenant.

2. Each State Party to the present Covenant may nominate not more than two persons. These persons shall be nationals of the nominating State.

3. A person shall be eligible for renomination.

Article 30
1. The initial election shall be held no later than six months after the date of the entry into force of the present Covenant.

2. At least four months before the date of each election to the Committee, other than an election to fill a vacancy declared in accordance with article 34, the Secretary-General of the United Nations shall address a written invitation to the States Parties to the present

Covenant to submit their nominations for membership of the Committee within three months.

3. The Secretary-General of the United Nations shall prepare a list in alphabetical order of all the persons thus nominated, with an indication of the States Parties which have nominated them, and shall submit it to the States Parties to the present Covenant no later than one month before the date of each election.

4. Elections of the members of the Committee shall be held at a meeting of the States Parties to the present Covenant convened by the Secretary-General of the United Nations at the Headquarters of the United Nations. At that meeting, for which two-thirds of the States Parties to the present Covenant shall constitute a quorum, the persons elected to the Committee shall be those nominees who obtain the largest number of votes and an absolute majority of the votes of the representatives of States Parties present and voting.

Article 31

1. The Committee may not include more than one national of the same State.

2. In the election of the Committee, consideration shall be given to equitable geographical distribution of membership and to the representation of the different forms of civilization and of the principal legal systems.

Article 32

1. The members of the Committee shall be elected for a term of four years. They shall be eligible for re-election if renominated. However, the terms of nine of the members elected at the first election shall expire at the end of two years; immediately after the first election, the names of these nine members shall be chosen by lot by the Chairman of the meeting referred to in article 30, paragraph 4.

2. Elections at the expiry of office shall be held in accordance with the preceding articles of this part of the present Covenant.

Article 33

1. If, in the unanimous opinion of the other members, a member of the Committee has ceased to carry out his functions for any cause other than absence of a temporary character, the Chairman of the Committee shall notify the Secretary-General of the United Nations, who shall then declare the seat of that member to be vacant.

2. In the event of the death or the resignation of a member of the Committee, the Chairman shall immediately notify the Secretary-General of the United Nations, who shall declare the seat vacant from the date of death or the date on which the resignation takes effect.

Article 34

1. When a vacancy is declared in accordance with article 33 and if the term of office of the member to be replaced does not expire within six months of the declaration of the vacancy, the Secretary-General of the United Nations shall notify each of the States Parties to the present Covenant, which may within two months submit nominations in accordance with article 29 for the purpose of filling the vacancy.

2. The Secretary-General of the United Nations shall prepare a list in alphabetical order of the persons thus nominated and shall submit it to the States Parties to the present Covenant. The election to fill the vacancy shall then take place in accordance with the relevant provisions of this part of the present Covenant.

3. A member of the Committee elected to fill a vacancy declared in accordance with article 33 shall hold office for the remainder of the term of the member who vacated the seat on the Committee under the provisions of that article.

Article 35 The members of the Committee shall, with the approval of the General Assembly of the United Nations, receive emoluments from United Nations resources on such terms and conditions as the General Assembly may decide, having regard to the importance of the Committee's responsibilities.

Article 36 The Secretary-General of the United Nations shall provide the necessary staff and facilities for the effective performance of the functions of the Committee under the present Covenant.

Article 37

1. The Secretary-General of the United Nations shall convene the initial meeting of the Committee at the Headquarters of the United Nations.

2. After its initial meeting, the Committee shall meet at such times as shall be provided in its rules of procedure.

3. The Committee shall normally meet at the Headquarters of the United Nations or at the United Nations Office at Geneva.

Article 38 Every member of the Committee shall, before taking up his duties, make a solemn declaration in open committee that he will perform his functions impartially and conscientiously.

Article 39

1. The Committee shall elect its officers for a term of two years. They may be re-elected.

2. The Committee shall establish its own rules of procedure, but these rules shall provide, inter alia, that:

(a) Twelve members shall constitute a quorum;

(b) Decisions of the Committee shall be made by a majority vote of the members present.

Article 40

1. The States Parties to the present Covenant undertake to submit reports on the measures they have adopted which give effect to the rights recognized herein and on the progress made in the enjoyment of those rights:

(a) Within one year of the entry into force of the present Covenant for the States Parties concerned;

(b) Thereafter whenever the Committee so requests.

2. All reports shall be submitted to the Secretary-General of the United Nations, who shall transmit them to the Committee for consideration. Reports shall indicate the factors and difficulties, if any, affecting the implementation of the present Covenant.

3. The Secretary-General of the United Nations may, after consultation with the Committee, transmit to the specialized agencies concerned copies of such parts of the reports as may fall within their field of competence.

4. The Committee shall study the reports submitted by the States Parties to the present Covenant. It shall transmit its reports, and such general comments as it may consider appropriate, to the States Parties. The Committee may also transmit to the Economic and Social Council these comments along with the copies of the reports it has received from States Parties to the present Covenant.

5. The States Parties to the present Covenant may submit to the Committee observations on any comments that may be made in accordance with paragraph 4 of this article.

Article 41

1. A State Party to the present Covenant may at any time declare under this article that it recognizes the competence of the Committee to receive and consider communications to the effect that a State Party claims that another State Party is not fulfilling its obligations under the present Covenant. Communications under this article may be received and considered only if submitted by a State Party which has made a declaration recognizing in regard to itself the competence of the Committee. No communication shall be received by the Committee if it concerns a State Party which has not made such a declaration. Communications received under this article shall be dealt with in accordance with the following procedure:

(a) If a State Party to the present Covenant considers that another State Party is not giving effect to the provisions of the present Covenant, it may, by written communication, bring the matter to the attention of that State Party. Within three months after the receipt of the communication the receiving State shall afford the State which sent the communication an explanation, or any other statement in writing clarifying the matter which should include, to the extent possible and pertinent, reference to domestic procedures and remedies taken, pending, or available in the matter;

(b) If the matter is not adjusted to the satisfaction of both States Parties concerned within six months after the receipt by the receiving State of the initial communication, either State shall have the right to refer the matter to the Committee, by notice given to the Committee and to the other State;

(c) The Committee shall deal with a matter referred to it only after it has ascertained that all available domestic remedies have been invoked and exhausted in the matter, in conformity with the generally recognized principles of international law. This shall not be the rule where the application of the remedies is unreasonably prolonged;

(d) The Committee shall hold closed meetings when examining communications under this article;

(e) Subject to the provisions of subparagraph (c), the Committee shall make available its good offices to the States Parties concerned with a view to a friendly solution of the matter on the basis of respect for human rights and fundamental freedoms as recognized in the present Covenant;

(f) In any matter referred to it, the Committee may call upon the States Parties concerned, referred to in subparagraph (b), to supply any relevant information;

(g) The States Parties concerned, referred to in subparagraph (b), shall have the right to be represented when the matter is being considered in the Committee and to make submissions orally and/or in writing;

(h) The Committee shall, within twelve months after the date of receipt of notice under subparagraph (b), submit a report:

(i) If a solution within the terms of subparagraph (e) is reached, the Committee shall confine its report to a brief statement of the facts and of the solution reached;

(ii) If a solution within the terms of subparagraph (e) is not reached, the Committee shall confine its report to a brief statement of the facts; the written submissions and record of the oral submissions made by the States Parties concerned shall be attached to the report. In every matter, the report shall be communicated to the States Parties concerned.

2. The provisions of this article shall come into force when ten States Parties to the present Covenant have made declarations under paragraph 1 of this article. Such declarations shall be deposited by the States Parties with the Secretary-General of the United Nations, who shall transmit copies thereof to the other States Parties. A declaration

may be withdrawn at any time by notification to the Secretary-General. Such a withdrawal shall not prejudice the consideration of any matter which is the subject of a communication already transmitted under this article; no further communication by any State Party shall be received after the notification of withdrawal of the declaration has been received by the Secretary-General, unless the State Party concerned has made a new declaration.

Article 42

1. (a) If a matter referred to the Committee in accordance with article 41 is not resolved to the satisfaction of the States Parties concerned, the Committee may, with the prior consent of the States Parties concerned, appoint an ad hoc Conciliation Commission (hereinafter referred to as the Commission). The good offices of the Commission shall be made available to the States Parties concerned with a view to an amicable solution of the matter on the basis of respect for the present Covenant;

(b) The Commission shall consist of five persons acceptable to the States Parties concerned. If the States Parties concerned fail to reach agreement within three months on all or part of the composition of the Commission, the members of the Commission concerning whom no agreement has been reached shall be elected by secret ballot by a two-thirds majority vote of the Committee from among its members.

2. The members of the Commission shall serve in their personal capacity. They shall not be nationals of the States Parties concerned, or of a State not Party to the present Covenant, or of a State Party which has not made a declaration under article 41.

3. The Commission shall elect its own Chairman and adopt its own rules of procedure.

4. The meetings of the Commission shall normally be held at the Headquarters of the United Nations or at the United Nations Office at Geneva. However, they may be held at such other convenient places as the Commission may determine in consultation with the Secretary-General of the United Nations and the States Parties concerned.

5. The secretariat provided in accordance with article 36 shall also service the commissions appointed under this article.

6. The information received and collated by the Committee shall be made available to the Commission and the Commission may call upon the States Parties concerned to supply any other relevant information.

7. When the Commission has fully considered the matter, but in any event not later than twelve months after having been seized of the matter, it shall submit to the Chairman of the Committee a report for communication to the States Parties concerned:

(a) If the Commission is unable to complete its consideration of the matter within twelve months, it shall confine its report to a brief statement of the status of its consideration of the matter;

(b) If an amicable solution to the matter on the basis of respect for human rights as recognized in the present Covenant is reached, the Commission shall confine its report to a brief statement of the facts and of the solution reached;

(c) If a solution within the terms of subparagraph (b) is not reached, the Commission's report shall embody its findings on all questions of fact relevant to the issues between the States Parties concerned, and its views on the possibilities of an amicable solution of the matter. This report shall also contain the written submissions and a record of the oral submissions made by the States Parties concerned;

(d) If the Commission's report is submitted under subparagraph (c), the States Parties concerned shall, within three months of the receipt of the report, notify the Chairman of the Committee whether or not they accept the contents of the report of the Commission.

8. The provisions of this article are without prejudice to the responsibilities of the Committee under article 41.

9. The States Parties concerned shall share equally all the expenses of the members of the Commission in accordance with estimates to be provided by the Secretary-General of the United Nations.

10. The Secretary-General of the United Nations shall be empowered to pay the expenses of the members of the Commission, if necessary, before reimbursement by the States Parties concerned, in accordance with paragraph 9 of this article.

Article 43   The members of the Committee, and of the ad hoc conciliation commissions which may be appointed under article 42, shall be entitled to the facilities, privileges and immunities of experts on mission for the United Nations as laid down in the relevant sections of the Convention on the Privileges and Immunities of the United Nations.

Article 44   The provisions for the implementation of the present Covenant shall apply without prejudice to the procedures prescribed in the field of human rights by or under the constituent instruments and the conventions of the United Nations and of the specialized agencies and shall not prevent the States Parties to the present Covenant from having recourse to other procedures for settling a dispute in accordance with general or special international agreements in force between them.

Article 45   The Committee shall submit to the General Assembly of the United Nations, through the Economic and Social Council, an annual report on its activities.

PART V

Article 46   Nothing in the present Covenant shall be interpreted as impairing the provisions of the Charter of the United Nations and of the constitutions of the specialized agencies which define the respective responsibilities of the various organs of the United Nations and of the specialized agencies in regard to the matters dealt with in the present Covenant.

Article 47   Nothing in the present Covenant shall be interpreted as impairing the inherent right of all peoples to enjoy and utilize fully and freely their natural wealth and resources.

PART VI

Article 48

1. The present Covenant is open for signature by any State Member of the United Nations or member of any of its specialized agencies, by any State Party to the Statute of the International Court of Justice, and by any other State which has been invited by the General Assembly of the United Nations to become a Party to the present Covenant.

2. The present Covenant is subject to ratification. Instruments of ratification shall be deposited with the Secretary-General of the United Nations.

3. The present Covenant shall be open to accession by any State referred to in paragraph 1 of this article.

4. Accession shall be effected by the deposit of an instrument of accession with the Secretary-General of the United Nations.

5. The Secretary-General of the United Nations shall inform all States which have signed this Covenant or acceded to it of the deposit of each instrument of ratification or accession.

Article 49

1. The present Covenant shall enter into force three months after the date of the deposit with the Secretary-General of the United Nations of the thirty-fifth instrument of ratification or instrument of accession.

2. For each State ratifying the present Covenant or acceding to it after the deposit of the thirty-fifth instrument of ratification or instrument of accession, the present Covenant shall enter into force three months after the date of the deposit of its own instrument of ratification or instrument of accession.

Article 50   The provisions of the present Covenant shall extend to all parts of federal States without any limitations or exceptions.

Article 51

1. Any State Party to the present Covenant may propose an amendment and file it with the Secretary-General of the United Nations. The Secretary-General of the United Nations shall thereupon communicate any proposed amendments to the States Parties to the present Covenant with a request that they notify him whether they favour a conference of States Parties for the purpose of considering and voting upon the proposals. In the event that at least one-third of the States Parties favours such a conference, the Secretary-General shall convene the conference under the auspices of the United Nations. Any amendment adopted by a majority of the States Parties present and voting at the conference shall be submitted to the General Assembly of the United Nations for approval.

2. Amendments shall come into force when they have been approved by the General Assembly of the United Nations and accepted by a two-thirds majority of the States Parties to the present Covenant in accordance with their respective constitutional processes.

3. When amendments come into force, they shall be binding on those States Parties which have accepted them, other States Parties still being bound by the provisions of the present Covenant and any earlier amendment which they have accepted.

Article 52

1. Irrespective of the notifications made under article 48, paragraph 5, the Secretary-General of the United Nations shall inform all States referred to in paragraph 1 of the same article of the following particulars:

(a) Signatures, ratifications and accessions under article 48;

(b) The date of the entry into force of the present Covenant under article 49 and the date of the entry into force of any amendments under article 51.

Article 53

1. The present Covenant, of which the Chinese, English, French, Russian and Spanish texts are equally authentic, shall be deposited in the archives of the United Nations.

2. The Secretary-General of the United Nations shall transmit certified copies of the present Covenant to all States referred to in article 48.

(Available at www.ohchr.org/english/law/ccpr.htm)

Optional Protocol to the International Covenant on Civil and Political Rights

Adopted and opened for signature, ratification, and accession by General Assembly resolution 2200A (XXI) of 16 December 1966, the protocol entered into force 23 March 1976, in accordance with Article 9.

The States Parties to the present Protocol,

Considering that in order further to achieve the purposes of the International Covenant on Civil and Political Rights (hereinafter referred to as the Covenant) and the implementation of its provisions it would be appropriate to enable the Human Rights Committee set up in part IV of the Covenant (hereinafter referred to as the Committee) to receive and consider, as provided in the present Protocol, communications from individuals claiming to be victims of violations of any of the rights set forth in the Covenant.

Have agreed as follows:

Article 1   A State Party to the Covenant that becomes a Party to the present Protocol recognizes the competence of the Committee to receive and consider communications from individuals subject to its jurisdiction who claim to be victims of a violation by that State Party of any of the rights set forth in the Covenant. No communication shall be received by the Committee if it concerns a State Party to the Covenant which is not a Party to the present Protocol.

Article 2   Subject to the provisions of article 1, individuals who claim that any of their rights enumerated in the Covenant have been violated and who have exhausted all available domestic remedies may submit a written communication to the Committee for consideration.

Article 3   The Committee shall consider inadmissible any communication under the present Protocol which is anonymous, or which it considers to be an abuse of the right of submission of such communications or to be incompatible with the provisions of the Covenant.

Article 4

1. Subject to the provisions of article 3, the Committee shall bring any communications submitted to it under the present Protocol to the attention of the State Party to the present Protocol alleged to be violating any provision of the Covenant.

2. Within six months, the receiving State shall submit to the Committee written explanations or statements clarifying the matter and the remedy, if any, that may have been taken by that State.

Article 5

1. The Committee shall consider communications received under the present Protocol in the light of all written information made available to it by the individual and by the State Party concerned.

2. The Committee shall not consider any communication from an individual unless it has ascertained that:

(a) The same matter is not being examined under another procedure of international investigation or settlement;

(b) The individual has exhausted all available domestic remedies. This shall not be the rule where the application of the remedies is unreasonably prolonged.

3. The Committee shall hold closed meetings when examining communications under the present Protocol.

4. The Committee shall forward its views to the State Party concerned and to the individual.

Article 6
The Committee shall include in its annual report under article 45 of the Covenant a summary of its activities under the present Protocol.

Article 7
Pending the achievement of the objectives of resolution 1514 (XV) adopted by the General Assembly of the United Nations on 14 December 1960 concerning the Declaration on the Granting of Independence to Colonial Countries and Peoples, the provisions of the present Protocol shall in no way limit the right of petition granted to these peoples by the Charter of the United Nations and other international conventions and instruments under the United Nations and its specialized agencies.

Article 8

1. The present Protocol is open for signature by any State which has signed the Covenant.

2. The present Protocol is subject to ratification by any State which has ratified or acceded to the Covenant. Instruments of ratification shall be deposited with the Secretary-General of the United Nations.

3. The present Protocol shall be open to accession by any State which has ratified or acceded to the Covenant.

4. Accession shall be effected by the deposit of an instrument of accession with the Secretary-General of the United Nations.

5. The Secretary-General of the United Nations shall inform all States which have signed the present Protocol or acceded to it of the deposit of each instrument of ratification or accession.

Article 9

1. Subject to the entry into force of the Covenant, the present Protocol shall enter into force three months after the date of the deposit with the Secretary-General of the United Nations of the tenth instrument of ratification or instrument of accession.

2. For each State ratifying the present Protocol or acceding to it after the deposit of the tenth instrument of ratification or instrument of accession, the present Protocol shall enter into force three months after the date of the deposit of its own instrument of ratification or instrument of accession.

Article 10   The provisions of the present Protocol shall extend to all parts of federal States without any limitations or exceptions.

Article 11

1. Any State Party to the present Protocol may propose an amendment and file it with the Secretary-General of the United Nations. The Secretary-General shall thereupon communicate any proposed amendments to the States Parties to the present Protocol with a request that they notify him whether they favour a conference of States Parties for the purpose of considering and voting upon the proposal. In the event that at least one-third of the States Parties favours such a conference, the Secretary-General shall convene the conference under the auspices of the United Nations. Any amendment adopted by a majority of the States Parties present and voting at the conference shall be submitted to the General Assembly of the United Nations for approval.

2. Amendments shall come into force when they have been approved by the General Assembly of the United Nations and accepted by a two-thirds majority of the States Parties to the present Protocol in accordance with their respective constitutional processes.

3. When amendments come into force, they shall be binding on those States Parties which have accepted them, other States Parties still being bound by the provisions of the present Protocol and any earlier amendment which they have accepted.

Article 12

1. Any State Party may denounce the present Protocol at any time by written notification addressed to the Secretary-General of the United Nations. Denunciation shall take effect three months after the date of receipt of the notification by the Secretary-General.

2. Denunciation shall be without prejudice to the continued application of the provisions of the present Protocol to any communication submitted under article 2 before the effective date of denunciation.

Article 13   Irrespective of the notifications made under article 8, paragraph 5, of the present Protocol, the Secretary-General of the United Nations shall inform all States referred to in article 48, paragraph I, of the Covenant of the following particulars:

(a) Signatures, ratifications and accessions under article 8;

(b) The date of the entry into force of the present Protocol under article 9 and the date of the entry into force of any amendments under article 11;

(c) Denunciations under article 12.

Article 14

1. The present Protocol, of which the Chinese, English, French, Russian and Spanish texts are equally authentic, shall be deposited in the archives of the United Nations.

2. The Secretary-General of the United Nations shall transmit certified copies of the present Protocol to all States referred to in article 48 of the Covenant.

Second Optional Protocol to the International Covenant on Civil and Political Rights, Aiming at the Abolition of the Death Penalty

This protocol was adopted and proclaimed by General Assembly resolution 44/128 of 15 December 1989.

The States Parties to the present Protocol,

Believing that abolition of the death penalty contributes to enhancement of human dignity and progressive development of human rights,

Recalling article 3 of the Universal Declaration of Human Rights, adopted on 10 December 1948, and article 6 of the International Covenant on Civil and Political Rights, adopted on 16 December 1966,

Noting that article 6 of the International Covenant on Civil and Political Rights refers to abolition of the death penalty in terms that strongly suggest that abolition is desirable,

Convinced that all measures of abolition of the death penalty should be considered as progress in the enjoyment of the right to life,

Desirous to undertake hereby an international commitment to abolish the death penalty,

Have agreed as follows:

Article 1

1. No one within the jurisdiction of a State Party to the present Protocol shall be executed.

2. Each State Party shall take all necessary measures to abolish the death penalty within its jurisdiction.

Article 2

1. No reservation is admissible to the present Protocol, except for a reservation made at the time of ratification or accession that provides for the application of the death penalty in time of war pursuant to a conviction for a most serious crime of a military nature committed during wartime.

2. The State Party making such a reservation shall at the time of ratification or accession communicate to the Secretary-General of the United Nations the relevant provisions of its national legislation applicable during wartime.

3. The State Party having made such a reservation shall notify the Secretary-General of the United Nations of any beginning or ending of a state of war applicable to its territory.

Article 3   The States Parties to the present Protocol shall include in the reports they submit to the Human Rights Committee, in accordance with article 40 of the Covenant, information on the measures that they have adopted to give effect to the present Protocol.

Article 4   With respect to the States Parties to the Covenant that have made a declaration under article 41, the competence of the Human Rights Committee to receive and consider communications when a State Party claims that another State Party is not fulfilling its obligations shall extend to the provisions of the present Protocol, unless the State Party concerned has made a statement to the contrary at the moment of ratification or accession.

Article 5   With respect to the States Parties to the first Optional Protocol to the International Covenant on Civil and Political Rights adopted on 16 December 1966, the competence of the Human Rights Committee to receive and consider communications from individuals subject to its jurisdiction shall extend to the provisions of the present Protocol, unless the State Party concerned has made a statement to the contrary at the moment of ratification or accession.

Article 6

1. The provisions of the present Protocol shall apply as additional provisions to the Covenant.

2. Without prejudice to the possibility of a reservation under article 2 of the present Protocol, the right guaranteed in article 1, paragraph 1, of the present Protocol shall not be subject to any derogation under article 4 of the Covenant.

Article 7

1. The present Protocol is open for signature by any State that has signed the Covenant.

2. The present Protocol is subject to ratification by any State that has ratified the Covenant or acceded to it. Instruments of ratification shall be deposited with the Secretary-General of the United Nations.

3. The present Protocol shall be open to accession by any State that has ratified the Covenant or acceded to it.

4. Accession shall be effected by the deposit of an instrument of accession with the Secretary-General of the United Nations.

5. The Secretary-General of the United Nations shall inform all States that have signed the present Protocol or acceded to it of the deposit of each instrument of ratification or accession.

Article 8

1. The present Protocol shall enter into force three months after the date of the deposit with the Secretary-General of the United Nations of the tenth instrument of ratification or accession.

2. For each State ratifying the present Protocol or acceding to it after the deposit of the tenth instrument of ratification or accession, the present Protocol shall enter into force three months after the date of the deposit of its own instrument of ratification or accession.

Article 9   The provisions of the present Protocol shall extend to all parts of federal States without any limitations or exceptions.

Article 10   The Secretary-General of the United Nations shall inform all States referred to in article 48, paragraph 1, of the Covenant of the following particulars:

(a) Reservations, communications and notifications under article 2 of the present Protocol;

(b) Statements made under articles 4 or 5 of the present Protocol;

(c) Signatures, ratifications and accessions under article 7 of the present Protocol:

(d) The date of the entry into force of the present Protocol under article 8 thereof.

Article 11
   1. The present Protocol, of which the Arabic, Chinese, English, French, Russian and Spanish texts are equally authentic, shall be deposited in the archives of the United Nations.
   2. The Secretary-General of the United Nations shall transmit certified copies of the present Protocol to all States referred to in article 48 of the Covenant.

Monitoring Bodies for Core Human Rights Treaties

The seven treaties considered to be the core human rights treaties, along with optional protocols, are listed below. The implementation of these treaties is monitored by committees, or treaty monitoring bodies, that were established by the treaties. The names of each of these seven bodies are presented below before the names of the treaties that created them. These "treaty monitoring bodies" are composed of independent experts of recognized competence in the field of human rights who are elected by states that are parties to the treaty. All treaty bodies are serviced by the Office of the High Commissioner for Human Rights in Geneva, with the exception of the Committee on the Elimination of Discrimination against Women, which is serviced by the Division for the Advancement of Women in New York.

Committee on Economic, Social and Cultural Rights (CESCR)

Convention on Economic, Social and Cultural Rights, 1966.

Human Rights Committee (HRC)

Covenant on Civil and Political Rights, 1966.

Committee on the Elimination of Racial Discrimination (CERD)

International Convention on the Elimination of All Forms of Racial Discrimination, 1965.

Committee on the Elimination of Discrimination Against Women (CEDAW)

Convention on the Elimination of All Forms of Discrimination Against Women, 1979.

Optional Protocol to the Convention on the Elimination of All Forms of Discrimination against Women, 1999.

Committee Against Torture (CAT)

Convention Against Torture and Other Cruel, Inhuman or Degrading Treatment or Punishment, 1984.

Committee on the Rights of the Child (CRC)

Convention on the Rights of the Child, 1989.

Optional Protocol to the Convention on the Rights of the Child on the Involvement of Children in Armed Conflict, 2000.

Optional Protocol to the Convention on the Rights of the Child on the Sale of Children, Child Prostitution and Child Pornography, 2000.

Committee on Migrant Workers (CMW)

International Convention on the Protection of the Rights of All Migrant Workers and Members of Their Families, 1990.

UN Electoral Assistance

UN electoral assistance is responsive to the Universal Declaration of Human Rights assertion that "[t]he will of the people shall be the basis of the authority of government; this shall be expressed in periodic and genuine elections which shall be by universal and equal suffrage and shall be held by secret vote." The UN Electoral Assistance Division, established in April 1992 in accordance with General Assembly resolution A/RES/46/137, is responsible for the coordination of the activities of the UN System in the field of electoral assistance. The division advises and assists the under-secretary-general for political affairs who serves as the focal point for UN electoral assistance activities. By the end of 2004, 101 states had requested assistance and 91 had been assisted.

There are two main categories of United Nations electoral assistance: standard electoral assistance activities and major electoral missions, which are normally conducted within the context of comprehensive peacekeeping operations.

Standard Electoral Assistance Activities are of four types:

1. Coordination and support of international observers. Although considerable international attention has been given to the role of the United Nations in supporting election components of peacekeeping operations, most electoral assistance provided by the United Nations is relatively small-scale assistance that does not require a mandate from the General Assembly or the Security Council. This type of assistance was first provided in Ethiopia and Kenya in 1992 and later provided to support the international observation of elections in Niger (1993), Lesotho (1993), Malawi (1993 and 1994), Tanzania (1995), Armenia (1995), Azerbaijan (1995), Sierra Leone (1996), Mali (1997), and Algeria (1997), among others.
2. Technical assistance. Technical assistance, the most frequently requested type of electoral assistance, involves a broad range of short- and long-term assistance to national election authorities responsible for administering elections in their countries. Various subsidiary bodies of the United Nations regularly provide advice and assistance to local electoral authorities for electoral administration and planning, voter registration, election budgeting, review of electoral laws and regulations, training of election officials, logistics, voter and civic education, procurement of election materials, coordination of international donor assistance, electoral dispute resolution, computerization of electoral rolls, and boundary delimitation. The range of technical assistance provided by the United Nations has expanded as its experience has grown.
3. Support for national election monitors. This form of assistance underscores the importance of building the domestic observation capacity of member states by supporting the activities of civil society to monitor elections on a nonpartisan basis. Following a government

request, technical assistance (e.g., training, advisory assistance) may be provided to a national network of domestic monitoring groups sponsored by local, nonpartisan civic organizations. This type of assistance is best utilized in countries that are relatively well developed and pluralistic and possess a viable community of civic organizations interested in undertaking national election observation activities. Support for national election observers was provided in Mexico in 1994 and 1997.

4. Limited observation. In special cases, a small United Nations observer team, usually composed of UN political affairs officers, may be sent to a country to follow the final phase of an electoral process and issue an internal report to the secretary-general on its conduct.

Major electoral missions are exceptional and require a mandate from the General Assembly or the Security Council. They are normally a central element of comprehensive peacekeeping operations. When the United Nations is mandated to organize and conduct an election or referendum, it assumes a role normally fulfilled by national electoral authorities. This requires the establishment of a system of laws, procedures, and administrative measures necessary for the holding of free and fair elections, as well as the actual administration of the electoral process, that is, the establishment of a legal framework, the registration of voters, and the proper conduct of elections in accordance with international norms. Due to the cost, scope, and lead time required, this type of assistance operation is undertaken only in special postconflict situations in which there is insufficient national institutional capacity to organize elections. Examples of major electoral missions are (1) the United Nations Transitional Authority in Cambodia (UNTAC) that was responsible for the organization and execution of national elections in Cambodia in May 1993 as part of a comprehensive peace plan and (2) the United Nations Transitional Authority in Eastern Slavonia, Baranja and Western Sirmium (UNTAES) that was requested to organize elections for all local government bodies in April 1997 in cooperation with Croatian authorities (www.un.org/Depts/dpa/ead/ea).

Examples of Human Rights Activities of Other UN Agencies

The activities and policies of organizations throughout the UN System affect a diversity of economic, social, cultural, civil, and political rights. As a result there has been a growing effort by those concerned with human rights to ensure that these activities and policies are consistent with human rights standards in the International Bill of Rights and other human rights treaties. Examples of this trend are offered below by the human rights involvements of four Specialized Agencies followed by those of three UN programs.

International Labor Organization (ILO); Labor Standard Conventions

The ILO labor standards take the form of international labor conventions and recommendations. They set standards for freedom of association, the right to organize, collective bargaining, abolition of forced labor, equality of opportunity and treatment, and other standards regulating conditions across the entire spectrum of work-related issues. The conventions are international treaties, subject to ratification by ILO member states. Recommendations are nonbinding instruments that set out guidelines that can orient national policy and action.

The two key elements of regular ILO supervision are the submission of government reports and their examination. Concerning the first, the ILO constitution contains provisions under which governments have to report to the ILO on measures taken to give effect to conventions they have voluntarily ratified. These reports are forwarded to a Committee of Experts on the Application of Conventions and Recommendations. Subsequently reports of the committee of experts are submitted to the annual session of the International Labor Conference where each is examined by a special tripartite conference committee made up of representatives of governments, labor organizations, and businesses.

The ILO considers eight conventions to be fundamental. The date provided is the date of adoption.

Freedom of association

1. Freedom of Association and Protection of the Right to Organize Convention, 1948 (No. 87).
2. Right to Organize and Collective Bargaining Convention, 1949 (No. 98).

The abolition of forced labor

3. Forced Labor Convention, 1930 (No. 29).
4. Abolition of Forced Labor Convention, 1957 (No. 105). United States ratified, 1991.

Equality

5. Discrimination (Employment and Occupation) Convention, 1958 (No. 111).
6. Equal Remuneration Convention, 1951 (No. 100).

The elimination of child labor

7. Minimum Age Convention, 1973 (No. 138).
8. Worst Forms of Child Labor Convention, 1999 (No. 182). United States ratified, 1999.

UN Educational, Scientific and Cultural Organization (UNESCO); Promotion of Education as a Fundamental Human Right

UNESCO views its mission as the promotion of education as a fundamental right.

The core purpose of UNESCO's education program is to achieve education for all (EFA) seen in its broadest sense: education for all, at all levels, throughout life. Education is the foundation of personal fulfillment, of economic growth, and of social cohesion. It is a critical factor in overcoming poverty and ensuring sustainable development. At the World Education Forum, held in Dakar, Senegal, in 2003, the 1,100 participants adopted the Dakar Framework for Action, a commitment to achieving education for all by the year 2015. The World Education Forum set an agenda for progress towards this aim expressed as six goals: (1) expanding and improving comprehensive early childhood care and education, especially for the most vulnerable and disadvantaged children; (2) ensuring that by 2015 all children, particularly girls, children in difficult circumstances, and those belonging to ethnic minorities, have access to and complete free and compulsory primary education of good quality; (3) ensuring that the learning needs of all young people and adults are met through equitable access to appropriate learning and life-skills programs; (4) achieving a 50 percent improvement in levels of adult literacy by 2015, especially for women, and equitable access to basic and continuing education for all adults; (5) eliminating gender disparities in primary and secondary education by 2005, and achieving gender equality in education by 2015, with a focus on ensuring girls' full and equal access to and achievement in basic education of good quality; and (6) improving all aspects of the quality of education and ensuring excellence of all so that recognized and measurable learning outcomes are achieved by all.

The five principal functions of UNESCO provide a useful context for its promotion of education. These functions are to be (1) a laboratory of ideas, (2) a standard setter, (3) a clearing house, (4) a capacity builder, and (5) a catalyst for international cooperation. The function of catalyst for international cooperation is particularly salient for the education program because UNESCO has the responsibility for coordinating the global movement to achieve education for all (EFA). Since 2000 it has developed links with four key stakeholder groups, namely governments of developing countries, multinational agencies, civil society, and bilateral development agencies. This has enabled UNESCO and the other agencies to develop their work in a complementary fashion so that each plays to its areas of strength and comparative advantage (www.unesco.org).

Food and Agriculture Organization (FAO); Guidelines on the Right to Food

The attention of the reader is drawn to the extensive connection between FAO's concern with the right to food and WHO's concern with the right to health that follows.

The Covenant on Economic, Social and Cultural Rights, which came into force in 1976, declares that "[t]he States Parties to the present covenant recognize the right of everyone to an adequate standard of living for himself and his family, including adequate food, clothing, and housing" (article 11). The right to food has been repeated in three subsequent international instruments:

1. Two articles in the Convention on the Rights of the Child, which came into force in 1990, address the issue of nutrition. Article 24 asserts: "States Parties recognize the right of the child to enjoyment of the highest attainable standard of health . . ." and shall take appropriate measures "to combat disease and malnutrition" through the provision of adequate nutritious foods, clean drinking water, and health care. Article 27 says: "States Parties shall in case of need provide material assistance and support programs, particularly with regard to nutrition, clothing, and housing."
2. The World Declaration on Nutrition, adopted at the Joint FAO/WHO International Conference on Nutrition (Rome, 1992), affirmed that "access to nutritionally adequate and safe food is a right of each individual" (www.fao.org/docrep/U9920t/u9920t0a.htm).
3. In the Rome Declaration on World Food Security (World Food Summit, 1996) heads of state and government reaffirmed "the right of everyone to have access to safe and nutritious food, consistent with the right to adequate food and the fundamental right of everyone to be free from hunger" (www.fao.org/DOCREP/003/W3613E/W3613E00.HTM).

In September 2004 the FAO Committee on World Food Security (CFS) adopted voluntary guidelines to "support the progressive realization of the right to adequate food in the context of national food security." According to the FAO, various nongovernmental and intergovernmental organizations contributed significantly to the preparation of the guidelines. These included the Office of the High Commissioner for Human Rights; the UN Special Rapporteur on the Right to Food; and the Committee on Economic, Social and Cultural Rights; and the North-South Alliance, which is a coalition of a large number of NGOs. The FAO says the guidelines are a "human rights-based practical tool addressed to all states." They cover the full range of actions that need to be taken at the national level to build an environment enabling people to feed themselves and to establish safety nets for those who are unable to do so. "The adoption of these Voluntary Guidelines constitutes a major breakthrough. This is the first time that an intergovernmental body agrees on what the right to food really means," said Giuliano Pucci, FAO legal counsel (www.fao.org/newsroom/en/news/2004/50821).

World Health Organization (WHO) and the Right to the Highest Attainable Health Quality

The preamble to the WHO constitution states that "[t]he enjoyment of the highest attainable standard of health is one of the fundamental rights of every human being." The WHO has reported that "every country in the world is now party to at least one human rights treaty that addresses health-related rights, including the right to health and a number of rights related to conditions necessary for health. UN Secretary General Kofi Annan has stated: 'It is my aspiration that health will finally be seen not as a blessing to be wished for; but as a human right to be fought for'" (www.who.int/hhr/en).

The WHO cites these international instruments as a basis for its human rights obligations:

1. The Universal Declaration of Human Rights (1948) asserted that "everyone has the right to a standard of living adequate for health and well-being of himself and his family, including food" (article 25 (1)).
2. This position is echoed in the constitution of the World Health Organization (1948), which affirms that promoting the improvement of nutrition (article 2) is among the specific ways that WHO can achieve its objective, "the attainment by all peoples of the highest possible level of health" (article 1).
3. In 1981, the World Health Assembly adopted the International Code of Marketing of Breast-milk Substitutes that emphasizes providing "safe and adequate nutrition for infants" (article 1). On this occasion, the member states of the World Health Organization affirmed "the right of every child and every pregnant and lactating woman to be adequately nourished as a means of attaining and maintaining health" (Code preamble, paragraph 1).
4. In the Convention on the Rights of the Child, which came into force in 1990, two articles address the issue of

nutrition. According to article 24, "States Parties recognize the right of the child to enjoyment of the highest attainable standard of health" and shall take appropriate measures "to combat disease and malnutrition" through the provision of adequate nutritious foods, clean drinking water, and health care.

The WHO website lists three main objectives in the field of health and human rights:

1. To strengthen WHO's capacity to integrate a human rights-based approach in its work
2. To support governments to integrate a human rights-based approach in health development
3. To advance the right to health in international law and international development processes.

It makes these points as evidence that protecting health and fulfilling human rights are inextricably linked:

1. Violations or lack of attention to human rights can have serious health consequences, for example, slavery, torture, and inhuman and degrading treatment.
2. Health policies and programs can promote or violate human rights in their design or implementation, for example, freedom from discrimination, individual autonomy, and rights to participation.
3. Vulnerability to ill health can be reduced by taking steps to respect, protect, and fulfill human rights, for example, ensuring freedom from discrimination on account of race, sex, and gender roles and establishing rights to health, food, and nutrition and to education and housing. (www.who.int)

UN Environment Program (UNEP) and the Right to a Pollution-Free Environment

On 27 April 2001 the UN Commission on Human Rights declared that everyone has the right to live in a world free from toxic pollution and environmental degradation. This was the first time the commission addressed the links between the environment and human rights. The UN high commissioner for human rights, and the executive director of the UN Environment Program (UNEP) were invited to organize an international seminar to explore how environmental and human rights principles can be strengthened. Klaus Toepfer, executive director of UNEP, welcomed the historic move by saying: "Many of the fundamental rights enshrined in the Universal Declaration of Human Rights have significant environmental dimensions." (The information and quotes in this section were acquired from UNEP Information Note 2003/05 at www.unep.org/Documents.Multilingual/Default. It is now available through a search of www.unep.org.)

On 25 April 2003 the UN Commission on Human Rights passed a resolution on Human Rights and the Environment as Part of Sustainable Development. This resolution was welcomed by the UNEP executive director with these words: "People can only achieve their full human potential when their natural environment is robust and respected. . . . The existence of clean air, clean water, a stable climate, thriving wildlife and well-managed natural resources determines the extent to which people can enjoy their basic rights to life, health, food, housing, livelihood and culture. . . . Today's decision on 'Human Rights and the Environment as Part of Sustainable Development' states that the 'protection of the environment and sustainable development can also contribute to human well-being and potentially to the enjoyment of human rights. Respect for human rights and fundamental freedoms are essential for achieving sustainable development. . . . Environmental damage can have potentially negative effects on the enjoyment of some human rights'."

This decision of the Human Rights Commission emphasizes the importance for states, in their environmental policies, to take into account the impact of environmental degradation on disadvantaged members of society. The UNEP website states that "[t]he Commission's decision provides a good basis for further cooperation between UNEP and the Office of the High Commissioner for Human Rights on promoting the linkages between human rights and the environment, including efforts to strengthen the role of the judiciary in supporting the goals of sustainable development."

UN High Commissioner for Refugees (UNHCR); Protection of Human Rights

In more than five decades the UNHCR has helped an estimated 50 million people restart their lives. In 2005 a staff of more than 6,000 people in more than 116 countries strove to help some 17 million displaced persons (www.unhcr.ch/cgi-bin/texis/vtx/basics).

In June 1994 Sadako Ogata, UN high commissioner for refugees, accepted the Human Rights Award from the International Human Rights Law Group. The edited excerpts from her acceptance speech that follow clearly illuminate the human rights dimension of the problems confronted by refugees:

> The Award is a tribute to the tireless efforts of more than 4,000 UNHCR staff members, many of whom are risking their lives daily to defend the human rights of those who are forced to flee their homes. Above all, the Award is an acknowledgment that the plight of refugees and the displaced is as much a human rights problem as it is a humanitarian one.
>
> There is growing support today for a comprehensive strategy which addresses the entire continuum of refugee flows from causes through emergency response, protection and eventual solution. This means not only responding to refugee situations in countries of asylum, but also focusing on the situation in the country of origin.
>
> How does such a strategy retain its human rights focus? Let me outline three areas. Firstly, it does so by ensuring that refugees continue to be protected, even on a temporary basis. All states parties to the 1951 United Nations Refugee Convention and its 1967 Protocol must apply these instruments fully and liberally. At the same time, I would also advocate a more temporary form of protection through which victims of war and generalized violence who are not covered by the Refugee Convention Protocol can find the sanctuary they badly need, while host governments can afford to be more generous in the expectation that they need to provide protection only for as long as it is needed.
>
> The second way in which the human rights aspect is upheld is through the protection of the internally dis-

placed. It should be perceived not as an alternative to asylum, but as an important complement, easing the protection of refugees, rather than undermining it. Although UNHCR does not have a general mandate for the internally displaced, we have assisted in specific cases, at the request of the Secretary-General, in northern Iraq, Sri Lanka, Ethiopia, Afghanistan, Central America, Bosnia-Herzegovina, and now in Georgia.

The third and final aspect of the human rights approach to refuge problems is the promotion of human rights so that people are not forced to flee, and those who have left home can safely return. We must prevent refugee flows, not by building barriers or border controls but by defending the right of people to remain in peace in their own homes and their own countries. When people have to leave their homes to escape persecution or armed conflict, a whole range of human rights are violated, including the right to life, liberty and security of person, the right not to be subjected to torture or other degrading treatment, the right to privacy and family life, the right to freedom of movement and residence, and the right not to be subjected to arbitrary exile. How do we secure people's right to remain at home, how can we promote tolerance and defend the human rights of all those who live among us: these are urgent questions facing the international community, to which, I regret to say, we have yet to find an adequate response. (www.unhcr.ch)

Habitat (UNHSP) and a Rights-Based Approach to Urban Poverty Reduction

At its seventeenth session in 1999, the Governing Council of Habitat (UN Human Settlements Program) adopted a new vision statement for Habitat. It charts a new course for Habitat by espousing a rights-based approach to urban poverty reduction. The vision statement endorsed three new initiatives with the goal of reducing urban poverty: the Global Campaign for Secure Tenure, the Global Campaign for Urban Governance, and the Cities Alliance (launched in partnership with the World Bank).

The Global Campaign for Secure Tenure promotes the security of tenure of the urban poor. The absence of the threat of eviction offers incentives for investment by slum dwellers, public authorities, and private individuals and corporations. Security of tenure improves the access of slum dwellers to urban basic services and credit. It can formalize governmental recognition of the right of slum dwellers to organize and make claims on and negotiate the use of public resources. The Global Campaign recognizes that, in many cases, the urban poor are not passively waiting for solutions from the government, the private sector, or nongovernmental organizations (NGOs). They are finding their own solutions that the Global Campaign seeks to learn from and support.

Grounded in human rights, the Global Campaign for Urban Governance promotes the right to development and the civil and political right of participation. Inclusive processes of decision making are recognized as the best means for the effective use of scarce development resources, for the equitable distribution of the benefits of development, and for ensuring the sustainability of hard-won benefits. The Global Campaign is committed to working with local governments and their associations to explore mechanisms for involving the urban poor, particularly women, in the decisions that affect their lives and their cities.

The Cities Alliance aims to improve the impact of international development cooperation efforts to reduce urban poverty. Admitting that there is not enough to show for money already invested in urban development, it recognizes the need for engaging and learning from the urban poor and from their partnerships with government at all levels. The Cities Alliance regards such engagement as necessary for improving the quality of living and working conditions of the urban poor. Focus is being placed on two approaches: slum upgrading and city development strategies, which are linked to the Global Campaigns and to the twin mandates of Habitat: "Shelter for All" and "Sustainable Urban Development" (www.unhabitat.org/HD/hdv6n4/advocacy.htm).

UN Peacekeeping Operations

The UN Charter stipulates that, to assist in maintaining peace and security around the world, all member states should make available to the Security Council necessary armed forces and facilities. From 1948 to 2005, close to 130 states have contributed military and civilian police personnel to peace operations. It is estimated that up to 1 million soldiers, police officers, and civilians have served the United Nations in the last 56 years. As of June 2004, 97 countries were contributing a total of more than 56,000 uniformed personnel—the highest number since 1995.

The initial peacekeeping missions tended to consist primarily of small units, lightly armed, patrolling cease-fire lines. More recently, after the end of the Cold War, peacekeeping missions have become larger and more complex. In addition, they now increasingly involve nonmilitary elements to ensure sustainability. The UN Department of Peacekeeping Operations was created in 1992 to support this increased demand for complex peacekeeping.

In 1993 annual UN peacekeeping costs peaked at some $3.6 billion, reflecting the expense of operations in the former Yugoslavia and Somalia. Compared to the costs of national police and military expenditures, peacekeeping costs very little. The United Nations spends less per year on peacekeeping worldwide than the City of New York spends on the annual budgets of its fire and police departments. UN peacekeeping cost about $2.6 billion in 2002. In the same year, governments worldwide spent more than $794 billion on arms. The approved UN peacekeeping budget for the year 2004–2005 is $2.80 billion (www.un.org/ Depts/dpko/dpko/faq/q6.htm).

In 2005 there were eighteen peacekeeping operations; in the Middle East (three), Asia (three), the Americas (one), Africa (eight), and Europe (three). In the past there have been forty-four completed peacekeeping operations, in the Middle East (six), Europe (seven), Asia (eight), the Americas (eight), and Africa (fifteen) (www.un.org/Depts/dpko/dpko/index.asp).

UN Peacekeeping Operations in 2005

Middle East (3):

UN Disengagement Observer Force (UNDOF) (Golan Heights)

UN Interim Force in Lebanon (UNIFIL) (Lebanon)

UN Truce Supervision Organization (UNTSO)
(Golan Heights, Lebanon, Sinai)

Asia (3):

UN Office in Timor-Leste (UNOTIL)

UN Military Observer Group in India and Pakistan
(UNMOGIP)

UN Assistance Mission in Afghanistan
(UNAMA)
Americas (1):
UN Stabilization Mission in Haiti (MINUSTAH)
Africa (8):
UN Mission in the Sudan (UNMIS)
UN Operation in Burundi (ONUB)
UN Operation in Côte d' Ivoire (UNOCI) (Ivory Coast)
UN Observer Mission in Liberia (UNMIL)
UN Organization Mission in Democratic Republic of the Congo
(MONUC)
UN Mission in Ethiopia and Eritrea (UNMEE)
UN Mission in Sierra Leone (UNAMSIL)
UN Mission for the Referendum in Western Sahara(MINURSO)
Europe (3):
UN Observer Mission in Georgia (UNOMIG)
UN Interim Administration Mission in Kosovo (UNMIK)
UN Peacekeeping Force in Cyprus (UNFICYP)

Past Peacekeeping Operations

Middle East (6):
UN Iran-Iraq Military Observer Group (UNIIMOG)
UN Observation Group in Lebanon (UNOGIL)
UN Emergency Force I (UNEF I) (Suez Canal, Sinai, Gaza)
UN Emergency Force II (UNEF II) (Egypt-Israel Border)
UN Yemen Observation Mission (UNYOM)
UN Iraq-Kuwait Observation Mission (UNIKOM)
Europe (7):
UN Confidence Restoration Operation in Croatia (UNCRO)
UN Transitional Administration for Eastern Slavonia, Baranja,
and Western Sirmium (UNTAES) (Croatia)
UN Civilian Police Support Group (UNPSG) (Croatia)
UN Protection Force (UNPROFOR) Croatia, Bosnia and
Herzegovina, and Republicc of Macedonia
UN Preventive Deployment Force (UNPREDEP) (former
Yugoslav Republic of Macedonia)
UN Mission of Observers in Prevlaka (UNMOP) (Area
disputed by Croatia and the Federal Republic of
Yugoslavia)
UN Mission in Bosnia and Herzegovina (UNMIBH)

Asia (8):
UN Good Offices Mission in Afghanistan and Pakistan
      (UNGOMAP)
UN Advance Mission in Cambodia (UNAMIC)
UN Transitional Authority in Cambodia (UNTAC)
UN Transitional Administration in East Timor (UNTAET)
UN Mission of Support in East Timor (UNMISET)
UN India-Pakistan Observer Mission (UNIPOM)
UN Mission of Observers in Tajikistan Civil War (UNMOT)
UN Security Force in Western New Guinea (UNSF)

Americas (8):
UN Observer Group in Central America (ONUCA)
      (Costa Rica, El Salvador, Guatemala, Honduras and
      Nicaragua)
Mission of the Representative of the Secretary-General in the
      Dominican Republic (DOMREP)
UN Observer Mission in El Salvador (ONUSAL)
UN Verification Mission in Guatemala (MINUGUA)
UN Mission in Haiti (UNMIH)
UN Support Mission in Haiti (UNSMIH)
UN Transition Mission in Haiti (UNTMIH)
UN Civilian Peace Mission in Haiti (MIPONUH)

Africa (15):
UN Angola Verification Mission I (UNAVEM I)
UN Angola Verification Mission II (UNAVEM II)
UN Angola Verification Mission III (UNAVEM III)
UN Observer Mission in Angola (MONUA)
UN Mission in the Central African Republic (MINURCA)
UN Aouzou Strip Observer Group (UNASOG) (Chad/Libya)
UN Operation in the Congo (ONUC)
UN Observer Mission in Liberia (UNOMIL)
UN Operation in Mozambique (ONUMOZ)
UN Transition Assistance Group (UNTAG) (Namibia)
UN Assistance Mission for Rwanda (UNAMIR)
UN Observer Mission Uganda-Rwanda (UNOMUR)
UN Observer Mission in Sierra Leone (UNOMSIL)
UN Operation in Somalia I (UNOSOM I)
UN Operation in Somalia II (UNOSOM II)

Civilian Police

United Nations civilian police officers were deployed for the first time in the 1960s in the UN peacekeeping operation in the Congo. They have been part of the UN force in Cyprus for more than thirty years. Beginning with the UN mission in Namibia in 1988, UN civilian police have become an increasingly important element of UN peacekeeping by helping war-torn societies restore social, economic, and political stability. The UN Civilian Police Division was set up in October 2000 as part of the Department of Peacekeeping Operations with a staff of experienced police officers from contributing countries. Goals of the Division are to: (1) support civilian police components of UN peacekeeping operations; (2) enhance planning capacity for police components of UN operations; (3) assist in strengthening the performance, effectiveness, and efficiency of local criminal justice systems, including police and corrections; and (4) enhance the ability to deploy rapidly a functional police force. More than 7,000 police officers from 80 countries were participating in 18 missions near the end of 2004 (www.un.org/Depts/dpko/dpko/civpol/4.htm).

UN Peacekeeping Fatalities

As of 31 October 2004, there were 1,945 peacekeeping fatalities from 106 member states. Fifteen member states had 40 or more fatalities (www.un.org/Depts/dpko/fatalities):

Bangladesh 53	Norway 41
Canada 106	Pakistan 82
France 95	Poland 45
Ghana 103	Sweden 64
India 109	United Kingdom 92
Ireland 85	United States 57
Nepal 50	Zambia 54
Nigeria 63	

UN Mine Action Service (UNMAS)

The UNMAS is part of the UN Department of Peacekeeping Operations, established in 1997 to serve as the UN focal point for mine action. The UNMAS chairs the UN Inter-Agency Coordination Group (IAGC), which includes representatives from the UN

Development Program, UNICEF, the UN Department for Disarmament Affairs, the UN Food and Agriculture Organization, the UN High Commissioner for Human Rights, the UN High Commissioner for Refugees, the UN Office for the Coordination of Humanitarian Affairs, the UN Office for Project Services, the World Bank, the World Food Program, and the World Health Organization. It also chairs a Steering Committee on Mine Action (SCMA), which includes IACG members as well as representatives from the International Campaign to Ban Landmines (ICBL), the International Committee of the Red Cross (ICRC), the Geneva International Centre for Humanitarian Demining (GICHD), and a number of operational nongovernmental organizations (NGOs). In partnership with the GICHD, the UNMAS also organizes an annual meeting of mine-action program directors and advisers from around the world (www.mineaction.org).

UN Peacemaking and Peace-Building Missions

Peacemaking refers to the use of diplomatic means to persuade parties in conflict to cease hostilities and to negotiate a peaceful settlement of their dispute. Peacemaking excludes the use of force against one of the parties to enforce an end to hostilities, an activity that in UN parlance is referred to as "peace enforcement." *Peace building* is employed by the United Nations to refer to external efforts to assist countries and regions in their transitions from war to peace and includes all activities and programs designed to support and strengthen these transitions. The United Nations' role is often focused on facilitating the implementation of a peace agreement. Effective peace building requires concurrent and integrated action of many different types: military, diplomatic, political, economic, social, and humanitarian. The UN Department of Political Affairs, under the secretary-general's direction, provides a broad political and policy framework for the UN System's response to postconflict situations in an effort to acquire participation of each of the components of the UN System that has a part to play.

The United Nations provides various means through which conflicts may be contained and resolved and their root causes addressed. The Security Council may recommend ways to resolve a dispute or request the secretary-general's mediation. The secretary-general may participate personally and by dispatching special envoys or missions for specific tasks, such as negotiation or fact finding.

In late 2004 there were fourteen UN peacemaking and peace-building missions:

> UN Observer Mission in Bougainville (UNOMB)
> UN Office in Burundi (UNOB)
> UN Office in the Central African Republic (BONUCA)
> Office of the Special Representative of the Secretary-General for the Great Lakes Region (Burundi)
> UN Verification Mission in Guatemala (MINUGUA)
> UN Peace-building Support Office in Guinea-Bissau (UNOGBIS)
> Office of the UN Special Coordinator for the Middle East Peace Process (UNSCO)
> UN Political Office for Somalia (UNPOS)
> UN Tajikistan Office of Peace-building (UNTOP)
> Office of the Special Representative of the Secretary-General for West Africa (UNOWA)
> UN Assistance Mission for Iraq (UNAMI)
> UN Assistance Mission in Afghanistan (UNAMA)
> Special Envoy for Mynamar
> Special Political Mission in Sudan

(Further information is available at: www.un.org/Depts/dpa/prev_dip/fst_prev_dip.htm)

International Criminal Tribunals

In 2005 there are two UN international criminal tribunals, the International Criminal Tribunal for the former Yugoslavia (ICTY) and the International Criminal Tribunal for Rwanda (ICTR), established in 1993 and 1994. Creation of these criminal tribunals continued the practice of establishing ad hoc tribunals to bring to justice exceedingly serious violations of international law, as in the case of the Nuremberg trials of German Nazi leaders after World War II. A permanent tribunal, the International Criminal Court (ICC), was approved on 17 July 1998 by 120 states participating in the United Nations Diplomatic Conference of Plenipotentiaries on the Establishment of an International Criminal Court.

International Criminal Court (ICC)

The ICC statute entered into force on 1 July 2002. When this was followed by the establishment of the Permanent Secretariat of the ICC in The Hague, the UN Secretariat ceased to serve as the Secretariat of the ICC on 31 December 2003. The International Criminal Court (ICC) is the first permanent, treaty-based international criminal court established to promote the rule of law and ensure that the gravest international crimes are punished. In February 2003 the Assembly of States Parties elected the eighteen judges of the court for a term of office of three, six, and nine years. Ninety-seven states had ratified the ICC Treaty by October 2004. By late 2004 two states, the Republic of Uganda and the Democratic Republic of the Congo, had referred situations to the chief prosecutor of the court. The prosecutor decided to open investigations into both situations (www.icc-cpi.int).

The U.S. government opposed the creation of the ICC. In December 2004 President Bush approved the Nethercutt Amendment, passed by the U.S. Congress, which suspends Economic Support Fund assistance to countries that have ratified the Rome Statute of the ICC and have not signed bilateral immunity agreements with the United States. Such agreements prohibit U.S. citizens and U.S. contractors from transfer to the ICC for investigation or prosecution.

International Criminal Tribunal for the former Yugoslavia (ICTY)

The International Criminal Tribunal for the former Yugoslavia (ICTY) was established by Security Council resolution 827, passed on 25 May 1993 in the face of the serious violations of international humanitarian law committed in the territory of the former Yugoslavia since 1991. The ICTY is located in The Hague, The Netherlands. The ICTY's mission is fourfold: (1) to bring to justice persons allegedly responsible for serious violations of international humanitarian law, (2) to render justice to the victims, (3) to deter further crimes, and (4) to contribute to the restoration of peace by promoting reconciliation in the former Yugoslavia.

The chambers consist of sixteen permanent judges and a maximum at any one time of nine ad litem judges. The sixteen permanent judges are elected by the General Assembly of the United Nations for a term of four years. They can be reelected. The judges are divided between three trial chambers and one appeals chamber. The judges represent the main legal systems in the world and bring to the tribunal a variety of legal expertise (www.un.org/icty).

International Criminal Tribunal for Rwanda (ICTR)

In response to the serious violations of humanitarian law committed in Rwanda, and acting under Chapter VII of the United Nations Charter, the Security Council created the International Criminal Tribunal for Rwanda (ICTR) by Resolution 955 of 8 November 1994. The purpose of the ICTR is to contribute to the process of national reconciliation in Rwanda and to the maintenance of peace in the region. The tribunal was established for the prosecution of persons responsible for genocide and other serious violations of international humanitarian law committed in the territory of Rwanda between 1 January 1994 and 31 December 1994. It may also deal with the prosecution of Rwandan citizens responsible for genocide and other such violations of international law committed in the territory of neighboring states during the same period. The tribunal consists of three trial chambers and an appeals chamber, composed of sixteen judges. The Office of the Prosecutor is divided into an investigation Section and a prosecution Section.

The Registry is responsible for the overall administration and management of the tribunal.

By resolution 977 of 22 February 1995, the Security Council decided that the seat of the tribunal would be located in Arusha, United Republic of Tanzania (www.un.org/ictr).

UN System Counterterrorism Efforts

Counterterrorism has long been on agendas of the UN System. In this section what the UN considers to be the twelve key UN anti-terrorism conventions that predate 11 September 2001 (9/11) are presented first. The Security Council, General Assembly, and Secretariat bodies that were established in response to 9/11 are then described. The last two sections provide information on the counterterrorism efforts of the IAEA, IMO, ICAO, ILO, OPCW, UPU, and WHO.

Twelve Key UN Antiterrorism Conventions That Predate 11 September 2001

1. Convention on the Prevention and Punishment of Crimes against Internationally Protected Persons, including Diplomatic Agents, adopted by the General Assembly of the United Nations on 14 December 1973.
2. International Convention against the Taking of Hostages, adopted by the General Assembly of the United Nations on 17 December 1979.
3. International Convention for the Suppression of Terrorist Bombings, adopted by the General Assembly of the United Nations on 15 December 1997.
4. International Convention for the Suppression of the Financing of Terrorism, adopted by the General Assembly of the United Nations on 9 December 1999.
5. Convention on Offences and Certain Other Acts Committed on Board Aircraft, signed at Tokyo on 14 September 1963. (Deposited with the secretary-general of the International Civil Aviation Organization)
6. Convention for the Suppression of Unlawful Seizure of Aircraft, signed at the Hague on 16 December 1970. (Deposited with the governments of the Russian Federation, the United Kingdom, and the United States of America)
7. Convention for the Suppression of Unlawful Acts against the Safety of Civil Aviation, signed at Montreal on 23 September 1971. (Deposited with the governments of the Russian Federation, the United Kingdom and the United States of America)
8. Convention on the Physical Protection of Nuclear Material, signed at Vienna on 3 March 1980.

(Deposited with the director-general of the
International Atomic Energy Agency)
9. Protocol on the Suppression of Unlawful Acts of
Violence at Airports Serving International Civil
Aviation, supplementary to the Convention for the
Suppression of Unlawful Acts against the Safety of
Civil Aviation, signed at Montreal on 24 February
1988. (Deposited with the governments of the Russian
Federation, the United Kingdom, and the United
States of America and with the secretary-general of
the International Civil Aviation Organization)
10. Convention for the Suppression of Unlawful Acts
against the Safety of Maritime Navigation, done at
Rome on 10 March 1988. (Deposited with the
secretary-general of the International Maritime
Organization)
11. Protocol for the Suppression of Unlawful Acts against
the Safety of Fixed Platforms Located on the
Continental Shelf, done at Rome on 10 March 1988.
(Deposited with the secretary-general of the
International Maritime Organization)
12. Convention on the Marking of Plastic Explosives for
the Purpose of Detection, signed at Montreal on 1
March 1991. (Deposited with the secretary-general of
the International Civil Aviation Organization.)

Counter-Terrorism Committee (CTC) of the Security Council

On 28 September 2001, acting under Chapter VII of the UN Charter (concerning threats to international peace and security), the Security Council adopted Resolution 1373 (2001), reaffirming its unequivocal condemnation of the terrorist attacks which took place in New York, Washington, D.C., and Pennsylvania on 11 September 2001, and expressing its determination to prevent all such acts.

Resolution 1373 also established the Counter-Terrorism Committee (known by its acronym, the CTC), made up of all fifteen members of the Security Council. The CTC monitors the implementation of Resolution 1373 by all states and tries to increase the capability of states to fight terrorism.

Counter-Terrorism Committee Executive Directorate (CTED)

Security Council resolution 1535 (2004) of 26 March 2004 established the Counter-Terrorism Committee Executive Directorate (CTED) in the UN Secretariat to enhance the committee's ability to monitor the implementation of Resolution 1373 (2001) and effectively continue the capacity-building work in which it is engaged. The CTED is headed by its executive director, Javier Rupérez, at the assistant secretary-general level.

General Assembly Ad Hoc Committee on Terrorism

The General Assembly Ad Hoc Committee on Terrorism in 2005 is drafting a comprehensive antiterrorism convention aimed at filling the gaps left by the twelve sectoral treaties listed below. It has been reported that committee members have agreed on the bulk of twenty-seven of the draft treaty's articles, leaving only three key articles and the preamble to be completed. The focus of ongoing discussions is agreement on exclusions to the treaty and its applicability to armed forces and to foreign occupation.

Most Relevant Activities of UN Agencies and Programs That Postdate September 2001

A report following this heading that appears at the UN website is fully quoted below (www.un.org/News/dh/infocus/overview.htm).

1. International Atomic Energy Agency (IAEA). IAEA considers the first line of defence against nuclear terrorism to be strong physical protection of nuclear facilities and materials. In March this year its Board of Governors approved an action plan designed to upgrade worldwide protection against acts of terrorism involving nuclear and other radioactive materials. "National measures for protecting nuclear material and facilities are uneven in their substance and application," the IAEA says. "There is wide recognition that the international physical protec-

tion regime needs to be strengthened." A number of States have subsequently pledged funds and resources to support the plan.

2. International Maritime Organization (IMO) regulations aimed at improving the security of ships on the high seas entered into force on 1 July 2002. These include a requirement that all new passenger ships and large non-passenger craft carry data recorders—black boxes similar to those used on aircraft—on all voyages. The black box recorders will allow investigators to review procedures undertaken and instructions given in the moments before any incident, and thereby better identify the cause of incidents at sea. In addition, ships will be obliged to carry automatic identification systems, so they can be identified and tracked. The mandatory regulations are among many amendments designed to further strengthen the 1974 International Convention for the Safety of Life at Sea.

3. International Civil Aviation Organization (ICAO) adopted strengthened in-flight security standards in March 2002 that require reinforced cockpit doors on civil aircraft, as well as other in-flight security measures. The reinforced doors are intended to prevent unauthorized persons from forcibly gaining access to the cockpit. They must be closed and locked from the time an aircraft's external doors are closed until the flight reaches its destination. The standards also require the installation of a system that allows pilots to monitor the area immediately outside their cockpits, and a system to enable flight attendants to discreetly notify pilots of suspicious activity or potential threats in the passenger cabins.

4. United Nations Office of Drug Control and Crime Prevention (ODCCP) has undertaken a series of "closed door" meetings of experts to develop new strategies to counter terrorism. The most recent, held in Turin (Italy), focused on the prevention of terrorism at major international events, such as the 2006 Turin Winter Olympics. Amongst those attending were high-level officials from Interpol, Europol, the United States Federal Bureau of Investigation (FBI), the U.S. Department of Justice Office for Domestic Preparedness, and HQ Allied Forces Southern Europe.

Other Counterterrorism Activities of ILO, IMO, OPCW, UPU, and WHO

The UN website also provides additional information on the anti-terrorism activities of these organizations and others in the UN System. We have extracted and edited information on five of these agencies and present it below (www.un.org/News/dh/latest/un-agencies.shtml).

1. International Labor Organization (ILO). The attacks of 11 September had severe consequences for the tourism industry, affecting its workers and particularly those holding temporary contracts. In response, the ILO organized a meeting of government, employer, and worker representatives to exchange information on ways to ease the social impact of this downturn. It also organized a think-tank meeting on the impact of 11 September for civil aviation because the strong fall in passenger demand led to airlines announcing 200,000 job reductions in the weeks immediately following the attacks. The meeting was attended by aviation industry experts, as well as industry and employee representatives.

2. International Maritime Organization (IMO). Twelve proposals to improve maritime safety and security have been developed by an IMO working group on maritime security, aimed at decreasing the likelihood of maritime terrorism and improving the ability of seafarers and others to respond to any crises that do arise. They include acceleration of the timetable for installing mandatory automatic identification systems on all ships over 500 tons working in international waters and changed regulations that would require such ships to have ship security plans and ship security officers. Development of guidelines and criteria for port vulnerability assessments have also been proposed, as has urgent action on an up-to-date seafarer identification document. New arrangements for cooperation with customs authorities and the prospect of secret antiterrorist alarm systems on ships were also raised. These proposals will be fleshed out by the IMO Maritime Safety Committee and then presented to member states for approval. The IMO is also seeking ways to strengthen the UN Convention for the Suppression of Unlawful Acts against the Safety of Maritime Navigation and its Protocol for the Suppression of Unlawful Acts against the Safety of Fixed Platforms Located on the Continental Shelf. The convention entered into force in 1992.

3. Organization for the Prohibition of Chemical Weapons (OPCW). A meeting of experts on mobilizing and coordinating international responses to chemical terrorism was hosted by the Organization for the Prohibition of Chemical Weapons. The OPCW also provides answers to questions like "How can chemical weapons be detected?" and "How can we protect ourselves from chemical attack?" on a special web page it maintains at the address www.opcw.nl/resp/index.html. The OPCW provides research and information on the use and potential use of chemical weapons, including by terrorists. It also tracks the movement of chemicals that can be used to make such weapons globally. If asked by a state that has signed the Chemical Weapons Convention, it can carry out expert "challenge inspections" to ensure that other states parties are not breaking their commitment not to develop, stockpile, or use such weapons.

4. Universal Postal Union (UPU). Following the United States' anthrax-by-mail terrorism experience in 2001, the UPU arranged for a special presentation on security to representatives of 189 postal services from around the world by the United States Postal Service. As the U.S. Post Office is the service with the most experience of bioterrorism, the UPU drew the attention of all other postal services to the updated U.S. guidelines, and a link to those guidelines is now on the UPU website (www.upu.int/about/en/postal_security_25.html). In 1989 the UPU established a Postal Security Action Group to raise awareness about security issues and the mail. It has established a world postal security network in partnership with regional and international authorities. Through this network it offers advice and training on ways to ensure not only that dangerous materials are not transmitted through the mail, but also on ways to eliminate the use of mail systems for drug trafficking, money laundering, fraud, and child pornography.

5. World Health Organization (WHO). In October 2001 the WHO identified three lessons from the outbreaks of anthrax: (1) public health systems have to respond promptly to the suspicion of deliberate infections, (2) these systems must continue to be vigilant, and (3) an informed and responsible public is a critical part of the response. On the same day, it released revised guidance for states on how to respond to suspected anthrax infections. Fact sheets on anthrax and other communicable diseases that could be used by bioterrorists, such as smallpox, are available to the public on the WHO's website (www.who.int/inf-fs/en/index.html).

Financing the UN System
Total UN System Expenditures: 1986–2004

The brief overview of UN System financing in Chapter 1 was based on information provided in Table 5.1. It indicates that the overall yearly budget in 2001 was US$ 11.9 billion, as compared to US$ 800 billion devoted to world military expenditures of UN member states. Less than half of the UN System budget, US$ 5.5 billion, came from assessments of member states, with the remainder coming from voluntary contributions. Approximately 49 percent of assessments, US$ 2.7 billion, was for peacekeeping operations.

Assessed expenditures are funded by payments assessed of all UN member states based on their capacity to pay. Voluntary contributions are made to specific UN agencies and Specialized Agencies.

The data presented does not include assessments for international tribunals, which are a separate but relatively small item. Nor do they include the Bretton Woods institutions (the World Bank Group and IMF), which are in practice quite distinct and rarely included in UN System data, because both their governance and their source of funds are very different.

Peacekeeping operation expenses rose rapidly from 1992 to a peak in 1994 of about $13.4 billion. System expenses declined by 1997 to about $10.4 billion, as peacekeeping dropped to $1.2 billion and other funding shrank. Nonpeacekeeping growth throughout the period is mostly accounted for by inflation and, after 1990, by emergencies, including spending for humanitarian relief. Spending for programs long in existence actually declined in this period, while new mandates for issues such as human rights, the environment, and women's rights, drew upon a fairly static pool of resources (adapted from Klaus Hüfner, www.globalpolicy.org).

The column in Table 5.1 labeled "UN Agncies" refers to Specialized Agncies. The major specialized agencies include the International Atomic Energy Agency (IAEA), the International Labor Organisation (ILO), the Food and Agriculture Organisation (FAO), the UN Educational, Scientific, and Cultural Organisation (UNESCO), the World Health Organisation (WHO), the Universal Postal Union (UPO), the International Telecommunication Union (ITU), the International Maritime Organisation (IMO), and the UN Industrial Development Organisation (UNIDO). The column labeled "UN Organs" includes the UN Conference on Trade

Table 5.1
Total UN System Expenditures, 1986–2004

Prepared by the Global Policy Forum from data provided by the United Nations.   **Revised March 2004**
Table created by Feisal Lakha, January 2004. Data compiled by Klaus Hüfner.

The following tables offer a summary of the total UN system expenditures. Assessed contributions expenditures are funded by payments assessed to all UN member states. Voluntary contributions are payments made to specialized UN organs and agencies not included in the assessed contributions of member states.

The data presented does not include assessed contribution expenditures for international tribunals, which are a separate but relatively small item. Nor do they include the Bretton Woods Institutions, which are in practice quite distinct and rarely included in UN system data, since both their governance and their source of funds are very different.

Of note, peacekeeping operations drove a rapid runup in system costs from 1992 to a peak in 1994 at about $13.4 billion. System costs declined by 1997 to about $10.4 billion, as peacekeeping dropped to $1.2 billion and other funding shrank. The non-peacekeeping growth throughout the period is mostly accounted for by inflation and, after 1990, by emergencies, including spending for humanitarian relief. Real program spending (for programs long in existence) actually declined in this period, while new mandates for issues such as human rights, the environment, and women's rights, drew upon a fairly static pool of resources.

	Assessed Contributions Expenditures				Voluntary Contributions Expenditures			
Year	UN Regular Budget	UN Peace-keeping Operations Budget	UN Agencies	Total Assessment Spending	UN Organs	UN Agencies	Total Voluntary Spending	Grand Total
1986	725	242	1,142	2,109	3,075	951	4,026	6,135
1987	725	240	1,178	2,143	3,266	931	4,197	6,340
1988	752	266	1,349	2,367	3,868	1,129	4,997	7,364
1989	765	635	1,359	2,759	4,078	1,182	5,260	8,019
1990	838	379	1,495	2,712	4,436	1,346	5,782	8,494
1991	999	449	1,509	2,957	5,401	1,360	6,761	9,718
1992	1,008	1,697	1,731	4,436	5,888	1,271	7,159	11,595
1993	1,031	3,005	1,713	5,749	6,091	1,216	7,307	13,056
1994	1,087	3,357	1,826	6,270	5,967	1,126	7,093	13,363
1995	1,181	3,281	1,847	6,309	5,778	1,159	6,937	13,246
1996	1,112	1,522	2,057	4,691	5,009	1,045	6,054	10,745
1997	1,112	1,226	2,033	4,371	4,936	1,057	5,993	10,364
1998	1,086	995	1,792	3,873	4,260	1,151	5,411	9,284
1999	1,217	1,321	1,787	4,325	4,300	1,123	5,423	9,748
2000	1,090	2,139	1,766	4,995	4,023	955	4,978	9,973
2001	1,074	2,700	1,772	5,546	5,282	1,092	6,374	11,920
2002	1,149	2,284	–	–	–	–	–	–
2003	1,409	2,260	–	–	–	–	–	–
2004	1,483	–	–	–	–	–	–	–

Notes:

1. Sums in $US millions, rounded to the nearest million.

2. Totals since 2002 are not included as some data is not yet available.
   (http://www.globalpolicy.org/finance/tables/tabsyst.htm)

and Development (UNCTAD), the UN Development Program (UNDP), the UN Environment Program (UNEP), the UN Population Fund (UNFPA), the Office of the UN High Commissioner for Refugees (UNHCR), the UN Children's Fund UNICEF), the UN Development Fund for Women (UNIFEM), and the United Nations University (UNU).

Assessments of the Fifteen Largest Contributors to the UN Regular Budget, 2003–2004

Table 5.2 presents 2003 through 2004 assessments to the UN regular budget of the fifteen largest contributors. Therefore, peacekeeping expenditures and voluntary contributions are not included. Assessments are based on the capacity to pay, measured by gross national product, with the exception of the United States, whose assessment has been lowered in response to a unilateral decision by the U.S. Congress. The United States and Japan have the largest assessments, followed by seven European countries (Germany, the United Kingdom, France, Italy, Spain, the Netherlands, and Switzerland), two from South America (Mexico and Brazil), two from East Asia (China and Korea), Canada, and Australia. Notable is the fact that the percentage of the budget paid by Switzerland, the fifteenth ranked, is slightly over 1 percent. This means that the other 176 members of the United Nations are assessed less than this amount. This is a dramatic indicator of the skewed distribution of the wealth of the world.

Alternative Sources of Financing

There are a growing number of proposals for alternative sources for financing the UN System through "global taxes" because of the extremely limited financial resources provided by member states. Here we can provide only a brief overview. (For a much more extensive discussion see Paul and Wahlberg 2002.) Despite the expanding demands placed on the UN System, recent growth in financial resources has been mostly attributed to inflation. In addition, the fact that more than half of this financial support comes from voluntary contributions inhibits effective long-term

TABLE 5.2
Assessed Contributions to the UN Regular Budget
of the 15 Largest Assessed Contributors 2004–2005

The following table lists the contributions of the 15 largest assessed contributors to the UN regular budget. The table also illustrates the percentage of the assessed contributions by these countries and compares the assessments from the previous year. The countries are listed in order of rank, from the high to low.

Country	Total Assessment 2005	Percentage Assessment 2005	Total of Assessment 2004	Percentage Assessment 2004	Change in Position (previous rank)
United States	440	24%	363	24%	1 (1)
Japan	346	19%	280	19%	2 (2)
Germany	154	8%	124	8%	3 (3)
United Kingdom	109	6%	88	6%	4 (4)
France	107	6%	87	6%	5 (5)
Italy	87	5%	70	5%	6 (6)
Canada	50	3%	40	3%	7 (7)
Spain	45	2%	36	2%	8 (8)
China	37	2%	29	2%	9 (9)
Mexico	34	2%	27	2%	10 (10)
Republic of Korea	32	2%	26	2%	11 (11)
Netherlands	30	2%	24	2%	12 (12)
Australia	28	2%	23	2%	13 (13)
Brazil	27	1%	22	1%	14 (14)
Switzerland	21	1%	18	1%	15(15)

Notes: *Sums in $US millions, rounded to the nearest million.*
Prepared by the Global Policy Forum from data provided by the United Nations (UN Documents)

planning. Furthermore, many states do not pay their assessments on time.

In addition to proposing global taxes as a source of revenue, some favor them as policy instruments that can steer a variety of international activities and transactions in directions that prevent undesirable and costly consequences. These proposals concentrate on two policy goals, taxation as a means to regulate carbon emissions into the atmosphere (carbon tax/energy tax) and taxation to reduce currency speculation (Tobin tax/currency transaction tax).

Proposals for global taxes as both revenue sources and policy instruments include taxes on (1) international monetary transactions, (2) e-mail or Internet activity, (3) arms sales, (4) extraction of natural resources, (5) carbon/energy use, (6) aviation fuel, and (7) airline tickets. Much of the information on these taxes that follows has been extracted from the Global Policy Forum website. For additional information go to www.globalpolicy.org/socecon/glotax/index.htm.

1. International Monetary Transaction Tax

James Tobin, a Nobel prizewinner in economics has proposed what is referred to as the "Tobin tax," which calls for levying a charge on international monetary transactions. A very limited 0.25 percent tax would generate over $300 billion per year (the total UN annual budget is about $12 billion). A global currency trade tax has been proposed primarily as a means for limiting disruptive speculation, but it would also bring in large financial resources. Global currency trade amounts to approximately US$ 1.3 trillion per day. Of this amount, cross-border purchases of goods and services that require foreign exchange account for only 2 percent ($5 trillion per year) of the total trading. Another $50 trillion per year (about 17 percent) of foreign-exchange trading takes place with futures options and derivatives to hedge against future exchange rate fluctuations. Exchange rate speculation—short- or long-term profit-seeking transactions—accounts for the remaining transactions, at least 80 percent. These speculative movements, which can take place rapidly and unpredictably, threaten to empty central banks' currency reserves. Ruby van der Wekken of the Helsinki-based Network Institute for Global Democratization (NIGD) has said that the proposal for a tax on currency transactions (CTT) is by far the most viable suggestion of all global tax initiatives (www.nigd.org/wsf/1103575739/index_html).

2. E-mail or Internet Tax

An e-mail or Internet tax, sometimes known as a "bit tax," would tax the amount of data sent through the Internet. A person sending 100 e-mails a day, each containing a 10-kilobyte document, would pay a tax of just 1 cent, according to one proposal. This tax does not seek to discourage use of e-mail but could raise funds that would be spent to make e-mail and web access available in poor communities and low-income countries.

The UN Development Report, 1999, estimated that such a tax would have yielded $70 billion (http://hdr.undp.org/reports/global/1999/en). Since then the number of Internet users has grown enormously. A very small tax could produce a large revenue. In 1998 the United States persuaded the Organisation for Economic Co-operation and Development (OECD), an organization of the thirty wealthiest states, to impose a moratorium on Internet taxation, but on 12 February 2002, European Union finance ministers approved sales taxes on Internet transactions.

3. Arms Sales Tax

A 1 percent arms sales tax each year paid into a global fund administered by the United Nations would raise hundreds of millions of dollars. Part of that money could then be used for postconflict rehabilitation and government building in less-developed countries (LDCs). Civil wars and related conflicts are some of the greatest causes of poverty and underdevelopment in LDCs.

4. Extraction of Natural Resources Tax

Daphne Davies of the Brussels-based LDC Watch, a nongovernmental organization (NGO) that monitors the world's fifty poorest states, has proposed a "polluter pays" tax for extracting natural resources. She has proposed that procedures be created under the auspices of the United Nations, and overseen by the U.N. Environment Program (UNEP). Companies that extract natural resources would pay a percentage of the value of the wealth they earn into a fund whose money would then be used to improve or to restore the environment in LDCs (www.un.org/ esa/ffd/media-ipsnews-0704.htm).

5. Carbon/Energy Use Tax

There is a large body of literature advocating the economic and environmental virtues of carbon/energy use taxes. These arguments rest on the assumption that economic activity, such as the combustion of fossil fuels, imposes costs on society, including damage to the climate system from carbon dioxide emissions. The goal of a carbon tax, and all environmental tax policies, is to enable the price of goods and services to reflect their environmental costs. Coal generates the greatest amount of carbon emissions (0.3 tons/million Btu) and would therefore be taxed in greater proportion than oil and natural gas, which have lower carbon concentrations (0.24 and 0.16 tons of carbon/million Btu respectively).

6. Aviation Fuel Tax

Although airplane travel accounts for only 3 percent of global carbon emissions, it is the fastest-growing source of emissions. The Intergovernmental Panel on Climate Change (IPCC), a joint activity of the World Meterological Organization (WMO) and the UN Environment Program (UNEP), expects airplane travel to account for 15 percent of all carbon emissions in 2050 (www.ipcc.ch). In 2005 airline fuel is the cheapest in the world because the industry is exempted from fuel taxes. The European Union has actively discussed an aviation fuel tax, beginning with the Dutch presidency of 1997. The Dutch transport minister has suggested that the European Union introduce an aviation fuel tax unilaterally. In December 2000 the European Parliament's Economic and Monetary Affairs Committee confirmed its support for a recommendation to allow the member states to impose a tax on domestic and intra E.U. flights. The committee also urged the commission to pursue negotiations through the International Civil Aviation Organization with a view to amending the 1944 ILO Convention, which allows an exemption from taxes on air fuel. Australia and the United States oppose a worldwide levy on aviation fuel, but many other countries have expressed interest.

7. Airline Ticket Tax

Nongovernmental organizations are also pushing for increases in the VAT (value added or sales tax) levied on airline tickets and increases in landing fees. The main purpose of this tax would be to prevent climate change. According to some calculations, a 1 percent charge on all air passenger tickets issued in 1989 would have generated about $1 billion, 75 percent of this sum would have been contributed by airlines from the seven major industrialized countries. A large number of countries, especially in the developing world, are already using departure taxes as significant revenue raisers and might be reluctant to see this source of finance preempted by an international charge or tax (Dean 2004; Wahlberg and Wahlberg 2002.

Secretaries-General of the United Nations

The secretary-general of the United Nations is appointed by the Security Council and then must receive the approval of the General Assembly. The secretary-general serves for five years with the possibility of being appointed for a second term. There have been seven secretaries-general of the United Nations, three from small European states, and one each from Myanmar, Peru, Egypt, and Ghana. They are:

Trygve Lie	1946–1952	Norway
Dag Hammarskjöld	1953–1961	Sweden
U thant	1961–1971	Myanmar
Kurt Waldheim	1972–1981	Austria
Perez de Cuellar	1982–1991	Peru
Boutros Boutros-Ghali	1992–1996	Egypt
Kofi Annan	1997–	Ghana

(Biographies available at www.un.org)

Presidents of the UN General Assembly

The General Assembly elects a new president of the General Assembly when its annual meeting convenes each September. The president presides over one of the annual sessions and over special sessions that may be convened during that year. In rotating the office among member states, special concern is given to ensuring that the office rotates across all regions of the world.

Each session of the General Assembly also has twenty-one vice presidents. These vice presidents, and the chairs of the six main committees of the General Assembly, are members of the general committee that is chaired by the president. After receiving a draft agenda from the Secretary General, this committee submits its draft agenda to the General Assembly plenary.

UN System Nobel Peace Prizes

Eight Nobel Peace Prizes have been awarded to a diversity of activities of the UN System across fifty-one years, from 1950 to

TABLE 5.3
Presidents of the United Nations General Assembly

Session	Year	Name	Country
First	1946	Mr. Paul-Henri Spaak	Belgium
First special	1947	Mr. Oswaldo Aranha	Brazil
Second	1947	Mr. Oswaldo Aranha	Brazil
Second special	1948	Mr. José Arce	Argentina
Third	1948	Mr. H. V. Evatt	Australia
Fourth	1949	Mr. Carlos P. Rómulo	Philippines
Fifth	1950	Mr. Nasrollah Entezam	Iran
Sixth	1951	Mr. Luis Padilla Nervo	Mexico
Seventh	1952	Mr. Lester B. Pearson	Canada
Eighth	1953	Mrs. Vijaya Lakshmi Pandit	India
Ninth	1954	Mr. Eelco N. van Kleffens	Netherlands
Tenth	1955	Mr. José Maza	Chile
First emergency special	1956	Mr. Rudecindo Ortega	Chile
Second emergency special	1956	Mr. Rudecindo Ortega	Chile
Eleventh	1956	Prince Wan Waithayakon	Thailand
Twelfth	1957	Sir Leslie Munro	New Zealand
Third emergency special	1958	Sir Leslie Munro	New Zealand
Thirteenth	1958	Mr. Charles Malik	Lebanon
Fourteenth	1959	Mr. Víctor Andrés Belaúnde	Peru
Fourth emergency special	1960	Mr. Víctor Andrés Belaúnde	Peru
Fifteenth	1960	Mr. Fblueerick H. Boland	Ireland
Third special	1961	Mr. Fblueerick H. Boland	Ireland
Sixteenth	1961	Mr. Mongi Slim	Tunisia
Seventeenth	1962	Sir Muhammad Zafrulla Khan	Pakistan
Fourth special	1963	Sir Muhammad Zafrulla Khan	Pakistan
Eighteenth	1963	Mr. Carlos Sosa Rodríguez	Venezuela
Nineteenth	1964	Mr. Alex Quaison-Sackey	Ghana
Twentieth	1965	Mr. Amintore Fanfani	Italy
Twenty-first	1966	Mr. Abdul Rahman Pazhwak	Afghanistan
Fifth special	1967	Mr. Abdul Rahman Pazhwak	Afghanistan
Fifth emergency special	1967	Mr. Abdul Rahman Pazhwak	Afghanistan
Twenty-second	1967	Mr. Corneliu Manescu	Romania
Twenty-third	1968	Mr. Emilio Arenales Catalán	Guatemala
Twenty-fourth	1969	Miss Angie E. Brooks	Liberia
Twenty-fifth	1970	Mr. Edvard Hambro	Norway
Twenty-sixth	1971	Mr. Adam Malik	Indonesia
Twenty-seventh	1972	Mr. Stanislaw Trepczynski	Poland
Twenty-eighth	1973	Mr. Leopoldo Benítes	Ecuador
Sixth special	1974	Mr. Leopoldo Benítes	Ecuador
Twenty-ninth	1974	Mr. Abdelaziz Bouteflika	Algeria
Seventh special	1975	Mr. Abdelaziz Bouteflika	Algeria
Thirtieth	1975	Mr. Gaston Thorn	Luxembourg
Thirty-first	1976	Mr. H. S. Amerasinghe	Sri Lanka
Thirty-second	1977	Mr. Lazar Mojsov	Yugoslavia
Eighth special	1978	Mr. Lazar Mojsov	Yugoslavia
Ninth special	1978	Mr. Lazar Mojsov	Yugoslavia
Tenth special	1978	Mr. Lazar Mojsov	Yugoslavia

Thirty-third	1978	Mr. Indalecio Liévano	Colombia
Thirty-fourth	1979	Mr. Salim A. Salim	United Rep. of Tanzania
Sixth emergency special	1980	Mr. Salim A. Salim	United Rep. of Tanzania
Seventh emergency special	1980	Mr. Salim A. Salim	United Rep. of Tanzania
Eleventh special	1980	Mr. Salim A. Salim	United Rep. of Tanzania
Thirty-fifth	1980	Mr. Rüdiger von Wechmar	Fed. Rep. of Germany
Eighth emergency special	1981	Mr. Rüdiger von Wechmar	Fed. Rep. of Germany
Thirty-sixth	1981	Mr. Ismat T. Kittani	Iraq
Seventh emergency special*	1982	Mr. Ismat T. Kittani	Iraq
Ninth emergency special	1982	Mr. Ismat T. Kittani	Iraq
Twelfth special	1982	Mr. Ismat T. Kittani	Iraq
Thirty-seventh	1982	Mr. Imre Hollai	Hungary
Thirty-eighth	1983	Mr. Jorge E. Illueca	Panama
Thirty-ninth	1984	Mr. Paul J. F. Lusaka	Zambia
Fortieth	1985	Mr. Jaime de Piniés	Spain
Thirteenth special	1986	Mr. Jaime de Piniés	Spain
Forty-first	1986	Mr. Humayun R. Choudhury	Bangladesh
Fourteenth special	1986	Mr. Humayun R.Choudhury	Bangladesh
Forty-second	1987	Mr. Peter Florin	German Dem. Rep.
Fifteenth special	1988	Mr. Peter Florin	German Dem. Rep.
Forty-third	1988	Mr. Dante M. Caputo	Argentina
Forty-fourth	1989	Mr. Joseph Nanven Garba	Nigeria
Sixteenth special	1989	Mr. Joseph Nanven Garba	Nigeria
Seventeenth special	1990	Mr. Joseph Nanven Garba	Nigeria
Eighteenth special	1990	Mr. Joseph Nanven Garba	Nigeria
Forty-fifth	1990	Mr. Guido de Marco	Malta
Forty-sixth	1991	Mr. Samir S. Shihabi	Saudi Arabia
Forty-seventh	1992	Mr. Stoyan Ganev	Bulgaria
Forty-eighth	1993	Mr. Samuel R. Insanally	Guyana
Forty-ninth	1994	Mr. Amara Essy	Ivory Coast
Fiftieth	1995	Mr. Diogo Freitas do Amaral	Portugal
Fifty-first	1996	Mr. Razali Ismail	Malaysia
Tenth emergency special*	1997	Mr. Razali Ismail	Malaysia
Ninteenth special	1997	Mr. Razali Ismail	Malaysia
Fifty-second	1997	Mr. Hennadiy Udovenko	Ukraine
Tenth emergency special*	1998	Mr. Hennadiy Udovenko	Ukraine
Twentieth special	1998	Mr. Hennadiy Udovenko	Ukraine
Fifty-third	1998	Mr. Didier Opertti	Uruguay
Tenth emergency special*	1999	Mr. Didier Opertti	Uruguay
Twenty-first special	1999	Mr. Didier Opertti	Uruguay
Fifty-fourth	1999	Mr. Theo- Ben Gurirab	Namibia
Twenty-second special	1999	Mr. Theo- Ben Gurirab	Namibia
Twenty-third special	2000	Mr. Theo- Ben Gurirab	Namibia
Twenty-fourth special	2000	Mr. Theo- Ben Gurirab	Namibia
Fifty-fifth	2000	Mr. Harri Holkeri	Finland
Fifty-sixth	2001	Mr. Han Seung-soo	Korea
Fifty-seventh	2002	Mr. Jan Kavan	Czech Republic
Fifty-eighth	2003	Mr. Julian Robert Hunte	Saint Lucia
Fifty-ninth	2004	Mr. Jean Ping	Gabon

*Resumed

(Adapted from www.un.org/ga/55/session/prdts)

2001. Ralph Bunche was the first to receive the award for his work as mediator in Palestine while a member of the Secretariat in 1950. One prize was awarded to a specialized agency, the International Labor Organization, in 1969. Three were awarded to UN programs, with the UN Children's Fund (UNICEF) receiving it in 1965, and the UN High Commissioner for Refugees (UN-HCR) receiving it twice—in 1955 and 1981. Two secretaries-general received the award, Dag Hammarskjold in 1961 and Kofi Annan in 2001. UN peacekeeping forces were awarded the Nobel Prize in 1988.

UN Conferences
1994–2004

The UN has held many global conferences, including over thirty between 1994 and 2004. These conferences have focused on a very broad array of global issues and have been held at many sites around the world. The United Nations says that these "conferences have made a long-term impact by: (1) mobilizing national and local governments and non-governmental organizations (NGOs) to take action on a major global problem, (2) establishing international standards and guidelines for national policy; (3) serving as a forum where new proposals can be debated and consensus sought, and (4) setting in motion a process whereby governments make commitments and report back regularly to the United Nations" (www.un.org/News/facts/confercs.htm).

In addition, the UN website asserts: "By involving Presidents, Prime Ministers and other heads of State—as pioneered at the 1990 World Summit for Children—these events have put long-term, difficult problems like poverty and environmental degradation at the top of the global agenda. These problems otherwise would not have the political urgency to grab front-page headlines and command the attention of world leaders. The participation of thousands of NGOs, citizens, academics and businesspeople, in both the official and unofficial meetings, has turned these conferences into true 'global forums.' The UN has encouraged this, knowing that the support of a wide spectrum of society is needed to implement the policies being discussed." (www.un.org).

Many of these conferences had one or more follow-up sessions. Some have been followed by special sessions of the UN General Assembly that are not included in the list below. In order to highlight the focus of each conference for the reader, it has been placed in italics.

2004:

Global Forum on *Internet Governance* (New York, 25–27 March)

International Conference on the *Reconstruction of Liberia* (New York, 5–6 February)

2003:

The World Summit on the *Information Society* (Geneva, Switzerland, 10–12 December)

World *Electronic Media* Forum (Geneva, Switzerland, 9–12 December)

High Level Political Conference for the Signature of the United Nations Convention against *Corruption* (Mérida, Mexico 9–11 December)

High-Level Dialogue on *Financing for Development* (New York, 8–10 September)

International Ministerial Conference of Landlocked and Transit Developing Countries and Donor Countries and International Financial and Development Institutions on *Transit Transport Cooperation* (Almaty, Kazakhstan, 28–29 August)

2002:

The World Summit on *Sustainable Development* (Johannesburg, South Africa, 26 August–4 September)

World *Food* Summit: five years later (Rome, Italy, 10–13 June)

Second World Assembly on *Ageing* (Madrid, Spain, 8–12 April)

International Conference on *Financing for Development* (Monterrey, N.L., Mexico, 18–22 March)

2001:

Conference on Facilitating the Entry into Force of the Comprehensive *Nuclear-Test-Ban* Treaty (New York, 11–13 November)

World Conference against *Racism,* Racial Discrimination, Xenophobia and Related Intolerance (Durban, South Africa, 31 August–7 September)

United Nations Conference on the *Illicit Trade in Small Arms and Light Weapons* in All Its Aspects (New York, 9–20 July)

Third United Nations Conference on the *Least Developed Countries* (Brussels, Belgium, 14–20 May)

2000:

United Nations Convention against Transnational *Organized Crime* (Palermo, Italy, 12–15 December)

World Summit for Social Development and Beyond: Achieving *Social Development* for All in a Globalized World (Special Session of the General Assembly, Geneva, Switzerland, 26–30 June)

Crime and Justice: Meeting the Challenges of the Twenty-first Century (Vienna, Austria, 10–17 April)

1999:

Third United Nations Conference on the Exploration and *Peaceful Uses of Outer Space* (UNISPACE III) (Vienna, Austria, 19–30 July)

Fighting *Landmines*: First Meeting of States Parties (Maputo, Mozambique, 3–7 May)

1998:

World Conference of Ministers Responsible for *Youth* (Lisbon, Portugal, 8–12 August)

UN Conference on the Establishment of an *International Criminal Court* (Rome, Italy, 15 June–17 July)

1997:

Earth Summit +5 (New York, 23–27 June)

1996:

Second United Nations Conference on *Human Settlements* (HABITAT II) (Istanbul, Turkey, 3–14 June)

1995:

Fourth World Conference on *Women* (Beijing, China, 4–15 September)

World Summit for *Social Development* (Copenhagen, Denmark, 6–12 March)

Conference on Straddling and Highly *Migratory Fish Stocks* (New York, March–April and August)

1994:
Global Conference on Sustainable Development of *Small Island Developing States* (Barbados, 25 April–6 May)
International Conference on *Population and Development* (ICPD) (Cairo, Egypt, September)
World Conference on *Natural Disaster* Reduction (Yokohama, Japan, 23–27 May)
World Summit on *Trade Efficiency* (Columbus, Ohio, 17–21 October, www.un.org/events/conferences.htm)

Former UN Trust Territories

The Trusteeship Council suspended operation on 1 November 1994, with the independence of Palau, the last remaining United Nations trust territory on 1 October 1994. On 25 May 1994, the council suspended its obligation to meet annually and agreed to meet as occasion required—by its decision or the decision of its president, or at the request of a majority of its members or the General Assembly or the Security Council. The former UN trust territories are listed below.

Togoland (United Kingdom) united with the Gold Coast (colony and protectorate), a non-self-governing territory administered by the United Kingdom, in 1957 to form Ghana.
Somaliland (Italy) united with British Somaliland protectorate in 1960 to form Somalia.
Togoland (France) became independent as Togo in 1960.
Cameroons (France) became independent as Cameroon in 1960.
Cameroons (United Kingdom) northern territory joined Nigeria and southern territory joined Cameroon (1961).
Tanganyika (United Kingdom) became independent in 1961. (In 1964 Tanganyika and the former protectorate of Zanzibar, which had become independent in 1963, united as a single state under the name of the United Republic of Tanzania).
Ruanda-Urundi (Belgium) voted to divide into the two states of Rwanda and Burundi in 1962.
Western Samoa (New Zealand) became independent as Samoa in 1962.

Nauru (administered by Australia on behalf of Australia, New Zealand, and the United Kingdom) became independent in 1968.

New Guinea (Australia) united with the non-self-governing territory of Papua, also administered by Australia, to become the independent state of Papua New Guinea in 1975.

Trust Territory of the Pacific Islands (United States):

    (a) Federated States of Micronesia became fully self-governing in free association with the United States in 1990.

    (b) Republic of the Marshall Islands became fully self-governing in free association with the United States in 1990.

    (c) Commonwealth of the Northern Mariana Islands became fully self-governing as a commonwealth of the United States in 1990.

    (d) Palau became fully self-governing in free association with the United States in 1994.

Remaining Non-Self-Governing Territories

Only sixteen non-self-governing territories outside the borders of member states of the United Nations remained in 2005 (Table 5.4). This growth in the number of independent states is largely responsible for the growth in UN membership from fifty-one original members to 191 in 2004. All remaining non-self-governing territories, except Western Sahara and Gibraltar, are small islands—nine in the Atlantic and Caribbean and five in the Pacific and Indian Oceans. Of course, it must always be remembered that many of the borders of former colonies that are now member states of the United Nations were drawn by colonial powers. Therefore, there are areas within many of these states in which the inhabitants are demanding self-government.

Public Links to the UN System

Public links to the UN System have escalated as a result of expanding membership, the broadening UN System agenda, and

TABLE 5.4
Remaining Non-Self-Governing Territories in 2005

Territory	Administration	Area (sq.km.)	Population (1)
Africa			
Western Sahara	(2)	266,000	(3)
Atlantic and Caribbean			
Anguilla	United Kingdom	96	11,960
Bermuda	United Kingdom	53	6,997
British Virgin Is.	United Kingdom	153	23,000
Cayman Islands	United Kingdom	260	39,410
Falkland Islands (Malvinas)	United Kingdom	11,961	2,391
Montserrat	United Kingdom	98	5,000
St. Helena	United Kingdom	122	6,000
Turks & Caicos Is.	United Kingdom	430	24,000
US Virgin Is.	United States	340	108,612
Europe			
Gibraltar	United Kingdom	6	26,703
Pacific and Indian Oceans			
American Samoa	United States	197	57,291
Guam	United States	549	154,805
New Caledonia (4)	France	35,853	215,904
Pitcairn	United Kingdom	5	46
Tokelau	New Zealand	10	1,518

(1) From estimates or censuses cited in United Nations documents issued in 2002.

(2) On 26 February 1976, Spain informed the Secretary-General that as of that date it had terminated its presence in the Territory of the Sahara and deemed it necessary to place on record that Spain considered itself thenceforth exempt from any responsibility of any international nature in connection with the administration of the Territory, in view of the cessation of its participation in the temporary administration established for the Territory. In 1990, the General Assembly reaffirmed that the question of Western Sahara was a question of decolonization which remained to be completed by the people of Western Sahara.

(3) Not available.

(4) On 2 December 1986, the General Assembly determined that New Caledonia was a Non-Self-Governing Territory

(www.un.org/Depts/dpi/decolonization/trust3.htm)

the development of new methods for global communication. Increased linkage is a result of both outreach efforts by UN agencies and efforts by public organizations to attain contact and influence in the UN System. Eight types of public links to the UN System are briefly described below:

1. The UN Department of Public Information has a network of public information offices in seventy-seven countries around the world.
2. The UN Department of Public Information also has an NGO section that provides a number of information services to NGOs at UN Headquarters.
3. The Cyberschoolbus project of the UN Global Teaching and Learning Project is an online service that provides a wide range of information on current activities of UN agencies for young people and teachers.
4. Efforts have emerged, with involvement of the secretary-general, to influence the norms and standards of international business.
5. The Non-Governmental Organization Liaison Service (NGLS), supported by several UN agencies, attempts to strengthen UN-NGO dialogue and cooperation.
6. The World Federation of UN Associations has chapters around the world whose goal is to enhance public knowledge about, and involvement in, issues on UN System agendas.
7. One chapter of the World Federation of UN Associations, the UN Association USA, is of particular relevance to people living in the United States.
8. As all local communities have developed growing linkages to the world, local authorities have begun to seek links to the UN System.

Network of UN Information Centers

The network of UN Information Centers (UNICs), UN Information Services (UNIS), and UN Offices (UNOs) links the headquarters with people around the world. Located in seventy-seven countries, these field offices of the Department of Public Information help local communities to obtain up-to-date information on the United Nations and its activities. Eleven offices are in the Americas, including Washington, D.C., and Mexico City.

The Non-Governmental Organization (NGO) Section of the Department of Public Information (DPI)

The Non-Governmental Organization Section of the Department of Public Information at UN Headquarters serves as the liaison between the department and close to 1,400 NGOs from all regions of the world that are associated with the DPI. The goal of this effort is to enable NGOs to disseminate information about the United Nations to their constituencies around the world and thereby enhance support for the United Nations at the grassroots.

Among the services it provides to associated NGOs, the DPI/NGO Section:

1. Organizes, in collaboration with the NGO/DPI Executive Committee, the annual DPI/NGO conference
2. Organizes weekly briefings on UN-related issues
3. Conducts an annual orientation program for newly accredited NGO representatives
4. Organizes quarterly communications workshops
5. Maintains the NGO Resource Center, which offers access to current UN documents, press releases, DPI and UN System publications, and a video-lending library with a collection of UN System videos
6. Provides monthly mailings of UN information materials to associated NGOs
7. Processes UN passes for NGO representatives
8. Processes NGO applications for associative status with DPI
9. Publishes the Directory of NGOs associated with DPI. (www.un.org/dpi/ngosection)

Cyberschoolbus

The United Nations Cyberschoolbus was created in 1996 as the online education component of the Global Teaching and Learning Project, whose mission is to promote education about international issues and the United Nations. The Global Teaching and Learning Project produces teaching materials and activities designed for educational use (at primary, intermediate, and secondary school levels) and for training teachers. The vision of this project is to provide educational resources (both online and in print) to students growing up in a world undergoing increased globalization.

The UN Cyberschoolbus disseminates information and resources about international affairs and brings together diverse communities of students and educators from around the world. The Cyberschoolbus site makes available a number of interactive activities and projects that teach students about global issues. The specific aims of the Cyberschoolbus are: (1) to create an online global education community, (2) to create educational action projects to show students that they have a role in finding solutions to global problems, (3) to give students a voice in global issues, and (4) to provide high-quality teaching resources to a wide range of educators in a cost-effective manner (www.un.org/Pubs/ CyberSchoolBus/index.htm).

Business and the United Nations

The UN relationship with the business community has become more important as the role of business in generating employment and wealth through international trade, investment, and finance has grown and as UN member states have increasingly stressed the importance of private investment in development. At the same time, the business community is dependent on UN efforts to provide norms and standards in such diverse areas as trade laws, shipping, aviation, telecommunications, postal services, and statistics for addressing issues of vulnerability, poverty, environmental degradation, and social conflict.

In an address to the World Economic Forum in January 1999, UN Secretary-General Kofi Annan challenged business leaders to join an international initiative—the Global Compact—that would bring companies together with UN agencies, labor, and civil society to support compact principles in the areas of human rights, labor, the environment, and anticorruption. Global Compact activities were launched at UN Headquarters in New York in July 2000. Global Compact leaders held a summit in June 2004 at UN Headquarters in New York.

The Global Compact seeks to advance responsible corporate citizenship so that business can be part of the solution to the challenges of globalization.

Established by Secretary-General Kofi Annan in March 1998, the UN Fund for International Partnerships (UNFIP) was set up as an autonomous trust fund, headed by an executive director and operating under the leadership of the UN deputy secretary-general. The UNFIP brings together representatives of corporations, foundations, civil society, and academia to work together with the United Nations for the common purpose of assisting those less fortunate around the world. With a $1 million fifteen-year contribution, Ted Turner established the UN Foundation (UNF). The UN Fund for International Partnerships (UNFIP), in partnership with the UNF, serves as an autonomous trust fund that encourages greater private-sector investment in high-impact initiatives.

Of particular relevance in the United States is the Business Council for the United Nations (BCUN), an activity of the UN Association-USA. The BCUN took the lead in organizing business for the 2002 Monterrey International Conference on Financing for Development, organized by the United Nations, IMF, World Bank, and WTO. A goal of the conference was to facilitate relationships between the United Nations and businesses in order to develop "business solutions for a better world" and private-sector leverage for the United Nations' Millennium Development Goals. A series of ongoing conferences and working groups brings the United Nations and UN specialized agencies together with investment banks, ratings agencies, pension and mutual fund managers, insurance companies, and other corporations to work on innovative means of mobilizing private-sector capital for development (www.un.org/partners/business/index.asp).

United Nations Non-Governmental Liaison Service (NGLS)

The United Nations Non-Governmental Liaison Service (NGLS) is a small interagency program with offices in Geneva and New York and a combined staff of ten. It was established in Geneva and New York in 1975 and 1976 respectively, with the aim of strengthening UN-NGO dialogue and cooperation. The NGLS is concerned with the entire UN development agenda, including economic and social development, sustainable development, humanitarian emergencies, human rights (including women's rights), and related issues such as disarmament and democratization. Reflecting its systemwide character, the NGLS is currently supported by seventeen UN System organizations and reports annually to its program and coordination meeting (PCM), held every spring and attended by representatives of those organizations. The coordinator of the NGLS reports to the UN Communications Group (UNCG), its governing body, and through the UNCG to the UN Chief Executives Board (CEB), the highest administrative committee of the UN System, chaired by the secretary-general (www.un-ngls.org).

World Federation of UN Associations (WFUNA)

The World Federation of UN Associations was created in 1946—one year after the establishment of the United Nations. Through UN associations in over 100 member states, it is now a global network of hundreds of thousands of people. The WFUNA enables people around the world to connect with each other on critical global issues that reach from peace and human rights to the spread of democracy, equitable development, and international justice. The WFUNA lists its goals as: (1) seeking to ensure that the United Nations is relevant to the lives of the peoples it exists to serve; (2) campaigning in support of the United Nations, particularly through priorities such as the Millennium Development Goals, human rights, peace and conflict prevention, and bridging the digital divide; (3) educating for global citizenship through research and publications, educational resources, and organizing Model UN events; and (4) partnering and building alliances with other organizations whose objectives include support for the United Nations and its development. The WFUNA has offices at UN Headquarters in New York City and Geneva (www.wfuna.org).

United Nations Association of the USA (UNA-USA)

The United Nations Association of the USA is a member of WFUNA. It has 175 community-based chapters and divisions, with more than 20,000 members nationwide. It also has a council of organizations, with over 100 organizations as members. The programs of UNA-USA include: (1) the Adopt-A-Minefield Campaign that aims to empower people everywhere to take action against the global landmine crisis—one of the world's most pervasive problems; (2) the American NGO Coalition for the International Criminal Court (AMICC), a coalition of nongovernmental organizations committed to achieving full U.S. support for the International Criminal Court; (3) the Business Council for the United Nations, a network of partnerships in economic development, health, education, and technology that advances the common interest of the United Nations and business in a more prosperous and peaceful world; (4) the Global Health Initiative to inform Americans about the United Nations' ongoing efforts to improve children's health; and (5) the Model United Nations, which has been broadened by the UNA-USA's Global Classrooms Program to bring the simulation into the classroom (www.unausa.org).

Local Authority Links to the UN System

Because of increasing awareness of their direct linkage to other cities around the world and the common interests they share with them, local authorities have developed a number of global and regional organizations. Representatives of some of these organizations have banded together to place their concerns on agendas of organizations of the UN System. At the same time, both members of secretariats of UN organizations and representatives of states have become increasingly aware that successful implementation of UN programs on issues such as development, environment, and human rights require cooperative involvement of city authorities, as well as governments of member states. Below are listed an array of efforts to place issues confronted by local authorities on UN System agendas. Of course, UN-Habitat, the UN Settlements Program (UNHSP), plays a key role because of its mandate from the UN General Assembly to promote socially and environmentally sustainable towns. But the list of programs below also reveals involvement of local authorities with the World Bank, UNDP, UNICEF, WHO, UNEP, UNESCO, UNAIDS, UNDP, UNFPA, and UNDCP (Alger 2003, 96–103).

TABLE 5.5
Local Authority Links to the UN System

UN Advisory Committee on Local Authorities, www.unchs.org/committee
UN Habitat (UNHSP), www.unhsp,org
    World Urban Forum (1st session, April–May 2002), www.unhabitat.org/uf.htm
      (Merger of Urban Environmental Forum and International Forum on
      Urban Poverty)
    Urban Managements Program (UMP)
    Sustainable Cities Program (SCP)
    Municipal Development Program (MDP)
    Global Campaign on Urban Governance
    Urban Sanitation and Solid Waste Management
World Bank/UN Habitat (UNHSP) Collaboration
    Cities Alliance, www.cities alliance.org
World Bank, Municipal Development Program, www.worldbank.org
    Local Economic Development Specialists (LED) in Urban Development Sector
UNDP Urban Mangement Program, www.undp.org
    World Alliance of Cities Against Poverty, http://mirror.undp.org/switzerland/wacap
    Initiative Facility for Urban Environment (LIFE)
    Colloquium of Mayors, 1995 (New York, before Copenhagen Social Summit)
UNICEF Mayors Defenders of Children Initiative, periodical meetings of mayors,
    www.unicef.org
International Child Friendly Cities, www.childfriendlycities.org
WHO: Regional Office for Europe
    Healthy Cities network
    Urban Governance Programme, Copenhagen
UNEP Environmental Management Systems (EMS) for Local Authorities
UNAIDS Alliance of Mayors Initiative for Community Action on AIDS
    at the Local Level, www.amicaall.or
UN Interim Administration Mission in Kosovo (UNMIK)
UNESCO Cities for Peace Network
World Summit on Sustainable Development, 2002, Local Government Session

Nineteenth-Century Roots of Organizations in the UN System

In 1954 Gerard Mangone republished a list of nineteenth-century conferences (Mangone 1954, 93–97) taken from a 1907 issue of the *American Journal of International Law* (Vol. 1, Part II, 1907, 808–829). The conferences listed below were chosen from this list with the aim of offering concrete evidence of the nineteenth-century roots of the present UN System. A few conferences have been added from other sources.

1851   First International Sanitary Conference, Paris

1853   General Conference as to Statistics, Brussels
        Maritime Conference for the Adoption of a Uniform System of Meteorological Observation at Sea, Brussels

1863   Conference of Paris on a Postal Union, led to Berne conference 1874

1864   First International Conference on Weights and Measures, Berlin
        Conference of London on Marine Signaling

1865   Conference of Paris on Marine Signaling
        Conference of Paris on Telegraphic Correspondence

1866   Conference of Paris as to Navigation of the Danube

1867   Monetary Conference of Paris

1870   International Commission on the Metric System, set up an International Bureau of Weights and Measures in Paris in 1875

1872   International Telegraph Commission Conference, Rome, convention signed by twenty-one states

1874   Conference on Postal Union, Berne. Permanent bureau at Berne since 1875

1875   Conference on International Telegraphy, St. Petersburg

1878   Conference on Industrial Property, Paris. Reconvened in 1883 and formed an International Union for the Protection of Industrial Property with a headquarters in Berne.
        Monetary Diplomatic Conference, Paris, initiated by the United States. Set up permanent international bureau in Berne

1879   London conference on International Telegraphy Convention, signed by nineteen states.

1880   International Penitentiary Commission

1883   London Conference on Navigation of the Danube

1884   Washington conference adopted Greenwich, England, as Prime Meridian.

1890   International Bureau for the Publication of Customs Tariff

1892   Berne Conference on Literary and Artistic Property, with a bureau in Berne, consolidated with that for protection of industrial property

1889   Conference on International Telegraphy, St. Petersburg

Berne Conference to promote the well-being of the
working classes
International Marine Congress on Uniform Rules to
Secure Life and Property at Sea, Washington on the call
of the United States. Pronounced against a permanent
international maritime commission.
1893   International Sanitary Conference for Repression of
Epidemic Disease, Dresden
1896   International Maritime Committee formed, Hamburg
Conference on Protection of Artistic and Literary
Property, Berne.
1898   Sanitary Conference against Plague, Venice
1899 Permanent Council for the Exploration of the Sea

References

Alger, Chadwick F., 2003, "Searching for Democratic Potential in Emerging Global Governance," in Bruce Morrison, ed., *Transnational Democracy in Critical and Comparative Perspective: Democracy's Range Reconsidered.* Ashgate, UK: Aldershot, 87–105.

American Journal of International Law, "Selected List of International Conferences 1850 to 1905," Vol. 1, Part II, 1907, 808–829.

Business Council for the United Nations (BCUN), www.un.org/partners/business/index.asp.

Citizens for Global Solutions, www.globalsolutions.org.

Cyber School Bus, www.un.org/Pubs/CyberSchoolBus/index.htm.

Dean, Thalif, 2004, "UN Global Taxes Centre Stage," Inter Press Service, July 8, 2004 (available at www.ips.org).

Global Policy Forum, www.globalpolicyforum.org.

International Bill of Human Rights, www.ohchr.org/english/about/publications/docs/fs2.htm.

International Court of Justice Statute, www.icj-cij.org/icjwww/ibasicdocuments/Basetext/istatute.htm.

International Criminal Court, www.icc-cpi.int.

International Criminal Tribunal for Rwanda (ICTR), www.un.org/ictr.

International Criminal Tribunal for the former Yugoslavia (ICTY), www.un.org/icty.

League of Nations Covenant, www.ola.bc.ca/online/cf/documents/1924LeagueNations.html.

Mangone, Gerald J., 1954, *A Short History of International Organizations.* New York: McGraw Hill.

Non-Self-Governing Territories in 2005, www.un.org/Depts/dpi/decolonization/trust3.htm.

Paul, James A., and Katarina Wahlberg, 2002, "Global Taxes for Global Priorities," published by Global Policy Forum, WEED, and the Heinrich Böll Foundation. (Available at www.globalpolicyforum.org). UN Action Against Terrorism, www.un.org/terrorism/.

United Nations Association of the USA, www.unausa.org.

UN Charter, www.un.org/aboutun/charter.

UN Civilian Peace, www.un.org/Depts/dpko/dpko/civpol/4.htm.

UN Dept. of Information, NGO Section, www.un.org/dpi/ngosection.

UN Financing, Alternative Sources, globalpolicy.org/socecon/glotax/index.htm.

UN Global Conferences, www.un.org/News/facts/confercs.htm.

UN General Assembly Presidents, www.un.org/ga/55/session/prdts.

UN Information Centers Worldwide Directory, www.un.org/aroundworld/unics/english/directory.htm.

UN Member States, www.un.org/Overview/unmember.html.

UN Peacekeeping, Overview http://www.un.org/Depts/dpko/dpko/index.asp.

UN Peacekeeping, Present and Past Operations www.un.org/Depts/dpko/dpko/text.htm.

UN Peacemaking and Peacebuilding Missions, www.un.org/Depts/dpa/prev_dip/fst_prev_dip.htm.

World Federation of UN Associations, www.wfuna.org.

Websites for all Agencies in the UN System: Go to un.org, click on "about the United Nations," then click on "Organization Chart of the UN System," then click on the name of the agency that you wish to access.

6

Alternative Futures for the UN System

Earlier chapters in this volume have emphasized ways in which ever-changing technology has made human linkage ever more rapid and distant. As a result of efforts to cope with these changes, the UN System has slowly undergone fundamental changes since its founding. In recent years there have been many proposals for changes in the UN System that are intended to enable it to more effectively cope with present challenges, as well as those that are foreseen in the future. Some of these proposals are focused on specific issues, such as development, and others are focused on specific organizations, such as the Security Council, but more recently several proposals, such as the Secretary-General's High-Level Panel on Threats, Challenges and Change, take a UN System view.

This chapter is essential in the light of the fact that continuing change in the UN System is inevitable and that efforts to cope with this change require a vision of a preferred UN System toward which this change should be guided. Earlier chapters have indicated that this vision must be focused on the entire UN System because experience has demonstrated that organizations throughout the system have roles to play in long-term peace building.

The proposals that follow quickly indicate that this is a very challenging task because, as earlier chapters have revealed, the actors in emerging global governance range from the local to the global. But they will acquaint readers with a feast of options and challenge them to begin defining their preferred future for the

UN System, one that will inevitably undergo constant change as their knowledge about the UN System and world linkages continues to grow. Despite the difficulty of this task it is one that responsible citizens in a democracy must undertake.

"Democracy is on trial in the world, on a more colossal scale than ever before," Charles Fletcher Dole, an American clergyman and author, wrote in his book, *The Spirit of Democracy*, in 1906. They are still very relevant in the present world.

The proposals that follow have been deliberately selected from many possibilities so that they reflect the thoughts of a diversity of sources. They come from a Millennium Summit of all UN member states, panels appointed by the UN secretary-general, officials of individual states, regional organizations of states, global and national NGOs, and from scholars from around the world. They also have been chosen to indicate that people involved in a great diversity of governmental and civil society activities can play roles in shaping the future of the UN System. This point is clearly made in the title of the last section of this chapter: "There Are Tasks for Everybody."

Table of Contents

The Millennium Project

At the UN Millennium Summit in September 2000, a high-level plenary meeting of the sixtieth session of the General Assembly, world leaders adopted the Millennium Development Goals (MDGs). They set targets for reducing poverty, hunger, disease, illiteracy, environmental degradation, and discrimination against women by 2015. In support of these goals, UN Secretary-General Kofi Annan and the administrator of the UN Development Program (UNDP), Mark Malloch Brown, launched the Millennium Project to recommend the best strategies for achieving the MDGs. The Millennium Project will develop a plan for enabling developing countries to meet the MDGs by 2015.

The Millennium Project's research focuses on identifying the operational priorities, organizational means of implementation, and financing structures necessary to achieve the MDGs. Ten thematically orientated task forces are comprised of representatives from academia, the public and private sectors, civil society organizations, and UN agencies, with the majority of participants coming from outside the UN System. The fifteen to twenty members of each task force are global leaders in their areas, selected on the basis of their technical expertise and practical experience. The Millennium Project will report its findings directly to the UN secretary-general and the administrator of the UNDP. The ten task forces focus on:

1. Poverty and economic development
2. Hunger
3. Education and gender equality
4. Child health and maternal health
5. HIV/AIDS, malaria, tuberculosis, and access to essential medicines
6. Environmental sustainability
7. Water and sanitation
8. Improving the lives of slum dwellers
9. Open, rule-based trading systems
10. Science, technology, and innovation

The Millennium Project is directed by Professor Jeffrey Sachs of Columbia University, who serves as special advisor to the secretary-general on the Millennium Development Goals. Through his involvement, some of the project's research is conducted at the Earth Institute of Columbia University, which Sachs directs. A UN experts group oversees UN participation in the project. This group consists of senior representatives from UN agencies, whose role is to ensure that the ten task forces of the Millennium

Project have access to and make full use of the knowledge, experience, and capacities of the UN System.

The Millennium Project is part of the broader UN strategy for implementing the Millennium Declaration. This strategy consists of four elements:

1. The Millennium Project, which analyzes policy options and will develop a plan of implementation for achieving the Millennium Development Goals.
2. The Millennium Campaign, which mobilizes political support for the Millennium Declaration among developed and developing countries. This is led by Eveline Herfkens, the secretary-general's executive coordinator for the MDG campaign.
3. Country-level monitoring of progress towards achieving the Millennium Development Goals, led by the UN Development Group.
4. Operational country-level activities, coordinated across agencies through the UN Development Group, which help individual countries implement policies necessary for achieving the Millennium Development Goals. (www.unmillenniumproject.org)

Secretary General's High-Level Panel on Threats, Challenges and Change

In a speech to the General Assembly in September 2003 Secretary-General Kofi Annan warned member states that the United Nations had reached a fork in the road and must now choose between rising to the challenge to meet new threats or risk erosion in the face of mounting discord between states and unilateral action by them. He asserted that "[t]his may be a moment no less decisive than 1945 itself, when the United Nations was founded" (www.un.org/News/Press/docs/2003/sgsm8891.doc.htm). In order to facilitate the development of UN capacity to cope with new threats the Secretary General appointed a High-Level Panel on Threats, Challenges and Change with sixteen members from Thailand (chair), China, Japan, Pakistan, India, Australia, Egypt, Ghana, Tanzania, France, Norway, the United Kingdom, Russia,

Brazil, Uruguay, and the United States. A text of the report "A More Secure World: Our Shared Responsibility" and an executive summary are available at www.un.org/secureworld.

The panel report "A More Secure World: Our Shared Responsibility" recommends 101 steps that are responsive to six "clusters" of threats:

1. Economic and social threats, including poverty, infectious diseases and environmental degradation
2. Interstate conflict
3. Internal conflict, including civil war, genocide, and other large-scale atrocities
4. Nuclear, radiological, chemical, and biological weapons
5. Terrorism
6. Transnational organized crime

Citizens for Global Solutions, which identifies itself as "a grassroots membership organization," with headquarters in Washington, D.C., has chosen these fifteen items as "some of the main recommendations of the report":

1. Define terrorism as actions "intended to cause death or serious bodily harm to civilians or non-combatants, when the purpose . . . is to intimidate a population or to compel a Government or an international organization to do or to abstain from doing any act."
2. Reform the membership in the Commission on Human Rights to be universal with prominent human rights figures as the heads of national delegations.
3. Establish a Peacebuilding Commission to identify and assist countries that risk sliding towards collapse and "marshal and sustain the efforts of the international community in post-conflict peacebuilding over whatever period may be necessary."
4. Endorsement of the emerging norm of a responsibility to protect civilians from large-scale violence. When a state fails to protect its civilians, the international community then has a responsibility to act to protect civilians as necessary and use force as a last resort.
5. Sets out five basic criteria for the Security Council to consider to legitimize the authorization of the use of

force: the seriousness of threat, the purpose for using force, if it is the last resort, proportional means, and what is the balance of consequences.

6. Create at the UN a small corps of senior police officers (50–100) to plan and organize the international civilian police operations.

7. Allow the UN to fund regional peacekeeping operations authorized by the Security Council with assessed contributions.

8. Re-engage on the problem of global warming and begin new negotiations on a new long-term strategy to reduce global warming beyond the period covered by the Kyoto Protocol.

9. UN Security Council should refer cases of suspected war crimes and crimes against humanity to the International Criminal Court.

10. UN Security Council should slow the spread of weapons using an explicit pledge of "collective action" against any state or group that launches a nuclear attack or even threatens such an attack on a non-nuclear-weapon state.

11. All states should "pledge a commitment to non-proliferation and disarmament," ratify the comprehensive test-ban treaty and support talks on a Fissile Material Cut-off Treaty.

12. A State's notice of withdrawal from the Treaty on the Non-Proliferation of Nuclear Weapons should prompt immediate verification of its compliance with the Treaty.

13. Reform the sanctions system to include routine monitoring mechanisms, develop improved guidelines and reporting procedures to assist states in sanctions implementation, and ensure an auditing mechanism is in place.

14. Two proposals to increase the size of the Security Council from fifteen to twenty-four members and a review of the composition of the Security Council in 2020.

15. Amend the UN Charter by deleting all references in the Charter to the World War II era concept of "enemy States" and eliminate the UN's outdated Trusteeship Council and the Military Staff committee.

(This summary is available at the website of Citizens for Global Solutions, www.globalsolutions.org/programs/intl_instit/UN_ref/HLP_analysis.html, and is reprinted with their permission.)

Cardoso Panel: United Nations–Civil Society Relations

The Cardoso Panel of Eminent Persons was established in February 2003 by Secretary-General Kofi Annan to review past and current practices in UN-civil society relations and make recommendations on how the United Nations' relationship with civil society, as well as the private sector (i.e., business) and parliaments, could be improved. The creation of this panel was responsive to significant growth in the number of civil society organizations now involved at headquarters of UN organizations, as well as the fact that UN conferences on women, racism, and the environment, for example, have encouraged a new type of interaction between the United Nations and civil society. Fernando Henrique Cardoso, a former Brazilian president, chaired a panel of eleven additional members affiliated with governments, nongovernmental organizations, academia, and the private sector: Bagher Asadi (Iran), Manuel Castells (Spain), Birgitta Dahl (Sweden), Peggy Dulany (United States), André Erdös (Hungary), Juan Mayr (Colombia), Malini Mehra (India), Kumi Naidoo (South Africa), Mary Racelis (Philippines), Prakash Ratilal (Mozambique), and Aminata Traoré (Mali). The panel issued its report in June 2004.

The report, "We the Peoples: Civil Society, the United Nations and Global Governance," advocates a shift in how the United Nations organizes its work, from a traditional approach in which governments of states develop agreements on global issues that are then transmitted to these governments for implementation, to a process that includes additional actors. It observes that the shift is already underway, with the traditional procedure for policy analysis and action being supplemented by "global policy networks" that bring together constituencies that include local governments, civil society, business, and parliamentarians with the traditional representatives of the executive branches of states.

Former Brazilian President Fernando Cardoso told corre-
spondents at a headquarters briefing on June 21, 2004: "The
world has changed, and the United Nations must change, too."
He stressed that "[c]onstructively engaging with civil society is
no longer an option for the United Nations, but a necessity."
(www.un.org/News/briefings/docs/2004/Cardoso062104.doc.
htm). He emphasized the need to expand the idea of multilateralism to include multiple actors, including civil society and business, as well as central and local governments. He advocated
stronger links between the local and global levels that he believed
would help overcome democratic deficits in global governance.

The panel proposed that the General Assembly, rather than
the Economic and Social Council (ECOSOC), become the entry
point for nongovernmental organizations to the United Nations,
in an accreditation process that depends less on politics and more
on skills and expertise. In addition, it suggested ways of reducing
the imbalance in access to UN organizations between civil society
groups in the "northern" and "southern" states, including recom-
mending that a fund be created to assist southern NGOs in attending UN activities.

The panel states that priority should be placed on engagement at the country level, mentioning both civil society organizations and involvement with elected representatives, including
both national parliaments and local authorities. It recommends
broadening from representative to participatory democracy by
asserting that traditional democracy aggregates citizens by communities of neighborhood (their electoral districts), but in participatory democracy citizens aggregate in communities of interest.
Modern information and communication technologies make it
possible for these communities of interest to be global as readily
as local. In his press briefing Cardoso observed that traditionally
governments came together to discuss a new issue, reach consensus, and then spur action by governments of states and interstate
organizations. But he noted that today it is increasingly likely
that a civil society movement and public opinion will bring a new
issue to global attention and that initial action will be taken by
coalitions of governments, civil society and others.

The report proposes increased involvement in the General
Assembly by civil society organizations. A correspondent asked
whether this could lead to tension between representatives of
state governments and NGOs in cases such as the invasion of
Iraq. Cardoso responded that the Security Council had already

established successful contact with civil society, especially in implementing humanitarian decisions following conflicts. He explained that civil society organizations would have no seat or vote in the General Assembly, but would simply be allowed a voice.

The report has brought a variety of responses. Not surprisingly the report has been endorsed by local authorities, who are pleased to be newly recognized as participants in UN politics. For example, the presidents of United Cities and Local Governments (UCLG)—the mayor of Paris, Bertrand Delanoë; the mayor of Pretoria (South Africa), Smangaliso Mkhatshwa; and the mayor of São Paulo (Brazil), Marta Suplicy—have endorsed the proposals of the Cardoso Report. The report singles out United Cities and Local Governments (UCLG) as an important means whereby people at the local level are represented in global governance. It proposes that the UN regard the UCLG as an advisory body on all governance matters. It proposes the adoption of a resolution affirming and respecting local autonomy as a universal principle. The presidents of the UCLG have called on governments to adopt these recommendations when they are debated in the UN General Assembly and have pledged to work closely with the United Nations to implement them.

On the other hand, broadening the recommended array of participants, including local authorities and the private sector (defined as profit-making activities) is seen by some NGOs as weakening the role of NGOs. A number of NGOs issued sharply critical statements over the summer of 2004, and some UN governmental delegations expressed strong displeasure too. Criticism was sharpened by rumors that the Non-Governmental Liaison Service (NGLS) might fall victim to the Cardoso process (www.un.org/reform/panel.htm).

Panel on UN Peace Operations (Brahimi Report on Peacekeeping)

Chaired by Lakhdar Brahimi, an Algerian former foreign minister, the UN Peace Operations Panel, with ten members from all six continents, issued its report in August 2000. This group of ten experts on UN peace operations was appointed by Secretary-General Kofi Annan to respond to peacekeeping challenges confronted by the UN. The first paragraph of the Executive Summary of the Brahimi Report includes this statement: "Without renewed commitment on the part of Member States, significant institutional change and increased financial support, the United Nations will not be capable of executing the critical peacekeeping and peace-building tasks that the Member States assign to it in coming months and years" (www.un.org/peace/reports/peace_operations).

Space permits only a brief summary of some of the main points of this "far-reaching report by an independent panel." A UN press release, 23 August 2000, issued the following brief summary of main points in the lengthy report. This summary is reprinted below. It is available at www.un.org/peace/reports/peace_operations, along with the full report.

1. *Doctrine and Strategy:* The Panel calls for more effective conflict prevention strategies, pointing out that prevention is "far preferable for those who would otherwise suffer the consequences of war, and a less costly option for the international community than military action, emergency humanitarian relief, or reconstruction after a war has run its course." It says peacekeepers must be able to defend themselves and their mandate, with "robust rules of engagement," against those who renege on commitments or seek to undermine peace accords by violence. And it urges the Secretariat to draw up a plan for developing better peace-building strategies. Peacekeepers and peace-builders, it says, are "inseparable partners," since only a self-sustaining peace "offers a ready exit to peacekeeping forces."

2. *Mandates.* The Secretariat "must tell the Security Council what it needs to know, not what it wants to hear, when formulating or changing mission mandates."

3. *Transitional civil administration.* A panel of international legal experts should explore the idea of an interim criminal code for use in places where the United Nations is given temporary executive powers (as currently in Kosovo and East Timor), pending the re-establishment of local rule of law and law enforcement capacity.

4. *Timelines:* "Traditional" United Nations peacekeeping operations (sent to monitor ceasefires and separations of

forces after inter-State wars) should be fully deployed within 30 days; more complex peace operations, sent to help end intra-State conflicts, within 90 days.

5. *Personnel:* Member States should work together to form "coherent, multinational, brigade-sized forces," ready for effective deployment within these timelines; and should each establish a national pool of civilian police officers. The Panel does not call for a standing United Nations army, but says the Secretariat should establish "on-call" lists of about 100 military and 100 police officers and experts, from national armies and police forces, who would be available on seven days' notice to establish new mission headquarters. Conditions of service for civilian specialists should also be revised so that the United Nations can attract more qualified personnel, and reward good performance with better career prospects.

6. *Speed and efficiency:* The Secretary-General should be allowed funds to start planning a mission before the Security Council approves it, so that when approved it can be deployed quickly. Field missions should be given greater freedom to manage their own budgets. Additional ready-made mission "start-up kits" should be maintained at the UN Logistics Base in Brindisi, Italy.

7. *Funding for peacekeeping support:* The Panel remarks that, after 52 years, it is time to treat peacekeeping as a "core activity" of the United Nations rather than a "temporary responsibility." Headquarters support for it should therefore be funded mainly through the regular United Nations budget, instead of the current "Support Account" which has to be justified year by year and post by post.

Security Council Reform

It is widely recognized that the Security Council requires reforms that reflect changes in the world during the sixty years that have passed since its founding. These changes include a fourfold increase in UN membership. In 1965 the UN Charter was amended to increase Security Council membership from eleven to fifteen, but the Council still offers permanent membership with a veto only to the five major victors in World War II. Despite the geographical representation of all global regions in the ten elected members, overall Security Council membership remains unbalanced in favor of the industrialized North. The ongoing Security Council reform debate includes many reform proposals. An effort has been made here to acquaint the reader with a range of perspectives in different parts of the world. They offer insight on why, despite many proposals and many debates, no agreement has yet been reached.

Expanding the Council from fifteen to twenty-four members is one of the main reform recommendations. There are two competing models. The first one would add six new permanent members without veto powers—two from Africa, two from Asia, and one each from the Americas and Europe. It would also add three nonpermanent members with a two-year term like the ones currently elected to sit on the body. The second option would add eight new seats for semipermanent members, which would be elected for four years and could have their terms extended. Africa, Asia, Europe, and the Americas would each get two of these seats and one additional nonpermanent member would also be added.

The first model is supported by Germany, with hopes that it would secure one of the new permanent seats. Japan, Brazil, and India also support this plan and hope for permanent seats for themselves. While Britain, France, and Russia have indicated support for the aspirations of these four countries, the United States has so far refused to give Germany a nod of approval. The Bush administration in Washington has, however, voiced its support for Japan. It is reported that Nigeria, South Africa, and Egypt would compete for the African seats.

Support for the second version includes Italy, a strong opponent of handing a permanent seat to Germany. Italy is concerned that giving a Security Council seat to Germany, in addition to the two permanent seats already occupied by France and Britain, would weaken its role in the European Union. Others favoring the plan to introduce eight semipermanent seats include Pakistan—which rejects India's place on the Council—and Mexico and Argentina, which oppose Brazil's claims.

The Ministry of Foreign Affairs of Japan has stated its position on Security Council enlargement with points that are quoted below.

1. It is absolutely necessary to expand the permanent membership with the addition of both developed and

developing countries which possess the ability and will to assume global responsibility for international peace and security. Japan is prepared to assume greater responsibilities as a permanent member of the reformed Security Council.

2. Considering the tremendous increase in the number of United Nations Member States, it is also essential to expand the non-permanent membership.

3. In order to maintain both effectiveness and representativeness, the appropriate size of the expanded Security Council should be twenty-four members, with the addition of two developed and three developing countries to the permanent membership and four non-permanent members.

4. When allotting the expanded Council a new permanent member and non-permanent seats to regional groups, it should be up to each group to decide how to elect the permanent member(s) from that group.

5. Concerning the veto, as a matter of principle, there should be no differentiation between new and old permanent members. In Japan's view, the resolution of this issue will require the political judgement of all nations at the final stages of negotiation.

6. The Security Council's work methods should be improved to increase transparency and accountability (www.mofa.go.jp/policy/un/reform/role21.html#2).

Africa's Position

The Institute for Global Dialogue (IGD), a South African non-governmental organization, has circulated a much more detailed proposal in its policy brief series *Global Insight*, published by the Institute. The extract that appears here is printed with the approval of the IGD. Information on IGD is available at www.igd.org.za.

Following the launch of the High-Level Panel Report, African Heads of State decided at the end of the 4th Ordinary Session of the Assembly of the African Union to set up a 15 member committee to hammer out a common stance for the continent on UN reforms. The committee, whose members were drawn from the continent's main regions, was to consider two main options that take into account the African common position. These are contained in the Harare Assembly Declaration of 1997, and include developments on the international scene since the adoption of the Harare Declaration and the essence of the debate in the AU Executive Council in Abuja on 28 January 2005. The AU committee met in Mbabane, Swaziland from 20–22 February 2005 to hammer out what has become the "Ezulwini Consensus." While side-stepping the issue of which African countries would represent the continent in a future reformed UN Security Council, the committee resolved that Africa would insist on getting two veto-wielding permanent seats in a reformed UN Security council. In principle, the AU is opposed to the notion of exclusive veto power, as it is undemocratic. However, the organization also argues that if other Security Council members have veto power, then as long as it exists, all members, old and new, should have it.

Aside from African governments' case for at least two permanent veto-wielding seats and five non-permanent, rotational seats, they have also insisted that in the event of approval of the proposed reform of the Security Council, it should be the exclusive prerogative of the African continent—the African Union more precisely—to decide on which African states should represent the continent in this august body. More importantly, African leaders have argued strongly against any attempt to discriminate between old and future (new) permanent members of the Security Council. Their position is that either the veto power is scrapped completely or it must be extended to all permanent members of a broadened Security Council, within the ambit of the UN Charters' emphasis on the equality of member states.

Prospects for Africa's Candidates

Egypt, Nigeria, and South Africa have emerged as three main contenders for the continent's two seats on the UN-SC. Underneath this spirit of entente between Africa's major role players lies the reality of interstate power politics—national interest—with one particularly aspiring candidate, Nigeria, intent on out-manoeuvring other rather muted aspirants, South Africa and Egypt. The attractiveness of securing a permanent seat (even one devoid of the undemocratic but strategic veto power privilege) might be sufficient incentive to bring about a divorce between Africa's leading states, particularly Nigeria and South Africa.

However, even a casual reading of the High Panel's reform proposals, reveals that the panelists were expressly against any broadening of the veto power to new members. In fact, in the proposed models ("A" and "B") they have made no allowance for the extension of the veto power to potential new permanent or/and non-permanent members of the Security Council. As a matter of fact, they seem to have placed an injunction on the extension of the veto power by declaring: "we recommend that under any reform proposal, there should be no expansion of the veto." The official argument against an extension of the veto is that it would blunt the instrument and weaken the Security Council. It would seem, however, that this position was forced into the reform agenda by the traditional veto-wielding powers, in a bid to protect and preserve their post-war privileges. From this perspective, it would seem that the High-Level Panel made attempts to pander to the interests of the powerful.

Conclusion

The momentum for the reform of the UN has come from a global consensus over the need to align the organisation with new global realities and power configurations. There is no denying the fact that the scope of the ongoing reform agenda is unprecedented in the history of the institution. However, while the proposed reforms appear to be ground-breaking in areas such as broadening the definition of "collective security" and shifting from unilateralism to broad-based multilateralism, they painfully fall short in meeting the yearning for the democratisation of the Security Council. Overall, the High-level Panel report's recommendations are based on political realism. Its recommendations are anchored largely in the fear of alienating the interests of the world's most powerful nations.

Significantly though, the report calls for donor countries to live up to the commitments they have already made to developing countries. Irrespective of how one views these reform proposals, they have set in motion underlying centripetal and centrifugal forces amongst regions and regional "actors." While the veto-wielding nations are determined to retain their privileges, emerging global and regional actors are bent on wresting them away or at the very least, sharing them.

In Africa, the struggle to influence the reform process has created a potentially destructive rift that has brought into sharp relief how the continent's lead states view each other. If this rift becomes manifest, a lot of work will be needed to rebuild destroyed diplomatic fences when the dust finally settles. Whichever state gets the nomination it will be representing Africa not its flag. Both candidates should be states accepted by Africans as their representatives rather than those chosen for them by outside forces and interests.

Policy considerations

(1) **For the champions of the UN reform agenda:**

Although there is little beyond an advisory opinion that Annan and his reform team can express, they would need to shed the fear of provoking the wrath of the great powers by insisting on genuine reforms. This will help boost the legitimacy of the UN and render it more effective and efficient. More precisely, they must adroitly address the issue of the anachronism of the veto power if the proposed reforms are to be taken seriously. Any reform agenda that shies away from this thorny issue will be cosmetic and would do little to reverse the perceptions of illegitimacy and effectiveness of the institution.

(2) **For the African Union:**

Without necessarily being constrained by the wishes of the more powerful current veto-wielding states, the AU must state its case in a manner that is not overtly confrontational to the interests and wishes of the P–5. And while Africa's claim is legitimate and not necessarily overly ambitious, the AU must be psychologically prepared to settle for non-veto wielding Security Council membership. One suggestion would be that more effort be put into building stronger multilateral groupings from the Global South to counter the effects of the rapacious power of the US and its allies.

(3) For African contenders:

While contending African states have a right to promote their respective national interests, they have an obligation to conduct themselves responsibly and in a manner that would not compromise the broader African agenda. They need to present a unified, common position as embodied in the "Ezulwini Consensu." Potentially disastrous rifts will open the continent to the divide and rule tactics by the North. Nigeria, South Africa and Egypt must, therefore, avoid all strategies that consist of undermining and backstabbing each other. Practices like labelling each other as being less African or being too corrupt to qualify for a seat at the UN must, as a matter of urgency, be avoided. For South Africa in particular, the foreign ministry must be aware that the odds do not appear to be totally in its favour. Therefore, there is need to double diplomatic efforts to engage the continent on the negative perceptions that haunt it.

(4) To Africa's potential spoilers:

To the extent that it remains their legitimate aspiration to strive for a democratic reform agenda that avails all African states equal opportunity to influence UN Security Council decisions, they must realise that the Security Council represents the pinnacle of global power politics, in which only stronger countries will hold sway. Their efforts must therefore be directed at supporting stronger African candidates for seats on the Security Council.

(5) To current veto-wielding states:

Although current veto-wielding states will try to maintain the status quo, they must not lose sight of the fact that the failure to democratise the UN in line with new global power realities will act as a real obstacle to multilateralism. They must, therefore, make a conscious effort to create space for new comers to the Security Council to share in the privileges that go with the huge responsibility of keeping global peace and preventing war (Ikome and Samasuwo, 2005).

Reform of the Economic and Social Council (ECOSOC)

On 6 May 2004, the UN Association-USA (UNA-USA) and the World Federation of UN Associations (WFUNA) convened a workshop to discuss the current challenges and opportunities facing ECOSOC under the title "How Can ECOSOC Reform Help Achieve the Millennium Development Goals?" The report on the meeting is available at the UNAUSA website (www.unausa.org). Part of the report is printed here with the permission of the UN Association of the USA, copyright 2004.

The proposals of the workshop focused on four broad goals: (1) Define ECOSOC's role and streamline its program of work, (2) Clarify and strengthen ECOSOC's relationships with other U.N. and related institutions, (3) Enhance ECOSOC's institutional capacity, and (4) Widen participation in ECOSOC's activities.

1. Define ECOSOC's Role and Streamline its Program of Work

Increase ECOSOC's status as a political forum for reviewing and evaluating the U.N.'s system-wide efforts to achieve the Millennium Development Goals (MDGs). This process should take into account the normative standards already set on human rights and sustainable development.

Make ECOSOC's program of work and annual agenda more flexible. Instead of concentrating most of the work of ECOSOC in July of each year, efforts should be made to make ECOSOC's response to current crises or opportunities more timely and free-flowing. For example, ECOSOC could hold more ad hoc focused sessions on critical issues.

Focus ECOSOC's activities on providing policy guidance to its subsidiary bodies. This would return ECOSOC to its original role as an overarching policy body for the numerous programs and commissions it oversees.

ECOSOC should create a segment on global macroeconomic strategy and management which includes a debate on the adequacy of funds for financing development and implementation of the MDGs. This type of debate is critical since the central challenge to achieving the Millennium Development Goals is the inadequacy of mechanisms for financing for development.

ECOSOC should actively promote the urgent need for all OECD governments to dedicate 0.7% of their GNP to development assistance.

2. Clarify and Strengthen ECOSOC's Relationships with other U.N. and Related Organizations

ECOSOC should establish a more meaningful relationship with the functional commissions, funds and programs that it oversees. It should pay more attention to the role ECOSOC could play in dealing with the problem of "mission creep" among the bodies that it nominally supervises. The program of work for each of the functional commissions in particular, should come from ECOSOC, and not the other way around.

ECOSOC should request that the World Bank, International Monetary Fund, World Trade Organization, etc. present their annual reports for comment and evaluation by ECOSOC. As a result, each organization's political accountability would be strengthened, and the role of ECOSOC as a coordinating body would be cemented.

ECOSOC should expand its coordination with the Security Council on specific economic security situations. ECOSOC should act in concert with the Security Council, as it has done in reference to Guinea Bissau and Burundi, both countries in post-conflict situations.

ECOSOC should seek to build partnerships with related institutions. Since ECOSOC cannot dictate or impose its will on other institutions, it should seek to build strong partnerships toward realizing common goals. The meetings ECOSOC convenes jointly with the Bretton Woods institutions illustrate the beginning of this kind of partnership.

3. Enhance ECOSOC's Institutional Capabilities

Each member-state that belongs to ECOSOC should be encouraged to appoint a representative whose portfolio includes direct responsibility for his/her government's ECOSOC participation. This representative should possess the experience, skills and networks key to enhancing the leadership role of ECOSOC.

ECOSOC should request governments to channel a portion of their development funds through ECOSOC to enhance its capacity to give vitality to the "global partnership for development."

ECOSOC should develop small working groups on specific substantive issues.

4. Widen Participation in ECOSOC Activities

ECOSOC should convene meetings with a diverse group of government ministers to promote cross-sectoral dialogue. As opposed to other intergovernmental bodies (e.g., World Health Organization, World Bank, etc.) ECOSOC does not have a natural constituency in national governments. On the surface, this might be perceived as an acute challenge for ECOSOC. However, it could also serve to better position ECOSOC as a body that brings together Ministers from various relevant portfolios and makes the inherent linkages between finance and health or other cross-sectoral economic and social development issues. In addition to a cross-section of governmental representatives, ECOSOC can strengthen its ability to engage both civil society and the private sector by identifying areas in which each can contribute to the policy debate.

ECOSOC should engage civil society and business leaders to draw on their knowledge, expertise, and capacity to promote development on the ground. ECOSOC should use consultative arrangements with civil society groups to bring expertise, local knowledge and the perspectives of otherwise neglected constituencies (particularly people living in poverty) to substantive discussions. ECOSOC should partner with the private sector as a source of innovation, ideas and capital. In particular, it should promote public/private partnerships. If civil society and private sector groups are included principally in deliberations, not decision-making per se, governments should welcome expanded participation.

ECOSOC should convene meetings of the financial and economic editors from leading news agencies during high level sessions of ECOSOC to expand media coverage of ECOSOC.

ECOSOC should improve its use of the internet to promote awareness of ECOSOC's activities and engage local actors in developing countries. (Reprinted with the permission of the United Nations Association of the USA, Copyright, 2004)

UN Parliamentary Assembly

In September 2004 the Committee for a Democratic United Nations, a German nongovernmental organization, released a strategy paper to mobilize support for the establishment of a UN Parliamentary Assembly (UNPA). The group's goal is to raise support for a global parliamentary body by the German Bundestag, the European Parliament, and the German public. The creation of a "parliamentary dimension" of the United Nations has been proposed by resolutions of the German Bundestag, the European Parliament, the Inter-Parliamentary Union (IPU) and the Parliamentary Assembly of the Council of Europe. The committee has noted that this proposal is being made in light of the growing cooperation of the United Nations and the Inter-Parliamentary Union (IPU) (www.uno-komitee.de/en).

This proposal is building on numerous earlier proposals for the creation of a second general assembly directly elected by the people in UN member states. Daniele Archibugi, Director at the Italian National Research Council (CNR), asserts that "the most elaborate and realistic proposal . . . and one which has gained the widest support was put forward back in 1982 by Jeffrey Segall and the International Network for a UN Second Assembly (INFUSA)." Assuming an evolutionary perspective, the proposal asks the General Assembly, using its authority to establish "subsidiary organs " (Article 22 of the Charter), to establish such an assembly. Its membership would be directly elected, with representation from each country based on population. This proposal was supported by ninety-four nongovernmental organizations in 1993 (Archibugi 1993, 308).

In the past, proposals for a second general assembly tended to be quickly rejected by many as unrealistic. But a changing climate was revealed in 1994 by the fact that two former members of the UN Secretariat with long experience proposed a UN Parliamentary Assembly (UNPA) because of their belief "that NGOs cannot fully and adequately represent 'We, the peoples of the United Nations.'" In making their recommendation, Erskine

Childers and Brian Urquhart quote a statement by Ernest Bevin, foreign secretary of the United Kingdom, to the House of Commons in 1945: "We need a new study for the purpose of creating a world assembly elected directly from the people of the world as a whole, to whom the governments who form the United Nations are responsible" (Childers and Urquhart 1994, 176).

The Childers/Urquhart proposal calls for an assembly elected by universal adult franchise "for complementing the knowledge and perspectives brought to intergovernmental organs by government delegations." It would not limit its agenda to intergovernmental business "but include its own original activities to develop policy and programme proposals for the UN" (Childers and Urquhart 1994, 177). It would issue its own reports and communications as UN documents. "While recognizing the challenge in creating a UNPA for 6 billion people, the authors note the precedent of the Indian Parliament representing 850 million people from a diversity of cultures and nations and the European Parliament representing 345 million. In February 1994 the European Parliament endorsed the proposed UNPA, and the Canadian House of Commons has offered to host an exploratory meeting focused on the creation of a UNPA" (Alger, 1996, 347).

In the Childers/Urquhart proposal, the process for establishing the parliament would also be originated by the General Assembly under its authority to establish subsidiary bodies. Parliaments of member states would select representatives to the first UNPA based on population. Initially, the UNPA would meet once a year after the General Assembly (GA) and debate and comment on the GA session. Eventually it would develop detailed proposals for its conversion into a directly elected assembly. This would require a Charter amendment. Childers and Urquhart foresee UNPA functions to be: (1) consultation by the General Assembly and ECOSOC; (2) discussion of major decisions before ECOSOC; (3) conveying opinions to the GA and ECOSOC; (4) holding "question times" with the secretary-general and the presidents of the GA, ECOSOC, and the Security Council; (5) requesting that policies adopted by the GA be extended or amended; and (6) proposal of new policies. It is believed that budgetary power would be unlikely but that the UNPA would convey its views on the budget to the GA.

As concrete examples of the expected contributions of a UNPA, Childers and Urquhart give early priority to "examining and selecting the best means of additional financing of the UN.

Parliamentarians would do this without the built-in resistance of executive government, and with a more sure touch regarding citizen involvement and support for any needed national legislation." And they note that "diplomats are not particularly well-suited to oversee and improve the UN's public information and education activities. A Parliamentary Assembly could co-opt communication specialists to help its members apply their own well-attuned insights into these extremely important activities which have suffered serious neglect for many years" (Childers and Urquhart 1994, 180).

"Obviously, the UNPA would not be expected to replace the multiple routes through which NGOs can link people in a diversity of territorial entities to the UN system. Instead, NGOs and a UNPA would be complementary. Indeed, even if the UNPA were an assembly of 1,000, each member would have a constituency of more than 6,000,000 people. Thus, while its members would no doubt bring to UNPA perspectives different from those of representatives of states, they would still tend to be a cosmopolitan elite. But they would have more local ties than professional diplomats. Certainly the proposal for a UNPA, combined with suggestions that NGOs develop a more self-conscious strategy for their multiple roles, reveals the emergence of images of the kind of global political process required if UN potential is to be liberated. Very important is the fact that these visions have been provoked by the *real* behavior of NGOs in many venues throughout the UN system, and the fact that they are perceived to be realistic by international civil servants with long experience" (Alger 1996, 348).

Asian Civil Society Forum (ACSF) Statement on UN–Civil Society Relations

The first Asian Civil Society Forum (ACSF) was held in Bangkok, Thailand, in December 2002 under the theme "UN-NGO Partnerships for Democratic Governance in Asia: Building Capacities and Networks for Human Rights and Sustainable Development." It was a pilot project of an organization of NGOs at UN Headquarters in New York City, the Conference of NGOs in Consultative Relationship with the United Nations (CONGO), in its effort to reach out to NGOs in the South, particularly in Asia, toward the end of furthering partnerships with the United Nations for common goals. This was followed by the Asian Civil Society Forum 2004, held in Bangkok in November 2004. This forum issued an "ACSF Statement on UN-Civil Society Relations." This statement offers a very informative overview of issues on the agenda of NGOs attempting to strengthen their capacity to have an impact on decisions made in agencies in the UN System. So that the information that follows accurately reflects the views of those from Asian civil society organizations, the report that follows is complete and unedited. It is printed here with the permission of the ACSF and is available at www.acsf.info.

Introduction.

1. We, more than 300 participants of the 2nd Asian Civil Society Forum (ACSF) 2004, representing over 100 local, national, regional and international NGOs and civil society organizations from more than 30 countries of the Asian region and the rest of the world gathered in Bangkok, Thailand from Nov. 21 to 25, 2004 to discuss the theme "Building UN/NGOs Partnerships for Democratic Governance through MDGs." The ACSF was facilitated by the Conference of NGOs in consultative relationship with the UN (CONGO) Working Group on Asia in cooperation with many regional civil society organizations and networks in Asia.

2. On the first day of the Forum, we discussed the report of the High-level Panel of Eminent Persons on UN-Civil Society Relations (Cardoso Panel) as well as on the Report of the UN Secretary General (SG) on the implementation of the Report (A/59/354) in the context of Asian civil society's effort towards, "building UN/NGOs partnerships for democratic governance." The day-long discussion consisted of some major presentations including one by Ms Mary Racelis, member of the Cardoso Panel, and three sub-regional group discussions (Northeast Asia, Southeast Asia and South Asia) and a concluding plenary.

3. The discussion on UN-CS relations was a follow-up to the Asian consultation of the Cardoso Panel held in Bangkok in October, 2003. The meeting formed part of the Panel's regional consultation process. The second consultation, held in Bangkok on Aug. 13, 2004, two

months after the release of the Report, was on the 30 proposals contained in the report of the Panel. Some participants of ACSF 2004 had attended all of these meetings.

4. During the deliberations, as participants, we expressed interest regarding the prospect of enhanced relations with the UN. Recalling the first three words of the UN Charter, "We the Peoples," we welcomed the spirit of the Cardoso Report in calling for greater access to inter-governmental processes for all peoples. Some of the proposals in the Panel's Report offer substantial potential for enhancing interaction at all levels between the UN system and civil society. Both the Panel's recommendations and the SG's Report to the UN General Assembly on its implementation provide opportunities for discussion and debate on democratic global governance.

Issues, Concerns and Recommendations.

Increasing Participation of NGOs in Intergovernmental Bodies

5. We acknowledge the nature of the UN as an intergovernmental organization and the role of member nations in it.

6. We, as members of civil society, positively respond to the SG's call to organize around broad networks to enhance civil society participation following recommendations in Proposal 23. However, given the diversity and logistical peculiarities in Asia, such networking should take place voluntarily, and with full respect for the diversity and specificity of civil society organizations.

7. We note the failure in both the reports of the Panel and the SG, to include our recommendations to enhance civil society's participation in the work of the UN with particular regard to the regional level. We also note that both the Panel's recommendations and the SG's Report failed to encompass the diversity of civil society's engagement in human rights issues within the UN intergovernmental processes.

8. We, therefore, recommend that UN Economic and Social Commission for Asia and the Pacific (ESCAP) take on a more proactive role in facilitating the development of regional models/frameworks for enhancing cooperation. We noted an overall lack of enthusiasm and

absence of strategies at regional level for engaging civil society. Therefore, we call upon the UN ESCAP and other UN agencies in Asia to:

> Review their existing mechanisms of engagement with civil society in line with the recommendations contained in the report of the UN SG with a view to enhancing interaction between governments, inter-governmental organizations and civil society towards the full implementation of the spirit and values embodied in the Millennium Declaration;
> Encourage more sub-regional and regional interaction and facilitate more internet-based fora to allow greater access to a broader range of CSOs to be involved and informed;

> Consider holding more international meetings outside New York and Geneva, perhaps holding meetings rotationally in regional venues.

9. We look forward to the regular civil society hearings to be initiated by the UN Secretary General before and during the UN General Assembly beginning with the 60th session of UN GA in 2005 to review the implementation of the UN Millennium Declaration. As civil society organizations we affirm our right to be involved in these deliberations and are prepared to play our part and bring local concerns to the UN agenda.

Establishing a Trust Fund to Increase the Participation of Representatives of Non-governmental Organizations from Developing Countries
10. We welcome the SG's commitment to the creation of a trust fund to rectify current imbalances in participation of civil society from developing countries. However, we remain concerned that the proposed fund would not undermine or eliminate existing trust funds that are operating well. We enjoin governments to contribute generously and consistently to this fund so that civil society participation is secured well into the future.

Improving Accreditation
11. The streamlining and simplification of accreditation is very welcome. We hope that the single process makes

NGO access to inter-governmental deliberations much easier. However, we are confident that the single process will not be used to exclude bona fide civil society representation. In this regard, we urge the SG to ensure that the principles of openness, transparency and accountability be put into practice to ensure effective and meaningful participation. In particular, we urge the SG to create a "complaints mechanism" with a transparent process within which representatives of NGOs such as the Conference of NGOs in consultative relationship with the UN (CONGO) has an active presence. This is imperative as a modality for redress of grievances of NGOs who may be denied access due to political considerations.

12. We hope that security considerations and space limitations are not used to deny access to legitimate civil society organizations, including those working in areas of conflict resolution, de-colonization and the right to self-determination, as this will further undermine participation.

Rights and Responsibilities Pertaining to Participation

13. We reiterate our firm commitment to the aims of the UN Charter. We acknowledge the need for appropriate correspondence with the rules of procedure and decorum of the UN.

Improving the UN Secretariat's Dialogue with NGOs

14. Among the steps to improve internal in-house measures, civil society appreciates the provision of free access to the Official Documentation System (ODS). It also welcomes the moves to establish a central database of NGOs and to develop best practices relating to NGO involvement in UN activities.

Enhancing Country Level Engagement with NGOs

15. The Millennium Development Goals (MDGs) are not likely to be met without active and effective CSO involvement at grassroots and local levels. In this regard, we urge the Resident Coordinators of UNDP to engage in a systematic, sustained and meaningful manner with CSOs with a view to mutually enhancing the capacities of all stakeholders.

Exploring the Enlargement of the Partnerships Office

16. We welcome the fact that the Non-Governmental Liaison Service (NGLS) will be upgraded within the institutional standing and funding stability of the UN. We hope that this process will make the NGLS stronger and enhance its capacity for it's [sic] independent functioning in order for it better to fulfill its role in supporting civil society participation from the developing countries. In particular, we warn against any attempt to divert funds, energies and other resources from NGLS to other activities. The process of upgrading should also not become an entry point for corporate funding of unrelated activities.

17. We firmly believe that the Global Compact Office should not be a part of the Partnership Office structure.

18. We particularly welcome the decision of the SG not to incorporate the Secretariat of the Permanent Forum on Indigenous Peoples into the Partnerships Office. We find it appropriate that it remain under the purview of the Department of Economic and Social Affairs (DESA).

Way Forward

19. We commit ourselves to the challenges identified in the Report:

To engage in a constructive and proactive dialogue with our respective national governments and UN bodies to seek their support for our recommendations, while always maintaining our critical and independent engagement with these issues from the perspective of the communities and sectors that we represent.

To monitor the ongoing development in the UN General Assembly as well as the UN Secretariat and to lobby inter-governmental processes to make sure that our concerns are taken into consideration.

To network strategically with civil society organizations at national, regional and global levels to advance the concerns of Asian people regarding peace and disarmament, human rights and social justice, sustainable development and livelihoods and to strengthen Asian civil society's participation in inter-governmental processes.

There Are Tasks for Everybody

In a volume entitled *The Future of the UN System: Potential for the Twenty-First Century* (1998), edited by Chadwick F. Alger, twenty-two scholars from all continents have written twelve chapters in their search for feasible opportunities for strengthening the capabilities of the UN System. They cover a broad array of subjects that range across controlling weapons, peacekeeping, human rights, economic development, refugees, advancement of women, ecological security, communication about the United Nations, peace education, roles for NGOs, and other issues. They illuminate the fact that there are many opportunities for strengthening the UN System. They are scattered throughout the system, many regarding issues that are significant for global governance that rarely command headiness. The authors have creatively revealed that strengthening of global governance can involve "tasks for everybody," a phrase used by Johan Galtung, a Norwegian scholar widely recognized as one of the founders of peace research, in his proposals for "individual activation" in the pursuit of preferred worlds (Galtung 1980). What is needed are people of vision in a wide array of occupations, institutions, and activities around the world devoted to employing multilateral processes in solving global problems.

Of fundamental importance is creative involvement not only of representatives of states and members of international secretariats, but also people in NGOs directly linked to the UN System, as well as a multitude of other NGOs, citizen groups, and provincial, urban, and rural governments. Global problems reach from towns and cities—in their smokestacks, economic depravity, torture and death squads, etc.—across state borders to regional organizations and eventually to the field offices, headquarters, councils, and assemblies of the UN System. Effective global governance must link local people who have knowledge about the UN System with people in the United Nations who are in touch with their local roots. We believe that somewhere in the recommendations of these twenty-two scholars there are possibilities for the involvement of all readers of this volume in enhancing the effectiveness of the UN System.

The recommendations of the twenty-two authors can be briefly summarized under five headings: (1) strengthen UN response capacity, (2) broaden the participating community, (3) strengthen institutional competence, (4) enhance knowledge, and (5) widen UN outreach.

   I. Strengthen UN response capacity
      1. Long-range planning
      2. Early warning
      3. Rapid reaction
      4. Extension of nonmilitary options
  II. Broaden the participating community
      5. Widen participation of nongovernmental organizations
      6. Widen participation of local governments and organizations
 III. Strengthen institutional competence
      7. Strengthen institutional infrastructure
      8. Enhance institutional memory
      9. New financing sources
 IV. Enhance knowledge
      10. Research
      11. Education and training
  V. Widen UN outreach
      12. Extend UN information collection and dissemination
      13. Extend publicity about UN activities and achievements
      14. Offer rewards for fulfilling UN standards
      15. Visions of the future

In the summary that follows, we have chosen only a few of the items suggested by the authors. They have been selected in order to illustrate the broad array of opportunities available for strengthening the UN System.

I. Strengthen UN Response Capacity

1. Long-range Planning

Pervasive in this volume are explicit and implied appeals for planning that would cope with underlying causes of endemic violence, the squalor of refugee camps, violations of human rights standards, and ecological disasters. For example, it is proposed that UNESCO collaborate with NGOs in helping national ministries of education to provide teacher training for peace education (Osseiran and Reardon 1998, 393–396).

2. Early Warning

An array of proposals would significantly extend the capacity of the United Nations to monitor world events, both through technological devices and human eyes and ears. It is proposed that the secretary-general employ more roving ambassadors, who would meet with those involved in festering conflicts. Their work would be supported by an international monitoring agency employing satellite high-altitude aircraft (Johansen 1998, 102–104). It is also proposed that early-warning capacity could be enhanced through conflict monitoring by NGOs (Boulding and Oberg 1998, 146–147).

3. Rapid Reaction

Enhanced long-range planning and early warning would enable reaction to extend into preventive modes. One suggestion is the creation of conflict resolution committees in each major world region and the preventive deployment of peacekeeping forces. Both would be supported by a UN institute for mediation and dispute resolution that would provide seasoned mediators (Johansen 1998, 102–104). These efforts could be complemented by a multifaceted rapid-response force, including military, police, civilian, and technical personnel.

4. Extension of Nonmilitary Options

Civilians have tended to play increasing roles in UN peacekeeping operations as observers, as unarmed police, and as deliverers of humanitarian services. This volume includes suggestions for extending and making some of these developments more formal. It is proposed that the United Nations have a corps of "White Helmets" to investigate gross human rights violations (Rupesinghe 1998, 175–176). Another proposal is the creation of a three-legged peacekeeping organization consisting of armed "Blue Helmets," unarmed peace teams, and humanitarian NGOs (Boulding and Oberg 1998, 137–146).

II. Broaden the Participating Community

5. Widen Participation of Nongovernmental Organizations

All of the authors in the Alger volume advocate extension of the participation of actors other than states as they search for solutions to global issues. It is recommended that NGOs develop rapid response teams composed of trained personnel who are available on a stand-by basis for quick dispatch to sites where seriously disruptive conflicts appear to be emerging (Boulding and Oberg 1998, 147). It is recommended that the role of indigenous NGOs, as well as a diversity of cultural and ethnic groups, be more creatively involved in the formulation and implementation of community development projects (Jeong 1998, 235). Others would have NGOs work with UNESCO in assisting ministries of education to provide teacher training for peace education (Osseiran and Reardon 1998, 404).

6. Widen Participation of Local Governments and Organizations
The array of perceived roles for local authorities is impressive. One example is an emphasis on roles for cities and other local authorities in efforts to cope with global ecological problems (Mische and Ribiero 1998, 335–336). Another example is the need for both national and local efforts by women if UN standards for women are to be implemented (Pietila and Vickers 1998, 273–275).

III. Strengthen Institutional Competence
7. Strengthen UN Institutional Infrastructure
Some advocate new machinery for a coordinated system to address major disarmament problems promptly, including an effective global conventional arms transfer regime that would include a small arms register, and a UN conversion projects register (Brauch, Mesjasz, and Moller 1998, 39–46). Another proposal is to restructure the Trusteeship Council and thereby strengthen capacity for response to demands of aggrieved minorities. This would include the possibility of establishing new UN trust territories (Rupesinghe 1998, 175). Others would have the UN High Commissioner for Human Rights serve as an oversight agency to direct and coordinate UN human rights machinery that would include regional components. The advocacy of regional components is based on "the belief that human rights have a cultural or regional aspect to their interpretation and promotion." Therefore, "a regional regime would help ease the acceptance of the legitimate enforcement of human rights" (Apodaca, Stohl, and Lopez 1998, 212–214).

8. Enhance Institutional Memory
Deep concern is expressed about the lack of "continuity and learning from past experience" by both the UN and member

states. "Because neither UN officials nor the new generations of diplomats are benefiting from the lessons of the past in relation to development and economic issues, there is inevitably a great deal of 'reinventing the wheel' within UN bodies. . . . The lack of an 'institutional memory' within the UN system is catastrophic. Because of it, UN bodies are doomed to learn the same lessons over and over again. It is desperately necessary for a full, analytical view of UN activities since its inception in 1944 to be undertaken, beginning even with the first attempts at international action under the League of Nations" (Pietila and Vickers 1998, 275–277).

9. New Financing Sources

Much concern is expressed about inadequate financing of the United Nations. One proposed solution is a tax on the US$ 900 billion international currency exchanges each day (Johansen 1998, 104–105). Another proposal is to tax or fine individuals, corporations, and governments who engage in transboundary pollution (Mische and Ribeiro 1998, 344).

IV. Enhance Knowledge

10. Research

A number of the authors observe that limited knowledge is inhibiting full attainment of the potential of the UN System. A need is seen for the people of the world to understand their personal linkages to the world and the significance of these linkages for global governance. In response, research is advocated on press coverage of the United Nations; on the communications dimensions of global problems such as unemployment, poverty, violence, discrimination, and drugs; on contradictions raised by globalization of finance, the economy, and the media, in contrast to individual quests for local identity and culture and group pursuit of self-determination; and on the implications of technological change for lifelong learning in all parts of the world (Varis 1998, 359, 367, 373, 377). Research is also advocated on the impact of the empowerment of women and on the relationship between women's equal rights and the achievement of a just and peaceful world (Pietila and Vickers 1998, 278). A need is also expressed for research on the links between environmental degradation and conflict (Mische and Ribeiro 1998, 351).

11. Education and Training

Some see a need to educate UN staffs in order to liberate them from the structure of competitive national visions to an international, global one. They are concerned that the spirit of the United Nations is not infused in the hearts and minds of all its staff. They believe that it has become elitist, like the governments that dispatch their officials to the United Nations. It is also asserted that the United Nations must be an intentional peace learner and peace educator, working to educate the peoples of the world to participate in this inquiry, and be proactive in movements for change. Toward this end reciprocal learning is advocated between NGOs and UN secretariats, based in the belief that NGOs versed in various approaches to peace education could share with UN staff how they have devised concrete resolutions to a particular problem. At the same time, UN personnel could deepen the insight of NGOs on practical problems that they continually confront (Osseiran and Reardon 1998, 405–406).

V. Widen Outreach

12. Extend UN Information Collection and Dissemination

A need is seen for gathering and disseminating information that would provide a knowledge base for strengthening conversion from armament production to production of civilian needs. It is proposed that a conversion projects register be created that would: (1) collect information provided by governments, corporations, and NGOs about conversion projects; (2) collect information on experts in conversion; (3) collect data on possible sources of assistance and investment for conversion; and (4) perform research and training on conversion (Brauch, Mesjasz, and Moller 1998, 46). There is a proposal for the creation of human rights field offices. These field offices would provide for more explicit partnership between NGOs and the United Nations in the belief that "NGOS enjoy the trust and respect of the common citizen needed to gather and document cases of human rights abuses" (Apodoca, Stohl, Lopez 1998, 209–212). It is advocated that the United Nations and NGOs cooperate in disseminating information on states that have not ratified, or have not adhered to, treaties and declarations. The same authors also would have the United Nations and NGOs collaborate in developing mechanisms for engendering wider adherence to these standards (Osseiran and Reardon 1998, 406).

13. Extend Publicity about UN Activities and Achievements

It is impressive that two women conclude that "[t]he record of the advancement of women during the 50 years since the UN was established—and particularly during the past 25 years—is astonishing. In all of this the UN System has taken the lead. On average it represents significantly more advanced norms and practices concerning women than those of its member states. . . . But the normative impact of the UN in the advancement of women could be vastly more efficient if its information and education programs were better" (Pietila and Vickers 1998, 273). Therefore, it is emphasized that it is essential that women be more widely informed about the programs, provisions, and conventions of the UN System on their behalf so that they can monitor their governments' implementation of what they have agreed to in the United Nations.

Two other women take an even more strident approach by urging that the United Nations call attention to: "national legislation that contradicts the spirit and principles of the Charter. Although the United Nations does not have the mandate or the power to take action to rectify the contradictions, it can serve the international community as an impartial teacher of universal norms and values, and so affect the behavior of a country in contradiction with those norms and values. . . . It has to be underlined here that the United Nations needs to attract the media more, especially television networks, so as to bring attention to its past achievements, the obstacles it needs to overcome, and appear to the public as capable of anticipating and responding to crises and challenges in all parts of the world" (Osseiran and Reardon 1998, 406).

14. Offer Rewards for Fulfilling UN Standards

Perhaps rewards for adherence to Charter goals and for implementation of UN standards for economic well-being, ecological balance, social justice, and nonviolence could be a more effective strategy than those that would be perceived as punishment by member states. One proposal advocates that economic benefits be offered to those states that lower military expenditures and demilitarize their societies (Johansen 1998, 116–117). It is also proposed that the IMF and World Bank might provide assistance to states that would facilitate conversion from military production to that which serves public needs (Brauch, Mesjasz, and Moller 1998, 45–46).

15. Visions of the Future
Every chapter of this book, *The Future of the UN System: Potential for the Twenty-First Century,* has offered a vision of a preferred future in the context of specific UN issue areas. Because these visions have emerged out of in-depth research and thought focusing on specific aspects of UN activities, we believe that many of these visions are realistic and plausible. On the other hand, dialogue is necessary between these partial visions and holistic preferred visions of the future. It is important that Reardon and Osseiran draw our attention to the need for holistic visions of the future by quoting from the Yamoussoukro Declaration (UNESCO, 1989):

Humans cannot work for a future they cannot imagine.

They ask the United Nations "to set out a vision of the future for the peoples of the world that can inspire them with hope, that can invigorate them with energy and pride about their cultures, and awareness of the common humanity they share with others" (Reardon and Osserian 1998, 407).

References

Alger, Chadwick F., 1994, "Citizens and the UN System in a Changing World," in Yoshikazu Sakomoto, ed., 1994, *Global Transformation: Challenges to the State System.* Tokyo: UN University.

———, 1996, "Thinking about the Future of the UN System," *Global Governance,* 2, 335–360.

———, 1998, "Conclusion: The Potential of the United Nations System," in Alger, ed., 1998, *The Future of the UN System: Potential for the Twenty-First Century.* Tokyo: UN University, 409–423.

Alger, Chadwick F., ed., 1998, *The Future of the UN System: Potential for the Twenty-First Century.* Tokyo: United Nations University.

Apodaca, Clair, Michael Stohl, and George Lopez, 1998, "Moving Norms to Political Reality: Institutionalizing Human Rights Standards through the UN System," in Alger, ed., 1998, *The Future of the UN System: Potential for the Twenty-First Century.* Tokyo: United Nations University, 185–220.

Archibugi, Daniele, 1993, "The Reform of the UN and Cosmopolitan Democracy: A Critical Review," *Journal of Peace Research,* 30, No. 3, 301–315.

Boulding, Elise, and Jan Oberg, 1998, "United Nations Peace-Keeping and NGO Peace-Building: Towards Partnership," in Alger, ed., 1998, *The*

Future of the UN System: Potential for the Twenty-First Century. Tokyo: United Nations University, 127–154.

Brahimi Report on Peacekeeping, www.un.org/peace/reports/peace_operations.

Brauch, Hans Gunter, Czeslaw Mesjasz, and Bjorn Moller, 1998, "Controlling Weapons in the Quest for Peace: Non-offensive Defence, Arms Control, Disarmament, and Conversion," in Alger, ed., 1998, *The Future of the UN System: Potential for the Twenty-First Century.* Tokyo: United Nations University, 15–53.

Cardoso Panel: United Nations–Civil Society Relations, www.un.org/reform/panel.htm.

Childers, Erskine, and Brian Urquhart, 1994, *Renewing the United Nations System.* Uppsala, Sweden: Dag Hammarskjold Foundation.

Citizens for Global Solutions, www.globalsolutions.org.

Committee for a Democratic UN, www.uno-komite.de/en.

Dole, Charles Fletcher, 1906, *The Spirit of Democracy.* New York: T. Y. Crowell.

Field, Shannon L., 1998, "UN Security Council Reform: A Challenge for the South," *Global Dialogue,* Vol. 3.3, December (available at www.igd.org.za/pub/g-dialogue/multilateral_analysis/security.html).

Galtung, Johan, 1980, *The True Worlds: A Transnational Perspective.* New York: Free Press.

Ikome, Francis Nguendi, and Nhamo W. Samasuwo, 2005, "UN Reform: Towards a More [In] Secure World?," *Global Insight,* No. 48 (April).

Institute for Global Dialogue (IGD), www.igd.org.za.

Jeong, Ho-Won, 1998, "The struggle in the UN System for Wider Participation in Forming Global Economic Policies," in Alger, ed., 1998, *The Future of the UN System: Potential for the Twenty-First Century.* Tokyo: United Nations University, 221–247.

Johansen, Robert C., 1998, "Enhancing United Nations Peace-Keeping," in Alger, ed., 1998, *The Future of the UN System: Potential for the Twenty-First Century.* Tokyo: United Nations University, 89–126.

McSpadden, Lucia Ann, and Anthony Ayok Chol, 1998, "Generating the Political Will for Protecting the Rights of Refugees," in Alger, ed., 1998, *The Future of the UN System: Potential for the Twenty-First Century.* Tokyo: United Nations University, 282–314.

Ministry of Foreign Affairs, Japan, position on Security Council enlargement, www.mofa.go.jp/policy/un/reform/role21.html#2.

Mische, Patricia M., and Mauricio Andres Ribeiro, 1998, "Sharing and Protecting the Commons: Ecological Security and the United Nations

System," in Alger, ed., 1998, *The Future of the UN System: Potential for the Twenty-First Century.* Tokyo: United Nations University, 315–356.

Osseiran, Sanaa, and Betty Reardon, 1998, "The United Nations' role in Peace Education," in Alger, ed., 1998, *The Future of the UN System: Potential for the Twenty-First Century.* Tokyo: United Nations University, 385–408.

Pietila, Hilkka, and Jeanne Vickers, 1998, "The UN System in the Vanguard of Advancement of Women: Equality, Development, and Peace," in Alger, ed., 1998, *The Future of the UN System: Potential for the Twenty-First Century.* Tokyo: United Nations University, 248–281.

Rupesinghe, Kumar, 1998, "Coping with Internal Conflicts: Teaching the Elephant to Dance," in Alger, ed., 1998, *The Future of the UN System: Potential for the Twenty-First Century.* Tokyo: United Nations University, 155–184.

UN Association-USA (UNA-USA), www.unausa.org.

UN Millennium Project, www.unmillennium project.org.

UNESCO, 1989, "Yamoussoukro Declaration on Peace in the Minds of Men." Paris: UNESCO.

Varis, Tapio, 1998, "Communications in the Future UN System," in Alger, ed., 1998, *The Future of the UN System: Potential for the Twenty-First Century.* Tokyo: United Nations University, 357–384.

Vayrynen, Raimo, 1998, "Enforcement and Humanitarian Intervention: Two Faces of Collective Action by the United Nations," in Alger, ed., 1998, *The Future of the UN System: Potential for the Twenty-First Century.* Tokyo: United Nations University, 54–88.

World Federation of UN Associations (WFUNA), www.wfuna.org.

7

Directory of Organizations, Associations, and Agencies

B ecause readers of UN literature are often frustrated by the appearance of undefined acronyms, this chapter begins with the acronyms of UN System organizations and activities, followed by acronyms of peacekeeping operations. Information on most of these organizations and activities have been provided in earlier chapters.

Readers of the earlier chapters have become quite aware that the evolving UN System has become increasingly involved with a growing number of other governmental and nongovernmental associations. The remainder of this chapter provides brief information on many of these organizations, along with indication of where further information can be found. The sections that follow move from global, to global region, to local associations. The appearance of all three geographic ranges is required because all three are finding the need to play a direct role in global governance. The basic intent of this section is to offer the reader concrete evidence that all governments, from the local to the global, are challenged with different dimensions of global policy problems. The same is true of different nongovernmental/civil society organizations whose focuses range from the local to the global. As a result, citizens in democracies are challenged to understand the worldwide dimensions of their responsibilities for the shaping of policies of governmental institutions that reach from the local to the global.

Table of Contents

UN System Acronyms

Information in various resources and reports on organizations and activities in the UN System frequently includes acronyms. This list includes acronyms for organizations, programs, commissions, committees, etc. The acronyms are listed in alphabetic order. Basic information on these UN System activities can be quickly obtained by going to www.un.org, choosing the search option, and placing the acronym in the search box. Acronyms for peacekeeping operations follow in the next section.

1. Advisory Committee on Administrative and Budgetary Questions (ACABQ)
2. UN Office in Central African Republic (BONUCA)
3. Committee Against Torture (CAT)
4. Committee on Elimination of Discrimination Against Women (CEDAW)
5. Committee on Elimination of Racial Discrimination (CERD)
6. Committee on Economic, Social and Cultural rights (CESCR)
7. Committee on Migrant Workers (CMW)
8. Commission on Narcotic Drugs (CND)
9. Committee on Rights of the Child (CRC)
10. PrepCom for the Nuclear-Test-Ban Treaty Organization (CTBTO PrepCom)
11. Counter-Terrorism Committee (CTC)
12. Counter-Terrorism Committee Executive Directorate (CTED)

13. Department for Disarmament Affairs (DDA)
14. Department of Economic and Social Affairs (DESA)
15. Department of Political Affairs (DPA)
16. Department of Public Information (DPI)
17. Department of Peace-keeping Operations (DPKO)
18. Economic Commission for Africa (ECA)
19. Economic Commission for Europe (ECE)
20. Economic Commission for Latin America and the Caribbean (ECLAC)
21. Executive Office of the Secretary-General (EOSG)
22. Economic and Social Commission for Asia and the Pacific (ESCAP)
23. Economic and Social Commission for Western Asia (ESCWA)
24. Economic and Social Council (ECOSOC)
25. Food and Agriculture Organization (FAO)
26. Human Rights Committee (HCR)
27. International Atomic Energy Agency (IAEA)
28. UN Inter-Agency Coordination Group on Mine Action (IACG-MA)
29. Inter-Agency Standing Committee and Executive Committee on Humanitarian Affairs (IASC/ECHA)
30. International Bank for Reconstruction and Development (IBRD)
31. International Civil Aviation Organization (ICAO)
32. International Criminal Court (ICC)
33. International Computing Center (ICC)
34. International Center for Settlement of Investment Disputes (ICSID)
35. International Court of Justice (ICJ)
36. International Civil Service Commission (ICSC)
37. International Center for Settlement of Investment Disputes (ICSID)
38. International Criminal Tribunal for Rwanda (ICTR)
39. International Criminal Tribunal for the Former Yugoslavia (ICTY)
40. International Development Association (IDA)
41. International Fund for Agricultural Development (IFAD)
42. International Finance Corporation (IFC)
43. International Labor Organization (ILO)
44. International Monetary Fund (IMF)
45. International Maritime Organization (IMO)

46. International Research and Training Institute for the Advancement of Women (INSTRAW)
47. International Telecommunication Union (ITU)
48. International Trade Center (ITC)
49. Joint Inspection Unit (JIU)
50. Multilateral Investment Guarantee Agency (MIGA)
51. UN Verification Mission in Guatemala (MINUGUA)
52. Non-Governmental Liaison Service (NGLS)
53. Office for the Coordination of Humanitarian Affairs (OCHA)
54. Office for Drug Control and Crime Prevention (ODCCP)
55. Office of the High Commissioner for Human Rights (OHCHR)
56. Office of the High Representative for the Least Developed Countries, Landlocked Developing Countries and Small Island Developing States (OHRLLS)
57. Office of Internal Oversight Services (OIOS)
58. Office of Legal Affairs (OLA)
59. Organization for the Prohibition of Chemical Weapons (OPCW)
60. Permanent Forum on Indigenous Issues (PFII)
61. Steering Committee on Mine Action (SCMA)
62. UN Assistance Mission in Afghanistan (UNAMA)
63. UN Assistance Mission for Iraq (UNAMI)
64. UN Compensation Commission (UNCC)
65. UN Capital Development Fund (UNCDF)
66. UN Commission on International Trade Law (UNCITRAL)
67. UN Crime and Justice Information Network (UNCJIN)
68. UN Center for Regional Development (UNCRD)
69. UN Conference on Trade and Development (UNCTAD)
70. UN Drug Control Program (UNDCP)
71. UN Development Program (UNDP)
72. UN Environment Program (UNEP)
73. UN Educational, Scientific, and Cultural Organization (UNESCO)
74. UN Fund for International Partnerships (UNFIP)
75. UN High Commissioner for Refugees (UNHCR)
76. UN Human Settlements Program—HABITAT (UNHSP)
77. UN Joint Staff Pension Fund (UNJSPF)
78. UN Children's Fund (UNICEF)
79. UN Interregional Crime and Justice Research Institute (UNICRI)
80. UN Institute for Disarmament Research (UNIDIR)

81. UN Industrial Development Organization (UNIDO)
82. UN Development Fund for Women (UNIFEM)
83. UN Institute for Training and Research (UNITAR)
84. UN Mine Action Service (UNMAS)
85. UN Monitoring, Verification and Inspection Commission (UNMOVIC)
86. UN Office in Burundi (UNOB)
87. UN Office on Drugs and Crime (UNODC)
88. United Nations Office at Geneva (UNOG)
89. UN Peace-building Support Office in Guinea-Bissau (UNOGBIS)
90. UN Observer Mission in Bougainville (UNOMB)
91. United Nations Office at Nairobi (UNON)
92. UN Office for Outer Space Affairs (UNOOSA)
93. UN Office for Project Services (UNOPS)
94. United Nations Office at Vienna (UNOV)
95. Office of the Special Representative of the Secretary General for West Africa (UNOWA)
96. UN Political Office for Somalia (UNPOS)
97. UN Research Institute for Social Development (UNRISD)
98. UN Relief and Works Agency for Palestine Refugees in the Near East (UNRWA)
99. Office of the UN Special Coordinator for the Middle East Peace Process (UNSCO)
100. Office of the UN Security Coordinator (UNSECOORD)
101. UN System Staff College (UNSSC)
102. UN Transitional Authority in Cambodia (UNTAC)
103. UN Transitional Authority in Eastern Slavonia, Baranja and Western Sirmium (UNTAES)
104. UN Tajikistan Office of Peace-building (UNTOP)
105. UN University (UNU)
106. UN Volunteers (UNV)
107. World Food Program (WFP)
108. World Bank Group (WBG)
109. World Health Organization (WHO)
110. World Intellectual Property Organization (WIPO)
111. World Trade Organization (WTO)
112. World Tourism Organization (WTO)
    (The Alphabetic Index of Websites of the United Nations System of Organizations, www.undp.org/toppages/unsys/unsframe.htm, includes only some of the entities listed above.)

UN Peacekeeping Operations Acronyms

Included here are acronyms for both past and present peacekeeping operations, listed in alphabetic order. Basic information on these operations can be quickly obtained by going to www.un.org, choosing the search option, and placing the acronym in the search box. Overview information on all UN peacekeeping activity can be acquired at www.un.org/Depts/dpko/dpko/index.asp.

DOMREP (Dominican Republic)
MINUSTAH (Haiti)
MONUC (Democratic Republic of the Congo)
MINUGUA (Guatemala)
MINURCA (Central African Republic)
MINURSO (Western Sahara)
MIPONUH (Haiti)
MONUA (Angola)
ONUB (Burundi)
ONUC (Congo)
ONUCA (Central America)
ONUMOZ (Mozambique)
ONUSAL (El Salvador)
UNAMIC (Cambodia)
UNAMIR (Rwanda)
UNAMSIL (Sierra Leone)
UNASOG (Chad/Libya)
UNAVEM I (Angola)
UNAVEM II (Angola)
UNAVEM III (Angola)
UNCRO (Croatia)
UNDOF (Golan Heights)
UNEF I (Middle East)
UNEF II (Middle East)
UNFICYP (Cyprus)
UNGOMAP (Afghanistan/ Pakistan)
UNIFIL (Lebanon)
UNIIMOG (Iran/Iraq)
UNIKOM (Iraq/Kuwait)

UNIPOM (India/Pakistan)
UNMEE (Ethiopia and Eritrea)
UNMIBH (Bosnia and Herzegovina)
UNMIH (Haiti)
UNMIK (Kosovo)
UNMIL (Liberia)
UNMISET (East Timor)
UNMOGIP (India-Pakistan)
UNMOP (Prevlaka Peninsula)
UNMOT (Tajikistan)
UNOCI (Ivory Coast)
UNOGIL (Lebanon)
UNOMIG (Georgia)
UNOMIL (Liberia)
UNOMSIL (Sierra Leone)
UNOMUR (Rwanda/Uganda)
UNOSOM I (Somalia)
UNOSOM II (Somalia)
UNPREDEP (Former Yugoslav Republic of Macedonia)
UNPROFOR (Former Yugoslavia)
UNPSG (Croatia)
UNSF (West New Guinea)
UNSMIH (Haiti)
UNTAC (Cambodia)
UNTAES (Croatia)
UNTAET (East Timor)
UNTAG (Namibia)
UNTMIH (Haiti)
UNTSO (Middle East)
UNYOM (Yemen)

Organizations of States Outside the UN System, Both Global and Regional

Listed below are seventy-five international organizations of states, both global and regional, that are outside the UN System. They are listed here because their agendas frequently require them to collaborate with agencies in the UN System. Some of these organizations are concerned with regional problems involving only a few states, such as the Andean Community. Some have global membership with a rather limited agenda, as with the International Institute of Refrigeration. On many occasions these organizations are coping with the regional dimension of policy problems that are also on agendas of UN agencies. Examples are the Asian Development Bank and the European Civil Aviation Conference.

Andean Community, www.Comunidadandina.Org
Asian and Pacific Coconut Community (APCC),
     www.Apcc.Org.Sg/Index.Htm
Asian Development Bank (ADB), www.Adb.Org/
Asian Productivity Organization (APO), www.Apo-tokyo.org/
Asia Pacific Economic Cooperation (APEC), www.Apecsec.Org.Sg/
Association of Southeast Asian Nations (ASEAN), www.Asean.Or.Id/

Baltic Assembly (BA), www.Baltasam.org
Baltic Marine Environment Protection Commission (BMEPC),
     www.Helcom.Fi/
Bank for International Settlements (BIS), www.Bis.Org

Cab International (CABI), www.Cabi.Org/
Caribbean Community (CARICOM), www.Caricom.Org/
The Columbo Plan for Co-Operative Economic and Social Development
     in Asia and the Pacific (Columbo Plan)
Commonwealth of Independent States (CIS),
     www.Cisstat.Com/Eng/Cis.Htm
Commonwealth Secretariat (COMSEC), www.Thecommonwealth.Org/
Council of Europe (CE), www.Coe.Int/Defaulten.Asp

Economic Community of West African States (ECOWAS),
     www.ecowas.int
European Bank for Reconstruction and Development (EBRD),
     www.Ebrd.Com
European Civil Aviation Conference (ECAC), www.Ecac/Ceac.Org/

European Conference of Ministers of Transport (ECMT),
    www.Oecd.Org/Cem/
European Free Trade Association (EFTA), http://Secretariat.Efta.Int/
European Laboratory for Particle Physics (CERN), www.Cern.Ch/
European Patent Office (EPO), www.European/Patent/Office.Org
European Space Agency (ESA), www.Esa.Int
European Union (EU), www.Eurunion.Org

Group of 77 (G77), www.G77.Org
Gulf Cooperation Council (GCC), www.Gcc-Sg.org

Inter-American Development Bank (IABD, IDB), www.Iadb.Org
Inter-American Tropical Tuna Commission (IATTC), www.Iattc.Org/
International Centre for the Study of the Preservation and the
    Restoration of Cultural Property (ICCROM), www.Iccrom.Org/
International Civil Defense Organization (ICDO), www.Icdo.Org/
International Cocoa Organization (ICCO), www.Icco.Org
International Coffee Organization (ICO), www.Ico.Org/
International Committee Of Military Medicine (ICMM),
    www.Cimm-Cimm.Org
International Cotton Advisory Council (ICAC), www.Icac.Org/
International Council for the Exploration of the Sea (ICES),
    www.Ices.Dk
International Criminal Police Organization (Interpol; ICPO),
    www.Interpol.Int/Default.Asp
International Energy Agency (IEA)
International Hydrographic Organization (IHO), www.Iho.Shom.Fr/
International Institute for Cooperation on Agriculture (IICA)
International Institute of Refrigeration www.Iifiir.Org
International Lead and Zinc Study Group www.Ilzsg.Org
International Maritime Satellite Organization (INMARS),
    www.Inmarsat.Org/Index2.Html
International Natural Rubber Organization (INRO),
    www3.Jaring.My/Inro
International Nickel Study Group www.Insg.Org/Index.Htm
International Office of Epizootics (OIE/WHO/FAO), www.Oie.Int
International Olive Oil Council (IIOOC),
    www.Internationaloliveoil.Org/
International Organization for Migration (IOM), www.Iom.Ch/
International Organization of Legal Metrology (IOLM),
    www.Oiml.Org/
International Pepper Community (IPC), www.Ipcnet.Org/
International Rubber Study Group (IRSG), www.Rubberstudy.Com
International Sugar Organization (ISO), www.Sugaronline.Com/Iso/
International Telecommunication Satellite Organization (INTELSAT),
    www.Itso.Int/

International Whaling Commission (IWC), www.Iwcoffice.Org/
Inter-Parliamentary Union (IPU), www.Ipu.Org
Islamic Development Bank (IDB), www.Isdb.Org

Latin American Integration Association (ALADI), www.Aladi.Org

NATO Parliamentary Assembly (NATO PA), www.nato-pa.int
Nordic Council and Nordic Council of Ministers, www.Norden.Org
North Atlantic Assembly (NAA) [See Nato Parliamentary Assembly]
North Atlantic Treaty Organization (NATO), www.Nato.Int
Northwest Atlantic Fisheries Organization (NAFO), www.Nafo.Ca/
Nuclear Energy Agency (NEA) (Specialized Agency of the OECD),
    www.Nea.fr

Organization of African Unity (OAU), www.africa-union.org
Organization for Economic Cooperation and Development (OECD),
    www.Oecd.Org
Organization for Security and Cooperation in Europe (OSCE),
    www.Osce.Org/
Organization of American States (OAS), www.Oas.Org/
Organization of Arab Petroleum Exporting Countries (OAPEC),
    www.Oapecorg.Org/
Organization of Petroleum Exporting Countries (OPEC),
    www.Opec.Org
Oslo and Paris Commissions (OSCAM; PARCM), www.Ospar.Org

Pan American Institute of Geography and History
Permanent Court of Arbitration (PCA), www.pca-cpa.org

Secretariat of the Pacific Community (SPC), www.Spc.Org.Nc/
Southeast Asian Ministers of Education Organization (SEAMEO),
    www.Seameo.Org

Western European Union (WEU), www.Weu.Int

Inter-Parliamentary Union (IPU)

Member states of the United Nations are primarily represented in
the United Nations by representatives of departments in their executive branches, although some do have members of parliament
on their delegations to the General Assembly and to the assemblies of the specialized agencies. In 1889 the parliaments of many
states established the Inter-Parliamentary Union (IPU), having
members from over 130 national parliaments in 2005. Five re-

gional parliamentary assemblies are associate members of the IPU with headquarters in Geneva. Recently the IPU has become involved with UNESCO, UNCTAD, ILO, WTO, UNHCHR, the UN General Assembly, and a number of UN conferences.

The IPU website describes its mission as follows:

> The Union is the focal point for world-wide parliamentary dialogue and works for peace and co-operation among peoples and for the firm establishment of representative democracy. To that end, it: Fosters contacts, co-ordination, and the exchange of experience among parliaments and parliamentarians of all countries; Considers questions of international interest and concern and expresses its views on such issues in order to bring about action by parliaments and parliamentarians; Contributes to the defense and promotion of human rights—an essential factor of parliamentary democracy and development; Contributes to better knowledge of the working of representative institutions and to the strengthening and development of their means of action.
>
> The IPU supports the efforts of the United Nations, whose objectives it shares, and works in close co-operation with it. It also co-operates with regional inter-parliamentary organizations, as well as with international intergovernmental and non-governmental organizations which are motivated by the same ideals. (www.ipu.org)

Here are a few examples of IPU involvements with the UN, UNESCO, UNCTAD, and ILO: A cooperation agreement between the IPA and the United Nations was signed in 1996. This has been followed by numerous joint conferences. In 2002 the IPU was granted observer status in the General Assembly and the right to circulate its official documents in the General Assembly.

In 1997 a cooperation agreement was signed between UNESCO and the IPU. At the signing, Ahmed Fathy Sorour, IPU Council President, declared that the agreement would "provide an institutional framework" for cooperation between the two organizations and "open up new possibilities for dialogue and interaction on the international level between the two branches of the State which are governments and parliaments." Then he added that it is now up to the two organizations to "make progress and move down this path by constant interaction. We have many projects to implement together—all of which will allow the Inter-Parliamentary Union to fulfill in practice its role of a consultative parliamentary assembly to UNESCO" (www.ipu.org/english/pressdoc/gen64.htm).

In October 2003 a joint UNESCO/IPU meeting was held at UNESCO headquarters during the thirty-second session of the UNESCO General Conference. The aim of the meeting was to launch a cooperation network between parliaments that are members of the IPU and national commissions for UNESCO.

In 2000 the Inter-Parliamentary Union organized a parliamentary meeting on the occasion of UNCTAD X in Bangkok, which indicated an effort by the IPU to attain active parliamentary involvement in international trade issues, with particular focus on the WTO and UNCTAD. This was followed by a similar meeting in 2004 at UNCTAD XI in São Paulo. The meeting was open to all members of parliaments attending UNCTAD XI as part of their national delegations, as well as to any other MPs delegated by IPU members to take part in the parliamentary event. The IPU asserted that "[t]he objective of the Meeting in São Paulo is to ensure that the voice of parliamentarians as legitimate representatives of the people is heard loud and clear during the intergovernmental forum. Participation in the Meeting will permit them to obtain first-hand information about the main issues and thrusts of the intergovernmental Conference, to contribute to the elaboration of parliamentary recommendations to UNCTAD XI, and to lay foundations for concerted parliamentary follow-up action at the national and international levels after UNCTAD XI" (www.ipu.org/Splz-e/unctadxi.htm).

In March 2004 a special panel of delegates from the Inter-Parliamentary Union (IPU) and the International Labor Organization (ILO) charged with helping mobilize international political will to eliminate the worst forms of child labor met in Morocco. The meeting coincided with the launch of a new booklet: "Eliminating the Worst Forms of Child Labour: A practical guide to ILO Convention No. 18." Prepared jointly by the IPU and the ILO, the guide aims at providing policymakers with the tools to translate international child labor legislation into effective action in a range of local contexts (www.ipu.org).

International Organizations of Local Authorities with Worldwide Members

As the connections between local communities and the world escalated, local authorities began meeting with their counterparts around the world to discuss their common concerns. This was followed by the creation of a number of international organizations of local authorities.

As early as 1913 the International Union of Local Authorities, that eventually had worldwide membership, was created. These organizations are now aware that there are many issues on the agendas of organizations in the UN System that are of great local importance. Therefore, they are becoming directly involved in efforts to place their concerns on the agendas of UN organizations. The broad range of their interests is indicated in the organizations listed below. Of particular interest is the fact that these organizations have established a coalition, the World Association of Cities and Local Authorities (WACLAC), to coordinate their efforts to make their concerns known to UN agencies.

World Association of Cities and Local Authorities (WACLAC)

WACLAC is the world alliance of international associations of cities and local authorities "committed to responsible and effective local self-government for sustainable development. Its mission is to represent the local government sector in the international arena and in particular with the United Nations" (www.camval.org).

United Cities and Local Government Organization (UCLG)

Formed in 2004 by a merger of the International Union of Local Authorities (IULA) founded in 1913, and the Federation Mondial des Cities Unies (FMCU) founded forty-five years ago, the UCLG has members from over 100 countries. Its website states: "United Cities and Local Governments is the global voice of cities and the main local government partner of the United Nations." UCLG has five regional associations (www.cities-localgovernments.org/uclg).

Metropolis (World Association of the Major Metropolises)

The organization Metropolis has become the metropolitan section of UCLG. It has eighty-four member cities. "The main goal of the association is to better control the development process of metropolitan areas in order to enhance the well-being of their citizens. To do this, Metropolis represents regions and metropolitan areas at the worldwide level and is recognized as a major player by large international organizations such as the UN, WHO, the World Bank and others" (www.metropolis.org).

Local Governments for Sustainability (ICLEI)

The "ICLEI's mission is to build and serve a worldwide movement of local governments to achieve tangible improvements in global sustainability with special focus on environmental conditions through cumulative local actions. It was founded in 1990 by local governments at the United Nations Headquarters in New York as the International Council for Local Environmental Initiatives (ICLEI). ICLEI is a democratically governed membership association of cities, towns, counties, metropolitan governments, and local government associations" (www.iclei.org).

Mayors for Peace

"On June 24, 1982, at the 2nd UN Special Session on Disarmament held at UN Headquarters in New York, then Mayor Takeshi Araki of Hiroshima proposed a new Program to Promote the Solidarity of Cities toward the Total Abolition of Nuclear Weapons. This proposal offered cities a way to transcend national borders and work together to press for nuclear abolition. Subsequently, the mayors of Hiroshima and Nagasaki called on mayors around the world to support this program." In January 2005 membership stood at 688 cities in 110 countries. The Mayors Conference is officially registered as a UN NGO related to both the Department of Public Information and the Economic and Social Council (www.pcf.city.hiroshima.jp/mayors/english/index.html).

Association Internationales des Maires Francophones (AIMF)

The purpose of the International Association of French-Speaking Mayors is to organize mayors and other responsible persons of cities where French is the official language, the language of regular communication, or where it is frequently used. The AIMF was founded in 1969 and has members from forty-six countries. The headquarters is in Paris (www.aimf.asso.fr).

Regional Organizations of Local Authorities in Global Regions Outside of Europe

Regional organizations of local authorities have emerged in all regions of the world, as well as an organization of cities in the Commonwealth, based in London, and one focused on HIV/AIDS in Africa. All of these organizations tend to have a common desire for stronger local governments.

Arab Towns Organization (ATO), Kaifan, Kuwaitwww.ato.net
Asia and Pacific (CITYNET) Yokohama, Japanwww.citynet-ap.org
Commonwealth Local Government Forum (CLGF), London,
   www.clgf.org.uk
Council of Cities and Regions of Africa (CCRA) Founded in May
   2005 in Pretoria, South Africa
Federación Latinoamericana de Ciudades, Municipios y Asocia-
   ciones (FLACMA), Quito, Ecuador, www.flacma.org
Organization of Islamic Capitals and Cities (OICC) Makkah and
   Jeddah, Saudi Arabia, www.oicc.org
Union des Villes Africaines (UVA), Rabat, Morocco
The Alliance of Mayors and Municipal Leaders on HIV/AIDS in
   Africa, Katutura, Windhoek, Namibia, www.amicaall.org

Organizations of Local Authorities in the European Region

The most extensive array of organizations of local authorities that cross state boundaries has been formed in Europe (Table 7.1). Very significant is the emergence of directly elected organizations of local authorities that have become governmental units in the Council of Europe and the European Union. Some, including members of the Inter-Parliamentary Union described earlier in this chapter, believe that this provides a model for a future role for a directly elected assembly in the United Nations.

In addition, there are a wide range of other local authorities' organizations in Europe. They offer illuminating insight on the fact that there is a diversity of territorial borders, in addition to those of states, that are important for different political issues. Some have members from throughout Europe. In addition, there are regional organizations with members from border regions, mountain regions, and maritime regions. There are also organizations focused on specific issues, such as recycling, climate and energy. One organization even links European local authorities with those in Latin America.

Nongovernmental Organizations/ Civil Society

Because of the very large, and growing number, of NGOs involved in the UN System and in those providing information on the UN System, the development of this section involved difficult choices. Diversity has been provided by choosing a few from each of these categories: (1) NGOs associated with the United Nations, (2) NGO organizations with broad agendas for furthering NGO effectiveness, (3) NGO issue networks, (4) NGOs with research and education focus, and (5) NGOs attempting to extend informed participation of people in the United States. The websites of each of those that appear below provide information on many more NGO websites.

TABLE 7.1
Organizations of Local Authorities in the European Region

Direct Participation of Cities and
Local Regions in Governance in Europe

Council of Europe
> Congress of Local and Regional Authorities of Europe (CLRAE), www.coe.int/cplre
>> Chamber of Local Authorities
>> Chamber of Regions

European Union
> Committee of the Regions (COR), www.cor.eu.int
> Created by the Maastricht Treaty of 1991, as a representative assembly with the job of giving local and regional authorities a voice at the heart of the European Union. Succeeded Assembly of European Regions (ARE).

Other Organizations of Local Authorities in European Region

1. *General Membership, Broad Agenda*
   > Assembly of European Regions (AER), Strasbourg, France,
   >> www.are-regions-europe.org
   > Council of European Municipalities and Regions (CEMR), www.ccre.org
   > Eurocities, Brussels (100 major cities in European Union),
   >> www.eurocities.org

2. *Membership from regions within Europe*
   (1) Border Regions in Europe
   > Asso. of Euro. Border Regions (AEBR) (1971), Gronau, Germany,
   >> www.aebr-ageg.de
   (2) Mountain Regions in Europe
   > Euro. Asso. of Local and Reg. Auth. of Mountain Regions (AEM),
   >> Strasbourg, Fr., www.sdv.fr/aem
   > Asso. of Working Communities of the Alpine Regions, Innsbruck, Aus.,
   >> www.argealp.org
   > Working Community of the Adriatic Alps (ALPEN ADRIA),
   >> www.alpeadria.org
   > Western-Alps Working Community (COTRAO), www.unil.ch/cotrao
   > Working Community of the Central Alps, www.argealp.org
   > Working Community of the Pyrenees (CTP), www.ctp.org
   > Jura Working Community (CTJ), www.cor.eu.int/document/activities/ctpen.pdf
   (3) Maritime Regions in Europe
   > Conf. on Peripheral and Maritime Reg. of Euro. (CPMR), Rennes, Fr.,
   >> www.cpmr.org
   > Atlantic Arc Commision, http://web8956.vs.netbenefit.co.uk
   > Mediterranean Commission on Sustainable Development (MCSD),
   >> www.planbleu.org/vanglaise/1-3a.htm
   > Medcities Network of Mediterranean Coastal Cities, www.medcities.org
   > Union of Baltic Cities, Gdansk, Poland, www.ubc.net
   > Transmarche region (Straits of Dover)

3. *Specific Issue Focus*
   > Association of Cities and Regions for Recycling, www.acrr.org

Climate Alliance, of European Cities with Indigenous Rainforest Peoples, www.klimabuendnis.org

Energie-Cites, Besancon, France, www.energie-cites.org

Airport Regions Conference (ARC), www.airportregions.org

European Industrial Regions Association (EIRA), www.eira.org

Association European Wine-Growing Regions (AREV), www.arev.org

Assembly of Euro. Fruit and Vegetable Growing and Horticultural Regions (AREFLH), http://areflh.com

Forum of Local Authorities for Social Inclusion, www.autoridadeslocais.com.br

Four Motors of Europe, Promoting R & D linkages among Catalonia (Spain), Baden-Württermberg (Germany), Rhône-Alpes (France), and Lombardy (Italy), http://62.101.84.82/4motori.nsf/framesweb/index

4. *State Capitals*

Union of Central and South-Eastern European Capitals

Union of Capitals of the European Union, www.cor.eu.int/document/activities/ucueen.pdf

5. *Links outside Europe*

European Commission

URB-AL Program for urban areas in Europe and Latin America, www.urb-al.com

NGOs Associated with the United Nations

The NGO Global Network (www.ngo.org) is the home page for nongovernmental organizations associated with the United Nations. It provides a listing of organizations focusing on these issues, listed in alphabetic order. Its aim is to help promote collaborations between NGOs throughout the world, so that together we can more effectively partner with the United Nations and each other.

Children and youth	Health and nutrition	Religion
Communications	Human resources	Science and
Conflict resolution	Human rights	technology
Disarmament	Law	Sustainable
Disaster relief	Natural resources	development
Drug abuse	and energy	Status of women
Education	Peace and security	Trade, finance and
Environment	Population and	transport
Ethics and values	human settlements	United Nations
Family	Refugees	

NGO Organizations with Broad Agendas for Furthering NGO Effectiveness

Global Policy Forum
"Global Policy Forum monitors policy making at the United Nations, promotes accountability of global decisions, educates and mobilizes for citizen participation, and advocates on vital issues of international peace and justice" (www.globalpolicy.org/ngos).

The Global Communication Center for Development Organizations
"Our aim is to facilitate collaborations between NGOs throughout the world, so that we can effectively partner among ourselves to create a more peaceful, just, equitable and sustainable world" (http://ngos.cc).

InterAction, American Council for Voluntary International Action
This is an alliance of U.S.-based international development and humanitarian NGOs operating in developing countries to overcome poverty, exclusion, and suffering by advancing social justice and basic dignity for all (www.interaction.org).

NGO Issue Networks

Alliance for International Conflict Prevention and Resolution (www.aicpr.org)
"A not-for-profit network of private and public organizations dedicated to increasing the effectiveness of the conflict management field and maximizing its impact on international peace building. Members are working in the Middle East, Asia, Africa, Latin America, and Europe."

Amnesty International (www.amnesty.org)
"Amnesty International (AI) is a worldwide movement of people who campaign for internationally recognized human rights. . . . In pursuit of this vision, AI's mission is to undertake research and action focused on preventing and ending grave abuses of the rights to physical and mental integrity, freedom of conscience and expression, and freedom from discrimination, within the context of its work to promote all human rights."

Citizens for Global Solutions (www.globalsolutions.org)

"Citizens for Global Solutions, a grassroots membership organization, envisions a future in which nations work together to abolish war, protect our rights and freedoms, and solve the problems facing humanity that no nation can solve alone. We invite you to work with us on our campaigns to promote the International Criminal Court, reform United Nations peace operations, and encourage a bipartisan national consensus on reforming the UN for the 21st century that emphasizes cooperation with international institutions and our allies." Created by a merger of the World Federalist Association and the Campaign for UN Reform.

Coalition for the International Criminal Court (www.iccnow.org)

"The Coalition for the International Criminal Court is a network of over 2,000 non-governmental organizations (NGOs) advocating for a fair, effective and independent International Criminal Court (ICC). . . . The Coalition for the ICC and its members have been actively supporting the establishment of the Court for 10 years, and are engaged in a range of activities—from participating in expert consultations on ICC-related matters to advocating for broader national support for and cooperation with the Court."

Coalition to Stop the Use of Child Soldiers (www.child-soldiers.org)

"The Coalition to Stop the Use of Child Soldiers works to prevent the recruitment and use of children as soldiers, to secure their demobilisation and to ensure their rehabilitation and reintegration into society. . . . Formed in May 1998 by leading international human rights and humanitarian organizations. It has regional and national networks in Africa, Asia, Europe, Latin America and the Middle East. The International Coalition has its headquarters in London."

Human Rights Education Associates (www.hrea.org)

"Human Rights Education Associates (HREA) is an international non-governmental organisation that supports human rights learning; the training of activists and professionals; the development of educational materials and programming; and community-building through on-line technologies. HREA is dedicated to quality education and training to promote understanding, attitudes and actions to protect human rights, and to foster the development of peaceable, free and just communities."

Human Rights Links (www.derechos.net/links/ngo)
Provides links to these categories: Issue-specific NGOs, Regional NGOs, All NGOs, Directories of NGOs, Foundations, NGO Networks, NGO Support Groups, Research Institutes, Resources for NGOs.

International Action Network on Small Arms (www.iansa.org)
"The International Action Network on Small Arms is the global network of civil society organisations working to stop the proliferation and misuse of small arms and light weapons (SALW). World attention is increasingly focused on the humanitarian impact of these weapons, and IANSA brings together the voices and activities of non-governmental organisations (NGOs) and concerned individuals across the world to prevent their deadly effects."

International Campaign to Ban Landmines (ICBL) (www.icbl.org)
"The Campaign calls for an international ban on the use, production, stockpiling, and transfer of antipersonnel landmines, and for increased international resources for humanitarian mine clearance and mine victim assistance program. . . . the campaign was awarded the Nobel Peace Prize in 1997, together with its then coordinator, Jody Williams. . . . Since the adoption of the Mine Ban Treaty, the ICBL has remained committed to capitalizing on the global political momentum that it helped to create. 'We will continue to work diligently . . . [towards] our goal of a world free of mines where all survivors can live in dignity' (Jody Williams, September 2002)."

International Federation for Human Rights (FIDH) (www.fidh.org)
"FIDH' s mandate is to contribute to the respect of all the rights defined in the Universal Declaration of Human Rights. FIDH aims at obtaining effective improvements in the protection of victims, the prevention of Human Rights violations and the sanction of their perpetrators. Its priorities are set by the triennial World Congress and the International Board (22 members), with the support of the International Secretariat (30 staff members)."

Search for Common Ground (www.sfcg.org)
"Our mission is very ambitious: to transform the way the world deals with conflict. We emphasize cooperative solutions, pursued on a realistic scale and with practical means. Current problems—

whether ethnic, environmental, or economic—are simply too complex and interconnected to be settled on an adversarial basis. . . . Although some of the conflicts we are currently dealing with may seem intractable, there are successful examples of cooperative conflict resolution that we can look to for inspiration— such as in South Africa, where an unjust system was transformed through negotiations and an inclusive peace process." Has thirteen field programs on four continents.

World Organization Against Torture (OMCT) (www.omct.org)
The World Organisation Against Torture is known also by its French acronym, OMCT. [It] "is the world's largest coalition of non-governmental organisations fighting against arbitrary detention, torture, summary and extrajudicial executions, forced disappearances and other forms of violence. Its global network comprises nearly 300 local, national and regional organisations, which share the common goal of eradicating such practices and enabling the respect of human rights for all."

NGOs with Research and Education Focus
Academic Council on the UN System (ACUNS) (www.acuns.wlu.ca)
"A principal goal of ACUNS is to strengthen the study of international organizations as they increase in number, activity, and complexity and to create strong ties between the academic community and officials and diplomats within the UN system and other international organizations. . . . Founded initially as a North American organization . . . ACUNS now has individual members as well as institutional sponsors from some 50 countries. . . . In 1995, ACUNS launched a new journal, *Global Governance: A Review of Multilateralism and International Organizations.*"

Carnegie Council on Ethics and International Affairs (http://cceia.org)
"We seek to engage the world's best minds in attempting to clarify the relationship between ethics and world affairs . . . provides educational experiences in which participants from a variety of backgrounds are encouraged to share their ideas and learn from one another."

Institute of World Affairs (www.iwa.org)
"Conducts a range of programs designed to prevent violent conflict and to advance post-conflict peace building," including

training seminars, both in the United States and abroad. "Operates several long-term development and postconflict reconciliation projects in the Middle East, West Africa, and the Eastern Mediterranean."

International Forum on Globalization (www.ifg.org)
"The International Forum on Globalization (IFG) is an alliance of sixty leading activists, scholars, economists, researchers and writers, representing over sixty organizations in twenty-five countries, formed to stimulate new thinking, joint activity, and public education in response to economic globalization."

The Population Council (www.popcouncil.org)
A research organization supporting a global network of regional and country offices. Seeks to improve the well-being and reproductive health of current and future generations around the world and to help achieve a humane, equitable, and sustainable balance between people and resources.

Union of International Associations (www.uia.org)
A clearinghouse for information on over 40,000 international organizations and constituencies. The site also includes information on *The Yearbook of International Organizations* and *The Encyclopedia of World Problems and Human Potential* (both now available on CD-ROM).

NGOs Attempting to Extend Informed Participation of People in UN Issues
Americans for UNESCO (www.amunesco.org)
Devoted to educating the American public about UNESCO and to involving them in efforts to extend U.S. government support for and involvement in UNESCO.

The Better World Campaign (BWC) (www.betterworldfund.org)
A project of the Better World Fund, created with support from businessman and philanthropist R. E. ("Ted") Turner as part of his historic $1 billion gift to support UN causes. It is a bipartisan, nonprofit national education and outreach effort dedicated to enhancing the awareness of and appreciation for the vital role the United Nations plays around the world.

United Nations Association of the USA (UNA-USA) (www.unausa.org)

The UNA-USA "supports the work of the United Nations and encourages active civic participation in the most important social and economic issues facing the world today. . . . UNA-USA offers Americans the opportunity to connect with issues confronted by the UN—from global health and human rights to the spread of democracy, equitable development and international justice. . . . UNA-USA educates Americans about the work of the UN, and encourages public support for strong U.S. leadership in the UN." UNA-USA is a member of the World Federation of UN Associations (WFUNA), with members in over 100 countries.

The Committee for a Democratic United Nations (CDUN) (www.uno-komitee.de/en)

The Committee for a Democratic United Nations is located in Germany. The committee and its member organizations support the democratization and strengthening of the UN System and of all global governance processes. The committee is mobilizing support for the establishment of a parliamentary assembly at the United Nations.

8

Biographical Sketches of Present Heads of UN System Organizations

This chapter provides biographical sketches of twenty-three people who are now (2005) heads of UN System organizations. Included are the UN secretary-general; eleven heads of UN Programs, Funds, and Other Entities; and eleven heads of UN Specialized Agencies. These biographies provide an informative overview of twenty-three people recruited to move out of roles in which they served a single state, or a lesser group, to roles in which they preside over an organization of people obligated to serve a worldwide membership. They come from nineteen member states around the world: Argentina, Belgium, Canada, Chile, France, Germany, Ghana, Greece, Italy, Japan, Korea (South), Saudi Arabia, Singapore, Senegal, Spain, Sweden, Tanzania, the United Kingdom, and the United States. Two heads of agencies come from Germany and Japan, and three come from the United States. Quite remarkable is the fact that six of the eleven heads of UN organizations designated as Programs, Funds and Other Entities are headed by women. They are from member states that circle the globe: Canada, Saudi Arabia, Singapore, Tanzania, and the United States. No women head a UN Specialized Agency.

It is significant that twelve of these twenty-three heads of UN agencies have had previous experience as members of UN secretariats. This includes the secretary-general and seven from UN Programs, Funds, and Other Entities, but only four from

Specialized Agencies. Of the remainder, four have been members of permanent missions to UN agencies, and one has represented a member state at meetings of decision-making bodies of the UN agency that they now head. The other six have had a wide array of backgrounds: member of a state supreme court, university professor, member of a provincial legislature, member of a state foreign service, member of a state government, and an official in a banking institution.

As you read through these biographies, you will quickly learn that this brief introduction reflects only a few aspects of these twenty-three UN System leaders. Most have had a wide array of background experiences that include a significant international dimension. These very brief biographical sketches of heads of UN agencies have been primarily drawn from information available at the website of the organization that they lead. Additional information is available at these websites.

UN Secretary-General

Kofi Annan, Secretary-General of the United Nations

Secretary-general of the United Nations since 1997 with a term running until 2006, Kofi Annan is the seventh secretary-general of the United Nations and the first secretary-general from the ranks of UN staff. He joined the UN System in 1962 as an administrative and budget officer with the World Health Organization (WHO) in Geneva. Since then he has served with the UN Economic Commission for Africa (ECA) in Addis Ababa; the UN Emergency Force (UNEF II) in Ismailia, Egypt; the Office of the UN High Commissioner for Refugees (UNHCR) in Geneva; and, at UN Headquarters in New York, as assistant secretary-general for human resources management and security coordinator for the UN System (1987–1990) and as assistant secretary-general for program planning, budget and finance, and as controller (1990–1992). In 1990, following the invasion of Kuwait by Iraq, Mr. Annan was asked by the secretary-general Perez de Cuellar as a special assignment to facilitate the repatriation of more than 900 international staff and citizens of Western countries from Iraq.

Annan served as assistant secretary-general for peacekeeping operations (March 1992–February 1993) and then as under secretary-general (March 1993–December 1996). His tenure as under-secretary-general coincided with unprecedented growth in the size and scope of UN peacekeeping operations, with a total deployment, at its peak in 1995, of almost 70,000 military and civilian personnel from 77 countries. From November 1995 to March 1996, following the Dayton Peace Agreement that ended the war in Bosnia and Herzegovina, he served as special representative of the secretary-general to the former Yugoslavia, overseeing the transition in Bosnia and Herzegovina from the UN Protection Force (UNPROFOR) to the multinational Implementation Force (IFOR) led by the North Atlantic Treaty Organization (NATO).

Annan was born in Kumasi, Ghana, studied at the University of Science and Technology in Kumasi, and completed his undergraduate work in economics at Macalester College in St. Paul, Minnesota, in 1961. From 1961 to 1962, he undertook graduate studies in economics at the Institut Universitaire des Hautes Etudes Internationales in Geneva. In 1972 he received a master of science degree in management from the Massachusetts Institute of Technology.

Heads of Eleven UN Programs, Funds, and Other Entities

António Guterres, High Commissioner, UN Refugee Agency (UNHCR)

António Guterres joined the UN High Commissioner for Refugees on June 15, 2005. "Before joining UNHCR, Mr. Guterres spent more than 20 years in government and public service. He served as the Portuguese prime minister from 1996 to 2002, during which he spearheaded the international effort to stop the atrocities in East Timor. As president of the European Council in early 2000, he co-chaired the first EU-Africa summit and led the adoption of the so-called Lisbon Agenda. He also founded the Portuguese Refugee Council in 1991, and was part of the Council of State of Portugal from 1991 to 2002.

"From 1981 to 1983, Mr. Guterres was a member of the Parliamentary Assembly of the Council of Europe, as well as chairman of the Committee on Demography, Migrations and Refugees. In addition, he has been active in Socialist International, acting as the organisation's vice-president from 1992 to 1999 before taking over as its president till June 2005" (www.unhcr.ch/cgi-bin/texis/vtx/admin?id=3bb311511a).

Louise Arbour, High Commissioner, Office of the UN High Commissioner for Human Rights (OHCHR)

Louise Arbour assumed her office in 2004 with the task of integrating human rights thinking and standards throughout the United Nations, including programs in peace and security, economic and social affairs, development cooperation, and humanitarian affairs. In 1996 she was appointed by the Security Council as chief prosecutor for the international criminal tribunals for the former Yugoslavia and for Rwanda. Her professional experiences include appointment to the Supreme Court of Canada (1999), conducting an inquiry as a single commissioner into certain events at the women's prisons in Kingston (1995), service on the Court of Appeals for Ontario (1990), service on the Supreme Court of Ontario (1987), and work in the Legal Department, City of Montreal (1970). Her academic positions include associate professor and associate dean, Osgoode Hall Law School, York University (1987), associate professor, Osgoode Hall Law School, York University (1977–1987), assistant professor, Osgoode Hall Law School, York University (1975), lecturer in Criminal Procedure, Osgoode Hall Law School, York University (1974), research officer, member of the Law Reform Commission, and member of the Criminal Procedure Project (1972). Her other professional activities include vice president, Canadian Civil Liberties Association (until December 1987), member of the International Council, and Institute for Global Legal Studies of Washington University School of Law, St. Louis, Missouri (2001).

Klaus Toepfer, Executive Director, UN Environment Program (UNEP)

In addition to being the executive director of UNEP, Klaus Toepfer has also served as UN under secretary-general, and director-general of the UN Office at Nairobi (UNON) since 1998. He was also acting executive director of the UN Center for Human Settlements (formerly UNCHS/Habitat, now UNHabitat) from July 1998 to August 2000. Before joining the United Nations, he was the federal minister of regional planning, building and urban development in Germany (1994–1998); the federal minister of the environment, nature conservation and nuclear safety (1987–1994); the state minister of environment and health of the German federal state of Rhineland-Palatinate (1985–1987); and state secretary at the Ministry of Social Affairs, Health and Environment for the same state (1978–1985). He participated in the Earth Summit in Rio de Janeiro in 1992, in the negotiations for the UN Framework Convention on Climate Change and the establishment of the Global Environment Facility (GEF). As executive director of UNEP, he has restructured the organization under five priority areas (environmental assessment and early warning, development of policy instruments, enhanced coordination with environmental conventions, technology transfer and industry, support to Africa). Before his political career he was a full professor at the University of Hannover, where he directed the Institute of Regional Research and Development (1978–1979).

Ann M. Veneman, Executive Director, United Nations Children's Fund (UNICEF)

Ann M. Veneman assumed the leadership of UNICEF on May 1, 2005, becoming the fifth Executive Director to lead UNICEF in its sixty-year history. At UNICEF Veneman directs a global agency of 10,000 staff and an annual budget of more than $2 billion, funded entirely by the voluntary contributions of governments, businesses, foundations, and individuals.

Prior to joining UNICEF, Veneman served as the 27th secretary of the United States Department of Agriculture. From 1991 to 1993, she was USDA's deputy secretary, the department's second-highest position. She also served as deputy undersecretary of Agriculture for International Affairs and Commodity Programs from 1989 to 1991. Veneman joined the USDA's Foreign Agricultural Service in 1986 and eventually served as associate administrator until 1989. From 1995 to 1999, she served as secretary of the California Department of Food and Agriculture (CDFA).

She began her legal career as a staff attorney with the General Counsel's office of the Bay Area Rapid Transit District in Oakland, California, in 1976. In 1978, she returned to her hometown of Modesto, where she served as a deputy public defender. In 1980, she joined a Modesto law firm as an associate and later a partner. She practiced law with a Washington, D.C., law firm from 1993 to 1995 before returning to California to serve as the state's secretary of Food and Agriculture.

Veneman earned her bachelor's degree in political science from the University of California, Davis; a master's degree in public policy from the University of California, Berkeley; and a juris doctorate degree from the University of California, Hastings College of Law.

Mark Malloch Brown, Administrator, UN Development Program (UNDP)

Mark Malloch Brown has held his position as administrator of UNDP since 1999, being elected to a second four-year term in 2003. He is also the chair of the UN Development Group, consisting of the heads of all UN funds, programs, and departments working on development issues. Earlier he served at the World Bank as vice president for external affairs and vice president for UN Affairs (1996–1999). He joined the World Bank as director of external affairs in 1994. He is credited with having helped the bank enhance its outreach and expand its partnership with the United Nations and nongovernmental organizations. In 1997 he chaired the UN secretary-general's task force on the reform of UN communications. Prior to joining the World Bank, Malloch Brown was the lead international partner from 1986 to 1994 in a strategic communications management firm, the Sawyer-Miller Group, based in New York and Washington, where he worked with corporations and governments. He worked for the UN High Commissioner for Refugees (1979–1983) in Thailand, where he was in charge of field operations for Cambodian refugees, and as deputy chief of UNHCR's Emergency Unit in Geneva, undertaking extensive missions in the Horn of Africa and Central America. A British citizen, he received a first-class honors degree in History from Magdalene College, Cambridge University, and a master's degree in political science from the University of Michigan.

Anna Kajumulo Tibaijuka, Executive Director, UN-Habitat (UN Human Settlements Program)

Since 2000 Anna Kajumolo Tibaijuka has held her post as executive director of UN-Habitat. She was elected to a four-year term in 2002. A Tanzanian national, she is the highest-ranking African woman in the UN System. From 1998 to 2000 she was the special coordinator for least developed countries, landlocked, and small island developing countries at UNCTAD. From 1993 to 1998 she was associate professor of economics at the University of Dar-es-Salaam. During these years she was a member of Tanzanian government delegations to the UN Conference on Human Settlements (1996), the World Food Summit (1996), the Fourth World Conference on Women (Beijing, 1995) and the World Summit for Social Development (1995). At the World Food Summit in Rome, she was elected coordinator for eastern Africa in the Network for Food Security, Trade and Sustainable Development (COASAD). Tibaijuka has also been a board member of UNESCO's International Scientific Advisory Board since November 1997. She holds a doctorate of science in agricultural economics from the Swedish University of Agricultural Sciences in Uppsala. During her first two years in office, Tibaijuka oversaw major reforms that led the UN General Assembly to upgrade the UN Center for Human Settlements to a full-fledged UN program, now called UN-HABITAT—the UN Human Settlements Program.

Noeleen Heyzer, Executive Director, UN Development Fund for Women (UNIFEM)

Director of UNIFEM since 1994, Noeleen Heyzer is the first executive director from the global South. She has served as chair of the UN Interagency Task Force on Women's Empowerment to implement the Cairo Plan of Action (1995–1996); chair of the UN Operational Working Group on the implementation of the Platform for Action of the Fourth World Conference on Women (1996–1997); cochair of the UN Council of the Micro-Credit Summit to reach the 100 million poorest families (1997–ongoing); chair of the UN Development Group on Gender to create guidelines and indicators for the UN Development Assistance Framework (1998–1999); head of the international delegation to engender the peace process in the Middle East

(2000); o-convener of the Round Table on Human Rights and HIV/AIDS during the General Assembly Special Session on HIV/AIDS (2001); and chair of the UN Interagency Task Force on Gender Equality and HIV/AIDS (1999–ongoing). She also served in the UN Economic and Social Commission of the Asia and Pacific Region, and was director of the Gender Program of the Asia and Pacific Development Center. She received her education at the University of Singapore and holds a PhD in social sciences from Cambridge University in the United Kingdom. She worked as a banker in Singapore and tutored sociology at the University of Singapore.

Hans J. A. Van Ginkel, Rector, United Nations University (UNU)

Rector of the UNU since 1997, Hans J. A. Van Ginkel became a member of the governing council of the United Nations University in 1992, of UNESCO's Advisory Group for Higher Education in 1996, and member of the Steering Committee for UNESCO's World Conference on Higher Education in 1998. In this last capacity he prepared and led, among others, the thematic debate on "Higher Education and Sustainable Human Development." He has contributed to numerous international organizations, including the governing board of the International Institute for Geo-Information Science and Earth Observation at Enschedé, the Netherlands (president 1990–1998); the board of the European Association of Universities (CRE, vice president 1994–1998), and the board of the International Association of Universities (IAU, vice president, 1995–2000; president, 2000–2004). From 1965 to 1968 he taught geography and history at the Thomas à Kempis College, Arnhem, the Netherlands. From 1968 to 1985 he was on the Utrecht University faculty of geographical sciences. In 1980 he was appointed full professor in human geography and planning. He was dean of faculty (1981–1985), became a member of the executive board of the University in 1985, and rector magnificus in 1986. Born in Kota-Radjah (Bandar Acheh, Indonesia), he received the M.Sc. in human and physical geography, anthropology, and history, and a PhD in social science.

Peter Piot, Executive Director, UNAIDS (Joint UN Program on HIV/AIDS)

Peter Piot has served as executive director of UNAIDS since its creation in 1995, and under secretary-general of the United Nations. In 1992 Piot joined the Global Program on AIDS of the World Health Organization, as associate director. Under his leadership, UNAIDS has become the chief advocate for worldwide action against AIDS. It has brought together nine organizations of the UN System around a common agenda on AIDS, spearheading UN reform. In the 1980s Piot launched and expanded a series of collaborative projects in Africa. Project SIDA in Kinshasa, Democratic Republic of the Congo, was the first international project on AIDS in Africa and is widely acknowledged as having provided the foundations for the understanding of HIV infection in Africa. He was a professor of microbiology and of public health at the Institute of Tropical Medicine, in Antwerp and at the Universities of Nairobi, Brussels, and Lausanne. Piot earned a medical degree from the University of Ghent, and a PhD in microbiology from the University of Antwerp, Belgium. After graduating from medical school, Piot codiscovered the ebola virus in Zaire in 1976. He is a member of the Institute of Medicine of the National Academy of Sciences of the United States.

Antonio Maria Costa, Executive Director, UN Office on Drugs and Crime (UNODC)

Appointed executive director of UNODC in 2002, Antonio Maria Costa is also director-general of the UN Office in Vienna (UNOV), holding the rank of under secretary-general of the United Nations. From 1969 to 1983, he served as senior economist in the UN Department of International Economics and Social Affairs in New York. He was later appointed under secretary-general at the Organization for Economic Cooperation and Development (OECD) in Paris, where he served until 1987. He was a member of the OECD Working Group for financial transactions (later called FATF), a member of the IMF/World Bank Interim

Committee and of the G–10 group for the coordination of economic policy. Between 1987 and 1992, he served at the Commission of the European Union as director-general for economics and finance. He then joined the European Bank for Reconstruction and Development (EBRD) in London as secretary-general, where he oversaw political issues, institutional affairs, corporate governance, and questions relating to shareholders. He holds a degree in political science from the University of Turin, Italy (1963), a degree in mathematical economics from the Moscow State University (1967), and a PhD in economics from the University of California at Berkeley (1971).

Thoraya Ahmed Obaid, Executive Director, UN Population Fund (UNFPA)

Appointed in 2001, Thoraya Ahmed Obaid is the first Saudi Arabian to be named head of a UN agency. From 1998 to 2001, she was director of the Division for Arab States and Europe of UNFPA. Before joining UNFPA, she was deputy executive secretary for the UN Economic and Social Commission for Western Asia (ESCWA) (1993–1998); chief of the Social Development and Population Division, ESCWA (1992–1993); and social affairs officer, responsible for the advancement of women (1975–1992). Working with governments to establish programs to empower women and develop their capacities as citizens with rights and responsibilities and with women's nongovernmental organizations (NGOs) to advocate for equality for women has been a central focus of her work. Obaid chaired the UN Inter-Agency Task Force on Gender in Amman, Jordan, in 1996. In November 1997 she was a member of the UN Inter-Agency Gender Mission to Afghanistan. Earlier that year, she was a member of the UN Strategic Framework Mission to Afghanistan. From 1984 to 1985 she was a member of the League of Arab States Working Group for formulating the Arab strategy for social development. She was the first Saudi Arabian woman to receive a government scholarship to study at a university in the United States, in 1963. She has a doctorate degree in English literature and cultural anthropology from Wayne State University, Detroit, Michigan.

Heads of Eleven UN Specialized Agencies

Juan Somavia, Director-General, International Labor Organization (ILO)

Juan Somavia is the ninth director-general of the ILO, reelected for a second five-year term in March 2003. An attorney by profession, he has had a long career in business, civil organizations, diplomacy, and as an academic. He was permanent representative of Chile to the United Nations in New York (1990–1999), president of the UN Economic and Social Council (1993–94, 1998–99), and representative of Chile on the UN Security Council (1996–1997). In 1999 he submitted his Decent Work Agenda to the ILO Conference, which was subsequently endorsed by the governing body and the conference. The work of the office has been reorganized around four strategic objectives that make it possible to establish targets and indicators to measure progress and provide the basis of accountability. He began his career as an academic. From 1967 to 1968, he was a lecturer on economic and social issues for GATT's trade policy courses in Geneva. In 1971 he was appointed professor of international economic and social affairs in the Department of Political Sciences at the Catholic University of Chile. Mr. Somavia participated actively in the restoration of democracy in Chile as president of the International Commission of the Democratic Coalition in Chile and founder and secretary-general of the South American Peace Commission (1986–1990). For his contribution to peace and human rights, he was awarded the Leonides Proano Peace Prize by the Latin American Human Rights Association.

Jacques Diouf, Director-General, Food and Agriculture Organization (FAO)

Jacques Diouf took office as director-general of the FAO in 1994 and was elected to a second six-year term in 2000. He had been the permanent representative of Senegal to the United Nations, New York (1991–1993); the special adviser to the governor of the Central Bank for West African States, Dakar, Senegal (1990–1991); the secretary-general of the Central Bank for West African States, Dakar (1985–1990); adviser to the president and regional director of the International Development Research Center, Ottawa, Canada (1984–1985); member of the Senegal Parliament (1983–1984); Senegal's secretary of state for science and technology (1978–1983); secretary of the West Africa Rice Development Association, Monrovia, Liberia (1971–1977); and the executive secretary of the African Groundnut Council, Lagos, Nigeria (1965–1971). He has also served as the representative for Africa to the Consultative Group on International Agricultural Research, Washington, D.C.; as a member of the Council of African Advisers of the World Bank; a member of the board of the UN University World Institute for Development Economics Research, Helsinki, Finland; and as a member of the Council of African Advisers of the World Bank. His education includes a PhD in social sciences of the rural sector (agricultural economics) at the Faculté de Droit et de Sciences économiques, Panthéon–Sorbonne; a master of science in tropical agronomy from École nationale d'application d'agronomie tropicale, Nogent-Paris, France; and a senior program certificate in management from the American Management Association, New York.

Koichiro Matsuura, Director-General UN Educational, Scientific and Cultural Organization (UNESCO)

Elected director-general of UNESCO for a six-year term in 1999, Koichiro Matsuura also served as chairperson of the World Heritage Committee of UNESCO (1998–1999). Earlier he served in the Japanese foreign service since 1961; as ambassador of Japan to France and concurrently to Andorra and Djibouti (1994–1999); as deputy minister for foreign affairs (MIF) (1992–1994); director-general of the North American Affairs Bureau, MIF (1990–1992); director-general of the Economic Cooperation Bureau, MIF (1988–1990); consul-general of Japan in Hong Kong (1985–1988); director of the General Affairs Division and deputy director-general of the Foreign Minister's Office (1982–1985); director of the Aid Policy Division, MIF (1980–1982); counselor of the Embassy of Japan in Washington (1977–1980); director of the Development Cooperation Division, MIF (1975–1977); director of the First North American Division (Political Affairs), MIF (1974–1975); various posts in the central administration, MIF (1972–1974); second secretary, then first secretary of the Japanese delegation to the OECD, Paris (1968–1972); he assumed various posts at the central administration, MIF (1963–1968); was third secretary of the Embassy of Japan, Ghana, and also was accredited to other countries in West Africa (1961–1963). Before entering the foreign service, Koichiro Matsuura had two academic teaching posts, on the faculty of economics at Haverford College, in Pennsylvania (1959–1961) and the faculty of law at the University of Tokyo (1956–1959).

LEE Jong-wook, Director-General, World Health Organization (WHO)

LEE Jong-wook took office as director-general of WHO for a five-year term in 2003. He has worked at WHO for twenty years at country, regional, and headquarters posts in technical, managerial, and policy positions, notably leading the fight against two of the greatest challenges to health and development: tuberculosis and vaccine-preventable diseases of children. After heading the WHO Global Program for Vaccines and Immunizations and serving as a senior policy advisor, in 2000 he became director of Stop TB, a coalition of more than 250 international partners including WHO member states, donors, nongovernmental organizations, industry, and foundations. He began his WHO career in 1983 as a leprosy consultant in the South Pacific, and a year later was appointed team leader for leprosy control in the South Pacific. In 1986 he moved to the Western Pacific Regional Office in Manila, initially in the Regional Leprosy Control Program and later as regional adviser on chronic diseases. Prior to joining WHO, LEE worked for two years at the LBJ Tropical Medical Centre in American Samoa. Born in Seoul, Republic of Korea, he received a medical doctor degree (MD) from Seoul National University and a master of public health degree from the University of Hawaii.

Efthimios E. Mitropoulos, Secretary-General, International Maritime Organization (IMO)

Mitropoulos began a four-year term as secretary-general at the International Maritime Organization in 2004. He joined the IMO in January 1979 as implementation officer in the Maritime Safety

Division and was appointed head of the Navigation Section (1985), senior deputy director for navigation and related matters (1989), director of the Maritime Safety Division and secretary of the Maritime Safety Committee (1992). Between 1989 and 1998, he led the IMO's efforts to establish a global search and rescue (SAR) plan. In 2000 he was appointed assistant secretary-general while continuing as director of the Maritime Safety Division. Between 1966 and 1977 he participated, initially as a member and later as head of the Greek delegation, in the Maritime Safety Committee of the IMO. He also participated in the Council and Assembly of the IMO as well as at the 1972 Collision Regulations and 1974 Safety of Life at Sea Conferences convened by the IMO. He attended the Third United Nations Conference on the Law of the Sea (1975–1977) as the representative of the Greek Ministry of Mercantile Marine in the multiministerial Greek delegation. In 2004 he was appointed chancellor of the World Maritime University (Malmo, Sweden) and chairman of the governing board of the International Maritime Law Institute (Malta). He is the author of several books on shipping economics and policy, types of merchant vessels, safety of navigation, and other shipping-related matters.

Yoshio UTSUMI, Secretary-General, International Telecommunications Union (ITU)

Yoshio Utsumi has held his post as secretary-general of the ITU since 1998, elected for a second term in 2002. In 1994 he was elected chairman of the ITU plenipotentiary conference. Before this he served as Japanese minister of posts and telecommunication (MPT). His involvement in the ITU began with three years in the Japanese Permanent Mission in Geneva where he served as first secretary of ITU affairs. He has been in the telecommunications business for over thirty years. His roles in MPT included professor of public administration at the MPT Postal College (1972), head of Japan's largest investment fund at the Postal Life Insurance Bureau of the MPT (1986), head of the General Affairs Division of MPT's Broadcasting Bureau (1988). He is credited with introducing a competition and liberalization policy at a time when such ideas were not widely accepted. He undertook a major restructuring of Japan's postal services with a staff of 200,000. He has played a very active role in many international negotiations, particularly those leading to the historic WTO agreement on basic telecommunications. He has a bachelor of law degree from the University of Tokyo and a master of arts degree in political science from the University of Chicago.

Michel Jarraud, Secretary-General, World Meteorological Organization (WMO)

Michel Jarraud was appointed secretary-general of the WMO for a four-year term in 2003, after serving as deputy secretary-general from 1995 to 2003. He devoted part of his career to the European Center for Medium-Range Weather Forecasts (ECMWF), where he was appointed deputy director in 1991, after having been director of the Operational Department since 1990. From September 1978 to December 1985 he was a researcher in numerical weather prediction at the ECMWF. He started his career with Météo-France, as a researcher (1976–1978). He joined the French National Meteorological Service again in January 1986 as director of the Weather Forecasting Department, and served there until December 1989. He is a meteorologist with degrees from the French Ecole Polytechnique and the Ecole de la Météorologie Nationale. For World Meteorological Day on 23 March 2005, he chose "the theme 'Weather, climate, water and sustainable development,' in recognition of the vital role and outstanding contribution of meteorology, hydrology, and related geophysical sciences to human progress, sustainable socioeconomic development, environmental protection, and poverty alleviation. . . . A significant threat to sustainable development is the increased impact of extreme weather and climate events. . . . In the longer term, sustainable development requires that the climate system is better understood, with the possibility to project future climate changes and their potential impacts" (www.wmo.ch/index-en.htm).

Carlos Magariños, Director-General, UN Industrial Development Organization (UNIDO)

Carlos Magariños has been director-general of UNIDO since 1997, reelected for a four-year term in 2000 and having concluded a two-year chairmanship of the High-Level Committee on Programs of the UN System Chief Executives Board for Coordination (CEB) in 2002. He was state secretary for industry and mining of Argentina (1993–1996) and national director for foreign trade (1991–1992). He also served as under-secretary of state for industry (1992–1993) and economic and trade representative of the Argentine government in Washington, D.C., with the rank of ambassador and state secretary (1996). His earlier academic career includes associate professor of microeconomics (1986), technical coordinator in research methodology of investigation (1987), and assistant professor of foreign trade institutions (1989) at the National University of Buenos Aires. He was also associate professor for Argentine and Latin American economic issues at Salvador University, Buenos Aires (1990), and taught on the subject of imports and exports by small- and medium-sized enterprises at the University of Belgrano, Buenos Aires (1990). He studied in Italy at the International Development Law Institute in Rome (1990) and at the Wharton School of the University of Pennsylvania (1997).

"He has consistently advocated the cause of multilateralism, and the need for a development agenda that better addresses the threats and opportunities the developing countries face with globalization" (www.unido.org/doc/3322).

Paul D. Wolfowitz, President, World Bank Group (WBG)

Wolfowitz became the tenth president of the World Bank Group on 1 June 2005, after serving as U.S. deputy secretary of defense, the Pentagon's number two post, since March 2001. He was previously dean and professor of international relations at the Paul H. Nitze School of Advanced International Studies (SAIS) of Johns Hopkins University. He has held a number of U.S. government posts. In addition to U.S. deputy secretary of defense, he served as under secretary of defense for policy, U.S. ambassador to Indonesia, and as assistant secretary of state for East Asian and Pacific affairs. He has also served as head of the U.S. State Department's Policy Planning Staff, as deputy assistant secretary of defense for regional programs and in the Arms Control and Disarmament Agency, as well as in the U.S. Bureau of the Budget. He also served on the 1998 Commission to Assess the Ballistic Missile Threat to the United States and the 1996 President's Commission on the Roles and Capabilities of the U.S. Intelligence Community. He taught previously at Yale (1970–1973) and John Hopkins (1981). He earned a bachelor's degree in mathematics from Cornell University in 1965 and a doctorate in political science from the University of Chicago in 1972.

Rodrigo de Rato, Managing Director, International Monetary Fund (IMF)

Rodrigo de Rato assumed office as managing director of the IMF in 2004. He was appointed vice president for economic affairs and minister of economy for the government of Spain in 1996, when he also served as governor for Spain on the boards of governors of the IMF, the World Bank, the Inter-American Development Bank, the European Investment Bank, and the European Bank for Reconstruction and Development. He regularly attended the European Union's (EU) economics and finance ministers' meetings and represented the EU at the Group of Seven Finance Ministers. He was also in charge of foreign trade relations for the government of Spain, and represented Spain at the World Trade Organization's ministerial meetings in 2001 and 2003. He was a member of Spain's parliament from 1982 to 2004. He has a law degree from the Universidad Complutense in Madrid, a master of business administration degree from the University of California at Berkeley, and a PhD in economics from the Universidad Complutense. In January 2005 he stated: "Surveillance will remain the centerpiece of our efforts. Over the past decade, there has been significant progress in strengthening our dialogue with member countries that aims to improve their economic policies and prevent financial crises" (www.imf.org/external/np/vc/2005/010105.htm).

Lennart Båge, President, International Fund for Agricultural Development (IFDA)

Lennart Båge has held his post as president of the IFDA since 2001. He had been involved in the activities of IFAD for ten years, during which time he served as chairman of the Governing Council of IFAD and cochairman of the High-Level Special Committee on IFAD's Resource Requirements and Related Governance Issues. He came to IFAD with nearly twenty-five years of experience in international development, and active involvement in the UN System and multilateral finance institutions. Prior to IFAD, he served as head of the Department for International Development Co-operation in Sweden's Ministry for Foreign Affairs in charge of budget and policy development for Sweden's US$ 1.6 billion International Cooperation Program, as well as responsibility for EU Affairs and international financial institutions. He has also served as Sweden's deputy for the International Development Association (IDA), vice chairman of the Development Assistance Committee of the OECD and Sweden's alternate governor for the Asian, African and Inter-American Development Banks. In December 2002 UN Secretary-General Kofi Annan designated Båge as chairman of the UN High-Level Committee on Programs (HLCP). Throughout his career, Båge has focused on a variety of issues central to IFAD's mission for poverty reduction, rural development, economic and social reform, capacity building, environmental management, and gender. He holds an MBA from the Stockholm School of Economics.

9

Selected Print and Nonprint Resources

S electing the print and nonprint resources to appear in this final chapter has been a very difficult task because of the extensive array of available resources. On the other hand, the
choices that appear will provide information that can lead readers to many more possibilities. The selections that follow begin
with "I. Books" and "II. Articles and Chapters." We have chosen
to list separately references on the future and on the history of
the UN System. The future is covered in "III. Future of the UN
System." United Nations history is covered by references and
books that compose "IV. The UN Intellectual History Project"
and "V. Other Recent Publications about UN System History."
Following these items is a brief list of "VI. Bibliographies," "VII.
Encyclopedias," "VIII. Yearbooks," and "IX. Journals."

"X. Educational Materials on the UN System" contains references to educational material provided by organizations in the
UN System for students ranging from grammar school through
high school and beyond. Many are available on UN websites and
some can be purchased. These educational materials are provided by the United Nations in New York, the International
Monetary Fund, the UN High Commissioner for Refugees, the
World Bank, the UN High Commissioner for Human Rights, and
UNICEF.

In December 2004 the UN secretary-general announced that
its official document system (ODS) was now available to the
public. "XI. Web Access to Full Text of UN Documents" indicates
how access to this vast resource can be achieved.

On 15 May 2000, UN Secretary-General Kofi Annan sent the leaders of the member states a letter identifying the twenty-five treaties most central to the spirit and goals of the United Nations. "XII. Twenty-Five Most Central UN Treaties" indicates how you can gain quick access to an overview of each of these treaties.

Finally, "XIII. Websites" provides addresses of (1) UN sites, (2) NGO organizations with broad agendas for furthering NGO effectiveness, (3) NGO issue networks, and (4) other sources of information.

Table of Contents

Books

Aksu, Esref, and Joseph Camilleri, eds., 2002, *Democratizing Global Governance.* New York: Palgrave Macmillan.

Alger, Chadwick F., Gene Lyons, and John Trent, eds., 1995, *The United Nations: The Policies of Member States.* Tokyo: United Nations University.

Alleyne, Mark D., 1995, *International Power and International Communication.* New York: St. Martin's.

Ariye, Akira, 2002, *Global Community: The Role of International Organizations in the Making of the Contemporary World.* Berkeley: University of California.

Armstrong, David, Lorna Lloyd, and John Redmond, 1996, *From Versailles to Maastricht: International Organizations in the Twentieth Century.* New York: St. Martin's.

Bennett, A. LeRoy, and James K. Oliver, 2002, *International Organizations: Principles and Issues,* 7th ed. Upper Saddle River, NJ: Prentice Hall.

Boulden, Jane, and Thomas G. Weiss, eds., 2004, *Terrorism and the UN: Before and after September 11.* Bloomington: Indiana University.

Brodie, Bernard, and Fawn Brodie, 1973, *From Crossbow to H-Bomb,* revised and enlarged ed. Bloomington: Indiana University.

Childers, Erskine, and Brian Urquhart, 1994, *Renewing the United Nations System.* Uppsala, Sweden: Dag Hammarskjold Foundation.

Claude, Inis, 1971, *Swords into Plowshares: The Problems and Progress of International Organization,* 4th ed. New York: Random House.

Coate, Roger A., 1988, *Unilateralism, Ideology, and US Foreign Policy: The United States in and out of UNESCO.* Boulder, CO: Lynne Rienner.

Coicaud, Jean-Marc, Michael W. Doyle, and Anne-Marie Gardner, eds., 2003, *The Globalization of Human Rights: The United Nations System in the Twenty-First Century.* Tokyo: United Nations University.

Commission on Global Governance, 1995, *Our Global Neighborhood.* New York: Oxford University.

Cortright, David, and George A. Lopez, with Linda Gerber, 2002, *Sanctions and the Search for Security: Challenges to UN Action.* Boulder, CO: Lynne Rienner.

Coser, Louis, *The Functions of Social Conflict, 1956, 1968.* New York: Free Press.

Daws, Sam, and Paul Taylor, eds., 2000, *The United Nations, Volume I: Systems and Structures; Volume II, The United Nations, Functions and Futures.* Dartmouth, UK: Ashgate.

Diehl, Paul F., ed., 2001, *The Politics of Global Governance: International Organizations in an Interdependent World.* Boulder, CO: Lynne Rienner.

Dole, Charles Fletcher, 1906, *The Spirit of Democracy.* New York: T. Y. Crowell.

Fasulo, Linda, 2004, *An Insider's Guide to the UN.* New Haven, CT: Yale University.

Fenton, Neil, 2004, *Understanding the UN Security Council.* Aldershot, UK: Ashgate.

Fulbright, J. William, 1966, *The Arrogance of Power.* New York: Vintage.

Galenson, Walter, 1981, *The International Labor Organization: An American View.* Madison: University of Wisconsin.

Galtung, Johan, 1980, *The True Worlds: A Transnational Perspective.* New York: Free Press.

Gregg, Robert W., 1993, *About Face? The United States and the United Nations.* Boulder, CO: Lynne Rienner.

Jacob, Philip E., Alexine L. Atherton, and Arthur M. Wallenstein, 1972, *The Dynamics of International Organization.* Revised ed. Homewood, IL: Dorsey.

Jessup, Philip, 1956, *Parliamentary Diplomacy: An Examination of the Legal Quality of the Rules of Procedure of Organs of the United Nations.* Leyden: A.W. Sijhoff.

Juda, Lawrence, ed., 1983, *The United States without the Law of the Sea Treaty: Opportunities and Costs.* Wakefield, RI: Times.

Karns, Margaret P., and Karen A. Mingst, 2004, *International Organizations: The Politics and Processes of Global Governance.* Boulder, CO: Lynne Rienner.

Kirton, John J., and Radoslava N. Stefanova, 2003, *The G8, the United Nations, and Conflict Prevention*. Aldershot, UK: Ashgate.

Krasno, Jean E., ed., 2004, *The United Nations: Confronting the Challenges of a Global Society*. Boulder, CO: Lynne Rienner.

Kull, Steven, and I. M. Destler, 1999, *Misreading the Public: The Myth of a New Isolationism*. Washington, DC: Brookings Institution.

Landy, E. A., 1966, *The Effectiveness of International Supervision: Thirty Years of ILO Experience*. London: Stevens and Sons.

Leonard, L. Larry, 1951, *International Organization*. New York: McGraw-Hill.

Luck, Edward, C., 1999, *Mixed Messages: American Politics and International Organization*. Washington, DC: Brookings Institution.

———, 2003, *Reforming the United Nations: Lessons from a History in Progress*. New Haven, CT: Academic Council on the UN Occasional Papers.

Malone, David M., ed., 2004, *The UN Security Council: From the Cold War to the 21st Century*. Boulder, CO: Lynne Rienner.

Mangone, Gerard J., 1954, *A Short History of International Organization*. New York: McGraw-Hill.

McNeill, William, 1963, *The Rise of the West: A History of the Human Community*. Chicago: University of Chicago.

Muldoon, James P., Jr., JoAnn Fagot Aviel, Earl Sullivan, and Richard Reitano, 2005, *Multilateral Diplomacy and the United Nations Today*, 2d ed. Boulder, CO: Westview.

Muller, Joachim, ed., 2001, *Reforming the United Nations: The Quiet Revolution*. The Hague: Kluwer Law International.

Murphy, John F., 2004, *The United States and the Rule of Law in International Affairs*. Cambridge, UK: Cambridge University.

Nye, Joseph, 2002, *The Paradox of American Power: Why the World's Only Superpower Can't Go It Alone.* Oxford, UK: University of Oxford.

Pugh, Michael, and Waheguru Pal Singh Sidhu, eds., 2003, *The United Nations and Regional Security: Europe and Beyond.* Boulder, CO: Lynne Rienner.

Reinsch, Paul S., 1916, *Public International Unions.* 2d ed. Boston: World Peace Foundation.

Rittberger, Volker, ed., 2001, *Global Governance and the United Nations System: The United Nations System in the Twenty-first Century.* Tokyo: United Nations University.

Rochester, J. Martin, 1993, *Waiting for the Millennium: The United Nations and the Future World Order.* Columbia: University of South Carolina.

Schlesinger, Stephen C., 2003, *The Act of Creation: The Founding of the United Nations: A Story of Superpowers, Secret Agents, Wartime Allies and Enemies and Their Quest for a Peaceful World.* Boulder, CO: Westview.

Schwartzberg, Joseph E., 2004, *Revitalizing the United Nations: Reform through Weighted Voting.* New York and The Hague: Institute for Global Policy, World Federalist Movement.

Scott, J. S., ed., 1917, *The Reports of the Hague Conferences of 1899 and 1907.* Oxford, UK: Humphren Milford.

Siddiqi, Javel, 1995, *World Health and World Politics: The World Health Organization and the UN System.* Columbia: University of South Carolina.

Sriram, Chandra Lekha, and Kiarin Wermester, eds., *From Promise to Practice: Strengthening UN Capacities for the Prevention of Violent Conflict.* Boulder, CO: Lynne Rienner.

Taylor, Paul, and A. J. R. Groom, eds., 2000, *The United Nations at the Millennium: the Principal Organs.* London: Continuum.

United Nations, 2004, *Basic Facts About the United Nations.* New York: United Nations.

United Nations, Department of Public Information, 1996, *The Blue Helmets: A Review of United Nations Peacekeeping.* 3d ed. New York: UN Department of Public Information.

United Nations Association of the USA, *A Global Agenda: Issues before the General Assembly of the UN* (an annual publication). New York: UNA-USA.

Urquhart, Brian, 1972, *Hammarskjold.* New York: Harper and Row.

————, 1993, *Ralph Bunche: An American Life.* New York: W. W. Norton.

White, Nigel D., 2003, *The United Nations System: Toward International Justice.* Boulder, CO: Lynne Rienner.

Whitsorth, Sandra, 2004, *Men, Militarism, and UN Peacekeeping: A Gendered Analysis.* Boulder, CO: Lynne Rienner.

Williams, Phil, and Ernesto U. Savona, 1996, *The United Nations and Transnational Organized Crime.* London: Frank Cass.

Williams, Phil, and Dimitri Vlassis, 2001, *Combating Transnational Crime.* London: Frank Cass.

Ziring, Lawrence, Robert Riggs, and Jack A. Plano, 2000, *The United Nations: International Organizations and World Politics.* 3d ed. Fort Worth, TX: Harcourt College.

Articles and Chapters

Agrawala, Shardul, and Steinar Andresen, 1999, **"Indispensability and Indefensibility? The United States in the Climate Treaty Negotiations,"** *Global Governance,* Vol. 5, No. 4, 457–482.

Alger, Chadwick F., 2003, **"Evolving Roles of NGOs in Member State Decision-making in the UN System,"** *Journal of Human Rights,* Vol. 2., No. 3, 407–424.

———, 2003, **"Searching for Democratic Potential in Emerging Global Governance,"** in Bruce Morrison, *Transnational Democracy in Critical and Comparative Perspective: Democracy's Range Reconsidered.* Ashgate, UK: Aldershot, 87–106.

———, 1999, **"Strengthening Relations between NGOs and the UN System: Towards a Research Agenda,"** *Global Civil Society,* Vol. 13, No. 4, 393–410.

———, 1995, **"The United Nations in Historical Perspective,"** in Chadwick F. Alger, Gene M. Lyons, and John E. Trent, eds., *The UN System: The Policies of Member States.* Tokyo: UN University, 3–40.

———, 1994, **"Citizens and the UN System in a Changing World,"** in Yoshikazu Sakomoto, ed., *Global Transformation: Challenges to the State System.* Tokyo: UN University.

Archibugi, Daniele, 1993, **"The Reform of the UN and Cosmopolitan Democracy: A Critical Review,"** *Journal of Peace Research,* Vol. 30, No. 3, 301–316.

Debiel, Tobias, 2000, **"Strengthening the UN as an Effective World Authority: Security versus Hegemonic Crisis Management,"** *Global Governance,* Vol. 6, No. 1, 25–42.

Lyons, Gene, 1999, **"The UN and American Politics,"** *Global Governance,* Vol. 5, No. 4, 497–512.

Nuscheler, Franz, 2002, **"World Conferences,"** in Helmut Vogler, ed., *A Concise Encyclopedia of the United Nations.* The Hague: Kluwer Law International, 684–688.

Ruggie, John Gerard, 2003, **"The United Nations and Globalization: Patterns and Limits of Institutional Adaptation,"** *Global Governance,* Vol. 9, No. 3, 301–321.

Stoll, Peter Tobias, 2002, **"WTO—World Trade Organization, GATT—General Agreement on Tariffs and Trade,"** in Helmut

Vogler, ed., *A Concise Encyclopedia of the United Nations*. The Hague: Kluwer Law International, 691–697.

Future of the UN System References

Alger, Chadwick F., 1998, **"Conclusion: The potential of the United Nations system,"** in Alger, 1998, 409–423.

——, 1996, **"Thinking about the Future of the UN System,"** *Global Governance*, Vol. 2, 335–360.

——, 1998, *The Future of the United Nations System: Potential for the Twenty-First Century.* Tokyo: United Nations University.

Apodaca, Clair, Michael Stohl, and George Lopez, 1998, **"Moving Norms to Political Reality: Institutionalizing Human Rights Standards through the UN System,"** in Alger, *The Future of the United Nations System: Potential for the Twenty-First Century.* Tokyo: United Nations University, 185–220.

Biermann, Frank, and Steffen Bauer, 2005, *A World Environment Organization: Solution of Threat for Effective International Environmental Governance.* Williston, VT: Ashgate.

Boulding, Elise, and Jan Oberg, 1998, **"United Nations Peacekeeping and NGO Peace Building: Towards Partnership,"** in Alger, *The Future of the United Nations System: Potential for the Twenty-First Century.* Tokyo: United Nations University, 127–154.

Brauch, Hans Gunter, Czeslaw Mesjasz, and Bjorn Moller, 1998, **"Controlling Weapons in the Quest for Peace: Non-offensive Defence, Arms Control, Disarmament, and Conversion,"** in Alger, *The Future of the United Nations System: Potential for the Twenty-First Century.* Tokyo: United Nations University, 15–53.

Debiel, Tobias, 2000, **"Strengthening the UN as an Effective World Authority: Cooperative Security versus Hegemonic Crisis Management,"** *Global Governance*, Vol. 6, No. 1, 25–42.

Jeong, Ho-Won, 1998, **"The struggle in the UN System for Wider Participation in Forming Global Economic Policies,"** in Alger,

The Future of the United Nations System: Potential for the Twenty-First Century. Tokyo: United Nations University, 221–247.

Johansen, Robert C., 1998, **"Enhancing United Nations Peacekeeping,"** in Alger, *The Future of the United Nations System: Potential for the Twenty-First Century.* Tokyo: United Nations University, 89–126.

McSpadden, Lucia Ann, and Anthony Ayok Chol, 1998, **"Generating the Political Will for Protecting the Rights of Refugees,"** in Alger, *The Future of the United Nations System: Potential for the Twenty-First Century.* Tokyo: United Nations University, 282–314.

Mische, Patricia M., and Mauricio Andres Ribeiro, 1998, **"Sharing and Protecting the Commons: Ecological Security and the United Nations System,"** in Alger, *The Future of the United Nations System: Potential for the Twenty-First Century.* Tokyo: United Nations University, 315–356.

Osseiran, Sanaa, and Betty Reardon, 1998, **"The United Nations' Role in Peace Education,"** in Alger, *The Future of the United Nations System: Potential for the Twenty-First Century.* Tokyo: United Nations University, 385–408.

Pietila, Hilkka, and Jeanne Vickers, 1998, **"The UN System in the Vanguard of Advancement of Women: Equality, Development, and Peace,"** in Alger, *The Future of the United Nations System: Potential for the Twenty-First Century.* Tokyo: United Nations University, 248–281.

Rupesinghe, Kumar, 1998, **"Coping with Internal Conflict: Teaching the Elephant to Dance"** in Alger, *The Future of the United Nations System: Potential for the Twenty-First Century.* Tokyo: United Nations University, 155–184.

Varis, Tapio, 1998, **"Communications in the Future UN System,"** in Alger, *The Future of the United Nations System: Potential for the Twenty-First Century.* Tokyo: United Nations University, 357–384.

Vayrynen, Raimo, 1998, **" Enforcement and Humanitarian Intervention: Two Faces of Collective Action by the United Nations,"** in Alger, *The Future of the United Nations System: Potential for the Twenty-First Century.* Tokyo: United Nations University, 54–88.

The UN Intellectual History Project

The project has two main components. One is a series of eighteen books, each focused on well-defined economic or social areas of UN activity or on key ideas and norms linked to international peace and security. The second main component of the project is a series of oral history interviews. All seventy-three of the interviews in the first phase have been completed. All of the books are being published as a special series by Indiana University Press.

"The persistent cynicism about the UN's record being a 'blank slate' is one of the principal arguments for this project, and it underscores the importance of disseminating our research findings as widely as possible. As project research shows, the UN has been the international incubator, advocate, and disseminator of many key ideas emerging out of debates about economic and social issues over almost 60 years, ideas that we now take for granted—human rights, full employment, sustainable development, gender equality, basic needs, and human development and human security, to name but a few. In short, the UN has greatly contributed in shaping development discourse and practice globally albeit with varied results, while it has itself been shaped by it" (www.unhistory.org).

Listed below are five volumes already published, seven to be published in 2005, two in 2006, and three for which the authors have not yet been commissioned. All are published by Indiana University Press.

Berthelot, Yves, ed., with Adebayo Adedeji, Leelananda de Silva, Paul Rayment, Gert Rosenthal, and Blandine Destremeau, 2003, *Unity and Diversity in Development Ideas: Perspectives from the UN Regional Commissions.*

Emmerij, Louis, Richard Jolly, and Thomas G. Weiss, 2003, *Ahead of the Curve? UN Ideas and Global Challenges.*

Jolly, Richard, Louis Emmerij, Dharam Ghai, and Frederic Lapeyre, 2004, *UN Contributions to Development Thinking and Practice.*

Toye, John, and Richard Toye, 2004. *The UN and Global Political Economy: Trade, Finance, and Development.*

Ward, Michael, 2004, *Quantifying the World: UN Contributions to Statistics.*

Jain, Devaki, forthcoming 2005, *Women, Development, and the UN: Sixty Years in Quest of Equality and Justice.*

MacFarlane, S. Neil, and Yuen Foong-Khong, forthcoming 2005, *Human Security and the UN: A Critical History.*

Normand, Roger, and Sarah Zaidi, forthcoming 2005, *The UN and Human Rights: The Unfinished Revolution.*

Sagafi-nejad, Tagi, in collaboration with John Dunning, forthcoming 2005, *The UN and Transnational: From Code to Compact.*

Schriver, Nico J., forthcoming 2005, *The UN and the Global Commons: Development without Destruction.*

Stokk, Olav, forthcoming 2005, *The UN and Development Cooperation.*

Weiss, Thomas G., Tatiana Carayannis, Louis Emmerij, and Richard Jolly, forthcoming 2005, *UN Voices: The Struggle for Development and Social Justice.*

Jolly, Richard, Louis Emmerij, and Thomas G. Weiss, forthcoming 2006, *The United Nations: A History of Ideas and Their Future.*

Thakur, Ramesh, and Thomas G. Weiss, forthcoming 2006, *The UN and Global Governance: An Idea and Its Prospects.*

Authors to be commissioned, *Collective Security and Peacekeeping.*

Authors to be commissioned, *Conflict Prevention.*

Authors to be commissioned, *Humanitarian Intervention.*

Other Recent Publications about UN System History

This copyrighted bibliography is available at the UN Intellectual History Project website (www.unhistory.org) and is presented here with the permission of the Ralph Bunche Institute for International Studies, Graduate Center, City University of New York.

Anstee, Margaret Joan, *Never Learn to Type: A Woman at the United Nations.* (London: John Wiley and Sons, 2003).

Batisse, Michel, *Demain l'Unesco/Unesco and the Years Ahead.* (Paris: Millios Group 1999).

Blanchard, Francis, *L'Organisation Internationale du Travail: de la Guerre Froide au Nouvel Ordre Mondial.* Preface de Philippe Seguin. (Paris: Le Seuil 2004).

Bøås, Morten, "Governance as Multilateral Development Bank Policy: The Cases of the African Development Bank and the Asian Development Bank." *European Journal of Development Research,* vol. 10, no. 2 (1998): 117–134.

Chabbott, Colette, *Constructing Education for Development: International Organizations and Education for All.* Reference Books in International Education. Edward Beauchamp, editor. (New York: Routledge Falmer 2003).

Emmerij, Louis, "An Intellectual History of the United Nations" *Development in Practice,* vol. 12, no. 5 (November 2002): 653–655.

Dil, Anwar, ed., *Hunger, Poverty and Development: The Life and Work of Sartaj Aziz.* (Lahore: Ferozsons 2000).

Jolly, Richard, ed., *Jim Grant: UNICEF Visionary.* (New York: UNICEF 2001).

Lewin, André, *L'ONU, pour quoi faire?* (Paris: Gallimard, 1995).

Lewin, André, ed., *La France et L'ONU depuis 1945,* with foreword by Alain Juppé (Paris: Arleéa/Corlet/Le Seuil, 1995).

Mackenzie, Archie, *Faith in Diplomacy.* (St. Paul, MN: Grosvenor Books, 2002).

Schlesinger, Stephen C., *Act of Creation: The Founding of the United Nations.* (Boulder: Westview, 2003).

Shaw, D. John, *The UN World Food Programme and the Development of Food Aid.* (Basingstoke: Palgrave 2001).

Shaw, D. John, *Sir Hans Singer: The Life and Work of a Development Economist.* (Basingstoke: Palgrave 2002).

Singer, Hans, and D. John Shaw, *International Development Cooperation: Essays on Aid and the United Nations System.* (Basingstoke: Palgrave, 2001).

Taniguchi, Makoto, *North-South Issues in the 21st Century: A Challenge in the Global Age.* (Waseda University Press, 2001).

Tokman, Victor E., *Una Voz en el Camino—Empleo y Equidad en America Latina: 40 Anos de Busqueda.* (Chile: Fondo de Cultura Economica, 2004).

Toye, John, and Richard Toye, "The Origins and Interpretation of the Prebisch-Singer Thesis," *History of Political Economy,* vol. 35, no. 3 (Fall 2003): 347–367.

Weiss, Thomas G., and Tatiana Carayannis, "The Role of UN Economic and Social Ideas," *Work in Progress: A Review of Research Activities of the United Nations University,* vol. 16, no. 3 (Summer 2002). United Nations University.

Weiss, Thomas G., and Tatiana Carayannis, "Whither United Nations Economic and Social Ideas? A Research Agenda," *Journal of Global Social Policy,* vol.1, no. 1 (April 2001): 25–47.

Bibliographies

Hajnal, Peter, "United Nations Reform: A Selected Bibliography." Revised 27 January 1997. (http://www.library.yale.edu/un/un2a6a.htm)

Spencer, Christopher, "Global Issues of the Twenty-First Century and United Nations Challenges: An Annotated Bibliography." Updated 29 November 2004 (www.global-challenges.org). It is recommended that users of this bibliography go first to "Why This Bibliography, and How to Use It."

Encyclopedias

Encyclopedia of Life Support Systems (EOLSS). Oxford, UK: EOLSS, 2001.

Encyclopedia of World Problems and Human Potential. Vol. 1: World Problems. Vol. 2: Human Potential, Transformation and Values. Vol. 3: Actions, Strategies, Solutions. 4th ed. Brussels, Belgium: Union of International Associations (UIA), 1994–1995.

Volger, Helmut, ed., *A Concise Encyclopedia of the United Nations.* The Hague, Netherlands: Kluwer Law International, 2000.

Who's Who in International Organizations. 3d ed. Brussels, Belgium: Union of International Associations (UIA), 1999.

Yearbook

Yearbook of International Organizations. Brussels, Belgium: Union of International Associations (UIA).

Journals

Global Governance

Global Networks

Global Society

Globalization

International Journal of Peace Studies

International Organization

International Peacekeeping

International Studies Quarterly

Journal of Human Rights

Journal of Peace Research

Millennium Journal of International Studies

Transnational Associations

United Nations Chronicle

World Politics

Educational Materials on the UN System

The United Nations, the International Monetary Fund, the UN High Commissioner for Refugees, the World Bank, the UN Environment Program, and the UN High Commissioner for Human Rights have made available educational materials on global issues and on efforts of the UN System to cope with them. These materials are available for primary, intermediate, and secondary schools. Easy access to these materials can be attained on the Internet.

1. *UN Global Teaching and Learning Project, Cyberschoolbus*
The UN Cyberschoolbus offers three kinds of materials: briefing papers, curriculum topics, and school kits on the United Nations.

(1) The *Briefing Papers* for students are based on the secretary-general's Millennium Report on the role of the United Nations in the twenty-first century. Each briefing paper provides information about a current world problem and the UN System's efforts to cope with it. The topics include preventing conflict, poverty, refugees, human rights, child soldiers, child labor, and a number of others. (Available at www.un.org/cyberschoolbus/briefing/index.asp)

(2) Each *Curriculum Topic* focuses on an issue on the agenda of organizations in the UN System. Examples are peace education, poverty, human rights, cities of the world, world hunger, indigenous peoples, rights at work, ethnic discrimina-

tion, racial discrimination, peace schools, women's rights, saving tomorrow's world, cleaner oceans, the United Nations in space, and health.

(Available at http://www.un.org/Pubs/CyberSchoolBus)

(3) *School Kits* on the United Nations are prepared by teachers for three different levels: primary, intermediate, and secondary.

The *Primary School Kit on the United Nations* introduces the work of the UN System to children seven to ten years old. An effort is made to indicate how issues on the agendas of the UN System have a connection to the lives of young children. Themes covered are learning to resolve conflicts peacefully, human rights, refugees, disarmament, disaster relief, the environment, and a number of other issues.

The *Intermediate School Kit on the United Nations* is for students between the ages of eleven and fourteen. Issues covered include the environment, the rights of the child, health and science, disaster relief, and refugees. The UN website states that "teachers of all subjects, from history and language to math, science and geography, will work easily with these units." The kits illuminate the fact that in courses on art, music, and mathematics it is possible to focus on aspects of the broad agendas of organizations in the UN System that are often overlooked.

The *Secondary School Kit on the United Nations* has the goal of presenting very complex global issues in a way that makes them understandable to high school students. Efforts to work for tolerance, development, and peace are illuminated through units on child labor, the struggle against apartheid, equal rights for women, cleaner oceans, and accessible health care, among other topics.

School Kits are sold for $4.95 each, plus shipping and handling. For further information and ordering go to http://cyberschoolbus.un.org/bookstor/kits, or call 1–800 253–9646.

2. *The International Monetary Fund "For Students" Information and Online Learning Activities about the IMF* opens with information on the IMF, frequently asked questions about the IMF, and criticism of the IMF and provides some photos. There is also a section on "EconEd Online" that offers "educational activities and resources, including teaching guides, to help students understand the history of money, macroeconomics, international monetary cooperation, and global trade." This is followed by educational material prepared especially for high

school students and also for fifth- and sixth-grade students. (www.imf.org/external/np/exr/st/eng/index.htm)

3. *The UN High Commissioner on Refugees, "For Teachers" Website,* has a special area just for those interested in teaching about refugee issues at the primary, intermediate, and secondary levels. Good for many different subjects. (www.unhcr.ch/children/index.html)

4. *The World Bank* website has a section, "Youthink," devoted to offering students and teachers "information about global issues that matter to young people today." Among the issues covered are conflict, corruption, development, education, employment, environment, and globalization. An effort is made to share the research, knowledge and experience gathered by World Bank experts on these issues. (http://youthink.worldbank.org)

5. *The UN Environment Program* website offers the *Children and Youth Program* that provides a variety of activities that encourage the involvement of children in environmental issues. There is only space here to present three examples. One is a book, *Pachamama: Our Earth—Our Future,* 1999. It has sections on "Our Earth" (Atmosphere; Freshwater, Marine & Coastal Areas; Land and Food; Forests; Biodiversity; Urbanization; and Polar Regions); "Our Future" (What Scientists Say, What Others Think), and concludes with "What You Can Do! How Green Are You?" Second, since 1990 UNEP has sponsored an annual International Children's Painting Competition on the Environment. It has received over 160,000 entries from children in over 100 countries. The competition in 2005 is the fourteenth and will focus on the theme "Green Cities." Third, UNEP is organizing the first Children's World Summit for the Environment in Japan from 26 to 29 July 2005 in conjunction with Expo 2005. The conference is for children between the ages of ten and fourteen.

(www.unep.org/Documents.multilingual/Default.asp?DocumentID=295)

6. *The UN High Commissioner for Human Rights* website has an extensive "Database for Human Rights Education." This database includes bibliographies, curricula, educational games, picture books, plans of action, and teaching/training guides. Items in this last category have been prepared by human rights organizations in various countries. A few examples of the titles are: "Handbook for Teaching Human Rights and Peace"; "First Steps: A Manual for Starting Human Rights Education"; "Fields

of Hope: Educational Activities on Child Labor"; "Teacher's Guide, Peace and War: A Resource for Teaching and Learning"; and "Shopping List of Techniques in Teaching Human Rights." (www.unhchr.ch/hredu.nsf)

Web Access to Full Text of UN Documents

In December 2004 the United Nations announced the availability of its official document system (ODS), the full-text web resource for official UN documentation to the general public via http://documents.un.org. The ODS covers all types of official UN documentation originating from duty stations worldwide, including selective documents of the regional commissions: Economic and Social Commission for Western Asia (ESCWA), Economic and Social Commission for Asia and the Pacific (ESCAP), Economic Commission for Latin America and the Caribbean (ECLAC), and Economic Commission for Europe (ECE).

Comprehensive coverage starts in 1993. Older UN documents are added to the system on a daily basis. Selective coverage of General Assembly and Security Council documentation currently reaches back to 1985. The ODS also provides access to the resolutions of the General Assembly, Security Council, Economic and Social Council, and the Trusteeship Council from 1946 onwards.

In December 2004 the ODS contained close to 800,000 files and approximately 100,000 new documents are added each year.

Users may take advantage of ODS benefits such as quick access to valuable UN official documents, easy-to-use search functionality, easy-to-print PDF documents, and user-friendly design.

An ODS Training Guide is posted at: http://www.un.org/ Depts/dhl/resguide/train.htm.

Twenty-Five Most Central UN Treaties

On 15 May 2000 UN Secretary-General Kofi Annan sent the leaders of the member states a letter identifying the twenty-five treaties most central to the spirit and goals of the UN Charter. He invited these leaders to make use of the opportunity provided by the Millennium Summit to rededicate themselves to the international legal order by signing and ratifying those treaties. They include treaties on genocide, safety of UN personnel, human rights, racial discrimination, torture, drought and desertification, nuclear test-ban, women's rights, migrant workers and their families, children's rights, global warming, antipersonnel mines, refugees, international criminal court, conventional weapons restrictions, chemical weapons, terrorist bombings, biodiversity, and the environment. Key provisions of these twenty-five treaties are available at: www.un.org/cyberschoolbus/treaties.

Websites

UN System

Quick routes of access to all organizations in UN System: www.un.org, www.unsystem.org

UN On-line Tour: New York, www.un.org/Pubs/CyberSchoolBus/untour/subgen

Geneva, www.unog.ch/frames/tour/tour.htm

Cyberschoolbus: Introduction to the UN, www.cyberschoolbus.un.org/unintro/unintro.asp

Cyberschoolbus: www.un.org/Pubs/CyberSchoolBus/index.asp
    Cyberschoolbus has curriculum on: Peace Education, Poverty, Human Rights, World Hunger, Indigenous People, Racial Discrimination, Ethnic Discrimination, Rights at Work, Schools Demining Schools, and Cities of the World.

NGO Organizations with Broad Agendas for Furthering NGO Effectiveness

Global Communication Center for Development Organizations: http://ngos.cc/

Global Policy Forum: www.globalpolicy.org/ngos

NGO Links: www.ngo.org/links

NGOs Network: www.ngos.net

United Nations Association of the United States of America (UNA-USA): www.unausa.org

World Federation of UN Associations (WFUNA): www.wfuna.org

NGO Issue Networks

Abolition 2000: www.abolition2000.org

Amnesty International: www.amnesty.org

Business Council for the UN: www.bcun.org

Coalition for the International Criminal Court: www.iccnow.org/

Coalition to Stop the Use of Child Soldiers: www.child-soldiers.org

Doctors without Borders: www.doctorswithoutborders.org

European Platform for Conflict Prevention and Transformation: www.euconflict.org

Global Partnership for the Prevention of Armed Conflict (GPPAC): www.gppac.net

Global Peace Services USA: www.globalpeaceservices.org

Greenpeace: www.greenpeace.org

Human Rights Links: www.derechos.net/links/ngo

Human Rights Watch: www.hrw.org

International Action Network on Small Arms: www.iansa.org

International Alert: www.international-alert.org

International Campaign to Ban Landmines (ICBL): www.icbl.org

International Federation for Human Rights (FIDH): www.fidh.org

Lawyers Committee on Nuclear Policy: www.lcnp.org

Nuclear Age Peace Foundation: www.wagingpeace.org

Oxfam: www.oxfam.org

Pugwash: www.pugwash.org

Safer World: www.saferworld.org

Search for Common Ground: www.sfcg.org

UN Watch: www.unwatch.org

World Organization Against Torture (OMCT): www.omct.org

Sources of Information

Americans and the World: www.americans-world.org

Americans Talk Issues Foundation (ATIF):
www.publicinterestpolling.com

Center for Defense Information (CDI): www.cdi.org

Program on International Policy Attitudes (PIPA), University of
Maryland: www.pipa.org

UNWIRE (Daily news on UN system issues): www.unwire.org

United States Government Websites

Bureau of International Organization Affairs (IO) Department of
State: www.state.gov/p/io

U.S. Mission to the United Nations, New York City:
www.un.int/usa

U.S. Mission to the United Nations, Geneva:
www.usmission.ch/index.html

U.S. Mission to the United Nations Agencies in Rome:
http://usunrome.usembassy.it/

U.S. Mission to International Organizations in Vienna:
www.usun-vienna.usia.co.at

Index

About the Author

Chadwick F. Alger is Mershon Professor of Political Science and Public Policy Emeritus at Ohio State University. His education includes a B.A. from Ursinus College; an M.A. from the School of Advanced International Studies, Johns Hopkins University; and a Ph.D. from Princeton University in Political Science. His personal experiences in world affairs began very soon after he graduated from high school, with service for three years in the U.S. Navy during World War II that included overseas service that ranged across the Pacific Ocean. From 1950 to 1954 he served as a civilian intelligence analyst in the Office of Naval Intelligence in the Pentagon during the Korean War. While a political science professor at Northwestern University, from 1957 to 1971, for many years he has conducted extensive field research at the UN Headquarters in New York City and at the headquarters of the UN and UN Specialized Agencies in Geneva, Switzerland.

Professor Alger's research and teaching has focused on three linked themes: (1) the UN System of some thirty organizations, with special interest in the roles of Non-Governmental Organizations (NGOs); (2) the development of long term strategies for peace building; and (3) the world relations of people and organizations in local communities. He believes that creative peace building requires the participation of people in local communities everywhere who understand the "world relations of daily life" and the opportunities that they offer for everybody to personally participate in peace building. He is editor of *The Future of the UN System: Potential for the Twenty-First Century*, UN University Press, 1998. He has served as president of the International Studies Association, and as secretary general of the International Peace Research Association, an organization of scholars located around the world who are engaged in peace research.